GunDigest® Book of SUPPRESSORS

Patrick Sweeney

Copyright ©2015 F+W Media, Inc.

All rights reserved. No portion of this publication may be reproduced or transmitted in any form or by any means, electronic or mechanical, including photocopy, recording, or any information storage and retrieval system, without permission in writing from the publisher, except by a reviewer who may quote brief passages in a critical article or review to be printed in a magazine or newspaper, or electronically transmitted on radio, television, or the Internet.

Published by

Gun Digest® Books, an imprint of F+W Media, Inc.
Krause Publications • 700 East State Street • Iola, WI 54990-0001
715-445-2214 • 888-457-2873
www.krausebooks.com

To order books or other products call toll-free 1-800-258-0929
or visit us online at www.gundigeststore.com

ISBN-13: 978-1-4402-4532-9
ISBN-10: 1-4402-4532-0

Cover Design by Kevin Ulrich
Designed by Sharon Bartsch and Rebecca Vogel
Edited by Corrina Peterson

Printed in the United States of America

10 9 8 7 6 5 4 3 2 1

Related titles from Gun Digest

Gun Digest Guide to Customizing Your AR-15

Gun Digest Guide to Maintaining & Accessorizing Firearms

Gunsmithing Pistols & Revolvers

Gunsmithing the AR-15

CONTENTS

Dedication

And as always, Felicia. Ever faithful, ever patient, ever with encouragement and understanding, I am, and remind myself repeatedly, the luckiest man, ever. Those who are keeping track, the poodle count is now down to two. Alas, our youngest, our ADHD poodle who also had Addison's, contracted a gastric cancer that has vague symptoms. So vague that even the specialty vet we took him to missed their importance. So, we have but the two dudes I have to regale with bon mots on walks.

Acknowledgments

Wow, where to start? First, let's give Greg Latka and Casey Foster, at Gemtech, a big shout. Not only did they patiently answer my technical questions and give me background on many things in the suppressor-verse, they let me wander around their production facility (both the old one and the new one), camera in hand.

A special thank you also to Owen Miller of Gemtech, not just Director of Sales, but also regulatory compliance guru and historian, who demonstrated Job-like patience in dealing with my questions, dispelling myths and in general keeping me from promulgating any more of the suppositions, urban legends and just plain wrong "facts" with which this area is already rife.

Dr. Phil Dater not only let me attend his fact-packed technical class (usually limited to evidence techs, investigators, secret-squirrel military types and such) but answered questions during and after the class, letting me essentially brush up my decades-old grasp of good old physics. And, the guys at Long Mountain Outfitters, who hosted the class, not only made the space available, but afterwards let me wander through the vault and even fondle some of the movie props they have.

John Hollister and Kevin Brittingham, now of Sig, were more than generous with their time, information, technical info, samples and historical products.

On the technical side of things, I'd like to thank James Higley of Purdue and Brian Vuksanovich of Youngstown State University for their patience in handling the questions of someone with an engineering education from the Paleolithic era (me).

Brooks Van Camerick and Richard Thompson of Thomson Machine were generous in sending me product to test, abuse and just about break, and giving lots and lots of info.

The crew at Yankee Hill Machine needs to be recognized for going not just above and beyond, but by not cringing when I told them, and then showed them, what I did to one of their suppressors. Even hardened SWAT cops and the guys at my gun club who are used to seeing me abuse gear flinched. The Yankee Hill Machine guys were practically giddy at the abuse. Thanks for the opportunity, guys.

Zak Smith of Thunder Beast Arms has been more than helpful in helping me understand long-range accuracy and precision shooting with suppressors. For most shooters, a gigglefest at the gun club, plinking at clumps of dirt and busted lengths of target stands constitutes "accuracy testing" with a suppressed rifle. For Zak and the crew, long-range practical shooting, compared to un-suppressed, is the measure.

All the manufacturers who sent me product to use, abuse, test, photograph and write up have been more than generous with their time and products, and if you see someone in here, you should search them out. (Not to say that others aren't as good, but these I know from experience.)

On the gunsmithing side of things, my old friend Ned Christiansen was more than happy to fit threaded barrels, or thread barrels, or answer technical questions on real-world aspects of fitting suppressors to firearms. Bill Wilson willingly took my crusty old CQB (which has, in its service life, been buried, submerged, fired under water, dropped, run over, and had other atrocities perpetrated on it) and fit a second, threaded barrel so I could do more suppressor testing.

I hope you all have fun, I sure did.

INTRODUCTION

Oh, what a brave new world. Shakespeare had that line in The Tempest from the mouth of Miranda when she first saw a man who was not her father. "O brave new world, that has such people in it."

When I started regularly going to the range, it was common to see all manner of deer rifles. Handguns were mostly revolvers, with some hard-core "combat" shooters using pistols, and the random sighting of a bullseye competitor now and then. Almost no one had a CPL (called a CCW back then), and if they did they mostly kept the news to themselves. ARs were rare, viewed with disdain, and considered inaccurate and unreliable. Machine guns? SBRs? Silencers? You must be kidding, nobody has one of *those.*

One of the wonders of the old Second Chance match was the Back Range. It was the practice range, and the location for the optional events that took up more room than the Front Range could handle. It was where everyone who had a machine gun could show up and shoot it. And if you had good ammo, or knew the owner, or bought their ammo, you could shoot machine guns. In the fifteen years I went, I had the chance to shoot a rogue's gallery of buzzguns, but hardly any suppressed firearms at all. It is hard to imagine a time when machine guns were more common than suppressors. But that was life back in the occasionally good old days.

Times change.

We now live in a time where in some states the number of CPL holders is over five percent of the adult population. ARs are common as dirt. My friend Dave Fortier reports from his flat, dusty, agricultural state that the farmboys no longer have lever-action 30-30s in the windows of their pickup trucks. They have tricked-out ARs behind the seat.

Were they not so ferociously expensive, I'm sure we'd see a lot more machine guns at ranges and gun clubs. What we do see are SBRs and silencers. They are now no longer a rarity, no longer an ultra-rare sight at ranges and gun clubs, that when I started would have been the talk of the gun club for months afterwards.

And yet, there are a lot of shooters who still don't know about suppressors, or don't know much. Or what they know just isn't true. That is about to change.

One thing I can also add is a quip I just read (for all I know, I wrote it): "Education is the opportunity to learn from the mistakes of others." There is a lot here, a lot that might not fit with what "everyone

Here you have a bunch of gun writers at work. It is fun work, and it is (sometimes) well-paid work, but it is not an encyclopedic education in all things firearms.

knows." In a lot of instances, that is most likely because what "everyone" knows just ain't true. And to add a bit of frosting on that cake, read the manual. No, I mean it, despite the alleged deductions from your man-card, read the manual.

Suppressor manufactures include info with your new can. It may be a simple handout sheet, it may be a close attempt at a military TM, but they send info, and you would be wise to read it.

In full disclosure, I'm going to extend the military approach, and I'm going to tell you what I'm going to tell you, then tell you, and then tell you what I told you. Why? Because this is all new to many readers. If you've read a dozen books on, just to pick one, the AR-15, you can skim over the text on a new title and let your eyes/brain pick things up again when you realize you are into something you haven't seen before. So much is familiar, you want to skip the overlap and "get on with the good stuff, the new stuff." Well, this is all new.

And as a result, I have to get deep into the weeds, explaining a lot of things that are background, because, well (stop me if you've heard this before), this is all new.

So, first we'll go through the basics, the history, function and use of suppressors. Then we'll cover the testing and descriptions of a bunch of them, from small to large, plain to exotic. And finally, for those who want it, I'll get really technical (or as technical as I can without putting the editor to sleep) and wrap up with the legalities and a few mistakes to avoid.

When we're done, you'll know more about suppressors than anyone who hasn't been to a technical class or engineering school, and have a broader understanding than a whole lot of end-users. Yep, that's right, just because someone has a nickname as their radio handle and gets paid by the government, doesn't mean they are an expert on the subject. Just an expert (we hope) user of the tool.

And I hope this book, while informing you, will also give you a bit of humility. Once you've read it, you will be better informed (if I may say so, in all modesty) than anyone else at the gun club. Anyone else in matches. And pretty much any police officer you might meet, or discuss the subject with. And, in a delicious bit of irony, you will probably know more than a lot of the gun writers you will be reading, or have read. While it is fun to point out that the SpecOps people who are adored in some circles are not all gun experts, just more-or-less trigger-pulling experts, it is also humbling to be reminded now and then that even the gun experts aren't experts in all things gun-related. And to cut them some slack, there's a truckload (literally, in some cases) of gear that that SpecOps guy knows how to use. Just because someone can use a radio, that does not make them an electrical engineer. In many instances, being able to quickly dial up a digital gizmo and rain ordnance down on the bad guy's head will net more dead terrorists than the best trigger-puller could manage with a rifle alone.

Be humble, because they will be where you were, before you started on Page One. Cut them some slack while they try to catch up.

"Time to take 'ole painless' out the bag." I know it isn't suppressed, but I just had to include this. Yes, the actual minigun used in the movies where you've seen miniguns. Don't know the quote? Shame on you.

Chapter One

WHY A SUPPRESSOR?

Why a suppressor? For a long time, the glib answer would be, "Why not?" In most states in the union they are legal to own and, barring local restrictions or mindless and irritating gun club rules, legal to use. (For a while, it was legal to own a suppressor in Washington State, but illegal to mount it on a firearm. Amusingly, in the first draft of this chapter, the thrice-damned auto-correct feature of this program spelled the state as "Washingtoon." Maybe it is smarter than I give it credit for.) Granted, they are still objects of mystery in many places, many gun clubs, and there are still a lot of police officers who don't know they are kosher, but so what else is new?

The not-so-glib answer? The biggest reason is noise, or the relative lack thereof when you use one properly.

Guns are noisy. Even .22 rimfires are too noisy for your hearing not to suffer from exposure. Oh, there are a lot of shooters who still don't believe it. There are hunters who tell you that shots taken at game don't "count" because your ears "shut down" under stress. Pardon my French, but those are both B.S. I've told this before, but it bears repeating, as it is quite illustrative. Many years ago, my Dad and brother and I were at the range "up north," plinking with .22s and happy to be there. It was the new summer two-week vacation plan, instead of the trek down to Florida. We were using the prescribed safety gear: glasses and plugs, in my case my prescription eyeglasses.

You see, my father was then, and was until he retired, an engineer for Ford. He'd gone to school on the G.I. Bill, and went to work for the Big Three. Safety procedures were drilled into him. Any prescription glasses we wore had to meet ANSI safety standards. (Yes, I was *that kid* in school.) We used foam plugs when shooting our rimfire rifles. Anything bigger in caliber, we used more protection.

Besides being a whole lot of fun, suppressors/silencers can save your hearing. Who wants to be the gun club's cranky old shooter, always going "Huh?"

A club member arrived to sight in his deer rifle. Dad saw that he didn't have any hearing protection, so we walked over to offer him some. (Dad made us stop firing when the other member arrived, so he'd have a chance to set up without our rapid-fire shooting.) At the offer, the other member declined. "That's all right, you get used to it."

As we walked off, I heard Dad mutter, "Yes, you get used to it by going deaf."

My Dad knew whereof he spoke. He was a combat vet in Europe, and I can't guess how many rounds he fired, all without protection. And he and his unit weren't slackers. (Not that many were, there and then.) His unit went into the fight in September of 1944, and pretty much stayed there to the end. He rarely talked about it, but when he did we were told casually of such details as "when you are blowing mouse-holes through building walls, offset the locations. Otherwise the German in

Not everyone who needs protecting from gunfire noise walks on two legs. Our canine friends and workmates have sensitive ears, and they need protection, too.

the last room you blew a hole into can poke his MG42 through the hole you just blew and run bullets the length of the block." You can figure out how he knew that.

After the war and a bit of hell-raising racing dirt bikes on flat dirt tracks, he went to work for the auto companies, first GM, then Ford, where he stayed for 35 years. He knew about noise. He taught us well, and that was a good thing.

In the course of practice, competition, gunsmithing and teaching shooting, I have personally fired well over a million rounds. I've been on the line at law enforcement classes, where pretty much everyone is shooting AR-15s, when there were another million rounds fired. And, I worked as an RO at my gun club for twenty years, plus was on the range with other competitors when they fired their stages, for at a bare minimum of another million. So, by the most conservative estimate possible, I've been shooting, or in close proximity to, three million rounds. Probably closer to four million. Of those rounds, I have subjected my ears (not always by my choice) to less than a dozen shots, unprotected.

My hearing? Just fine, thank you. And thanks, Dad.

But even with protection, there has been some cost. What a suppressor does is take enough of the edge off of the sound that the cost becomes pretty much nothing. But it isn't completely nothing. To understand why, let's take a look at what noise is, and how your hearing works.

Noise

The old philosophical question, "If a tree falls in the forest, and there's no-one there, does it make a noise?" is a trap for the unwary philosophy student. What the professor wants the student to think about is the meaning of meaning. If we don't experience it, since we are the be-all and end-all of existence, then clearly we can't be sure it happened. After all, without us there to define it, it hasn't been defined. Philosophers have debated this for centuries, nay, millennia, and there's no telling how many Master's and PhDs have been issued, arguing over the details. All of it, utter nonsense, at least from an engineering viewpoint.

Let's instead shift from philosophy to physics and engineering. Falling things make noise. They disrupt the air through which they pass. They impact the surface on which they come to rest. Exploding things make noise. Noise is a compression wave of the air involved. Noise travels at the speed of sound, which is self-defined as the speed that sound travels through air. (Students of logic will recognize that as circular reasoning. Good, you're paying attention.) The wave travels through air by means of each molecule being pushed by the energy in the wave, and transferring that energy to the next molecule, and so on. How tightly bound the molecules happen to be determines both the maximum energy the system can transfer and the speed at which that transfer occurs.

In air, at standard conditions, sound travels at 1,126 feet per second.

The speed of sound in water, for example, depends on what kind of water: fresh or salt? In fresh water, the speed of sound is 4,910 fps. In sea water, it is 5,116, depending on density, salinity, sediments, etc. When Krakatoa exploded in 1883, the noise generated was so loud it was heard 3,000 miles away, on the island of Rodrigues, Mauritius. Through the air, the sound took almost four hours for the sound to travel that far through the air, but only 52 minutes for it to arrive by seawater.

Part of that is the mode of transmission. Through air, the energy of sound can only be transferred by means of the compression wave. However, some liquids and all solids (metal, rock, etc) offer an additional means of energy transmission, transverse waves. Here, the molecules do not vibrate in a linear fashion, that is, they do not vibrate away from and toward the source. In transverse vibration, they move at a right angle to the direction of energy travel. They travel at different speeds. Those of you who live in earthquake-prone areas now know why you feel the quick "up-down" of the compression wave (arriving sooner) then the arrival of the side-to-side wave, the transverse wave.

Sound travels faster in water, rock and metal due to density.

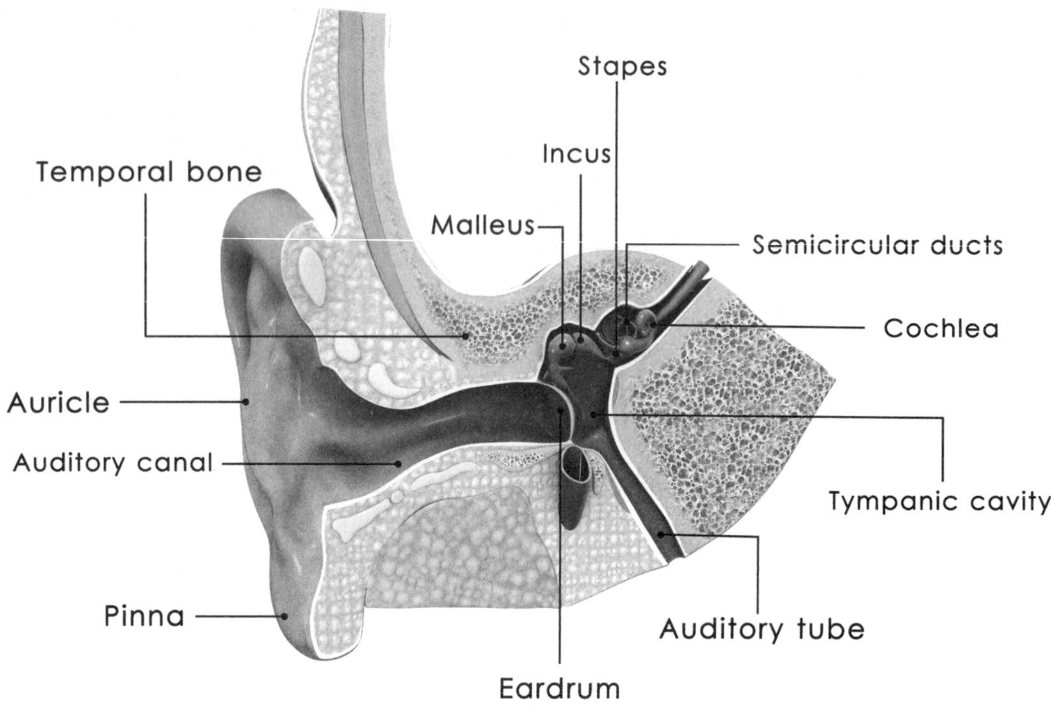

A marvel of bio-engineering, the ear is amazingly sensitive, and amazingly rugged. But once abused, it can't be overhauled and made like new. So, save your hearing, use a suppressor.

Since we are not going to be doing much shooting, if any, underwater, and earthquakes have nothing to do with suppressors, we'll simply refer to "the speed of sound" as its value in air from now on.

Measuring sound

We need a means of recording the compression of the air, to determine the intensity of a sound. The bel, named in honor of Alexander Graham Bell, is a unit of energy. The bel scale is defined as starting at the threshold of human hearing, or 0.0002 dynes per square centimeter. We use as our measuring system, one-tenth of a bel: the decibel. One awkward part of measuring sound is the scale. The pressures don't seem that different, but the energy in the compression wave varies by orders of magnitude. For those who have used it incorrectly, in slang, an "order of magnitude" is ten times, or a tenth of, the previous measured value.

To properly measure and record sound in a way we can grasp, the decibel scale is logarithmic, and each ten decibels represents an order of magnitude of the energy difference. So, if you go from 60 dB to 70 dB for example, you have ten times more energy at the higher sound level. Going from 70 to 80, you now have a hundred times more energy in the compression wave, than you had at 60 dB.

The ear

Ears do a couple of things, besides provide me a parking place for glasses and irresistible targets to jewelers who specialize in piercings. The shape of the ear channels noise down into the ear canal. The time differential between your ears (one ear will be closer to the sound than another) also provides directional information.

The part that matters is inside. Down at the end of your ear canal is the eardrum. That thin sheet of tissue vibrates to the sounds that come into your ears. Your external ears are there to add sensitivity, and to aid in directional orientation, but why? Sharp hearing, in the

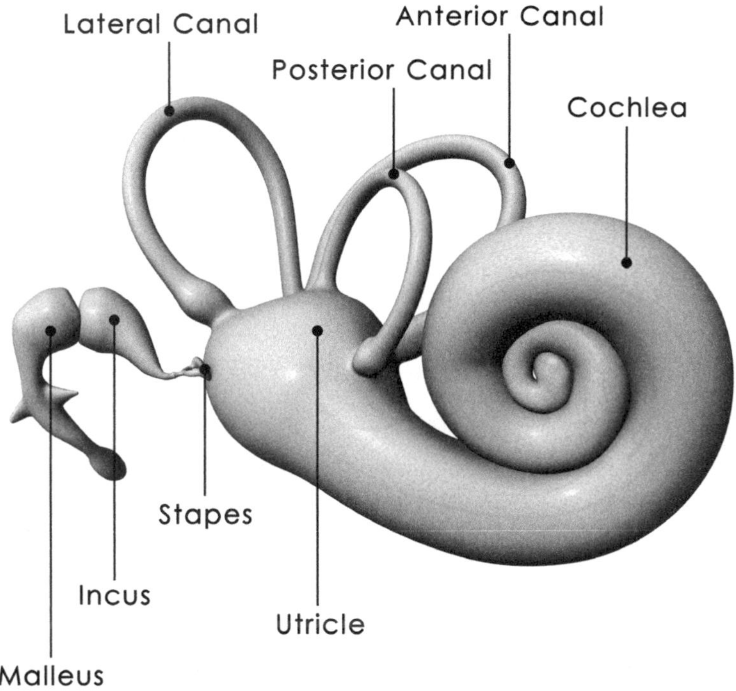

Your ear is more than just a hearing tool, the circular canals also work to keep you on balance. The bones (incus, malleus, stapes) are the transmitters of sound to the cochlea.

jungle when everything wants to eat you, is good; but even better is knowing from which direction the danger comes. So we have very directional hearing, Your brain can analyze the time differential between your ears and figure out where the sound came from. With practice, you can even get a sense of absolute distance.

The movement of the eardrum is "read" by three tiny bones in your inner ear: the malleus, incus and stapes. The three bones form an intricate linkage, and leverage, and the result is that they transmit the pressure they feel to the three-part tube inside your ear, the cochlea, the actual inner ear.

The inner ear provides both balance and hearing. Separate from your hearing are the three semi-circular canals. As the fluid in them sloshes around, your brain reads the fluid movements via small hairs inside the canals, called cilia, and the feedback tells you if you are upright, lying down, or falling.

The three bones transmit the vibrations of sound to the inner ear, and the waves in the fluid moves also to the cochlea, where you hear. Here's the clever part, but also the weak link; the cochleal hairs are different lengths, corresponding to different frequencies of sound. So, when a sound of a particular frequency hits your tympanic membrane, your eardrum, the vibration gets transmitted to the cochlea, and the hair or hairs that correspond to it (and not the other hairs) are moved by the fluid wave.

Of course, if the hairs for that particular frequency are dead, missing, damaged or otherwise incapable of response, you don't hear that frequency.

Good hearing is also a matter of good brain-wiring. You can teach yourself to identify particular noises. In music, there are people who have perfect pitch, they can hear a note and tell you what it is. Note sounds, "That's A flat." Then you have people who have trained to reproduce that note. The Oboist (the most difficult instrument to tune) hits a note, and the rest of the orchestra tunes to it.

The first is genetic, the second is training. Then there are the rest of us: "Oh, that sounds nice."

Now, good hearing and training or practice will provide other information. For instance, having stood on the line while a crew of police officers loaded their ARs, I can tell when someone has an empty chamber. The sound of a chambered round and that of a bolt crashing down on an empty chamber are different. "You, third from the end, Lakeview is it? Your chamber is empty." When he checks, finds it empty, and I wasn't even looking at him, he thinks I'm some sort of magician. Nope, just practiced, and not even unique in this acquired skill. Just protective of my hearing when I was younger.

Ok, so far, so good.

Now, if you over-work your cilia, they do not get stronger. They aren't muscles. If you overwork them, they get brittle, break or die. When that happens you can no longer hear that frequency (the one that particular cilia "heard") and your overall hearing suffers. You can over-work them with a single impulse, sound. Something that is massively too loud will over-work them, and they die in one or two exposures. Less than the impulse that kills them outright, but too much for too long, and they will also die.

So, when you were a teenager, you stood right in front of the bass speakers of your favorite band? Good for you. That explains why I have to shout.

This is also a good time to point out the differences between hardware and software, at least in the human body. The hardware is the ears, the various parts, all the way through the cilia, until your ear sends the nerve signal to the brain. Then software takes over. Your brain hears the various signals coming in, identifies them, assigns priority, and then constructs the "sound" for your conscious mind to use.

Your hearing is an interesting situation of "use it and lose it" because you will lose some as you get older. Part of that is simply getting old, but part of that is that anything that is used gets used up, even if it gets regenerated along the way.

Those of you with good hearing, ever wonder how you can follow a conversation in a crowded room? Your brain assigns those particular noises priority, and not the rest of it. So there you are, in a crowd, and someone calls your name. You hear it, almost as an electric jolt. Your brain did that, not your ears. Oh, and clever detectives and investigators also use it. If someone is trying to pretend they don't understand English, or is using an assumed name, they will react to their name, or particular words in English, despite wanting not to. And those of you who can't hear well, wonder why you can't follow a conversation in a crowded room? Because the gaps in your hearing frequencies, the now-dead cilia, mean your ears deliver insufficient information to your brain to patch together the words that got muffled, overwhelmed or muddied by outside noises. Which leads us to hunters.

There is a steadfast belief, incorrect, that the stress of hunting causes your ears to "shut down" and not "hear" the shot. Therefore, your ears aren't as damaged by hunting shots as much as they are at the practice range.

The reason you don't "hear" the shot, or don't perceive it as being as loud as it is, is because your brain has "discounted" the value of that information. Just like it filters out, via the equivalent of software, the background noise in a party so you can follow the conversation, your brain decides the sound of the shot isn't as important as the rest of what you are focusing on.

But that doesn't mean your ears don't take the hit. They still do. Just like the tree still makes noise when it hits the ground.

I did a survey of fellow gunwriters at one of our magazine title's gatherings. The most common response was, "I wish I'd taken more care of my hearing, back when I was younger." Even then, they quite often did not fully grasp how much hearing they had lost. I mean, when a gunwriter who has written his answer on the survey question "estimated remaining hearing" at 80%, and later that night you have to practically shout across the dinner table so he can hear you, he hasn't grasped the actual loss.

Sometimes it has been in a single, awful experience. Fellow gunwriter Craig Boddington shared how he lost a lot of hearing in one incident. He was hunting, in the field with a guide and a fellow hunter. The other guy had a muzzle brake on his rifle and, swinging at game, he swung close to Craig. Before Craig could move or cover his ears, the other guy shot. Only a few feet away and to the side of the muzzle, Craig's ear caught the directed muzzle blast of a big-bore hunting rifle, with muzzle brake attached. "It was days before the ringing went away."

That ringing noise? That is the death throes of the cilia that had been damaged, signaling the brain in true operatic fashion (long, repeated, and usually in the tenor and soprano regions): "We're outta here."

Typically, the damage happens in the higher frequencies. For some reason they are the weaker cilia, or we just get exposed to more high frequency noise than low frequency noise. So exposure to gunshots accelerates the ageing loss, in the top of our hearing frequencies. In a cruel quirk, women's voices have more register in the higher frequencies than men's do, and as a result, yes, shooting does make you less able to hear your wife's voice.

How good is our hearing? Consider the following example. A couple of decades ago, the neighbors around our gun club decided that the township would be better without a gun club. Long story short, after a couple of years of wrangling, legal expenses and court appearances, the township lost. Lost big, and even precipitated a change in state law that made noise no longer actionable when it came to gun ranges.

At one point, early on in the process but after the first injunction, we were standing on our club property, with the judge and attorneys, discussing gunshot noise. The neighbors had been complaining that bullets were leaving the property, and that the noise was too great. We had built a test stand, an overhead structure that would keep bullets from leaving our property, and the judge and attorneys were there to see how it worked.

We heard gunshots. Immediately the judge asked, "Who is that?" and, said more than a bit testily, "I said no shooting here until I've had a chance to inspect these baffles you've made." I knew the cause, it was one I'd heard many times over the previous years. "Your Honor, that is the gun club to the north. They are a mile and a quarter away. I believe that is the State Police practicing with their machine guns."

The judge looked at me, at the attorneys, and said, "As long as you build these baffle things, so bullets can't leave, you can resume shooting until we've settled the case."

The untrained or inexperienced could not tell that the gunshots they heard were more than a mile off, and had thought them just a couple of hundred yards away, perhaps even on the club property. In the course of this book I will conduct tests and do calculations to determine the decibel level of gunshots from roughly 2200 yards away. It won't be much over the background noise a country day has as a matter of course. And, it certainly isn't harmful to hearing. Not so much good for the enjoyment of your barbeque, maybe, but hey, as I said (perhaps amusingly, but perhaps also unwisely) to one of our neighbors who complained, "That's something your realtor should have told you about."

Again, you can damage the cilia in one impulse, one awful event. Or you can over-work them with a lesser, but continuous exposure, longer than they can recover from. Which leads us to health standards.

OSHA

The Occupational Safety and Health Administration determined what levels of noise are safe. That is, the level you can be exposed to and still retire with your hearing relatively intact. (Always remember; you're going to lose some just from ageing.)

In 1981, OSHA adopted a requirement that all workers be protected from noise above a weighted average noise level of 85 dB, over an eight-hour work period. If your work station has an ambient (constant, non-stop, ever-present, you get the idea) sound level above 85 db, then the company has to provide you with hearing protection. I'd hope you'd be smart enough to use it, and/or smart enough to provide your own if the place you work is noisy.

The exposure you are subjected to, plus the duration, determines the safe level of noise. Safe, as in, you won't lose hearing, but it may not be safe if you can't hear danger coming. The upper limit of 140 dB for impact or impulse noises is not time-limited. The allowable time for exposure to that level is "none."

As a quick check, how loud is 85 decibels? And can we figure out a rule of thumb to use? Yes, and yes. 85 dB is the noise level such that you have to raise your voice to conduct a conversation at normal, conversational distances. Or, you have to lean in to be heard or hear. I worked for few years in the printing industry. Printing presses are loud. When any press went on, we all put on hearing protection.

"This is all well and good," you say, "but we're talking guns here." Yes, we are. And each impulse over 140 dB is an event that OSHA would not allow, were it a work environment. But this isn't work, and OSHA also has limited purview over members of the Armed Forces. So, we have to go by a different standard here.

Military and hearing

There is, and has been for a long time, a decided bias against the use of hearing protection. At first, the reason seems good, "I don't want to use earplugs, because I might miss hearing something that could save my life." OK, that's good as far as it goes.

Let's, just for the sake of argument, pick a number, say, 10% as the amount of hearing lost/hidden by hearing protection, when worn. You wear plugs, you "lose" 10%, but only as long as you have them in/on.

So, what do you do when the normal damage (and I

Manufacturers can enclose machines to dampen noise, but there is a limit to that, and there are limits to worker exposure.

use "normal" only in the meaning of that's what happens when you undergo the abuse) of not wearing hearing protection has cost you 10% of your hearing? 10% that you won't get back, ever?

The better-equipped of the military units, and the sharper members who can get away with it, use electronic ear muffs. These buffer your ears from outside noise, but have built-in microphones that hear the sound, clip the peaks above 85 dB, and then project it to speakers inside the muffs. You get the best of both worlds, as long as the batteries last.

But, the services have been looking into the use of suppressors both for hearing-protection and tactical advantages.

My father's combat in Europe, and after the war working in the auto industry, led to hearing loss. But as soon as it was possible to protect himself from further hearing damage/loss, he used the tools available. And he made the rest of us use them.

Hearing-safe

There is a general standard used in the suppressor industry, referred to as "hearing-safe." What it means is that the suppressor or silencer on the firearm, in the given caliber, in a non-constricted environment, provides a sound signature below the 140 dB level.

Example: you park an effective 5.56-rated suppressor on a 20-inch AR and shoot it in the open. The unprotected muzzle blast of the rifle is (let's just pick a number) is 162 dB. The suppressor (let's just pick another) provides 28 dB of sound reduction. That means the sound, as measured by our instruments, is reduced to 134 dB. Cool. And as a bonus, which we'll get into later in detail, but which I have to mention now, you get a db or two of extra reduction because the 20-inch barrel puts the muzzle farther from your ear.

Now, let's start making this a bad thing. First, we'll shorten to a carbine-length barrel. That does two things. It makes the noise louder because the shorter barrel makes for greater bore pressure at bullet release, and it is now closer to your ear. Let's arbitrarily add 2 dB to the muzzle blast, and deduct the 2 dB you got as a bonus for the 20-inch barrel. Oops, we're right at the 140 dB threshold. Now, let's put you under a covered firing line. This doesn't add to the 140 dB you get hit with, but it does create a secondary sound impulse on each and every shot. You get hit with the 140 dB from the muzzle, and a micro-second later you get slapped with the (again, snatching a number out of the air) 136 dB echo off the ceiling. Indoors, you'd get hits with 3, 4, 5 or more echoes, off the ceiling, the sidewalls of the shooting booth, the back wall, etc.

Remember, exposure is cumulative. Out in the open, with your suppressed rifle-length AR, you've gone from one shot at 136 dB, to indoors with your SBR, each shot creating multiple exposures, and they add up.

Modern popularity

Why the recent upsurge in suppressor use and acquisition? If you don't know, the current wait time for approval of a transfer form is something over nine months. That is either a transfer or a build, however you want to do it. That long wait has caused a surge in the forming of Trusts, a subject we'll get into in a bit.

There was a time, not too long ago relatively speaking, when a transfer was approved in a couple of months. What happened?

One thing that changed was the number of states where suppressors were permitted. It used to be, back in the Dark Ages when I first started professionally in firearms, that not two dozen states approved suppressor ownership for their residents. Now it is over 40, and many of them allow the use of suppressors in hunting. Using suppressors in vermin control isn't covered in a lot of them, as it isn't "hunting." The companies are making and selling a lot of "cans."

The main reason is simple: the Hughes Amendment to the Firearm Owners Protection Act of 1986. By a dubious voice vote, at the literal last minute, an amendment (named after Hughes, curse him) was added prohibiting the manufacture of new transferable select-fire firearms. In short, the number of machine guns was frozen. No new ones could be made for commercial sale. Manufacturers could make new ones for the government and for law enforcement, but the rest of us were shut out.

Anyone who has not slept through Econ 101 will tell you what happened. In 1986, an AR-15 from Colt cost you maybe $500. You could build one, if you knew how, for maybe $400 or a bit less, depending on the source/quality of the parts you used. A transferable (a term of art, meaning not LE-owned, not a salesman's sample, not a military item) M16 cost you maybe $600. Colt was really pissy about selling them, and really didn't want to be in the business of selling icky "machine guns," so many people (relatively speaking) would file a Form 1, a form that when approved, allowed them to build an AR into an M16. This cost them the $200 tax, plus the work, plus the cost of the rifle. They could end up spending almost a grand to make an M16, when Colt wouldn't sell one.

Enter FOPA 1986, and *viola*, no more Colt, no more Form 1; only what is there is there.

Fast-forward to 2014. You can buy all manner of AR-15 rifles, from vanilla-plain for $6-700, to custom-build, best-parts, and in high-tech materials far superior to mil-spec, for $3500. I walk into a gun shop that deals in select-fire firearms, and I see a transferable M16 on the wall, with a price tag of $25,000. No, that is not a typo, and no, I did not mis-place the decimal point. It is a transferable, meaning there are only so many, and that means that if you want one, you have to pay more than anyone else at the moment who wants one, in order to own one.

I have no idea what suppressors cost back in 1986, because my home state didn't allow them. But, the Hughes Amendment didn't cover them (you have to thank god, or someone, sometimes for the ignorance of the anti-gun set) so they have only increased in cost with the rate of inflation, and maybe not even that. After all, the cost of ARs has not kept up with inflation. We can now buy ARs, and good ones, for about half the price, in adjusted dollars, than I could back in 1986.

So, for the cost of one transferable M16, you can buy up to a dozen ARs, and equip each of them with its own suppressor. How cool is that?

Practical uses

OK, they are cool, but they also serve a purpose. In a shooting situation, the noise of gunfire drowns out everything else. In a law enforcement setting, when a shot goes off, "Who was that?' becomes paramount. If the police are using suppressors and the bad guys aren't, then the sound of the shot tells those involved a lot more.

There's also the matter of K9. The hearing of dogs is a lot better than ours. If it is better, then the sound of gunshots has to be a lot more painful and more damaging. Why not take it easy on Fido, and make sure the K9 officers are equipped with suppressors?

And for the rest of us, while it may seem a bit "out there" to use a suppressor on a home defense firearm, why not? Hearing is hearing, and hearing loss is still loss. Yes, the local DA is going to be beside himself, but if it is a lawful and proper shooting, and everything you use is lawfully owned, what's the problem?

Law enforcement

Coolness aside, there are also good reasons law enforcement has been shifting towards suppressors. Although I have to say (Hey, those of you who have read me, when have you ever known me to avoid a chance to point out the obvious?) that law enforcement is lagging behind us, as they have before.

IPSC shooters learned how to shoot, and taught police. IPSC competition proved pistols were dependable, and law enforcement shifted. Now, we are going whole-hog into the hearing-protection aspects of silencers, and the police are paying attention.

Imagine yourself a city administrator, and the SWAT team of your department has been busy for the last few years. You've had to deal with a recent upsurge in meth-heads, tweekers, and the crime that comes with them. However, you've managed to "convince" them to move on.

Just when you're ready to bask in the glory of the good work you and yours have done, a massive pile of paperwork hits your desk. The SWAT team is retiring, almost to a man. And on top of the large retirement income they are going to collect, due to the overtime they had to put in over the last few years (we'll avoid the book-length inquiry into municipal pension funding that arises at this point) they are all filing for medical disability. In short, hearing loss.

What? How? Simple. There's the team, entering a building on a raid. Back in the crack cocaine days, the bad guys knew that getting arrested was simply part of the cost of doing business. Getting into a shoot-out simply got them shot, and added a hospital visit plus extra charges to the rotation they were going to do in County lockup and the prison afterwards. Tweekers aren't so smart, nor patient. More often than in the old days, the raid ends up in gunfire. Back then, the teams were using MP5s, in 9mm, and the bad guys were using pistols and revolvers. When there was gunfire, it wasn't as loud to the participants.

Now, the teams go in with short-barreled AR-15s or M16s. Bad guys use whatever they've got. A few bursts of 5.56, in a narrow hallway crowded with police, preceded or followed by flash-bangs, and everyone's ears are ringing. Ringing means damage, and repeated damage means early-onset deafness. *Viola*, medical disability on retirement.

And, just as other things have changed, we're more aware of hearing loss issues today, and the team members are more likely to file medical disability claims over it. (And rightly so.)

For you, the administrator, the issue is simply one of economics, and not even very complicated arithmetic at that. A silencer issued to every team member costs the department/municipality a thousand dollars each, and lasts longer than their careers do. (Maybe more money, maybe less, depending on which ones the municipality buys.) A medical disability claim is going to cost you, the city financial officer, a thousand dollars a month, until the end of time. And, it is money that does not come out of the pension, it has to be paid for out of some other part of the budget. If you expect to stay on the job in the city, the quick response, "How fast can we get them all equipped with silencers?" should be asked.

There's also the matter of liability. If you, the SWAT team leader, know that your members can suffer hearing loss, and perhaps are, then you have to ask for gear to preclude damage. If you don't, the courts may find you partly responsible, and financially responsible. If the SWAT team leader asks his boss and gets turned down, the SWAT team leader is legally protected. And so on, up the ladder. The first one to say "no" may find his or her pension or IRA paying for the team's disability. If you're on a team, ask for silencers.

If the Hughes Amendment had included silencers, we would not have them available to us. And they would not come to the fore so quickly for law enforcement use. So, the logic is simple; if you are a law enforcement officer, and you can still hear when you retire, you can thank two things; the ignorance of Senator Hughes, and the need for cool, status and fun of the non-sworn (don't use "civilian") shooters at the gun clubs across the country.

Chapter Two

HISTORY

This was hi-tech automotive engineering when Maxim introduced his first firearms silencer. This REO Runabout, sold new for about $500, and is now worth $100,000.

When did silencers come about? Before we can answer that, there's a couple of things we have to make clear; one, it wasn't possible to *have* silencers until the invention of smokeless powder. Oh, you say "of course" but think about it; the percentage of black powder that is actually combusted is small, compared to that of smokeless. Lots of smoke, lots of powder residue, and lots of cleaning afterwards. But then there is also the matter of noise. Having fired black powder firearms (I was heavily into black powder when I was starting the journey that lead to here) I can attest to the noise being distinctly different, lower-pitched and perhaps at a lower decibel level as well. That is one thing I intend to look into when I have the time, and fully wring decibel levels out with the sound meter.

The second thing is the apparent temporal dysfunction of many anti-gunners. From listening to them, you'd think that "assault weapons" came about in the 1980s, that mass shootings didn't happen until Reagan was elected to the Presidency, and that silencers were unknown before spy movies became popular.

The invention of silencers occurred in the first decade of the 20th century, patented by a fellow named Maxim. No, not the machine-gun Maxim, but his son. Hiram Percy Maxim was not one to go slowly. Even at a time when precocious young men could attend college at an early age, he not only attended MIT early, but graduated early. He patented his first firearms silencer in 1909. We have to be specific, because the Maxim Silent Firearms Company later changed its name and pretty much only made mufflers for internal combustion engines.

Which, when I found out about it, allowed me to connect a few dots. OK, let's look at the first decade of the 20th century, firearms-wise and other inventions as

Until there was smokeless powder, there could not be suppressors or silencers. Imagine trying to deal with all that smoke, in a suppressor?

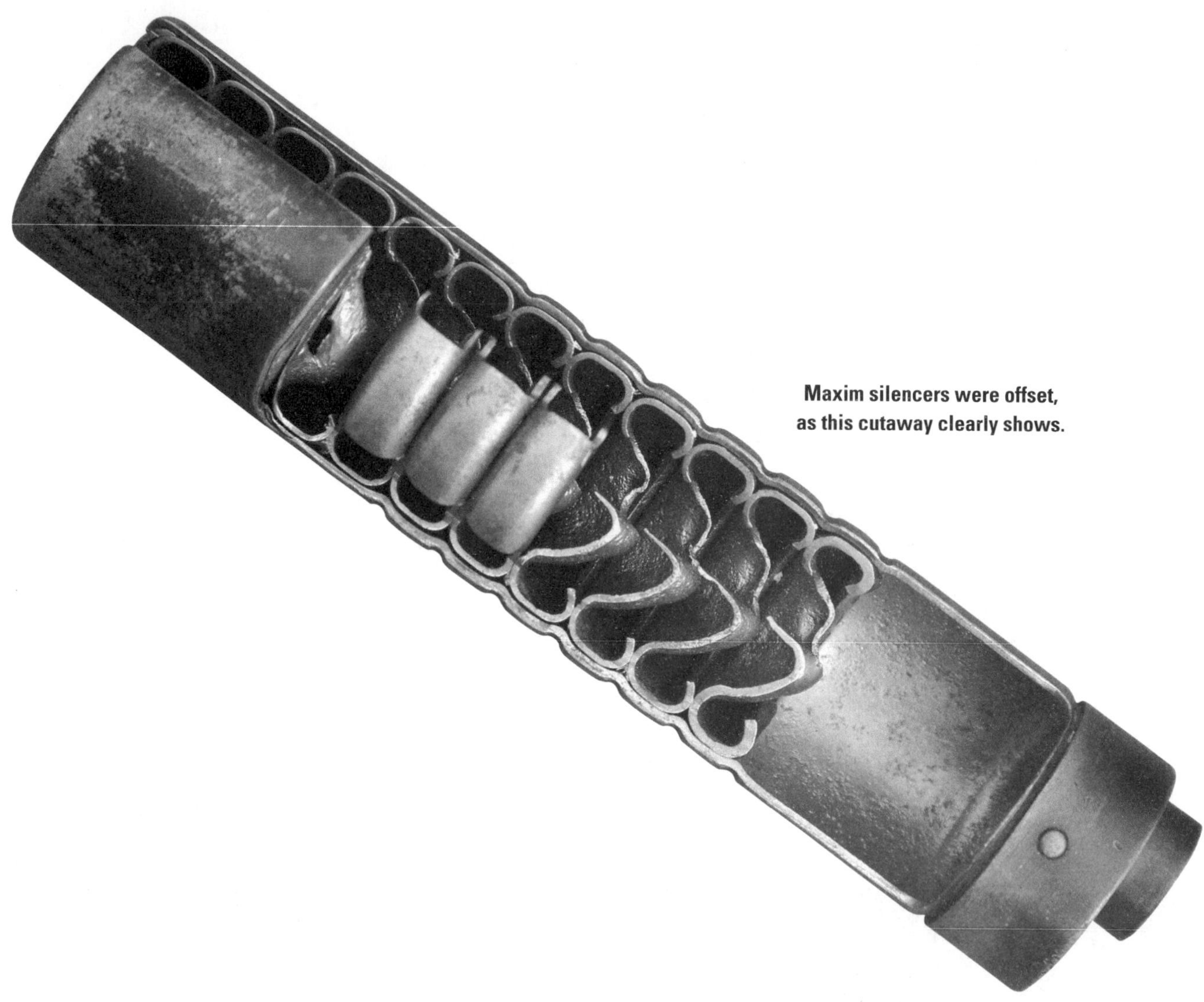

Maxim silencers were offset, as this cutaway clearly shows.

well. With Roosevelt in office, we've now had about a generation of shooters who are familiar with smokeless powder. And it is noisier than black powder. While no one has thought to actually invent hearing protection (at least, not that I've been able to find) they had to have noticed that these new cartridges, and smokeless powder, made your ears ring more than grand-dad's old black powder rifle.

But what was really making everyone cranky were these new-fangled horseless carriages. Not to pick on them, but we've all been standing on the corner when a Harley goes by, right? Noisy? You betcha. Ok, imagine an early automobile, granted not with the horsepower of a Harley, but completely un-muffled. Even your lawnmower has a muffler. Early automobiles got a reputation for scaring horses, disturbing the peace, making a racket, and generally being unpleasant. And deservedly so. Early autos weren't all that powerful, it took time to get even the most powerful engines up out of the teens as far as horsepower was concerned. But un-muffled, your average city street corner in 1905-1910 sounded like the parking lot of a Harley dealership. As a comparison, a Harley motor can develop on the order of 65-70 horsepower.

Cadlillac won the Dewar Trophy in 1914, with a racing car whose engine developed a thundering 40 to 50 horsepower (records vary). Your average automobile in 1914 probably had half that at its disposal. But by 1914, there would have been thousands on city streets. Noisy? Like you can't imagine, in this era of

And you thought modern suppressors were compact? This is the shipping container (mailing, actually) of a Maxim silencer.

If you ordered a Maxim silencer, it would come by way of the U.S. Postal Service. Well, back before the Depression, anyway.

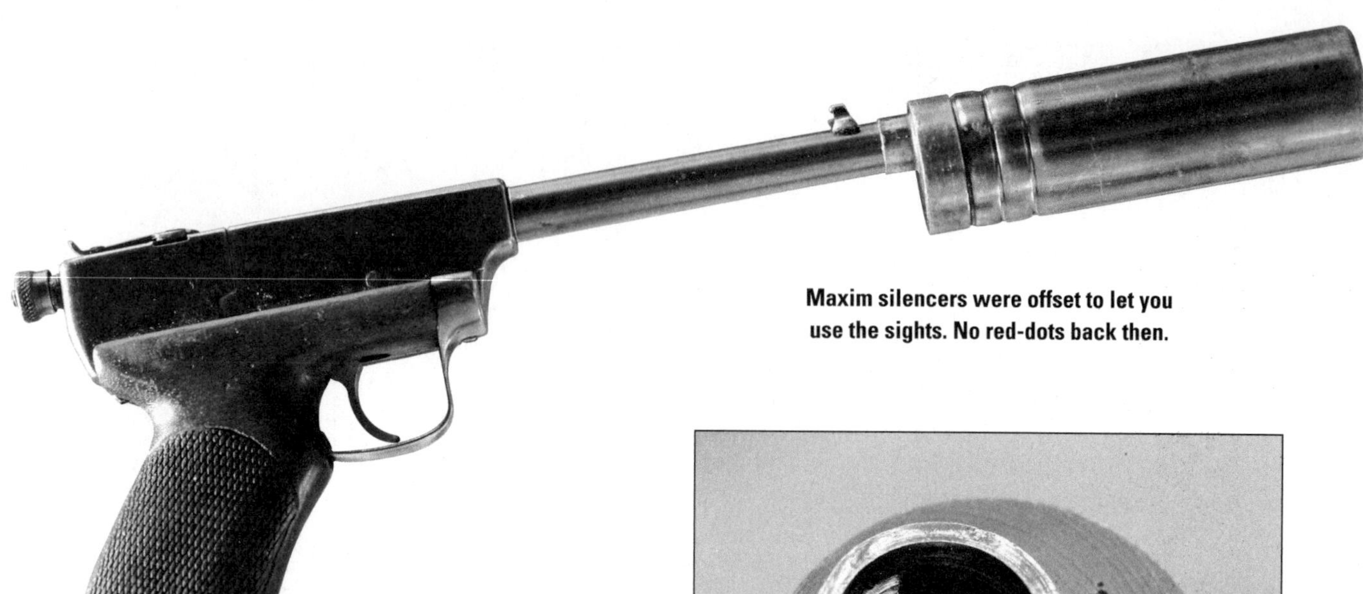

Maxim silencers were offset to let you use the sights. No red-dots back then.

Just to mess with your mind, notice where Maxim was based: New York.

hybrids and electric cars.

Maxim designed mufflers to tame engine noise. And, since each cylinder combustion was a separate noise event, doing the same to firearms was easy. After all, even an early engine ran at a higher rpm than one of his father's machine guns, right? If he could tame the noise of a 1,000 rpm engine (when you add in the firing of all the cylinders, and not consider just the rotation of the crankshaft) then a single gunshot was a piece of cake.

I've seen early magazine ads for silencers, showing properly dressed gentlemen plinking in their parlors, not even waking up the sleeping dog. If you wanted to buy a silencer back then, you simply sent a check or other funds to the Maxim Company and they mailed you a silencer. (You could probably have simply enclosed cash, since the basic ones were maybe twenty dollars.) Well, they mailed you one if you lived in a rational place. New York City had passed the Sullivan Act in 1911, controlling the purchase of firearms. Meant to keep those unruly southern-European immigrants from getting their hands on guns, I'd be surprised if it didn't address silencers sooner or later, probably sooner.

I can't say I've had a chance to look at a large number of Maxim suppressors, but I'm not sure anyone alive *can* say that, with the possible exception of Kevin Brittingham. They were not exactly common when they were new, and time has taken its toll. That, and stupid legislation. But the ones I have seen had some characteristics that jumped out at me. For one, they are all small. I mean, a Maxim silencer meant for use on a '03 Springfield, in .30-06, is not much bigger than what we now make for a .22LR. He clearly didn't believe in making them any larger than he had to, or else the end-users were so happy to have something this glorious, it didn't occur to them to ask, "Can you make it quieter still?"

Second, I have only ever seen a direct-thread mount on a Maxim silencer. I wouldn't be surprised to find he had done some work to make a quick-connect system of some kind, but the only ones I've ever seen were direct-thread. This is solid, simple, easy to understand, and something any competent gunsmith of the time

A Maxim box.

could have managed. Well, a competent gunsmith with a lathe big enough to hold the rifle barrel, perhaps. Now, don't quote me on that, because as much as I've seen, I haven't seen a lot of Maxim suppressors. Heck, I'm not sure anyone alive has seen a lot of them, they are rare.

Last, his designs were all offset. That is, the bullet path was not down the center of the tube, but traveled along a path above the centerline of the tube. This meant the silencer would not obscure the sights. Interesting, and a reminder that back then, iron sights were the only sights.

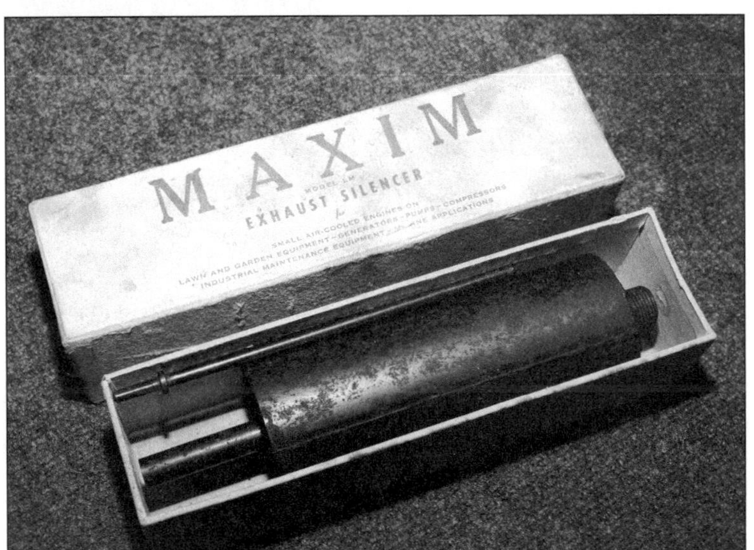

Maxim made automotive silencers, also.

Things change

During Prohibition, silencers weren't much of a problem, but they became so when it was "necessary" to find a "solution" to an existing problem. Look at it this way, if you are in the business of breaking the law, and you are trying to keep the competition out of your territory, you *want* to make a noisy, splashy, memorable event out of it. Plus, the liquor gangs were so much in control of the political process in many areas that making a scene really didn't matter. Imagine yourself across the street from that particular garage on the day the St. Valentine's Day Massacre happened. What do you hear? Machine guns going

Compared to today's mufflers, the Maxim is quite small. Then again, there's no catalytic converter in there, either.

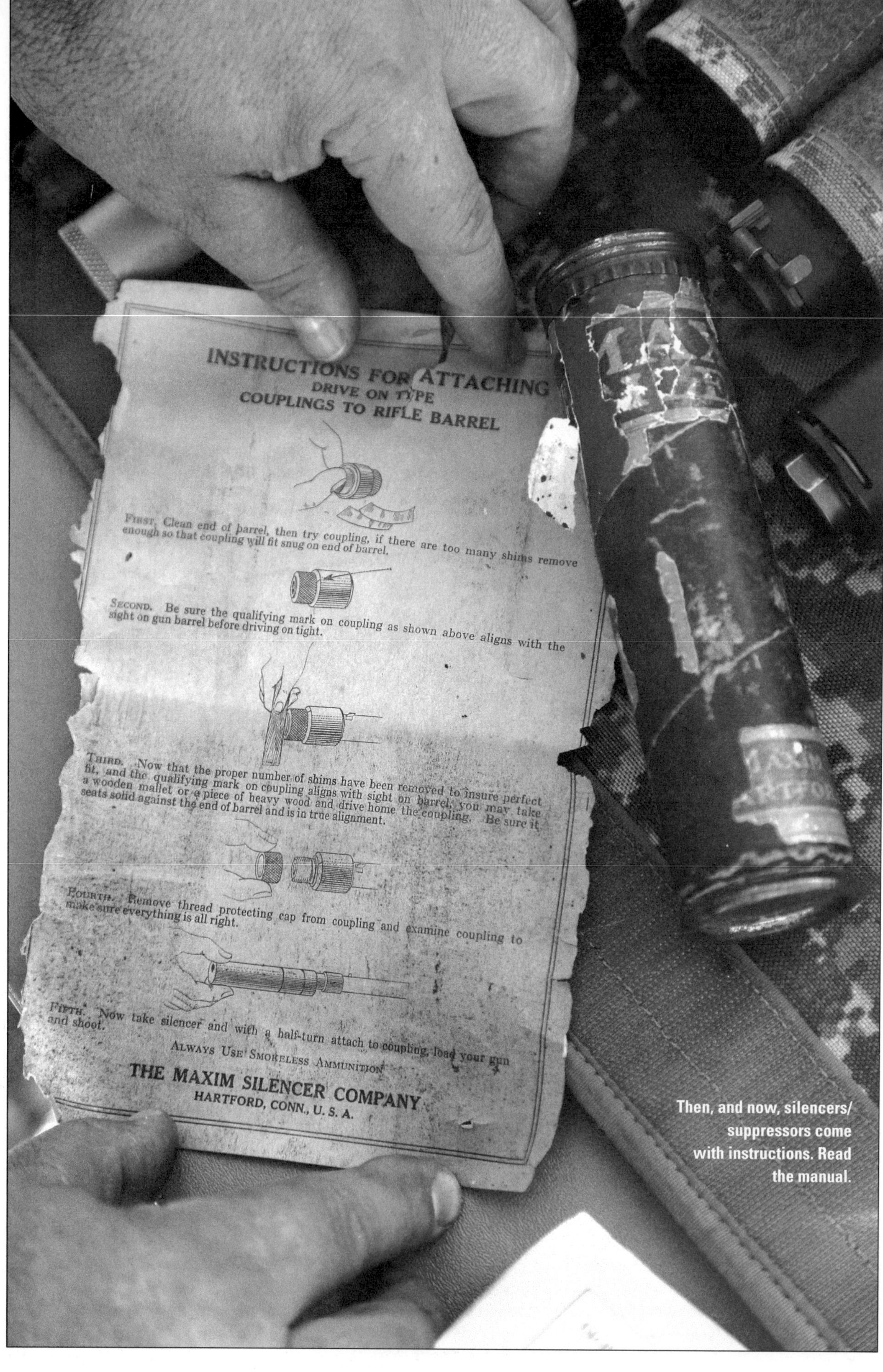

INSTRUCTIONS FOR ATTACHING
DRIVE ON TYPE
COUPLINGS TO RIFLE BARREL

FIRST. Clean end of barrel, then try coupling, if there are too many shims remove enough so that coupling will fit snug on end of barrel.

SECOND. Be sure the qualifying mark on coupling as shown above aligns with the sight on gun barrel before driving on tight.

THIRD. Now that the proper number of shims have been removed to insure perfect fit, and the qualifying mark on coupling aligns with sight on barrel, you may take a wooden mallet or a piece of heavy wood and drive home the coupling. Be sure it seats solid against the end of barrel and is in true alignment.

FOURTH. Remove thread protecting cap from coupling and examine coupling to make sure everything is all right.

FIFTH. Now take silencer and with a half-turn attach to coupling, load your gun and shoot.

ALWAYS USE SMOKELESS AMMUNITION

THE MAXIM SILENCER COMPANY
HARTFORD, CONN., U. S. A.

Then, and now, silencers/suppressors come with instructions. Read the manual.

Not only were Maxim silencers sent by mail, they even said what was in the tube.

Postage for a silencer, back in the day? Less than a quarter.

off, shotguns roaring, shooting, screaming. A moment of silence, then people running, cars starting and roaring off. Are you going to poke your head in the door to see what is happening? Are you going to stick around and give an eyewitness account to the police? Or are you going to be a prudent person back then, fade into the woodwork, and pretend like nothing happened? That's what I thought.

No, bootleggers had no use for suppressors.

Later, silencers got swept up in the impetus to deal with bank robbers. Crime had been bad enough when gangsters were getting rich supplying everyone with bootleg liquor, but after the Crash of 1929, bank robbers were all across the middle of the country, stealing with abandon. And remember, this was before the formation of the FDIC, the Federal Deposit Insurance Corporation. When a bank robber stole the money in the bank, he was stealing your money. Your neighbor's money. The town's money. And if he got away, there was no getting it back. Once he/they were out of sight, they were *gone*. As a result, when the alarm went off, lots of people with guns might (and often did) show up, and shoot anyone

DEPARTMENT OF THE ARMY
FRANKFORD ARSENAL
Philadelphia, Pa. 19137
SILENCERS
PRINCIPLES AND EVALUATIONS
REPORT R-1896
AUGUST 1968

The government has been looking at silencers for a long time, but is still very much undecided about them.

who looked like a robber.

Since you could (if you had the cash) buy a machine gun at the local hardware store, what showed up could be impressive, indeed.

Faced with this, the legislators did something good, and something stupid. Anytime someone stands up and says, about a problem they or the group is facing, however earnestly "We've got to do *something*" the proper response is to drown them. Or at least waterboard them until they promise to behave. "Doing something" in response to a problem, real or imagined, typically means "do anything that makes everyone involved feel better" and has invariably ended up badly, and taken years, decades or a lifetime to set right.

The good thing that Congress did was to form the FDIC, so when bank money gets stolen, it gets replaced from the U.S. Treasury. "Hey, they're robbing the bank." Let them go, we'll get the money replaced, and the Feds can hunt them down and arrest them. That is the FBI's job, and they became so good at it that only the terminally stupid rob banks today.

The second thing Congress did, and this came from the "we've gotta do something" side of the ledger, was to try and get a handle on "gangster guns." They passed a law, the National Firearms Act of 1934, that controlled and taxed "gangster guns." What, exactly were gangster guns? They were the "scary" guns: machine guns, rifles and shotguns that were too short, and silencers. There was some effort in the initial phases of the law-making process to include handguns in that group, with some extra agitation for that behind the scenes on the part of J. Edgar Hoover, but wiser heads prevailed.

You see, they could not ban them, so they taxed them. And the tax, in 1934, was set at $200 per transfer. A good-quality handgun back then cost less than $50, (the catalog price of a Colt 1911A1 then was $35) while a Colt 1928 Tommy gun could sell for pretty much $200. The idea that the entire population of handgun-owning-and-using Americans would pay such a tax on handguns was finally disabused before passage. Those who had a clue knew the tax would be widely ignored, and that anyone prosecuted could count on a jury of his peers to dismiss the case, perhaps even with a strong jury vote to tar and feather the prosecutor. Given enough publicity, with a string of failed prosecutions, there was a risk that later the whole law would be repealed, as Prohibition had just been. So they left handguns out, thank goodness.

Luckily for us, the tax was not indexed to inflation and, as a result, it is now a mere inconvenience. Had it been indexed, it would currently be something on the order of $3500, and creeping up still.

Procrustean legislation

You've all heard of the bed of Procrustes, right? No? What are they teaching in schools these days? He offered travelers a room and bed for the night. What he didn't tell them was that the bed was one size. If a traveler was too tall, he'd be shortened. If too short, he'd be stretched. This was the origin of "one size fits all" for clothing, but one size does fit when the clothing is a toga.

When the National Firearms Act of 1934 was passed, there was a grace period in which you could register your covered items and pay the tax. There was no internet in 1934, and unless you noticed the mention in

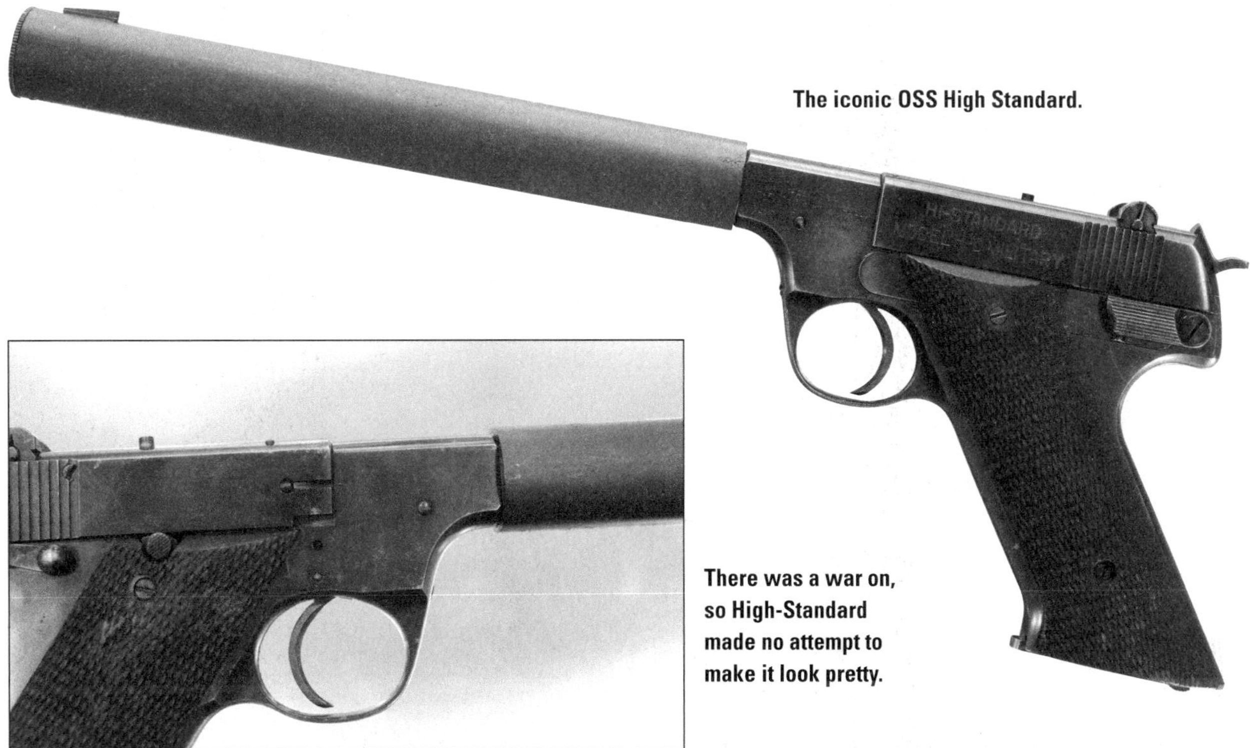

The iconic OSS High Standard.

There was a war on, so High-Standard made no attempt to make it look pretty.

the newspapers, you missed it. Once the grace period was over, that was it. Now, the Treasury Department (who handled things back then) had and has had in its successor agencies full authority to announce and implement an amnesty period. Which they did, once, for one month, back in 1968. If a firearm that is covered by NFA-34 wasn't registered back in 1934, or when it was made later, nor during the amnesty, it is illegal.

"Made later?" you ask. From 1934 to 1986, if you wanted to make a machine gun, you simply filed a Form 1, and when it was approved you got to work with the tools. Since May of 1986, you can't. During that whole time, you could buy or make a suppressor, provided you filled out and had approved a Form 1 (to make) or a Form 4 (to buy). If, however, something existed that hadn't been registered, you can't now. So, the tommy gun in the attic that grandpa brought back from (fill in the blank) war? Illegal. In this instance the old adage "it is easier to get forgiveness, than permission" is dead wrong.

So, a missed chance to register a Maxim suppressor in 1934 meant that as each one turned up it was confiscated, and either ended up in a museum or shoved into a furnace.

That's procrustean legislation; one size fits all, no forgiveness and suffer the consequences.

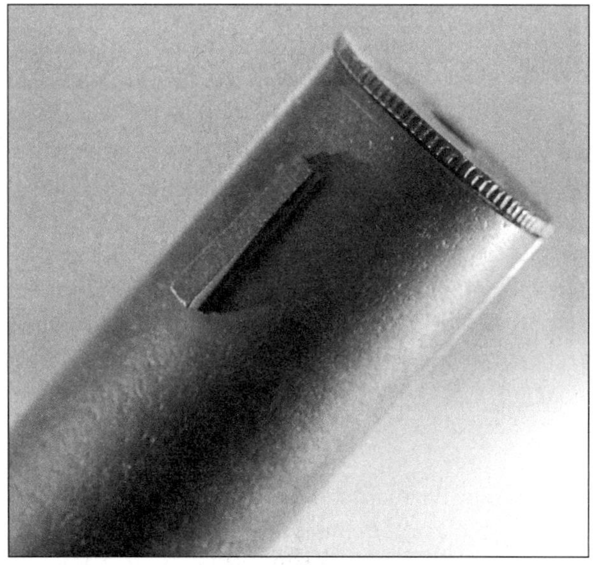

But, unlike other silencer-equipped firearms, they did give it a pair of sights.

Life moves on

This, as you can imagine, put something of a crimp in silencer R&D, sales and innovation. Which is how we ended up with silencer design being stalled for more than half a century after 1934. Who spends time and money to improve a product when the, in effect, sales

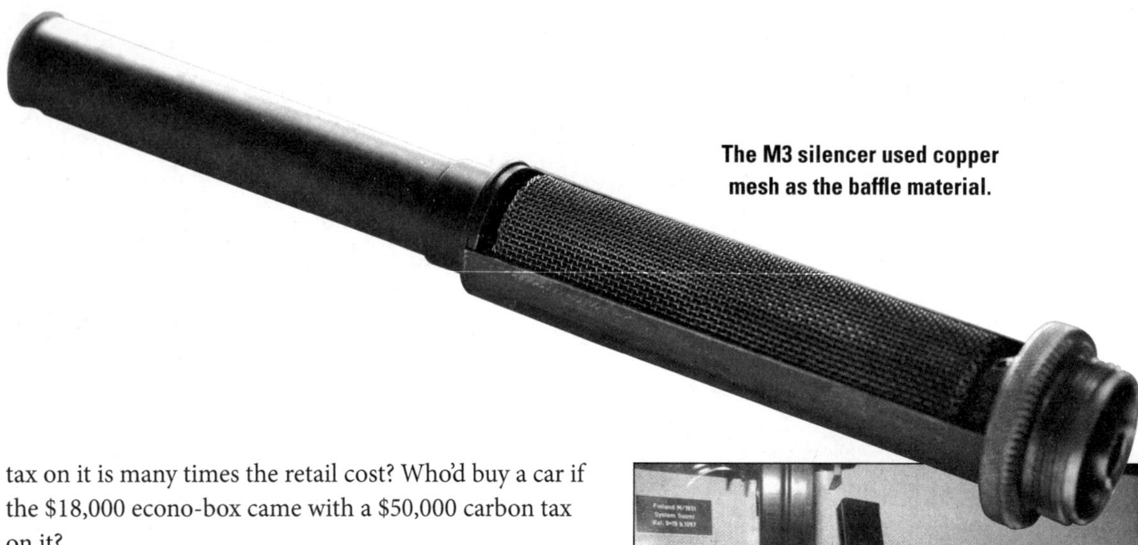

The M3 silencer used copper mesh as the baffle material.

tax on it is many times the retail cost? Who'd buy a car if the $18,000 econo-box came with a $50,000 carbon tax on it?

At the time of the depression, designers were still working on various approaches, mostly involving wipes and copper mesh. The idea was simple; if you used a rubber washer, you could keep more of the gases in the tube, longer, and thus decrease noise. And the copper offered lots of surface area to break up the shock front and mass to soak up heat.

Two silencers of WWII, one famous, one not, are illustrative: the OSS-issued High Standard and the M3 "Grease gun." The High Standard was their regular .22LR USA Model H-D (MS) pistol, the "MS" standing for military-silent. The barrel of the MS was drilled for vents, and the entire length was a suppressor tube. Inside it was packed with copper mesh. This was so quiet that, allegedly, the head of the OSS, "Wild" Bill Donovan, took one into the Oval Office and, while Roosevelt was distracted, emptied the magazine into a sandbag and then placed the pistol on the President's desk. (Hey, there was a war on, Donovan was a trusted guy, and the Secret Service hadn't yet made a career out of ramping paranoia to 11.)

The High Standard was made with a vented barrel and, inside the tube that was the suppressor, they (High Standard and the War Department) had baffled it by means of copper mesh. What they did was take screen-door like material, but made out of copper, and stamp little washers out of it. By sliding a fistful of these washers over the barrel, before tightening on the tube, they provided both gas expansion and a heat sink.

The brass was cheap, easy to manufacture, worked reasonably well, and if it got too caked up and you had spares, was easy to change. If you didn't have spares, you could clean the copper mesh. In all, the government

Since the Sten was made in small shops all over England during the war, we should not be surprised that silencers for them have a variety of looks.

ordered 2,500 of these little gems, and continued to use them for decades afterwards. (They ordered 34,000 non-suppressed ones for general training and marksmanship.) U.S. Air Force pilot Lt. Gary Powers was shot down over the Soviet Union in 1960, and part of his equipment was a suppressed High Standard. (Which, curiously, wasn't in the serial number list of pistols sold to the Army in WWII.)

But wars are not fought with pistols, and even when you have to be quiet, you need something bigger. The M3 has a steel tube around the barrel as long as the receiver itself, and this was packed with layers of copper mesh. Here, instead of cutting the copper mesh into washers, they simply folded sheets of it into the tube, before assembling the suppressor portion.

The British did their part for suppressed goodies during WWII. One approach was to build a suppressor onto a Sten gun. They did these for several models of the Sten, which is kind of like painting racing stripes on different years production of the Yugo. Oh, I admit it,

The DeLisle carbine came in its own shipping crate.

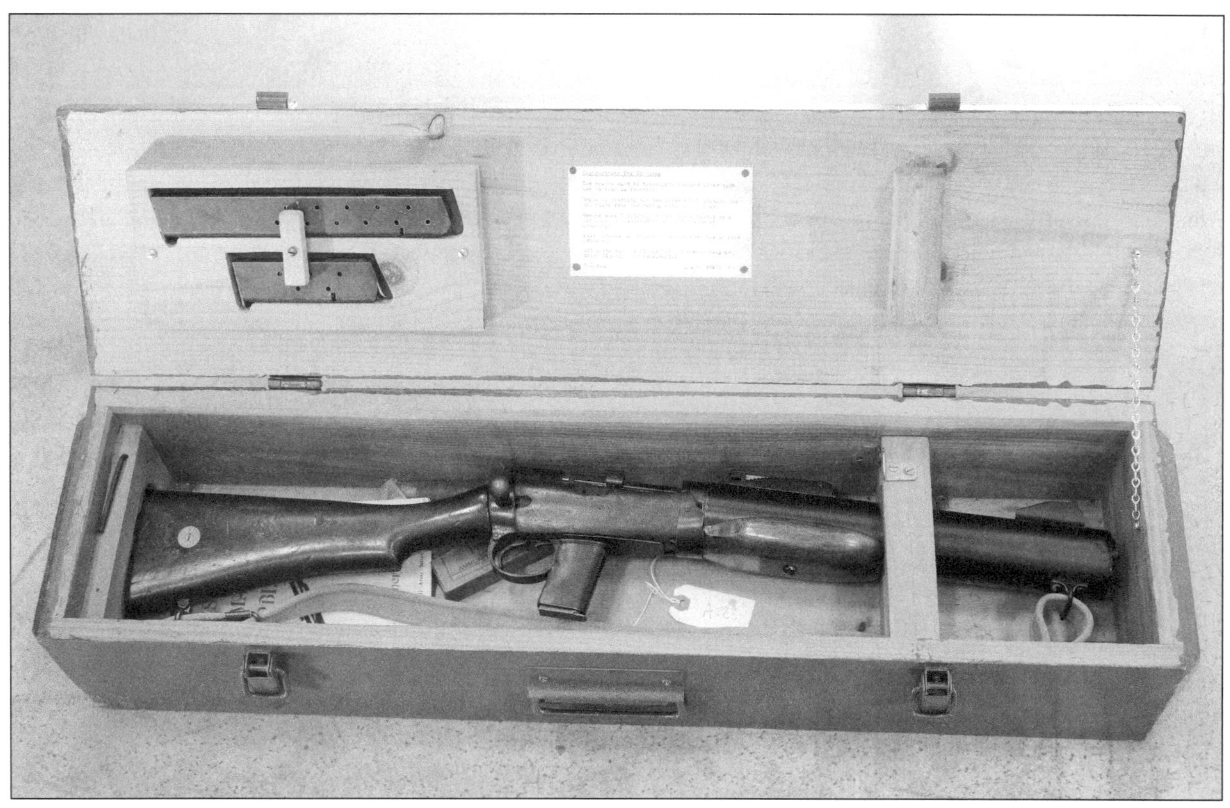

Silenced carbine, magazines, instructions. Are you jealous?

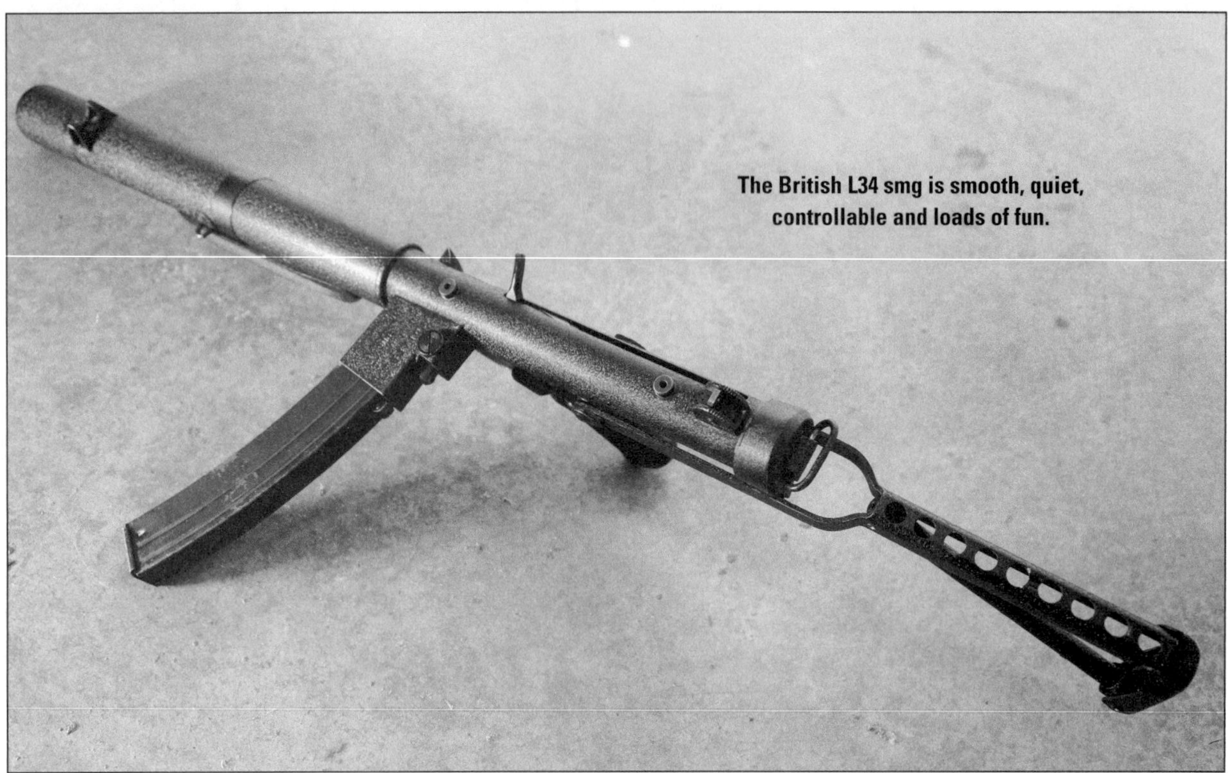

The British L34 smg is smooth, quiet, controllable and loads of fun.

the Sten works a whole lot better than, and for longer than, a Yugo. But really? The Sten versions were both integrally suppressed and external suppressed models. I had a chance to see one of the latter in the Military Museum in Copenhagen, and the maker of the suppressor seemed to have been more invested in looking good, than the maker of the Sten it was attached to.

The British also made the DeLisle carbine. Or rather, DeLisle made the initial prototype, and convinced the British that no, it would not be better, were it made in 9mm. A converted SMLE, built to be .45 ACP, and integrally suppressed, the DeLisle is a fabled bit of history. In all, there were maybe 130 of them made. Given the three-quarters of a century since, multiple wars and other scraps, not many have survived. I was talking to a serious collector and historian about this, and there are eight known original ones to exist. And if a ninth were to appear, the collector frenzy would be amazing.

The British did update their suppressed smgs after the war, and the L34 Sterling was the result. Where the Sten is crude, bulky, awkward and ugly, the Sterling is as smooth as a civilized sports car. And quiet.

While the wartime designs were an improvement over the previous designs, we did not continue improving after the war. Yes, the High Standard and the M3 both worked, but they were not as effective as we now know a silencer can be, they were heavy, and due to institutional inertia and the tax, they hung on forever. Both of these were still in use in Vietnam and afterwards, and the next step, the silencers of Mitch WerBell, were not much better.

A quick side-step here, before we go delving into dead ends. If you ask a firearms cognoscenti – a real maven of the spec-ops field – about "hush puppy," they'll be happy to tell you. In Vietnam, the existing suppressors from WWII were still in use, but they were showing their age. And the latest, hottest, hot dogs were the SEALs. They needed something better than a ten-shot .22 pistol (the High Standard), or an elderly .45 smg that was just about the size and weight of an M1 Garand (the M3 "Grease" gun). The tool they got was a S&W pistol, with a suppressor on the barrel, and the suppressor was amazingly small, light and effective. At least for 1969 it was. It was called the "hush puppy" because one of the tasks was to eliminate guard dogs at VC compounds (or so the stories go). One aspect that was insisted upon, for reasons that are still head-scratch inducing, was a way to remove the noise of the cycling slide. So, the frame of

The famous Hus Puppy from Vietnam.

the pistol had a lever installed, when moved, that could be used to lock the slide closed.

Now, I wasn't there. I've never been in that situation. But it seems to me that a falling, shot body makes noise. And if you want to shoot again, you have to hand-cycle the slide, which makes noise (albeit, not as much). In any event, the pistol is now known as much for its fabled uses, and its rarity, as for any effectiveness it might have had.

Oh, the Soviets were not letting any grass grow under their feet, either. I've seen suppressed Makarovs and a suppressed Czech Scorpion. The Scorpion used an interesting approach to attachment: a collet. The simple axial clamp held the suppressor on, but with some help. You see, even in .32 ACP (yes, a suppressed, select-fire .32 ACP sub machine gun. Wow, what where they thinking?), the forward thrust of the muzzle blast would blow a suppressor off the barrel. So they machined the barrel with a small lip, and the collet ran over this lip and clamped behind it, staying put when fired.

On the same trip where I saw the Sten in Copenhagen, I had my eyes opened about the Soviets. Part of the trip had us visiting Talinn, and while there I saw a newspaper notice about a nearby town, Paldiski. Paldiski was the eastern-most ice-free port on the Baltic that the Soviets had access to, so they put a nuclear submarine training base there. They moved in the staff, families and trainees, expanding the population from 4,000 to almost 20,000. When the Soviet Union fell, they moved out.

The locals, all 4,000 of them, were left with an immense pile of rubble. No, I'm not kidding. The buildings that had been built as housing were miserable copies of buildings. They appeared to have been built with whatever showed up on the train each week (and the town was at the literal end of the line).

They moved into buildings that were in the best shape and scavenged materials from others to keep theirs livable. I'm a pretty nosy guy and fearless in a lot of respects. I took one look inside the doorway of one of the buildings they left and decided "I'm not going in there." Despite being masonry and concrete and only ten years empty, it was dangerous. I've seen buildings in Detroit, empty longer than that, that were safer to enter.

On a later trip, I had a chance to visit another secret Soviet sub base (there were four main bases, I've been to three of them now, pretty much just by chance) in the Black Sea. It is tunneled out of a mountain, with

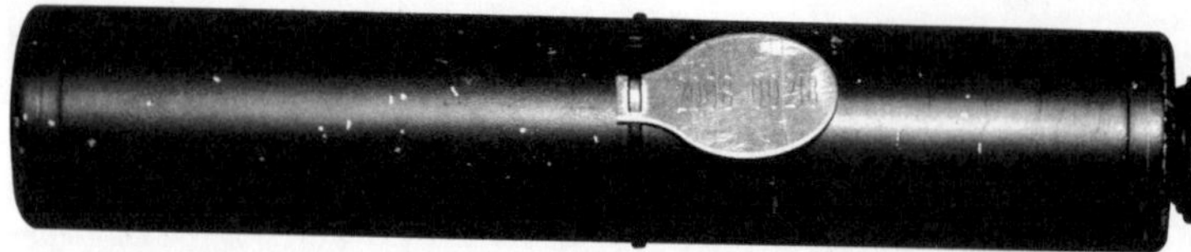

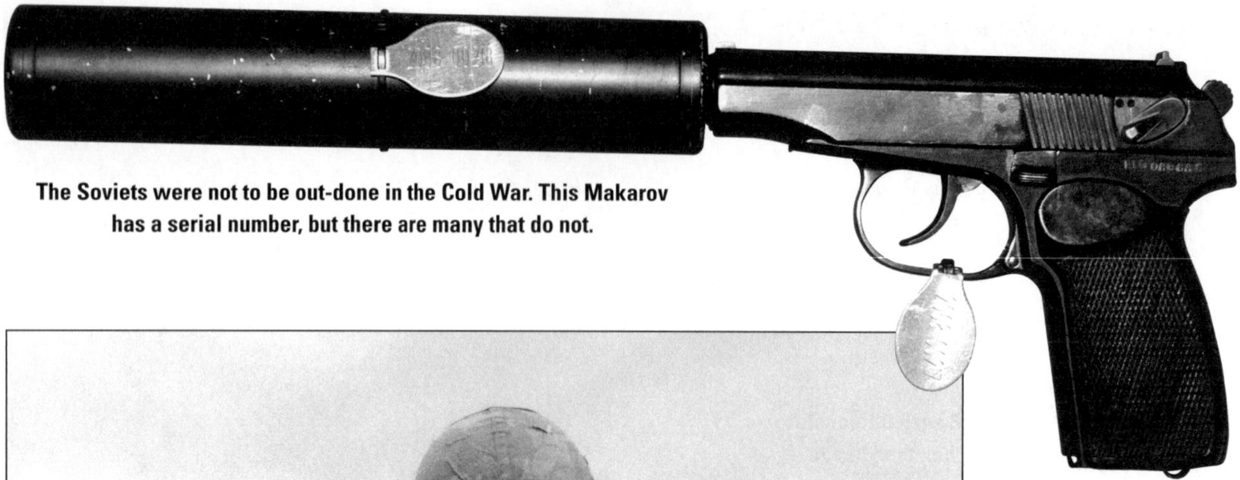

The Soviets were not to be out-done in the Cold War. This Makarov has a serial number, but there are many that do not.

As if the M16 wasn't light, short or handy enough, the Army, even though they didn't want the M16, wanted more. Here, a Vietnam grunt is packing an XM177 of one or another variant. Hope he made it home.

A Czech Skorpion, a .32 ACP smg, complete with silencer.

a secret, underwater exit. All very James Bond-ish, if James Bond and the crew had had to work on a shoe-string budget. I've learned more about the former Soviet Union from those two visits than I had in years of reading before.

They could make big, strong, crude weapons in volume, yes. Everything else? Epic fail.

The MAC-10 smg was the brainchild of Gordon Ingram. Mitch WerBell is the designer of the suppressor to fit on the Mac-10, and the founder of Sionics, the company that built the suppressors. The two are now-and-then conflated, that is, if you ask people who made the Mac-10, the answer you get is "Mitch Werbell" or "Sionics." Nope, but since the two always went together, in the movies at least, like peanut butter and jelly, it is easy to see why.

If you've seen one or both of a couple of movies, you've seen them in action: John Wayne in "McQ" and Robert Redford "Three days of the Condor." In McQ, which is the first movie the Mac-10 appears in, John Wayne is a police officer who investigates the murder of a friend. As was common for police movies then, he uncovers a conspiracy involving dirty cops, drug dealing, and lots of big cars. In Three days of the Condor, the bad guy is using the Mac-10.

This was state-of-the-art Soviet housing for the staff, family and students of the nuclear submarine program. This is one of the sturdier abandoned buildings, and I wouldn't go into it.

In both movies, the vigorous cyclic rate of the Mac-10 was part of the cinematic appeal. When revolvers were still the norm for defense, seeing a hand-held buzzgun clip through ammo at 1200 rpm or faster was eye-opening.

Anyway, the real star at the time was the Sionics suppressor. Except, looking back, it wasn't much. I've since seen the insides of one, and the idea that Werbell had

The Mac-10, a buzzgun of historical significance.

A secret Soviet sub base in the Black Sea. Now a tourist destination, and all clearly James Bond on a shoestring.

was to machine the baffles as two opposed aluminum spirals; that is, to make one half spiral one way, and the other half the other way, so the two waves of gas would crash into each other and cancel out. Nice try, but not so. Oh, and that's the front half, the smaller-diameter tube. The larger-diameter tube of the assembly? That's the expansion chamber, and it is filled with, are you sitting down? Shoe eyelets. Yep, the brass circles that the shoe maker clamps into the sides of your shoe, that you run the laces through.

Essentially what gives it its function is its size, being a lot bigger that we now accept for 9mm, 40 and .45 cans. Today, a normal 9mm suppressor is petite compared to the Sionics. The Sionics is nearly a foot long, and has two diameters, nearly 2.5 inches and two inches, and it tips the scales at nearly two pounds. It had a steel tube, not aluminum or titanium. A common modern-day 9mm suppressor is 1-3/8 inches in diameter, eight inches long, and weighs seven ounces. (The specs of a Thompson Machine ISIS-2, by the way.) The Sionics suppressor is bigger and heavier than a modern suppressor made for the .338 Lapua, but not as big and heavy as one for .50 BMG. That should give you an idea of the progress designers have made.

One very cool thing that came from all that was the "briefcase gun." This was a Mac-10 with suppressor that fit into a salesman's sample case or fat attaché case. And, you could even fire the gun without taking it out of the case.

I have to make a slight correction here, not all silencer development stalled. There was one advance, during the Vietnam War, but in typical government/Colt clumsiness, the end result wasn't entirely successful, as a rifle, as a silencer and as a continued item of government property. And, it wasn't even developed with the idea of being a silencer in mind. The M16 was brand-new, and the army was already not satisfied with it. Having moved from a rifle that was almost four feet long and ten pounds, to one that was three feet long and six pounds, they wanted something even smaller and lighter.

Mitch Werbell thought he could increase efficiency by making the gas fronts cancel each other out. He was wrong, but the suppressor worked anyway.

A salesman's sample case, right?

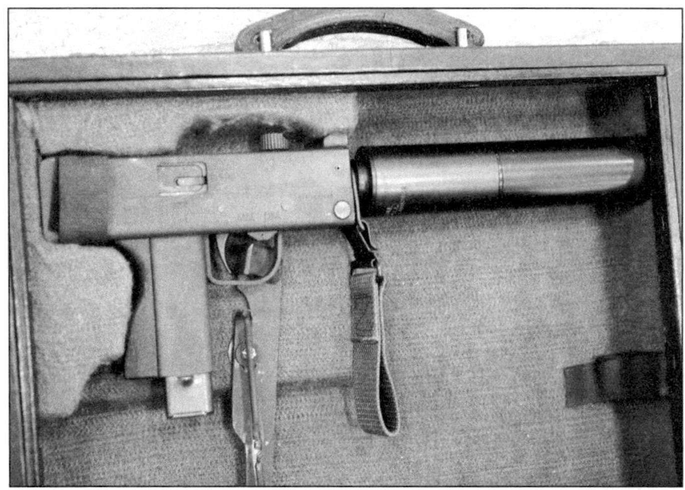

Inside is a Mac-10, with suppressor, room for a magazine, and it can be fired without removing it.

Talk about low-tech. The baffle stack in this Soviet silencer is a length of plastic rod, drilled with a hand-held power drill.

So Colt took the rifle, moved the gas port back, chopped the barrel back to ten inches, and installed a new, telescoping stock. One problem (among many): there wasn't enough gas system dwell time. The distance from port to muzzle was so short they found it difficult to properly regulate gas flow. Lengthening the barrel to eleven and a half inches helped, but what Colt did was construct a "moderator" and install it.

The idea was to slow down gas exit enough to boost the gas system, without adding more inches of barrel length to do it. (Hmmm, slowed gas release, is this sounding familiar?) They were successful, and the XM177 in its various modification designations (A1, A2, etc.) were used for a long time. The Air Force calls the carbine the GAU-8 (Gun, automatic unit) and has used them since.

The XM177 moderator had the beneficial effect of also dampening the noise a bit, but not nearly to the extent of one of the same size properly designed and built today. But, if it knocks off noise (and the interesting culprit here came about when it was tested with .22LR) then it is a silencer, and has to be treated as such. An interesting side note: once the XM177 moderator was declared a silencer, Colt could not export it without a real hassle. Rifle without silencer, no problem. With silencer you might as well be trying to export a tank, a helicopter, something that was a real war item. Colt, in one of their rare moments of rational thought and planning, decided that if they were going to export carbines without silencers, they might as well do a proper engineering work-up, and did.

The end result was the M4 carbine. And, since Colt had done all the work on its own dime, the M4 technical data package was not government property. If the government wanted it or the M4, they had to pay Colt for it, they could not put it up for competitive bid, as they later did with the M16.

The XM177 moderator is/was complicated to make, not user-serviceable, and didn't knock many decibels off the sound, but it did serve its intended purpose: give gas system dwell time a bit of a boost, and improve reliability of the CAR. As a silencer it is not as effective as a modern design. As a means of adding gas dwell time, it works.

Silencer design took a big step forward in the late 1970s and early 1980s, when experimenters began wringing out the particulars of baffle design, shape, spacing and internal diameters. I inadvertently found myself in part of this, early in the 1980s, when I went to work for a short time for the Marex Corporation. We imported the Spectre smg (with plans to make it a semi-automatic pistol and carbine), the Panther 9mm smg, and a suppressor for the Panther.

A rare and expensive suppressor from the Gulf War era, complete with unused wipes. Unused and very expensive-to-replace wipes.

By today's standards, the suppressor was too long, too heavy and probably not as quiet, but it seemed like magic back in 1983. Alas, it and the Panther were made in South Africa, and the import plans foundered on the rocks of sanctions and import restrictions placed on the apartheid government. The Spectre? I never found out why it didn't make it as an imported firearm, but when the sample came back to me again in the rotation (there were only a few in the country, and they had to be rotated amongst the staff) the firing mechanism was out of order. I took it apart, took a look, deemed it on-par with Italian automotive engineering at the time, and figured that was that.

One experimenter who raised the bar was Dr. Phil Dater, who started making silencers, selling them and then improving them. In an interesting convergence of life, engineering and arcane, when I was in Dr. Dater's suppressor class, he had a sectioned Panther suppressor for show. It was every bit as big and heavy as I had remembered.

And, old ideas got recycled and appeared as "new" ideas. When the crack cocaine epidemic was raging across America, the DEA and a lot of police departments found themselves not just raiding drug dealers, but drug labs. Drug labs, at least those run by amateurs (and not professional chemists) have all kinds of dangerous vapors. Muzzle flash can set off the flammable vapors. So, Colt made a suppressed 9mm smg for the police. It was integrally suppressed, it is heavy, it works OK, and it isn't as useful as the modern external ones. But it was what there was, in the 1980s.

When it came to buying silencers, the government either made the mistake of doing things right, or by mistake did the right thing; they bought existing designs from existing companies. The suppressors you see on the rifles of the SpecOps troops? The silencers you see in photos from Iraq and Afghanistan? Those are off-the shelf cans. Oh, the end-users gave feedback as to weight, size and durability, but the government never drove suppressor design by issuing requests for proposal with size, weight, etc. performance standards.

Thank goodness.

But, the track record of the small arms we have adopted over the previous century goes a long way to explaining why a radiologist, Dr. Dater, was the initial force moving the suppressor R&D meter off of "dormant."

Next up was Reed Knight, Jr. the owner of Knight's Armament. He jumped in, and started making suppressors for the "secret squirrel" organizations of the military. OK, you need a bit more background, if this is to make sense.

The normal methods of procurement for the military are arcane, byzantine and lengthy. Basically, the government entity that has a need for something, anything, once they get provisional funding for that something (let's just call it "an automobile"), then issues a blizzard of paperwork. It may start out as a "Draft solicitation for [Item X]" or "Request for Proposal," depending on god only knows what. The exact types aren't important (but many will obsess over them) but think of it this way:

Gov need cars.
Gov issues provisional notice to buy cars.
Gov prints specifications for cars.
Manufacturers propose cars to spec.
Lowest bidder wins contract.
Gov amends specs, manufacturer amends price.

Once the car, now weighing nine tons, running on approved, renewable fuels, complete with issued maintenance manuals weighing thirty-seven pounds, is purchased in bulk by Gov for $317,000 each, military units can request to be issued one.

If the unit has the "money" (really just accounting fictions, for a lot of this they don't really have a checkbook to use) and its assignment calls for them, they can "buy" the cars from government inventory. If they need any changes made, they have to do the changes themselves, provided the changes are approved by regulation.

The spec-ops guys found this to be unworkable. They needed things not in "the system", and in some instances the things they needed were things that they didn't want just anyone who could pore through a copy of the federal budget to read about. And they needed them faster than the multi-year process of acquisition that was "normal" for the government.

So they were granted budgeting authority outside of the system. And this was a real checkbook, with real money to use, not intra-office accounting figures. They could ask a particular company (i.e. not put it out for bid) to make them something to test. If it worked, they'd buy a bunch. If they still worked after being abused, they'd buy a metric buttload and issue them to all the operators. So, they could go to a company like Knight's, say, "We need something to do this, whatcha got?" buy test samples and use them until they were used up.

They'd either, depending on the performance and feedback from the operators, tell the company "No thanks" or "Can you make this better, here?" or "These things rock, here's a check for a whole bunch more of them."

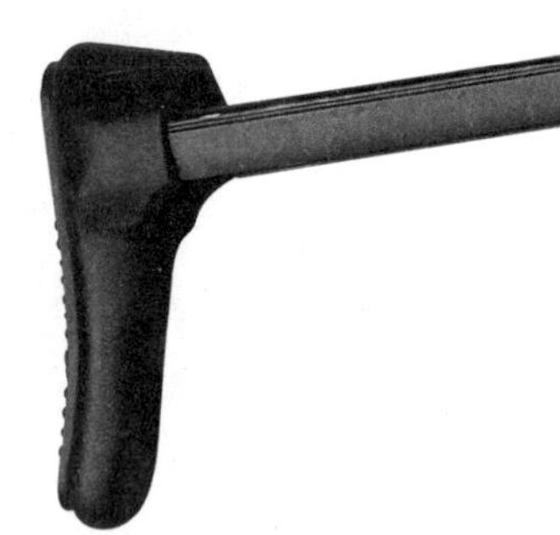

This of course is just the kind of system the whole creaky edifice of procurement was constructed to avoid. Because in the past, this was an avenue for crony contracts and was to be avoided. How does the modern system avoid that? Pretty much through modern communications. If someone gets too cozy, charges too much, etc., the end-users know that they are being denied better gear or being over-charged for gear. And it just takes a few words into a Congressman's ear to bring the whole oversight mechanism down on miscreants. Not that problems don't crop up, but it is harder to pull off these days.

The independent budgetary authority had an inadvertent good effect, however. The spec-ops people were not isolated from the line troops. In a lot of their jobs, they were simply there first, but counted on back-up from regular infantry units and others. The regular infantry could see what the "cool" guys were using. If it was a matter of placing an order with Blackhawk (just to pick one), then guys who could afford it, would. Soon, a new category of gear cropped up: COTS. Commercial, Off The Shelf gear got approved for use in a lot of instances. A unit commander could, as another example, see that his guy's boots were not good for their deployment. He'd approve other boots. If someone bought something that worked, the rest would too. And vice-versa, if someone bought a piece of crap, no one else would buy it. This was extended to unit budgets. A unit commander could request budgetary authority, real money, and then buy his crew the right rucksacks for their job.

Well, we're now out of a shooting war. In a real all-hands-on-deck combat situation, local commanders have a lot more leeway. The COTS approach is still used, but more and more the old ways are coming back. As I write this there's a lot of pushback on one of the

The HK MP5SD. Since HK only sold these to police departments, your chances of owning one are slim to none.

Maxim made silencers in a host of calibers, just as we do today.

examples I gave. The army is now trying to find a way to put the boot genie back in the bottle. Soon, it will be "wear issue boots or pay the penalty." And if the issue boots don't fit your feet? Hey, if the Army wanted you to have those non-standard feet, they would have issued them to you.

Which is why, despite all the good and rational reasons for suppressors to be general-issue on small arms in the military, I despair of it ever happening. Because, the spec ops people will get the ones they want, but the regular infantry will have to settle for whatever manages to survive the procurement process. Mark my

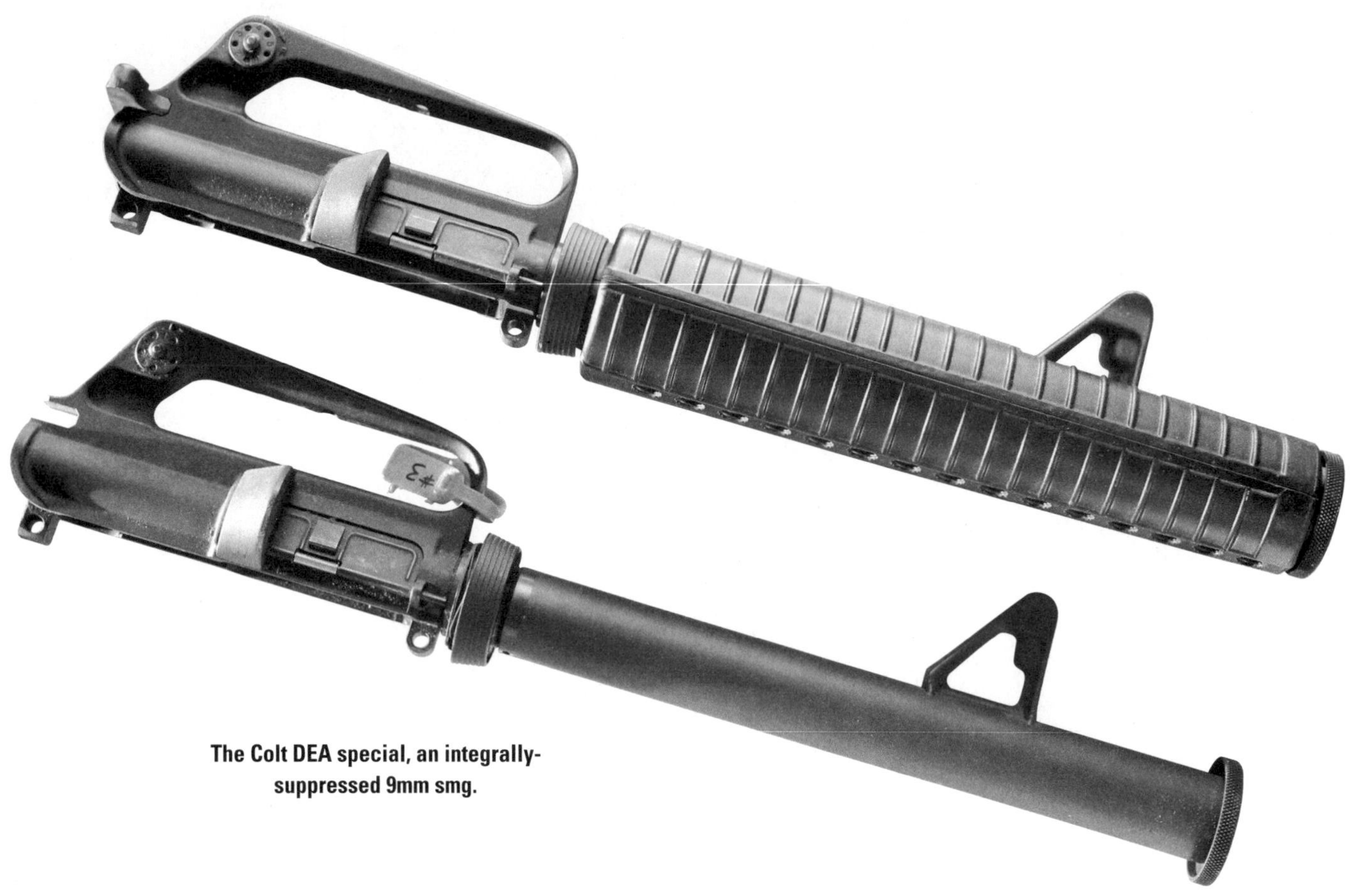

The Colt DEA special, an integrally-suppressed 9mm smg.

words, if the Army does ever adopt a suppressor, it will be a mess. Where a regular rifle suppressor costs about a grand, and weighs maybe 18 ounces, once the Ordnance process is done, the Army-adopted suppressor will cost more than twice that, and weight at least twice that. Oh, and there will be an insistence that the new Army suppressor be adaptable to all weapons in all calibers. (You think I jest, but in your heart, you know it to be true.)

But back to our tale.

The beginning of the new era of suppressors came in the 1990s, with the advances by Knight's and others. But what really threw it into high gear was 9/11. All of a sudden, all the old pejoratives of being a "survivalist" and other similar deprecatory descriptors fell by the wayside. A lot of people realized that if there was going to be help, it had to start at home. Katrina kicked it into overdrive.

It was during those and other discussions that I came up with the phrase, "You are the first responder to your emergency," and I still think it applies. So, how did this affect suppressors? Simple, when people decide they need something that will help them through hard times, they get serious about laying hands on it. Or them. Or the skills. People decided that having an AR-15 was a pretty smart thing to do, which drove the AR market through the roof, past a couple of crashes, and back to steady and higher-than-before sales. And since machine guns were prohibitively expensive (to buy, and to feed), they looked for what other tools could help. And lo and behold, suppressors were poised to be the next tool. By the 'oughts inflation had reduced the sting of the transfer tax to just about nothing. OK, another bit of perspective. When we started buying and building ARs, back in the 1980s, the transfer tax was $200 and you could buy a case of ammo to feed your AR for not much more than $100. Less, if you bought imported ammo. I did the calculations, and I could reload for less than that, so I could reload .223 ammo for maybe $75-80 a thousand rounds, which is how I came to get relatively good at shooting an AR, and wear out a number of barrels.

I remember sitting in a law enforcement instructors meeting later, this just after 9/11, where the State

Bid ammo prices were announced. This is the volume-buy ammo price for which police departments could buy ammo. The price for 5.56 (not just .223) was $143 per thousand rounds. Now, as individuals, we'd have had to pay the 11% Federal Excise Tax that the departments wouldn't have to, but at that price, the extra $16 was hardly an imposition. Within a few years the price would double, and then go up some more.

At one point, before the ammo crisis eased, a group of us instructors were talking about that time and commiserating. "If I had known, I'd have cashed out my 401K, and stuffed my garage full of ammo." Well, we didn't, we didn't, and we're still in possession of our 401Ks, so it wasn't all that bad.

So, we came to a time when a suppressor costs less than a grand, the transfer tax is $200, and a case of 5.56 was selling for something like $350, and suddenly a suppressor didn't seem like such an expensive purchase.

There was another variable that added to the number of suppressors. Since the late 1980s, when Florida changed its concealed carry licensing laws, the spread of "Shall Issue" carry laws across the country has come to this: there is now almost no place left where concealed carry is unlawful. Oh, there are places where you have to be wealthy and politically connected, but for most of the rational parts of the U.S., concealed carry is the norm. The grass roots campaigns to get the laws changed had not just the desired effect, but also the effect of energizing the populace.

"Hey, if we convinced the legislature to allow concealed carry, what about suppressors?" And so it spread. Now there are 42 states where suppressors are legal to own. And if we keep in pressing, there will be more. More states means more potential buyers, which creates a marketplace for more suppressor manufacturers. It is a parallel to the AR-15 market. When I started working on ARs, there was Colt, and a few others, plus some OEMs who made stuff for Colt and the others. Now you can't go fifty feet at the SHOT show without seeing either an AR-15 or an accessory for same.

At this rate, in a few years or a decade or so, we won't be able to keep track of all the companies that make suppressors. I mean, when Remington buys a company that makes suppressors (AAC) to add to their lineup, you know there is a market for cans.

Oh, and the subjects I raised in the beginning? Silencers, assault weapons and mass shootings? We've already looked at silencer history, and found that they long pre-dated James Bond and Three Days of the Condor. OK, if we use the basic anti-gunners definition of an assault rifle, a self-loading rifle with a magazine you can change, then "assault weapons" have been around since 1906, when the John Moses Browning-designed Remington Model 8 first hit the racks of hardware stores across the country. If that won't do, then there were lots and lots of rifles, smgs and others designed in The Great War, so the earnest but ignorant at VPC have missed the mark by three quarters of a century.

Mass shootings? My friend Dave Fortier takes the credit for finding this bit of history of a school shooting in Bremen, Germany, in 1913. The bad guy showed up with a literal bag of revolvers, and when the shooting started, the teachers, staff and passersby swarmed the school, and despite some of them being shot in the process, overwhelmed the gunman. The police then had to rescue the gunman from them, as the crowd was more than willing to take him to the roof and throw him off.

Compare that to the "modern" response. It is to weep.

No, history is long, reading it takes time and effort, and you can learn things. A lot of people don't want to run that risk, or so it seems.

Chapter Three

SILENCER MYTHS

Illegal? Never. Some states have prohibited them within their borders, but they have always been legal, federally-speaking.

Fair warning, this chapter will be stuffed full of snark, mockery, derision, scorn and even a little bit of pity.

Some of the myths out there are really, really, stupid. Epically stupid. And we have the movies to blame for a lot of them. Plus, the movies feed these myths to Washington, and there they get turbo-charged and sometimes fed right back to Hollywood. And sadly, we have only ourselves to blame. Every time we bought a ticket to a movie where James Bond stylishly screws his elegant silencer onto his PPK, we teach the producers that we'll settle for style over substance. In that vein, my wife has complained that I have ruined action movies for her, as she now sees all the bad gun-wrangling presented to us on-screen.

It has been worse. Watch an old spy or detective movie from the 1950s or so, and sooner or later you'll see someone screw a silencer onto a revolver. "Phhht, phht, phht" and the deed is done. Apparently, and for a long time, no one in Hollywood had a clue that there was a gap between cylinders and barrels, and that gas escaped from them. Making it even more ridiculous was the size of the silencer, typically about as big as a D-cell battery, screwed onto a snub-nosed revolver.

Now, there have been suppressed revolvers. One revolver you really can suppress (but why would you want to?) is the Russian Nagant. You see, the operation of that revolver is peculiar. As the cylinder rotates, the last action is to cam the cylinder forward, over the rear of the barrel. The cartridge case is longer than the seated length of the barrel. So you have multiple overlaps; the case mouth sticks into the forcing cone, while the cylinder slides over the exterior of the barrel stub. Thus sealed, you can count on much, much less of the gas escaping than you would on a real revolver.

Still, after all that, you have the 7.62 Nagant to depend on; a .30 bullet of 95 grains or so, not really breaking the sound barrier. Not your magnum stopper, and it is still a Nagant revolver, too. Meaning it is not exactly ergonomic, it isn't elegant (and we do care about fashion) and if something breaks, no one can fix it.

Reed Knight made a silenced revolver for the Navy, the agency, someone, we really don't know, back in the late 1980s. This was built on the hell-for-tough Ruger Super Redhawk, using a proprietary cartridge based on the .44 Magnum. The bullet was .30, and the reason for all this was to meet some pretty particular requirements. The un-named agency that asked for this wanted reasonably rapid follow-up shots, as low a sound signature as possible, and no brass left behind. What, they never thought of a canvas bag over the ejection port? It had a shoulder stock, it was integrally suppressed, and it used the Ruger scope mount system to clamp whatever the spy guys wanted on top. After Knight's made an unknown number of prototypes, the project was dropped.

If and when you see a silenced revolver in a movie, you have permission to laugh out loud.

Another myth is that high-end assassins check into luxury suites across the street from their targets, and there assemble their suppressed rifles from an attaché case. First, the idea of high-end assassins is laughable in and of itself. Second, anyone who might fit that job description would be far too smart to check into the hotel across the street, in this day of CCTV, facial recognition and instant ID and credit card checks.

I wish I had photos to go with these, but alas, I believe in intellectual property rights. I'd have to ask the studios for permission to use their photos and, once I start describing the mockery that will ensue, they'll never give it. Oh, to be carefree and oblivious to trademarks.

Another myth is that anyone can make a suppressor from stuff lying about. Oh, you can kludge together a reasonable silencer, that's for sure. But aside from Steven Segal, in "Fire Down Below" where he uses a two-liter pop bottle as a silencer (and in the noisy environment he uses it in, it would be moderately effective), most scenes of silencer making are pretty bad. One comes to mind: "The American" with George Clooney, who makes a silencer for a rifle with plumbing washers and a drill press. Well, OK, maybe. For a few shots, but not to the level of effectiveness they show in the movie. How does he thread the barrel, and does he really think no-one knows why he's buying pipe, washers, renting a machine shop, and taking long walks in the country by himself?

And then there are the really old, silly and "where'd they think of that?" ideas: the potato-stuffed-over-a-muzzle "silencer." Oh, when used on a .22LR it will probably work for a while, with little-to-no accuracy, but the scene I remember with great derision was one where a gang-banger shoves a spud over the flash hider of an M14. First, there's the thought of a gang-banger even having an M14. And knowing how to use it? Oh, that combination is going to work just fine, dude. And pillows? Really? Does no one in Hollywood realize that for a couple of generations at least, pillows have not been stuffed with goose down, but various synthetic foams? Sure, decrease the sound by a whopping 2 dB, but it will also set fire to the pillow, and make the fire alarm in the hotel go off. That'll lower your profile, now, won't it?

Which brings us to sound levels. Everyone who owns a suppressor knows how much it really decreases the sound. And everyone aspires to, and many load ammo to, movie levels. You know, the "Phht, phht, phht" sound. You can do it in certain situations. One is a subsonic load in a .22LR firearm. Or subsonics in a .300 Whisper or 9mm/45. But when you see someone using a bolt-action, center-fire rifle, (again, from the luxury hotel across the street) or a military rifle, and you hear the mouse-fart "sound" of it going off, you know you are deep into Hollywood sound production fantasyland.

Even with a suppressor, there's an audible crack, the supersonic crack of the bullet in flight. The supersonic sound can't be avoided, except by going subsonic. There's the brass flying, if it is a self-loading rifle. The noise of the action as it cycles. It would be nice if they spent even half as much time on those details as they did fussing over the exact shade of lip gloss on the starlet, whose lips we aren't even looking at, anyway.

Hollywood, alas, doesn't just fill viewers heads with fantasy and myth. They also inform the opinions of staffers who write executive summaries for Senators and Congressmen. And they see silencers as tools of the assassins. I guess, if I'm going to be fair (and where's the fun in that?), if you are a well-known politician and you've crossed a few, or more than a few, powerful people, you may well believe that someone out there just might be able to find a high-cost assassin willing to be in the luxury suite across the street from yours. As if. Not to be crude about it, but the potential hit-man money would be far better spent with a private investigator, in order to uncover dirt, and then use that information as leverage.

But, it is a child-like belief in political circles that some of the things they think are true about firearms are actually true. (And life in general, as well.) If you believed the political class, every drug gang out there is equipped like a Marine Force Recon fire team, with all manner of high-tech gear, firearms, organization and planning. I guess none of them have read Freakonomics, where we find out that drug gangs have an economic structure amazingly similar to that of a fast-food franchise. Money always flows up, talent sometimes flows up, but no extra cost is incurred unless it can bring in more revenue. When it comes to guns, the street staff uses what they can buy or steal, and they use them (if they expect to stay in their present positions) "on the job" only when the bosses feel it is cost-effective.

Shooting the opposition to "keep" a street corner tends to be counter-productive, especially when the police show up, take ownership of the entire block for the ensuing investigation, and make selling impossible until they and the various news show trucks leave.

But, to a gun-control pol, it is a matter of faith that every four-man drug "gang" has a warehouse of machine guns and silencers. And if they don't, there's a gun-runner with a big-box-store-like warehouse they can choose from.

Oh, I almost forget about that one: the "guns for hire" entrepreneur, who has a warehouse full of goodies to choose from, for a price. Nope, not the case. Criminals buy guns from other criminals, who stole them or got their girlfriends to buy them, and they aren't shopping out of the "criminal suppliers catalog."

The reason we see so many "stupid suppressor tricks" on TV and in the movies mainly comes down to the hothouse environment of script writing. What works (i.e.; gets ratings or critical acclaim) gets done to death, and anything new is avoided, mostly because it doesn't have a track record.

The ten seconds it takes to see a fit man wearing sunglasses walk into a hotel room, open an attaché case, and begin assembling a rifle is all the "writer" needs, and all the Director wants, to tell the audience that this is a bad man. Soon, someone will get shot, thus propelling the story forward. Nowadays, an hour-long TV show only has 42 minutes in which to tell its story. Every second wasted beyond the cliché of the hit man and hotel room is time taken from telling the rest of the story.

The reason we hear so much nonsense from politicians about guns in general, and silencers in particular, is that many of them have one skill: getting elected. For the majority of them, actually being able to run a business is not a skill they've had to learn, and when your "information" comes mostly from executive summaries, summaries written by people whose job depends on pleasing the boss, then no one writes anything other than what the boss wants to hear. The rest of the "position" on a subject is often based on the biggest campaign contributor. If someone just deposited a big old pile of money into your re-election campaign, there's a powerful incentive to at least pay lip service to their cherished notions on things like guns.

Historically, you will run into the myth that "silencers are against the law." Nope, not ever, at least not at the federal level. Before 1934 they were not even addressed by federal law, and since then they have been controlled and taxed, but not illegal. Some states have made them unlawful to own, but in the last couple of decades we've seen that change, and the tide is now towards more and more permission. As of writing this chapter, the number of lawful-to-own-a-suppressor states clicked up to 42.

That doesn't mean that just because it is lawful, it is easy. Some states make it allowed on paper, but the process is onerous enough to be next to impossible. The CLEO sign-off is one aspect of that. Then there are places like Illinois, where until recently, they were simply illegal. Not even the police, or even police departments could own suppressors. Oh, the Feds operating in Illinois could issue them, but only as agency equipment. If you were an FBI agent in Illinois, and you owned personal suppressors, you'd best leave them back in your home state.

That changed recently, and now Illinois allows suppressors for departmental use, but only when issued to "teams." That is, if your department has a SWAT team (or whatever it might be called), the department could acquire and issue suppressors, but only to the assigned team members. This, of course, and in proper political fashion, was not well thought-out. I mean, let's suppose your department isn't very big, and your "Emergency Response Team" is your whole department. That is, every officer is trained for the ERT, and when something happens, whoever is on duty switches into team mode. Does that mean your whole department is authorized to be issued suppressors, under state law? (sigh.)

Or can they only have them when they are actually assembled as a team? And if so, do they have to store them at the station when not assembled as a team? The city next door is bigger, and has a full-time ERT. Can the ERT members perform non-ERT duties, and still have the suppressors installed on their rifles? This is what happens when non-technical people start exerting authority into technical areas.

And lest you think I'm picking on Illinois, the "average" attitude towards suppressors in state legislatures is more toward irrational than rational. Thank goodness for the states that held the line, kept them legal and obtainable, and thus saved them for the rest of us when we came to our senses.

Then there are the purchase myths. Yes, the government does a background check on you when you apply for a transfer. Are you put on a list? Probably. It will be just one of the hundreds of lists you are already on, most of which you put yourself on. Every rewards program you've ever signed up for is a list, every credit card you've ever owned has you a list, and so-on and so-on.

The Feds are checking up to make sure you don't have a criminal record, using the hundreds of databases to which they have access. Once they have assured themselves that you don't have a record, they pretty much forget about you.

The same can't be said for the airline you bought tickets from seven years ago, to go to Wallyworld, or for Wallyworld itself. They never forget, and will never stop emailing you, despite what the moose out front told you. So forget about "the lists" as a problem to worry about.

Should the government be keeping lists? No. But given all the other ways they have to figure out who has what, if you own a "papered" firearm, something that has gone through the 4473 process, they can figure that out.

Once you have your silencer, you do not give up your Fourth Amendment right against search and seizure. If the BATF&E ever gets it into their head that you might not still have possession of the silencer you bought a decade ago, they'll just phone up and ask. If they want to see it, you can meet them at your front door, show it and the tax form, and be done. Or go there with your lawyer, and show them the item. Make an appointment.

If they show up at your door one dawn with a SWAT team behind them, it will be for something a lot more serious than the notion that you might have misplaced your suppressor.

That, or you've been *swatted*, and wouldn't it be nice if we could find the people who did that, and flog them until our arms got tired?

So, no, ATF agents will not be knocking on your door insisting on "inspecting" the silencer, and they cannot do a sweep of your house, just to see what's there.

The same holds for the local, county and state law enforcement agencies of your jurisdiction, but I can't say that with the same assurance as I can the Feds. You see, it is entirely possible that you live some place where the local laws say they *can* come and inspect your suppressor anytime they want. Unconstitutional? Probably. But until a case gets in front of a judge who says that it is unconstitutional, the LEOs of your area (if you live someplace like this) will keep on insisting. They'll probably keep insisting even after a judge says they can't, until he starts removing their qualified immunity and fining/imprisoning those who won't pay attention. (Good luck with that, and the legal expenses.)

Here's an interesting detail of your paperwork; your approved transfer form has on it your Tax Stamp, and as a result is technically part of your tax records. So, if you are at the range or traveling to or from the range, and a police officer insists on seeing your "paperwork," you can show him. But, the ATF and the IRS would take a dim view of him "making a copy for my report." Not that you should push this, but he's on the same grounds here as he would be, were he looking to make a copy of your 1040.

You should have a copy of the form with the suppressor, just in case. A lot of shooters simply make a reduced-size color copy, and even laminate it, to keep it in the case with the suppressor or the suppressor-equipped firearm.

To show you just how far things can go, when something is unobtainable, we used to joke around the gun shop that we didn't want to have a machine gun, or a suppressor, anyway. Who wanted an ATF agent sleeping at the foot of your bed each night, for the first six months you owned it? Yes, gallows humor, but that's how urban myths start.

Trusts

The process of acquiring a suppressor involves the "Chief Law Enforcement Officer" signature, also known as the CLEO sign-off. This is a holdover from the time the NFA/34 was enacted. In 1934, there were no centralized records. The FBI had just gotten approval to be armed. They were starting a database, but it was of felons and their fingerprints. The idea was simple: if anyone knew there was a good reason you shouldn't own something like a "gangster gun," it would be the local sheriff, or the chief of police in your small town.

So, the law simply put the signature in as a last-step measure to keep things under control, a "just in case" to keep everyone happy back in the Depression.

All the relevant portion of the NFA/34 asks of the CLEO is that they do not know of any particular reason you should not own a suppressor. It doesn't ask them to attest to your character, vouch for you or toast you at your wedding or retirement. It also does not create any liability on them for their signature. It verifies only one thing: that they don't know of any reason. And in most jurisdictions, this ends up being a "wants and warrants" check on the computer. The chief, sheriff, whomever, lets the forms pile up on his/her desk for a week, then a staffer does a "W&W" check on the computer. Those that passed (typically, all of them) get signed or rubber-stamped in one session and returned, and that's it.

But then there are the political law enforcement people. The ones who feel it is simply "wrong" for anyone not in the police force to own such a device, and as a result will refuse to sign any applications.

There's still an option. You see, the law does not define exactly who is, and isn't, the "chief law enforcement officer" of any given jurisdiction. That depends on the wording of state law where you live. So, if your chief of police won't sign, how about the county sheriff? The local state police post commander? I have heard of jurisdictions where the district attorney, coroner, medical examiner or others are acceptable.

Who is accepted by the Feds, and who will sign, is something the dealer from whom you are buying the suppressor will know. Ask them. If no one will sign (and you have to be living within the jurisdiction of the signee for their signature to be valid, you can't get a valid signature form the next county over) then there is always the "trust."

A trust is a legal instrument that acts to hold property, land, money, but not in the hands of a particular individual. Those are held by the trust. A trust can inherit a house, for example, and the officers of the trust can then rent the house or use it, and not pay inheritance taxes on ownership of it. (They do pay income taxes on the rent, however, it's a trust, not a golden ticket.) This is pretty common where houses can be very expensive and grandpa is getting on in years. You don't want to lose the house, and you can't agree on who gets what, since gramps was too crusty to make out a will. He won't sell ahead of time. Rather than have him sell it to one of the kids/grandkids (and who is the lucky one who gets that?), and pay the taxes, and incur the ramped-up tax consequences of the new value (established by the sale price), the family forms a trust and the trust owns/inherits the house. Then, someone can live in it, or later the trust sells it when they have come to full agreement on just how to divide the income without starting fistfights at the family Christmas party.

So, an NFA trust is the owner of the suppressor, and the officers of the trust have use of the suppressor (or more likely, suppressors). Here's the quirk that makes it useful: trusts aren't required to submit the transfer application for a suppressor for the CLEO sign-off. The form goes straight from the dealer to the ATF examiner.

Here's the catch; the officers are still required to be law-abiding people. You cannot form a trust, with one or more of the officers an otherwise prohibited-from-owning-suppressors-person, and have the trust shield them from the consequences.

In plain English, if one of the trust officers is a convicted felon or is otherwise prohibited from owning a suppressor, and you as another trust officer knowingly allow them to handle, use, possess or otherwise fondle the suppressor, they and you have committed another felony.

The Feds have been a bit touchy about this of late, as a lot of people new to the game have thought incorrectly that the trust shields them from this. Or, didn't think about it at all.

So, if you go the trust route, don't screw it up for the rest of us. Control who has access to the suppressor or suppressors, with the question always being, "Do I know if there is some good reason this person should not own a suppressor?" Yep, you just became the CLEO sign-off, for your trust. Welcome to the world of responsible adulthood.

Chapter Four

HOW THEY WORK

There is an expanding bubble of hot gas that comes out of the muzzle every time you shoot. Let's see if we can diminish its effect.

I have a confession to make. When I first began this chapter, I thought it would be a lot simpler. My writing method is a bit strange. (Which would come as a surprise to no one who knows me, as there are more than a few things I do differently than the group.) Before I go to write something, a chapter, an article, whatever, I first amass a big old pile of details, info, facts, figures and images. I then let them rattle around inside my head for a while, before then hammering out text. Then I re-write and re-write.

Well, my first attempt at this was straightforward and simplistic. Then, after consulting a few experts in various aspects of suppressor design and mathematics, I realized that it was a lot more complex than that. It didn't hurt that a bit of my calculus and other higher math started becoming familiar again. However, not everyone who wants to learn about suppressors, and buy and use them, is prepared (or willing) to sit through a Master's dissertation on the mathematics and physics of gas flow inside a suppressor in the microseconds of its function.

And I'm not sure I am, either, any more. So, with that in mind, I will keep things simple, with occasional forays into the more involved aspects of suppressor function for those who want to see what the next step might entail. I have to warn those who are looking forward to being the next great suppressor designer, you will be well into your second year of engineering school before you start acquiring the tools to get a handle on what is going on. Until then you'll simply be learning the basics. If, however, you simply want to make, test, adjust and re-make suppressors, you don't need a degree. Just machine tools and approved forms or a license.

Every time you fire a round, you burn gunpowder. This is a low-level explosion. (For shipping purposes gunpowder is classified as a low-grade explosive. As far as the fire department is concerned, it is merely a highly flammable solid, and not nearly as dangerous as the can of gasoline in your garage.) The primer initiates the event, the burning powder creates pressure and heat, and the pressure pushes the bullet down the bore. The heat is simply an unavoidable byproduct of the combustion process, but an annoying one that firearms and suppressor designers have to deal with.

The bullet accelerates down the bore until it leaves, or until the pressure drops below the frictional force experienced, at which point the bullet begins to slow down or fails to leave the bore. The second instance is a case of a too-long barrel. (For instance, a 20-inch barrel on a 9mm carbine will usually produce less velocity than a 16-inch barrel, which produces less than a 10-inch). The third is usually not enough, or no, powder in the case, leaving a bullet stuck in the bore.

When the bullet leaves the muzzle, the uncorking allows the full pressure of the expanding gases to escape *at that moment*, in a shock wave that you hear, and which we call sound. The greater the pressure of the gases at uncorking, the greater the decibel level of the noise. This is why an SBR is louder than a regular rifle, and a rifle chambered in a magnum cartridge is louder than one that is not, given the same barrel lengths. So, we take a rifle with a given chambering, and we replace the barrel with one that is longer. Have we reduced the muzzle blast, and as a result, the noise? Yes. So, if you want to, go ahead and replace your carbine barrel with a 20-inch barrel, and don't sweat it. No one else will.

Another approach that would appear to be a suppressor is the "bloop tube." This is a tube fixed onto the end of a barrel in target competition, to create a longer sight radius. Why not just use a longer barrel? In smallbore and airgun competition, the transit time of the bullet in the bore matters. No matter how steadily you hold it, the barrel is moving even while the bullet is

ON THE SUBJECT OF "LONGER BARRELS MAKE IT QUIETER," if you have a papered SBR, installing a carbine-length or longer barrel on it does not change its legal status. It remains an SBR on paper. You can't just swap barrels and then sell it as if it were like any other rifle. You have to write to have it de-listed. The de-listing won't cost you anything but time, there's no tax on it.

traveling down the bore. The shorter you can make that transit time, the less error is introduced into the system by your wobble. Error, in this instance, means not aimed at the "X" ring. With a bloop tube, once the bullet leaves the bore, the rifle, and the tube, can move and not influence the aiming of the bullet.

Since it is longer, and as a result the system is quieter, why isn't it a "silencer?" I can only speculate on this; and the inner workings of the ATF and, before them, the Treasury Department, are secret, but I can easily see that lacking any baffles at all, it would be a particularly dim judge who would buy the claim that it is a "silencer." Not that there is any lack of dim judges, but do you want to risk your career on being able to get one of them sitting on your case, solely on the luck of the draw?

The rifle or handgun is also what we call a "system" in physics. The system is designed to combust a solid, turn it into gases and heat, expand the gases, eject the bullet, and dissipate the gases and heat into the outside air. Anything that interferes with the operation of the system is bad. Anything that improves it (and we can have a host of variables when it comes to describing "improvements," up to and including the cost of the firearm and the ammo it consumes) is good. The history of firearms is rife with attempts to "game" the physics system.

What the suppressor does is multi-faceted. First of all, it slows the release of the gases. Think of a drinking fountain. If the pressure from the fountain is the same as the pressure in the mains, you don't get a drink, you get a shot of cold water in the face. The valves between the mains and the nozzle slow the water so you can take a drink, not become the subject of an amusing cell-phone video. That, in part, is what a suppressor does. By essentially and temporarily trapping the gases inside the can, it slows the rate at which they leave the can, and thus the compression of the shock wave of the sound.

A less-compressed sound wave is not necessarily one with less energy, but one with fewer decibels. What hurts our ears is the peak, not the total energy. In the course of a relaxing day on the beach, the sound of the waves crashing on the shore probably subjects your ears to as much audio energy as a single gunshot. But the gunshot hurts, and the beach doesn't. (Unless you forgot sunscreen.)

But that isn't all the suppressor does. It also, by allowing the gases to expand into the can, cools them. This is one of the gas laws, which will be referenced again and again. We've all used an aerosol spray can on a hot summer day. Probably paint, maybe insect repellant, those of you who work on computers or cameras will have used compressed air, but they are all the same, as far as a bunch of 18th century French experimenters are concerned. When you expand or contract, heat or cool, a volume of gas, the relationships between pressure, temperature and volume must remain a constant. So, when you expand a gas, the volume goes up. The mass of the gas remains the same, so the temperature must go down. Also, the suppressor body, being cooler than the gases, acts to suck heat out of the mass of gas, reducing its energy, and thus its temperature.

Cooling the gases expelled from the muzzle removes energy from that mass. Less energy, less noise. Basically, a suppressor, in this instance, turns noise into heat. Theoretically, a super-heated suppressor is less efficient at reducing muzzle blast, but even if the suppressor is a thousand degrees it is still cooler than the gases, and thus removes some heat, thus energy, from the gases. The cleverer among you might be thinking at this point, "Hey, a refrigerated or water-cooled suppressor would be more effective, longer, than one that isn't." Correct. However, the amount of water needed, or refrigerating capacity required, to cool a suppressor fast enough to keep up with any kind of a firing rate, would be too much.

As an example, on a TV episode devoted to suppressors, I did full-mag full auto dumps. I blasted eight, 30-round magazines through an SBR with a suppressor on it. At the end, the suppressor was so hot that the IR thermometer I had zoomed past 1,000 degrees so fast I couldn't see the numerals.

What you need to take away from all this is simple: expanding gases cool. Cooler gases have less energy to compress the air to create noise, thus lowering sound levels. Add the temperature-lowering aspects of the gas laws to the delaying action of the suppressor and the turbulence the baffles contribute, and you have a quieter gunshot.

Now, the simplest method of reducing muzzle blast, of suppressing noise, is to take a large tube, affix it to the muzzle, and then put a cap on the end, with a clearance hole for the bullet. We'll call this our Mark 1 can. Simple but not very effective. The problems are timing and pressure. The gases, as they exit the muzzle, have an initial speed of over 5,000 fps. In effect, they pressurize our simple suppressor before the bullet can escape, and the end result is little, if any, slowing of gas release. It all squirts out the front cap pretty much as if the Mark

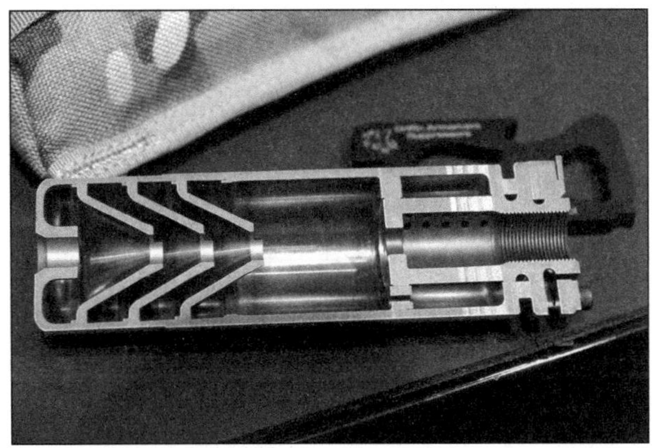

The inside of a suppressor. The angled walls are the baffles, and they delay gas release from the system.

There is also gas that comes out of the ejection port.

1 had not been there. This, of course, is the case if we use a tube that is in line with the modern design of a suppressor, a tube that is an inch-and-a-half in diameter. We can make the Mark 1 suppressor more effective if we greatly enlarge it. If we make the internal volume of the can so great that the air inside of it buffers the escaping gases, and slows them down enough to contain them, we can gain efficiency. The classic here is the one you see in movies, and which, surprisingly, actually works, that being the large plastic pop bottle. With enough internal space to slow down the gases, the plastic bottle does decrease sound. It is, however, large and clumsy. Fragile. Useful for one or two shots. And, *not* surprisingly, it is against the law unless you have a license to build suppressors and have filed the appropriate paperwork.

So, the next step to making our theoretical suppressor more efficient is obvious, add extra plates inside, called "baffles." Baffles act to slow down the gases and make the sound less than it would be in our Mark 1. The baffles now add yet another way suppressors work, by causing turbulence in the system. If the gases flow smoothly, they will not be slowed, at least not much. If you divert the gases, but the divergence is not turbulent, they will flow smoothly, albeit a bit more slowly, and continue on their way. (That's how a muzzle brake works, with a smooth divergence of gas flow pathways.) If you introduce turbulence, you soak more energy out of the system, and this both slows the release of gases and extracts energy out of those gases, cooling them and decreasing sound.

Nothing in life is without cost, however. Adding baffles adds weight. This is good, in that it provides more mass to soak up heat. It is bad in that it is not just more weight, but it is weight out at the end of the muzzle. This changes balance, makes the rifle/handgun/shotgun longer, and can alter accuracy.

Now, the gases are released more slowly but they still get out. This is not immediately obvious, and people can get hurt not knowing it. You'd think that would be obvious, "Hey, it is a firearm, sticking anything in front of it is dangerous." You're right. But for some reason people have been encouraged to be less careful, and more dependent on outside authority. Think for yourself. There's still noise. There's still a bullet leaving the area. The gases get out, quickly, just not noisily. The business end of a suppressor is still a hazardous place to be, or to put your hand, fingers or other valuable objects.

Then there is the matter of the heat. Even a few rounds of a rifle caliber can heat up a suppressor by a couple of hundred degrees. One of the first surprises you'll get, as a new owner of a suppressor, is to discover that the suppressor is hotter than the barrel. Stop and mull that over for a moment: the suppressor is hotter than the barrel. Were it not, it wouldn't be working properly. You can shoot a few magazines and make the suppressor so hot it instantly raises a blister, and still have a barrel that is warm but not so hot it will burn you. In the instance of the TV segment with the eight full-auto mag dumps, the barrel was a "mere" 300 degrees or so, with the suppressor glowing red.

You can seriously burn yourself even after a single magazine of ammo, and not even shooting quickly.

OK, so much for the simple stuff. On to the complicated stuff, details that require either lots and lots of experimenting, or lots and lots of computer simulation time.

NOT ALL DIVERGENCE OF GAS FLOW IN MUZZLE BRAKES IS SMOOTH. And please, it is "brake" not "break." Some of the gas crashes directly into the front plate of the expansion chamber, and that forward thrust decreases some of the felt recoil (the backwards force you feel on your shoulder or in your hands). The more gas you can crash forward, or the more of what is present you can capture, the greater the reduction, a simple matter of Newtonian physics.

If some of the gases are jetted back at an angle, this decreases felt recoil to a greater extent. The more gases you divert and the more smoothly they flow, the greater the reduction.

Some of the gases are directed upwards, and this counteracts the rotation of the rifle around your shoulder. The more of this, the greater the reduction in muzzle flip. When I first began experimenting with muzzle brakes, my initial design diverted so much gas up and sideways, and crashed so much into the front plate, that the test AR pulled off my shoulder and the muzzle was driven down below the target. It was too good.

Muzzle brake designers fuss over the details. A design that drives more forward is declared to be "softer" to shoot. One that diverts more gas up is declared to be "flatter" to shoot. Handgun brakes, or compensators, don't have a lot of gas to work with, and it is typically not possible to make one that is both soft and flat. There, it is one or the other. Rifles, on the other hand, can be both.

But, the guy next to you pays for it, as the gases have to go someplace. Outdoors, muzzle brakes are annoying. Indoors, they are obnoxious.

Many who shoot with suppressors feel they are also effective muzzle brakes. No, they are not. They are better than nothing, but they are not at all comparable to a real muzzle brake, just a whole lot quieter.

Now *this* is a muzzle brake. And a clear example of how they work. Lance Corporal Samantha L. Jones, USMC.

Suppressors are quiet, but they are not without hazards. There is a jet of gas that comes out. Diminished from un-suppressed, yes, but still a hazard.

Very quiet, the HK MP5SD makes you pay for it by stealing velocity.

How big? How long? How many baffles? What spacing between them? How big/small of a clearance hole can you have down the center, and still be certain that bullets won't strike the baffles? And how are you going to mount it? Let's start with the easiest, the first chamber, or expansion chamber.

The bullet leaves the muzzle, enters the chamber, and the gases get released. The shock front moves forward, initially at the maximum speed its pressure creates, let's call it 5-6,000 fps. The bullet is going half that, so the bullet is halfway across the expansion chamber when the shock front crashes into the first baffle.

At this point you're thinking of it like a smooth, expanding bubble. Alas, no. As it expands, the bubble it creates hits the walls inside of the tube, and the wave bounces off them and continues forward, but now at an angle to the bullet's travel. The shock front is decelerated by the air in the expansion chamber. The front edge of it becomes turbulent. By the time the bullet gets near the clearance hole of the first baffle, it has been, is being, buffeted by multiple shock fronts from its own gases. So, how long do you make that first chamber? And how does the internal diameter of the suppressor tube influence that length? And how big does the entrance hole have to be, to be sure the bullet will have clearance?

OK, a quick digression here, into an arcane aspect of suppressors – first-round "pop." Depending on the dimensions of the first chamber, a suppressor can have a first-shot sound signature that is greater than it will be in subsequent, soon-in-time shots. However, if you have a suppressor (and I'm speaking very, very generally here) with a louder first-round pop, it will typically have a much better decrease on subsequent shots.

This is not something that happens (the decrease) when the shot spacing is long enough for the system to re-set. That is, for the firing gases to leave, and be replaced with normal, ambient air. So, as an example, we have a rifle with suppressor, high first-round pop, five shots, one second apart, that we measure: 142 dB, 132, 132, 132, 132. Average; 134 dB. Now, we take another one, designed to minimize the first-round-pop: 136 dB, 136, 136, 136, 136. Average; 136 dB.

If you go by the averages, then the first one is "better." If you go by the initial shot, the second one is

If you want the quietest, you have to go with a manual action, to remove the bolt cycling from the noise component. You still have to work the bolt, however.

"better." In actuality, they are both pretty good, but you can hear the difference, because our ears can discern the change.

The first-round pop is influenced by the amount of oxygen in the air, in the suppressor. So, those who desire the absolute quietest first shot, for operational purposes, will go through a peculiar ritual. They will load their firearm. (And no, I *do not* want you doing this, even as I explain it.) They then use an aerosol can of some inert gas to spray a shot of the gas into the suppressor, and then affix a circular seal over the front cap. They purge the oxygen from the can, and then seal it. No oxygen means greatly reduced or eliminated first-round pop.

I explain it as part of the background on the first round pop, but I do not want you putting anything out in front of the front cap of your loaded firearm. Hey, I may tell you that navy SEALs swim in the open ocean, but that doesn't mean I think you should, too.

Even in daylight, you can sometimes see the muzzle flash of a suppressed firearm.

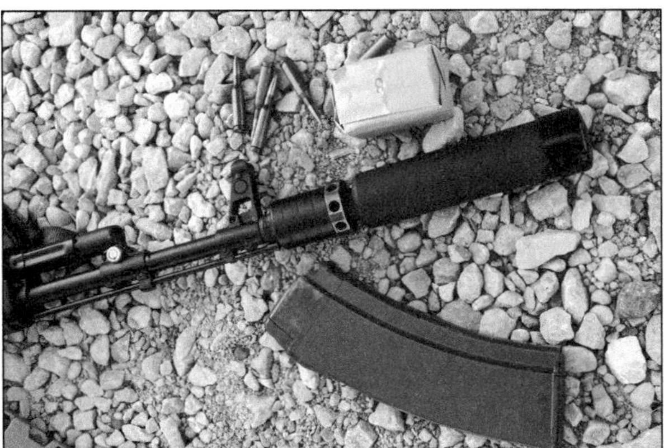

Not all firearms can be easily suppressed.

The gas system of the AK vents to the atmosphere. (See the holes in the tube above the barrel?) The owner of this AK installed a valve to meter gas, work the system and be as quiet as possible.

OK, let's address wipes. No, not baby wipes, or the moistened towlettes you get handed on the airline, before they serve you the alleged food they've been steaming for hours. Wipes in silencers are rubber or other synthetic membranes that let bullets pass through, but keep sound/gases in. They were an early attempt at efficiency, but they had some pretty serious downsides. One was they weren't really efficient, the sound still got out. And second, they were bad for accuracy. Why?

When your bullet gets forced down the bore, it is rotated by the rifling. When it gets spun up and still in the bore, it is rotated around its center of form (Cf). When it leaves the muzzle, it begins free flight, and once in the open air it must rotate around its center of mass (Cm).

No matter how good the bullet maker is, there will be some microscopic difference between Cf and Cm, and it takes time for the bullet to shift from one to the other. During the time interval/distance that elapses until the bullet "settles down" it is unstable. This time extends from the muzzle to whatever distance it takes for the bullet to stop yawing. This was covered thoroughly by Franklin Weston Mann in his book "The Bullet's Flight" more than a century ago.

Wipes are obstacles the bullet has to squirm through, right at the beginning of its yaw phase.

Modern, well-made fmj bullets do not suffer nearly as much from wipes, partly because of bullet quality and partly because of wipe material uniformity, but there is still some disturbance. Back in the early days, bullets were not so good, and wipes were thick, stiff and irregular. Accuracy could, and did, suck.

Oh, and softpoints and hollowpoints? They can be problematic. After all, they are supposed to expand when they encounter resistance, and just what do you think a wipe is? Some might expand, some might not, and some might take 2-3 wipes before they begin expanding. It depends on the bullet, the wipe material, and the velocity.

Limitations

Not all of the noise that your firearm makes comes out of the muzzle. (We'll ignore for the moment the giggling that usually follows one's first experience with a suppressed firearm.)

Also, not all of the noise you hear is simply that of the gases escaping as the bullet leaves the bore. There are seven sources, and not all of them occur in both suppressed and un-suppressed firearms. They are, in order, precursors, projectile exit, exit gases, blow-by, jetting, action and supersonic.

Precursor is the compressed air that was in the bore, being pushed ahead of the bullet. Suppressors, or at least good ones, scavenge a lot of this before the bullet has entered the suppressor.

Bullet exit is the sound of the bullet exiting the muzzle, or exiting the suppressor. A suppressor with a wipe as the last baffle can have the sound of the bullet squirming through the wipe as a noticeable part of the noise.

Gas exit is the big one, the one we are most interested in controlling. Depending on the cartridge, there can be a little or a lot of gas to deal with.

Blow-by is what happens in the suppressor, as the

Suppressors are messy enough, without adding wet to them. Wet suppressors splatter like there's no tomorrow.

gases exit the muzzle with more velocity than the bullet does. This can lead to gas escape, or pressurization of gas in the suppressor, and a "jolt" of gases out the suppressor before the bullet gets out.

Jet noise is the turbulence and harmonics of gases inside the suppressor, and whistling as it exits. This can be good or bad. If the frequency of the turbulence causes the noise to be shifted out of human hearing, then it is good. It still makes noise, but who cares if dogs can hear it? (That's a joke.) If the turbulence causes a pronounced increase in the human hearing range, we would tend to say it isn't a very good suppressor.

The bolt clacking back and forth and the brass being flung out to strike the ground, pavement, wall, whatever, is the fifth source of noise. The AR-15, just in closing the bolt, generates a sound of 120 dB, more or less. Other firearms can be worse. And then there is the venting gas of the gas system itself, an entirely different source than the main ones we have laid out. Obviously, bolt-action rifles are not subject to this source of noise.

The gas that the system uses is not all that the system bleeds off of the bore. Some are worse than others. The AR bleeds the gas back into the receiver, by which time the pressure has been greatly reduced.

The AK has gas vents right on the front end of the piston tube. The gas pressure there is much higher than the gas pressure in the AR receiver. Another egregious design (when considering suppressors) is the FAL. The gas system is adjustable, but the adjustment is how much gas gets bled off into the air. Less bleed, more thrust. More bleed, less thrust.

That gas comes pretty much directly out of the bore, so it is at high pressure. If you want to suppress an FAL, you have to deal with that extra gas.

One rifle that doesn't have this problem is the HK G3 and its derivatives. Of course, it has a whole host of its own problems, so suppressing it isn't high on the list of "must do" for the tactical set.

The end result is simple, you don't get as much reduction. Let's say you have a super-duper .308 suppressor, and on your 24-inch bolt action rifle it gives you a 40 dB reduction (which is very good, by the way). If you park it onto your 20-inch-barreled FAL, you aren't going to see a 40 dB reduction. The gas, venting out of the gas adjustment, will be a noise the suppressor can't address or reduce. And it gets worse. When you are firing unsuppressed, you are using a certain gas setting and only venting so much gas. When you install the suppressor, you need less gas (the increased dwell time of the gas, remember?) and to keep from making recoil harsher, or over-working the parts, you need to vent more gas. More vented gas means more noise. Some firearms are just noisier than others, and you find this out when you try to make them quieter.

Last on our hit parade is the supersonic crack, but the solution there is simple: either live with it, or load subsonic ammunition.

Wet vs. dry

There's one more way we can increase the efficiency of a suppressor, and that is to add heat-absorbing materials. The one in question is a good one – water. Water soaks up heat. That heat can be put to good use.

A BTU, or British Thermal Unit, is the amount of energy needed to heat one pound of water by one degree Fahrenheit. A calorie (aka a small, or gram, calorie) is the amount of heat needed to raise the temperature of one gram of water by one degree Celsius. A kilo-calorie, or food calorie, is the amount of heat needed to raise a kilogram of water one degree Celsius.

OK, good enough as it goes. But here's the best part; once you have heated water to the boiling point, it takes a whole lot *more* heat to turn it into steam.

The "latent heat of vaporization," as it is known, is impressive. It takes one calorie to raise the temperature of a gram of water from 99 degrees Celsius to 100 degrees Celsius. But to turn that same gram of water into steam takes another 540 calories.

So, we can see that we can get an inexpensive boost to the efficiency of our suppressor with water, right? Just add some water on the inside (outside doesn't do any good) and things will be quieter. Where do I sign up?

Alas, there is no free lunch.

First, there is the weight. A gram of water adds weight to a suppressor. Granted, we are talking about a teaspoon of water, five grams, in a suppressor that weighs over a pound. This is on a rifle that weighs ten pounds. Not a big deal. But make it stay. If it drains out, you lose the efficiency boost. If it drains back into the bore, you have a potential over-pressure problem. So, you need a cap or a seal on the muzzle, and you have to remember to keep the muzzle down, or some water will slosh where you don't want it.

But, the other over-pressure effect is the one we worry about. You see, water in the suppressor takes up space. And water is a non-compressible medium. Were it compressible, hydraulics wouldn't work, at least not those filled with water.

Fill a rifle suppressor with water and then fire it, and you can double pressure inside the suppressor. That is not good, unless the manufacturer made it tough enough to withstand those pressures, in which case it is heavier than it would be otherwise.

Manufacturers will list a suppressor as being either "wet" or "dry" and in some instances will say their product works both ways. If you want use it wet or dry it will always be quieter when wet. However, since the water is a sacrificial element in this operation, as the water evaporates, the decrease goes away.

What won't go away is the splatter.

Shooting a wet suppressor is a messy experience. You will find that you, the bench, your hands and arms, maybe even your face get splattered by wet, steamy, powder residue and oily bits. Short of wearing a tarp, there is no way to avoid this. For goodness sake, if you are in charge of demonstrating suppressors to higher-ups, don't let them shoot wet suppressors. If you do, make sure they have their "work" clothes on.

One way to deal with the possibility of draining, either out of the muzzle or into the bore and chamber, is to use a gel. The typical product is a water-based, wire-drawing lube. The gel is about the consistency of petroleum jelly. You squeeze a bit out, and using a wooden stick, rub it onto the baffles. It won't run out, and it will evaporate when the heat hits it. Once it gets hot enough, and the water has been evaporated, the gelling agent gets burned out. This is all good, until you go to shoot. Gel splatters more than water.

Wet is quieter, but wet is messy, and wet doesn't last. And, depending on the particular model and application, being too wet can break your suppressor. But the lure of 540 calories per gram is there, no doubt about it.

Chapter Five

WHAT THEY ARE MADE OF AND HOW THEY ARE MADE

Maxim made his silencers out of mild steel. Today we have many exotic alloys to choose from.

You need bar stock to make baffles on your lathe. Manufacturers need truckloads of bar stock.

For a long time, for a lot of us, it didn't matter what suppressors might were made of, because we could not get them. But now we can, and what they are made of is of vital importance. We've each of us spent a lot of money, time and effort acquiring a silencer, and we want it to last. So, metal matters. The Big Four are steel, aluminum, titanium and Inconel. I have no doubt that someone is working on carbon-fiber, and there are other metals that could be used, but let's take a quick look at suppressor anatomy before we look at these.

The guts of a can

On the outside we have a tube. It holds the internals together, keeps them aligned and provides an anchor place for the end caps. The ends caps, front and rear, do two things; they provide a means of disassembly (if the suppressor is a take-apart design) and they give a mounting location and gas seal.

Mounts we'll cover in the next chapter, but for now you need to know that the rear cap is mount-specific, either threaded or some sort of quick-attach system.

Inside is the baffle stack. Baffles come in a number of flavors. They can be flat, contoured, unitized or monocore. One thing they are not is unidirectional. They will all have a designed direction for most effective suppression. Some will be machined so they can only be assembled in a given orientation or order.

And, it has to be mentioned repeatedly, they will be caliber-specific, or caliber restricted. That is, you can only use them on a firearm chambered in the designated caliber, or smaller ones.

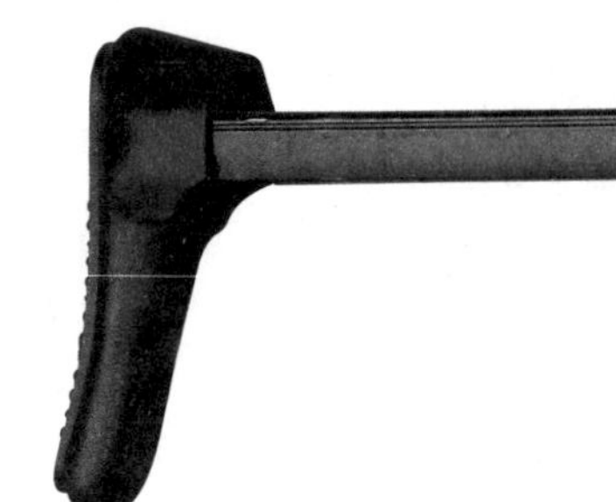

Steel

Steel is, at its essence, iron with a certain amount of carbon in it. Mild steel has a

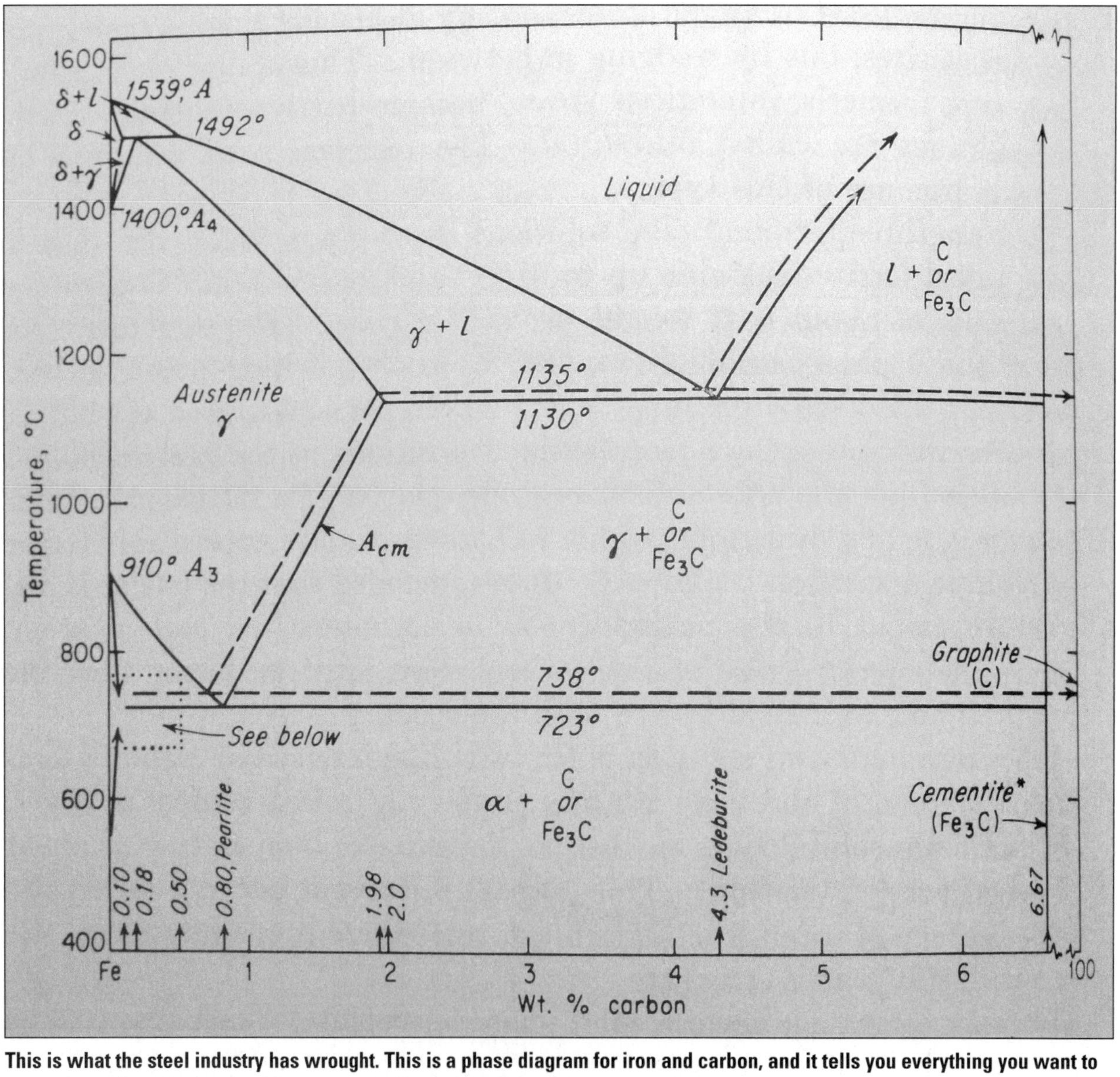

This is what the steel industry has wrought. This is a phase diagram for iron and carbon, and it tells you everything you want to know. Compiling the data for this chart probably produced a couple of dozen PhDs.

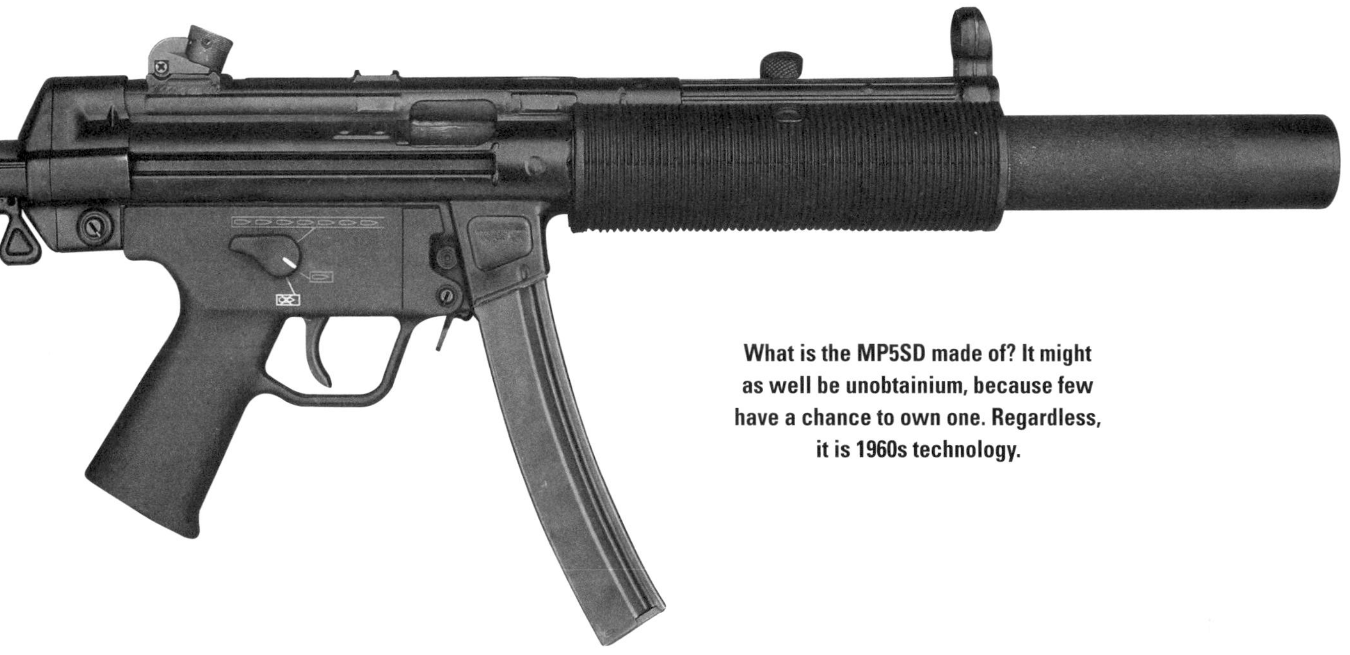

What is the MP5SD made of? It might as well be unobtainium, because few have a chance to own one. Regardless, it is 1960s technology.

little carbon, and "carbon" steel can have a little or a lot, depending on just who is using it. "A lot" of carbon, in steel terms is one percent, by the way. A high-carbon steel could be one with little more than half a percent of its composition being carbon, the rest iron and/or other alloying metals.

Alloy steels are those with other metals mixed in with the iron and carbon. An alloy can be selected or formulated to make it stronger, corrosion-resistant, easier to machine, and any mix of, or all of the above.

Due to the industrial revolution, and accelerated by the auto industry, steel has been studied extensively. It is possible to know what alloys (mixtures of iron and other metals) do when subjected to various heat-treatment methods, and how they will react to given loads in varying circumstances, and their corrosion rates in given environments.

Common, hard alloys are recipes like 4140 ("ordnance steel") and 4150, the alloy used in M16/M4 barrels. The four-numeral SAE designation tells you how much of what is in it, but not the heat-treatment, mixing process, heat-soak times or other variables. Think of the SAE number as a list of ingredients, but lacking a recipe. Mild steel would be something like SAE 1050. The number is just a starting point. It is possible, but highly unlikely in the modern competitive steel market, to buy bad 4140, and good 1050, and have the 1050 be a superior metal.

"Stainless" steel is simply alloy steel with so much nickel or chromium or both added to it that it more-or-less won't rust. Except it will, if you abuse it enough. One aspect of stainless steel that is unfortunate is that rust-proofing and heat-treatment/hardening are antagonistic. That is, the more rust-proof you make your alloy, the less you can harden it, and vice-versa. By the time you have added enough nickel and chromium to a steel to make it truly rust-proof, it isn't very hard. Look at your stainless tableware for an example of that. You can bend it, if you aren't careful. Your silverware will have a maker's name on it, and maybe an indication of the alloying in it. Numerals such as "8-18" or "9-10" indicate the relative amounts of nickel and chromium.

In firearms and suppressors, we use stainless alloys like 316 (common stainless alloys get a three-numeral SAE code) or 17-4PH.

These have enough alloying in them to be very corrosion resistant, but still hardenable. Firearms and suppressor manufacturers increase the stainless ability of stainless steel by a process known as "passivation." What they do is simple; they use a chemical or other process to bind to, and thus lock up, the microscopic sites on the surface where oxygen would attack the steel. If there's no place, in effect, that oxygen can get a bite, it can't oxidize.

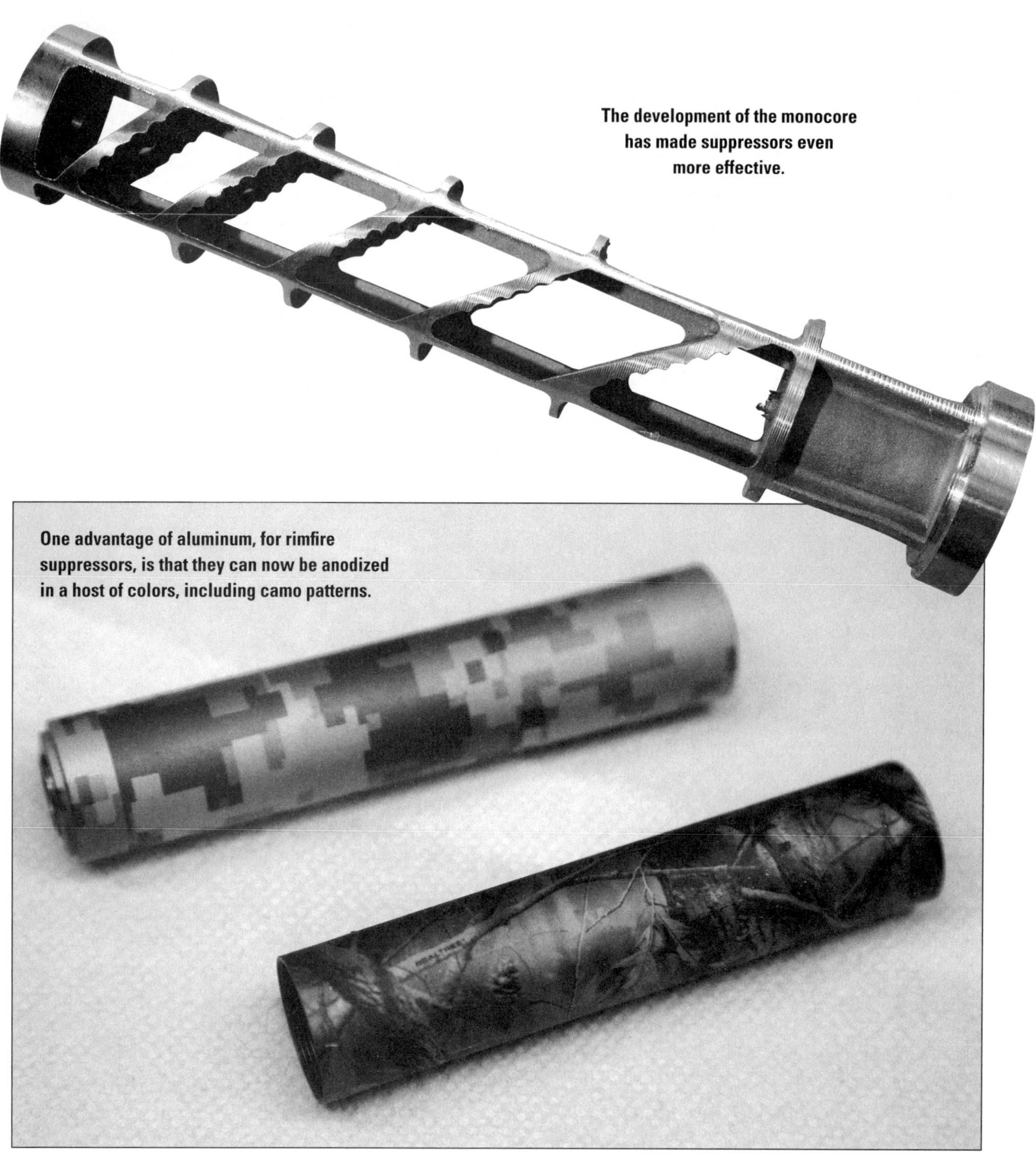

The development of the monocore has made suppressors even more effective.

One advantage of aluminum, for rimfire suppressors, is that they can now be anodized in a host of colors, including camo patterns.

Think of it as taking up all the parking spaces, and there's no room for the carload of party-crashing oxygen.

Steel has a density, depending on the alloy, that varies from 7.7 grams per cubic centimeter up to 8.1. (Ounces per cubic inch? That conversion gives us 4.45 oz/in^3 to 4.68 oz/in^3. Does that help?)

Steel is immensely strong. Well, the carbon steel and alloy steels. Stainless, no so much. Steel, depending on the alloy, may have a yield strength of only 40,000 PSI. 4140 alloy has a yield strength of 60,000 PSI. 4150, the barrel steel of mil-spec ARs, has a yield strength of 65,000 PSI.

Aluminum

Now common, aluminum for a long time was unknown, and even once discovered, remained rare. It so tightly binds to its oxidation partners that it was prohibitively expensive to smelt, despite being as common as dirt in the planet's makeup.

The two common alloys here are 6061, also known as "aircraft" aluminum, and 7075, known for being used in AR-15/M16 receivers.

Aluminum is quite soft, and bare aluminum is not something you would want to make suppressors out of. The softness is addressed by a process known as anodizing. This is a chemical and electrical treatment that creates a hard surface. The hardness adds enough strength that an anodized part is more than strong enough for some suppressor applications. (It is still far too soft for use in rifle-caliber suppressors, for example.)

Aluminum is used where great strength or heat resistance is not needed, or lightness is greatly desired. You'll find aluminum mostly in rimfire and pistol-caliber suppressors.

The density of aluminum is a little more than a third of that of steel. The yield strength of aluminum depends on the alloy. 6061, also known as "aircraft" aluminum, has a yield strength of 35,000 PSI. 7075. The alloy used in AR receivers, and many suppressors, has a yield strength of 62,000PSI.

The sharp-eyed reader will look at the yield numbers and wonder, "Has Sweeney lost his mind?" Everyone knows steel is stronger than aluminum. Yield strength is a different measure of strength than tensile strength. When it comes to tensile strength, steel is four times as strong as aluminum or stronger.

Inconel

Inconel is a family of alloys so laden with non-corrosive metals that they really can't corrode, outside of an acid bath of impressive strength. Its main attribute, besides non-corrosion is its resistance to heat. Most metals, and even alloys, lose a significant percentage of their strength when they become red-hot. Inconel does not. Of course, it does not start out as a high-strength alloy,

Some silencers don't need exotic, high-strength alloys. The calibers they deal with aren't that robust.

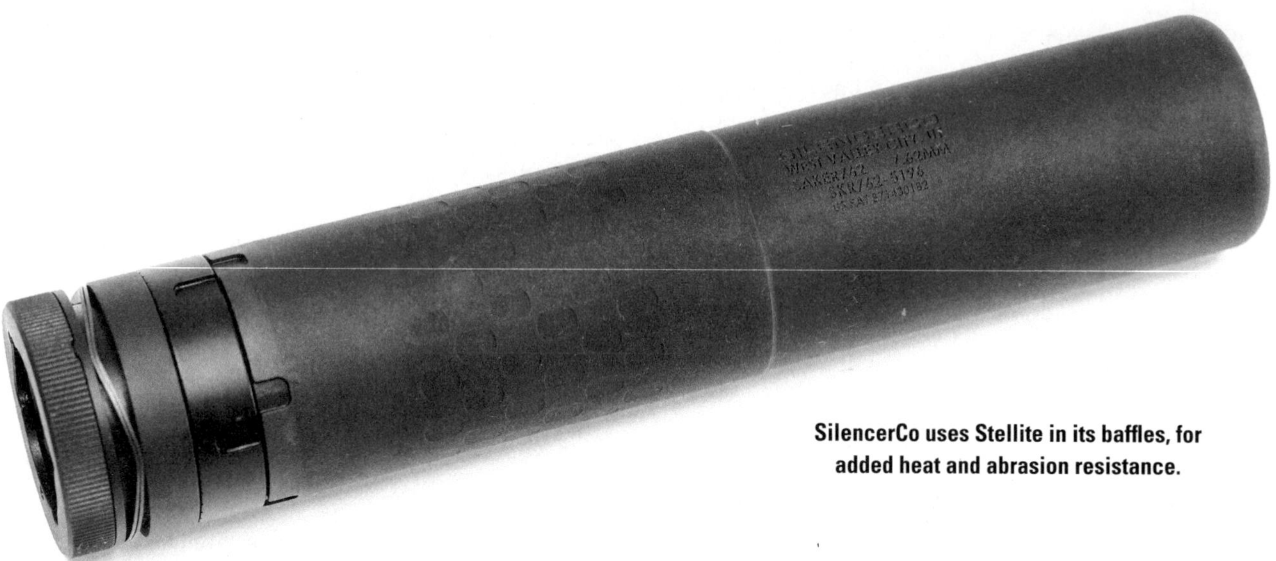

SilencerCo uses Stellite in its baffles, for added heat and abrasion resistance.

so you will find Inconel on the inside of a suppressor, used in baffles, but not for the external tube. It has a high cost, and is extremely difficult to machine.

In addition to the useful attribute of heat resistance, Inconel has great abrasion resistance. Some formulas of Inconel have been developed to emphasize the corrosion resistance, others to aid in weldability. Inconel, depending on the particular alloys being compared, can have a density 10% to 30% greater than that of steel. However, there isn't so much used in a suppressor that you could pick them up and tell which had identically-shaped baffles of Inconel vs. steel.

In researching Inconel, I came across papers on welding and corrosion testing of Inconel that dated back to the 1960s. It may be a new alloy for us in the firearms end of things, but to aerospace engineers and in marine applications, it is an old friend.

Titanium

When it comes to cost, titanium is king here. Also, when it comes to strength, heat-resistance, non-corrosion and light weight, titanium is king.

One interesting aspect of titanium is its weldability. If you take two pieces of steel, identical in composition, and weld them together with a "stick" of the same alloy, the join is the same alloy, but it will in all likelihood not have the same crystalline structure as the rest of the part or parts, those being the non-welded areas. The weld will be different – different in color when blued, in

YIELD, TENSILE, WHAT'S THE DIFFERENCE?

It depends on what you are measuring. The tensile strength of a material is the maximum load it can withstand before it breaks. The yield strength is when it first demonstrates plastic deformation. So, you put a load on a steel bar and it bends. That is its yield strength. You keep loading on weight until it bends enough to break. That is its tensile strength.

Does it matter? Yes. Soft steel will bend early, but hold on until it breaks. A very hard steel, one we might even call brittle, does not bend at all until the moment it breaks, or shatters.

Aluminum has a tensile strength not much greater than its yield strength, maybe 20% greater. So, for example, an alloy could have a yield strength of 40,000 PSI and a tensile strength of 50,000. Steel, on the other hand, can, but not always must, have a much higher tensile. So, you could have steel with a yield strength of 40,000 PSI and a tensile strength of 60,000, and you can have another alloy with a yield strength of 50,000 and a tensile strength of 200,000 PSI. It is all in what you want the part to do, and how you want it to fail, if and when it does.

The simplest suppressor can be made with plain old flat washers, and ring spacers of the correct sizes.

surface texture when bead-blasted, in hue when it heats up. Welding is a heat-treatment process, and steel reacts accordingly. So, the weld will differ as a result of the heating and cooling. Titanium, when welded properly, will not differ. You can weld (if you are a good welder, and know what you are doing) titanium, and the area welded will not differ in appearance or strength.

Let me amend that. Titanium is so reactive to oxygen and nitrogen that as a metal it creates a hard, self-healing oxide layer on the surface. This is good. But, if oxygen or nitrogen gets in while you are welding, well, that is bad. Oh, the inclusion of contaminants increases tensile strength, but it does so at such a prodigious rate that it makes the parts so brittle they will crack under even a moderate load. So, you have to use a TIG, MIG or plasma-MIG welding setup, and you have to be just about OCD or you will make a mess of things.

The density of titanium is a bit over half that of steel, again depending on which alloys we're comparing titanium to. The great attraction of titanium is its light weight, combined with its strength. You have, in essence, the weight of aluminum with much, much greater strength and corrosion and abrasion resistance.

The yield strength of titanium is scary, coming in at 120,000 PSI in the Grade 5 alloy. If you want the maximum corrosion resistance, you have to "step down" to Grade 2, with a yield strength of only 40,000 PSI.

Stellite

SilencerCo makes some of their suppressors with baffles made of Stellite. Those of you who are up on your machine gun history might remember this, but for the rest of the shooting community, this is a "huh?" metal.

Stellite is an alloy that isn't steel, despite the name. "Stellite" is a trademarked name, owned by the Kennametal Company. It has a pretty low percentage of iron, only a maximum of about three percent, in some alloys of Stellite. (Yes, there is more than one, in fact, there are more than fifty.) It is mostly cobalt, with a bunch of chromium, and then leavening amounts of iron, nickel, and trace amounts of tungsten, carbon and molybde-

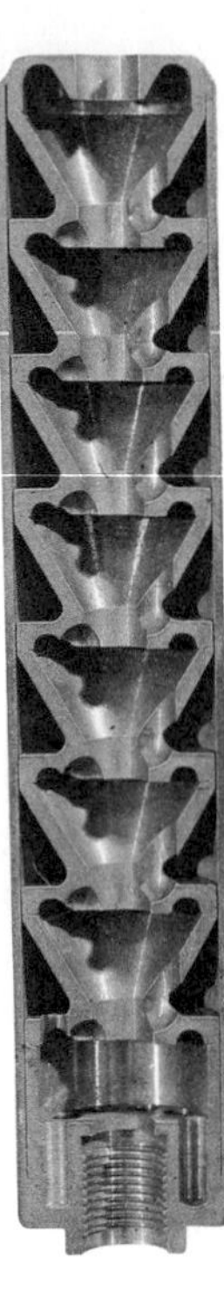

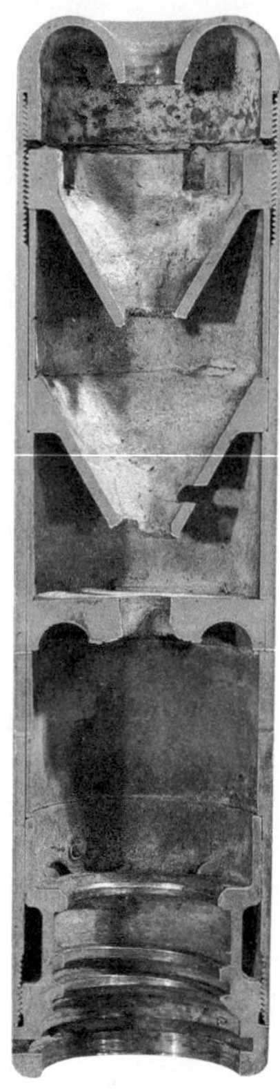

There are many solutions to the problem of noise. Designers use as many baffles, of whatever material, that they think will work.

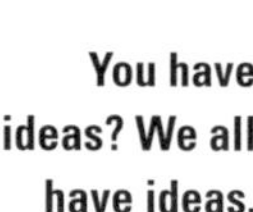

You have ideas? We all have ideas.

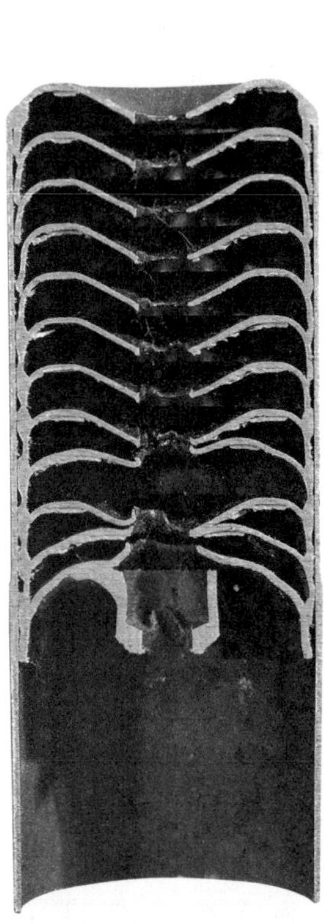

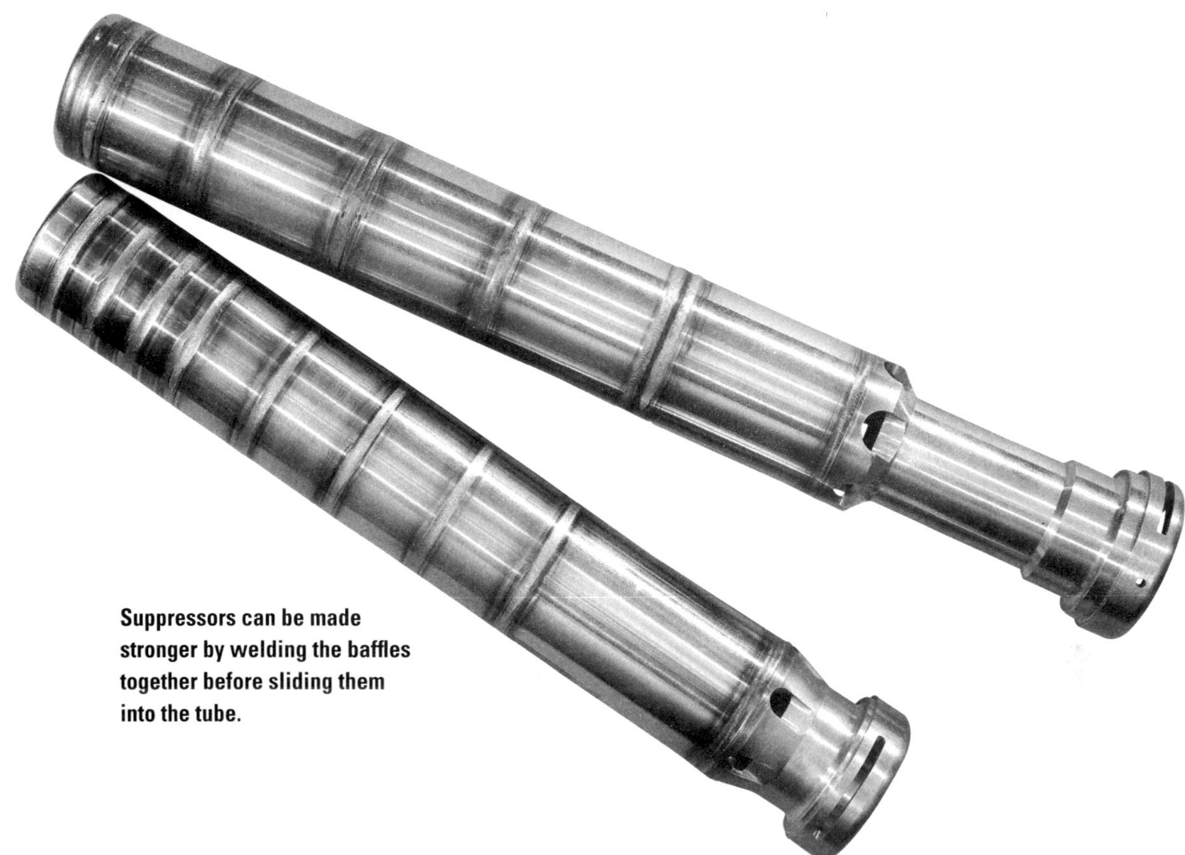
Suppressors can be made stronger by welding the baffles together before sliding them into the tube.

num, as needed for specific applications.

Stellite is used because it is amazingly resistant to abrasion and corrosion, it does not harden under use or stress, and does not anneal when subjected to high temperatures and cooled. It is so resistant to everything that it isn't even machined as are other metals. It is mostly cast and then ground to shape, instead of lathe-turned or milled. It is used as the teeth on cutting tools, and in chemical and industrial applications where its properties are useful.

Some machine guns had stellite liners in the first third of the bore, there to be strong when the barrel was heated red-hot in use.

In suppressors, a few companies use it for baffles, but the difficulty of shaping it means it is unlikely to become a common material used in the industry. However, you are probably around Stellite every day and don't know it. The hard seats of valves in the engine block of the car you drove today were probably Stellite, as it resists erosion, heat and, as long as the valve is properly timed, impact.

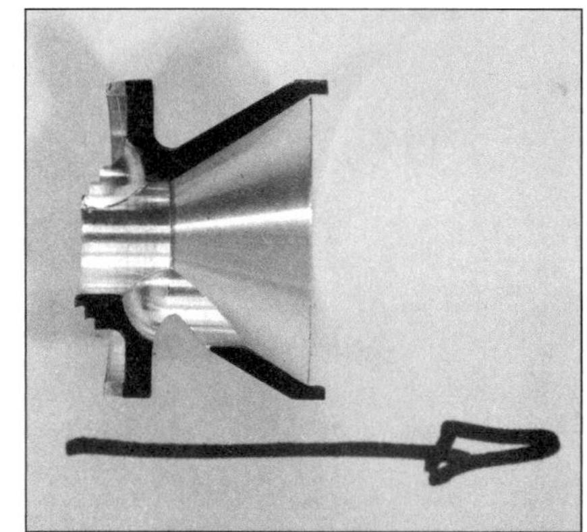
If you took a baffle and sectioned it (only a manufacturer would do this, no-one else wants to destroy a baffle), a "K" baffle looks like the letter K with a hole through it, and that's what the bullet passes through.

The "M" baffle is a little harder to parse, because you have to turn it on its edge to see the M.

What is best?

Someone out there is asking, "Why can't I have it all? Why can't I have an all-Inconel suppressor? Or a titanium-tube suppressor with Inconel baffles, or some other combo?" Why do the manufacturers all seem to have the same combinations? Well, they don't, but you can get that impression because they are all more than a little careful about telling exactly what alloys they use. As well they should be. Once you know how suppressors are made, what goes into cobbling one together, we'll discuss some of the limitations a designer has to deal with.

Designing a suppressor

OK, let's drag out a few new terms, poke them with sticks, and do a little mental suppressor design and fabrication. You may have heard the terms "K" and "M" baffles. This is a descriptor of what those baffles would look like, if cross-sectioned. The "K" like the capital K but with a hole right where all the lines meet. (Think-bullet going sideways.) The "M" is an M laid on it's side, and with a hole at the sharp point in the middle.

I'm going to add a couple more – the flat baffle and the funnel. The flat baffle is easy; think of a washer. Yep, that's it, all there is. The funnel is just that also, a funnel, with the bullet passing through the hole in the middle.

Next, we'll warm up the brain, do some mental 3-D design and fabrication, and make a suppressor. Oh, I know we did some of that in the previous chapter, but since most baffles are sealed, we have to keep doing this, so you can get a good grasp of what is going on inside.

First, take a pair of cylinders, one slightly smaller in diameter than the larger one, so it slips smoothly inside the other, but without a lot (best if there is none) wobble. Take the smaller one, and in a lathe, chop it into sections, let's make each of them an inch in length.

Depending on their application, these K baffles could be made of stainless steel, aluminum, titanium, even inconel.

This is one corner of a suppressor manufacturer's shop floor, with multiple CNC machining centers at work.

These are modified K baffles.

Now, we take a set of washers that just happen to have the same outer diameter as the inner diameter of the larger cylinder. Take a washer and weld it to one end of a six-inch length of the larger tube so it seals the end except for the hole in the middle.

Now, slide one, one-inch section of the smaller tube down into the bigger tube, until the washer on the end stops it. Drop in a washer. Slide in another smaller-tube section. Continue until you nearly have the tube filled, and then you add the only complex part involved: the threaded rear cap. This is threaded to fit the threads on the muzzle of your firearm. Weld the rear cap in place.

Congratulations, you've just made your very own suppressor, let's call it (as we did in the previous chapter) the Mark 1. You've done a number of things, mentally. You've gotten a 3-D idea of the interior of a suppressor. You've also skipped right over, oh, about 17 different engineering and manufacturing problems. If you have done this for real, you have committed a federal felony (unless you filed for a Form 1, and received approval) and you've made a suppressor with a service life of less than 100 rounds of centerfire ammo.

Your flat-baffle suppressor does not have the baffles secured. Depending on the spacing, the first baffle, the one that forms the expansion chamber, will begin to bend, hammered by the gas pressure that impacts it. Once it bends enough (it will be bent into a cone shape) it will come loose, be driven forward, and if you are

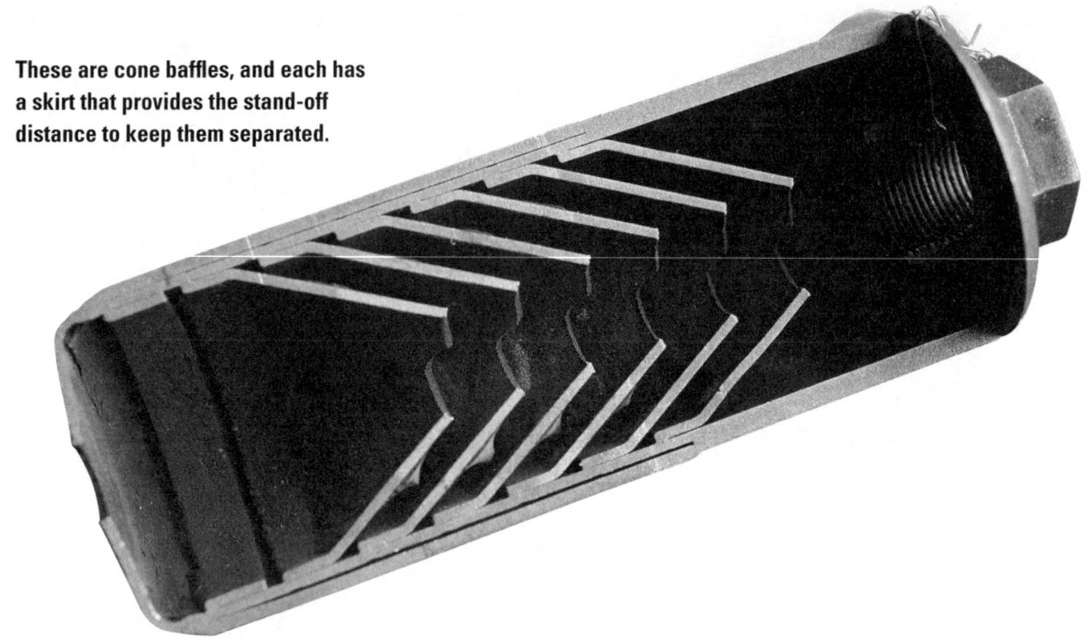

These are cone baffles, and each has a skirt that provides the stand-off distance to keep them separated.

Making your own is easy, with one lathe. Making them in volume, as a manufacturer, means *volume*.

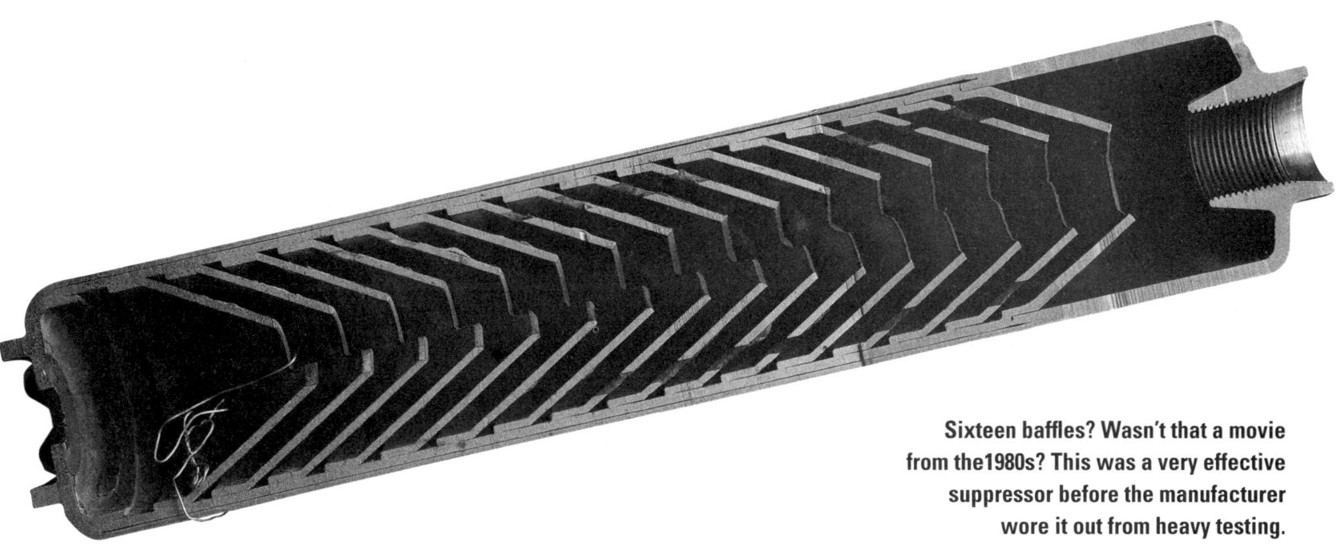

Sixteen baffles? Wasn't that a movie from the1980s? This was a very effective suppressor before the manufacturer wore it out from heavy testing.

unlucky, will block the bullet's passage.

In that case there will be extra noise, recoil, foul language, and maybe even an injury or two.

So, to improve it, we do a bit of measuring and calculating. We'll drill four holes around the external tube, at the point where each joint where the inner cylinders and the washers meet. Then, once the stack is assembled, we'll weld through the hole, sealing the holes and welding the inner cylinders and the washers in place. Call this the Mark 1A.

This will probably last a thousand rounds, instead of the previous hundred. The first baffle will still break loose (depending on the quality of the welding job) and may even break loose in three of the four welds, causing the baffle to pivot, inducing a baffle strike even sooner.

More holes, more welding, longer service life, let's call it the Mark 1B.

What can we do to up service life?

We upgrade the baffle material. Instead of using a stamped washer made of mild steel alloy from the hardware store, we fire up the lathe. We take bar stock of a better alloy, and we lathe-turn and bore center holes through the baffles that are a bit thicker, and then we heat-treat them to be stronger. We're now up to Mark 2.

When we have reached the service life of the Mark 2, we then improve the alloys of the inner and outer cylinders. We're now up to Mark 3. This one probably would last long enough for corrosion to be a problem, but that is a more difficult problem to deal with than simply upgrading materials or welds.

As a last step, we also add to the wall thickness of the outer cylinder, so we can get more of a "bite" in our welding, and lock the baffles in place with greater assurance. We can proudly call this our Mark 4 suppressor, and take pride in having gotten about to WWII in our technology and design.

What? Waitaminit, we can't be that far behind.

Actually, you have done very well. A flat-baffle suppressor, with 4-5 baffles in it, will be more than 80% effective compared to a current state-of-the-art design. One aspect in which it will fail utterly is if you use in on a full-auto firearm. Your Mark 4 will fail, probably spectacularly, if you heat it to red-hot on a full-auto or belt-fed. You just haven't built enough strength into it to handle the heat.

How do we next improve it? From here we have to take the leap to real manufacturing, real design and real alloys. In other words, we have to step up from home-workshop, resistance-level crudities to actual machine shop standards.

First, we lathe-turn all the components. The baffles will have to be bored, turned to O.D, and parted. The inner and outer tubes have to be bored and lathe-turned, then honed and polished. Then all the parts have to be

Here are bins full of turned baffles, welded into stacks and awaiting their trip to the centerless grinder to be made the exact size to fit into suppressor tubes.

A welded baffle stack, ready for the next step in manufacturing.

heat-treated, most likely after they have been continuously welded.

Next, the baffle stack, instead of being assembled inside the tube, is assembled outside the tube, and all the joints are fully welded, each of them the full diameter of the joints. This makes a rigid tube. The tube than has to be either lathe-turned on centers, or surface ground on centers, to bring the weld lines back down to the internal I.D. of the tube.

Finally, the baffle stack assembly is pressed into the external tube, the front end welded in place, and the rear cap welded on.

As a final measure, the finished suppressor is placed

in a fixture that indicates axial center and alignment off of the threads of the rear cap, and performs a finish-ream of the passage holes of the baffle stack.

Congrats, you've just doubled the cost of your suppressor, increased the amount of labor that went into it by maybe four or five times, and upped the capital investment in machine tooling by an order of magnitude at least. You've also magnificently demonstrated the law of decreasing returns on investment, because your previous 80% effective suppressor, with all the same design and dimensions, is perhaps 85% effective, and that's mostly due to being able to more-precisely controlled clearance diameters of the bullet passage.

If you want more, you need something more effective than flat-baffle design.

K and M

K and M baffles were the big design and efficiency step up from flat baffles. Basically, when advances in machining processes allowed, it became possible to lathe-turn an open-cup K with a hole down the middle, a dead space behind the arms of the K, and then cut the finished product off the bar and repeat.

The M baffle design is simply the M turned sideways, but also lathe-turned on automated machines or by a really good operator with a turret lathe.

You then stuff a stack of Ks or Ms into a tube, seal the ends, and you have a better-than-flat suppressor.

Each K (or M) spaces off of the ones on either side, KKKKKK with a hole down the middle, and you have a series of expansion chambers. Ditto the Ms, think of them as being laid on their sides, top-to-bottom, and if I could figure out how to do it as a text operation, I would.

The K and M approach is also amenable to refinements. It didn't take long to figure out that if you drilled lateral holes in the arms of the K, or the "nose" of the M, you could bleed gas into the dead space between the Ks

Front and rear caps can be welded on, or in this case, threaded for disassembly.

If a suppressor can be taken apart, that is a clue the manufacturer is giving you. Clean it.

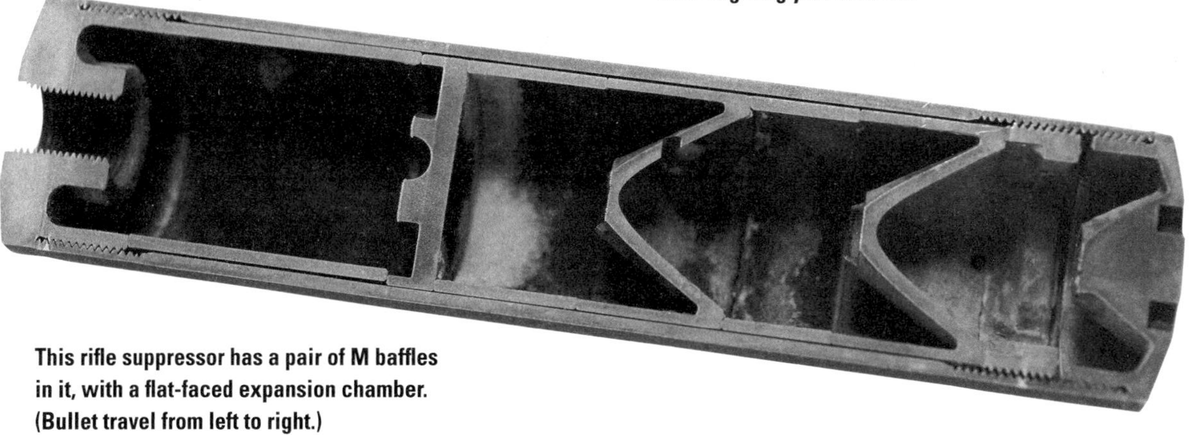

This rifle suppressor has a pair of M baffles in it, with a flat-faced expansion chamber. (Bullet travel from left to right.)

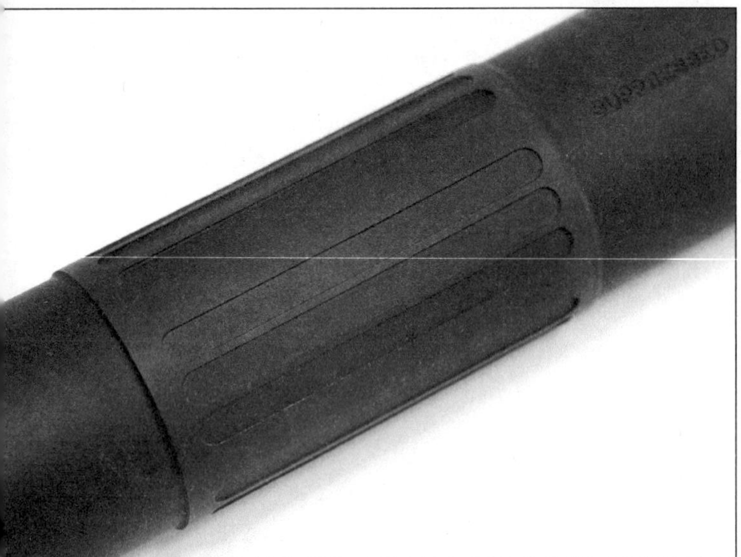

Here is a reinforcing band, around a Suppressed Armaments Systems suppressor.

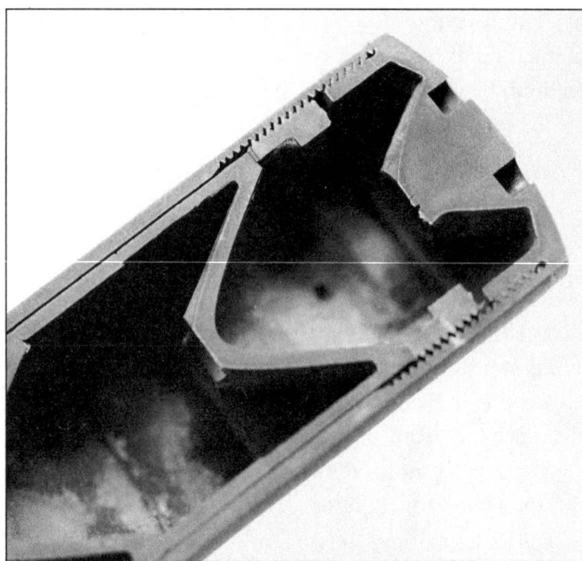

Here you can see the many threaded segments of the baffle and tube assembly, at the muzzle end.

and behind the Ms.

On the M, you could get another boost in efficiency if you notched the edge of the hole through the tip of the M, whereby you created turbulence, and that improved efficiency and sound-dampening effect.

The K and M suppressor designs rapidly went through the same processes that your flat-baffle stack did: loose, then tack-welded, then assembled outside, full-circumference welded, ground and press-fit. Of course, the really clued-in manufacturers didn't bother to go through the whole progression from flat to K and M, they simply adapted K and M baffles to their process, however much welding that required. Then they moved up from there.

As an extra note, it should be obvious that the investment in lathe tools alone (the cutters, and the lathes if greater output was needed) to make the K or M is a lot greater than that needed to make flat baffles. Also, you are much more in need of a skilled and efficient operator. But the results get you a markedly better product.

Some baffle stacks are only spot-welded. Some are continuous welded.

Cones

There's another way to make Ks and Ms, and that is to simply make cones. Think of a funnel. But, they are cones with an attached section of cylindrical skirt on them, above the part where you'd pour your soup through. Also, the cylindrical portion is stepped, that is, it is as if someone were to attach a cylinder to a funnel. That way, when they stack in the tube, they have their own stand-off section, and they create expansion chambers in-between the cones. Then it is a relatively simple matter to notch them at the entrance hole, in the tip of the funnel/cone for turbulence, arrange them prior to welding (different arrangements of turbulence orientation will alter the first-round pop, for instance) and produce a better suppressor.

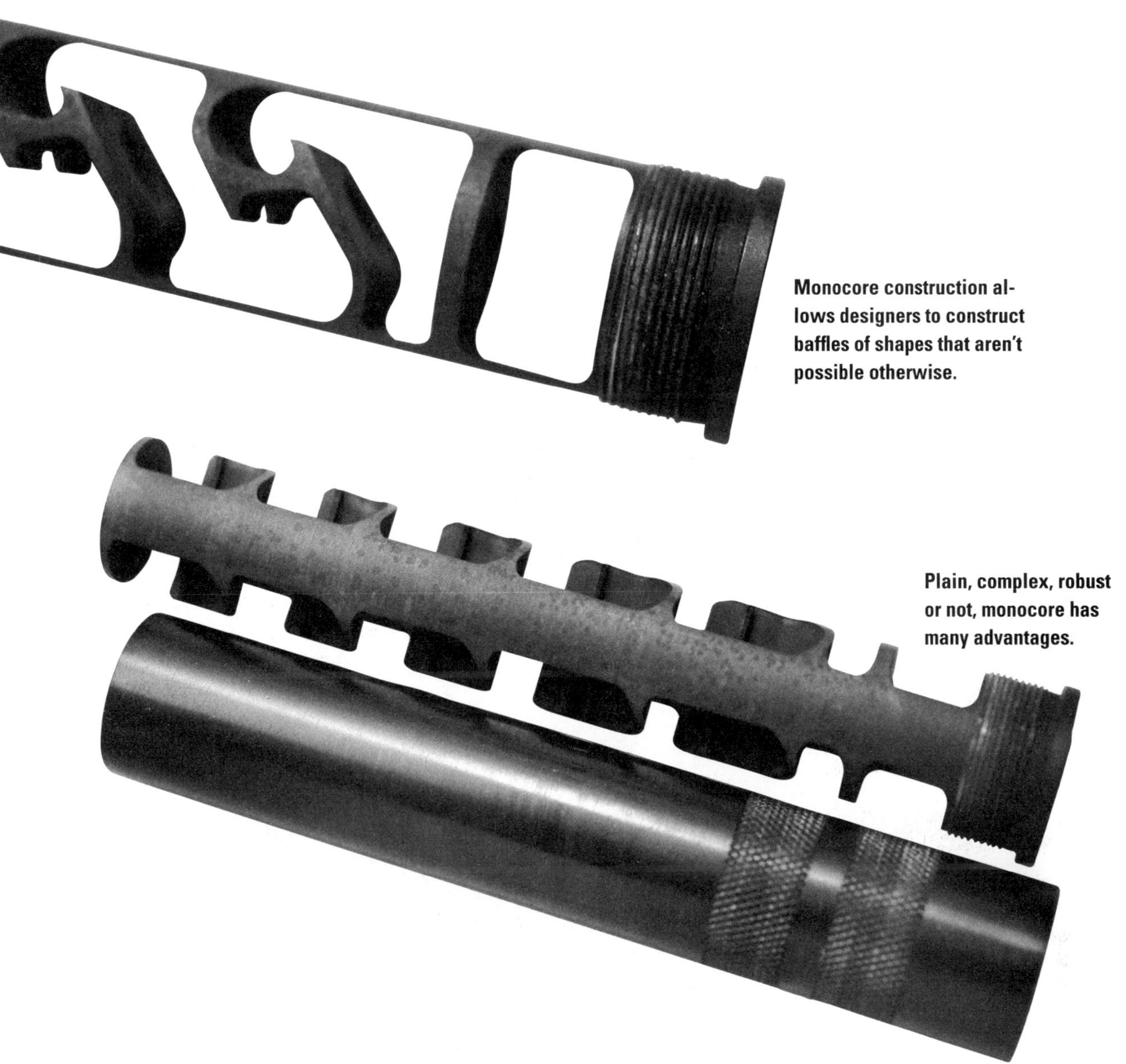

Monocore construction allows designers to construct baffles of shapes that aren't possible otherwise.

Plain, complex, robust or not, monocore has many advantages.

Now I'm baffled

These are not all of the designs that have been made over the decades. The varying designs, including slanted baffles, slanted holes in flat baffles, slightly cupped baffles, and combinations of curves, cups, slots, turbulence-generating angles, cuts, and so-on, are a combination of many things. First, the inventors' ideas and grasp of the physics involved. Second, the manufacturing capacity available. As an example, if you ask a machinist and a punch-press operator how to make a baffle, they will come up with different ideas. You can guess which each will favor.

How many baffles?

That depends. What kind of performance do you desire? First-round pop and a follow-on better average, or consistent performance? Durability? Weight? Full-auto service? Oh, and you can also, if you are really a good designer and manufacturer, have the baffles investment cast for you. As rough castings they are not suppressor parts, and thus the caster does not need to have an NFA file in the accounting office.

Once cast and delivered, you then do the final machining and welding to make a suppressor. What are the advantages? For one, you can spec a much, much tougher alloy. Since you only have to do a little machining, not carve it out of cylindrical stock, cutting a

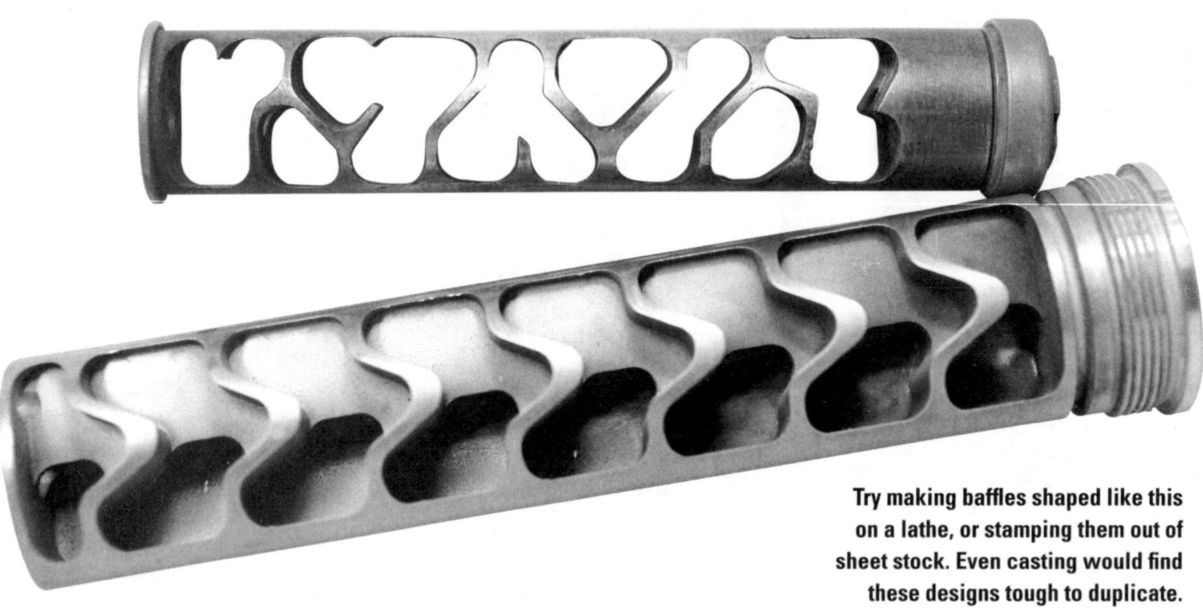

Try making baffles shaped like this on a lathe, or stamping them out of sheet stock. Even casting would find these designs tough to duplicate.

There's a lot to be said for straightforward and simple. These K baffles are robustly made, and expansion is not going to be a problem here.

tougher alloy isn't a big deal. You can also make the baffle contours as complicated as you want, because again, you aren't machining it.

And you can have your cast baffles made of exotic alloys at a lower cost because you aren't collecting and recycling nearly as much material from machining. Look at it this way, if you machine off 5% from cast parts, small losses in collecting and recycling the exotic alloys aren't a big deal. If you are turning 95% of each bar into scrap, small losses in recycling can break you.

Do we need this?

With all that as description, I have a small confession to make: you could make a pretty darned good suppressor with a minimal amount of welding. In fact, you could do it without any welding in the baffle stack. It would take some precise machining, though.

When you heat a cylindrical piece of metal, it expands. That is, it becomes a larger-diameter cylinder than it had been. That's how, in the days of the covered wagon, they made steel or iron-bound wheels. They'd make the steel hoop the same internal diameter that the

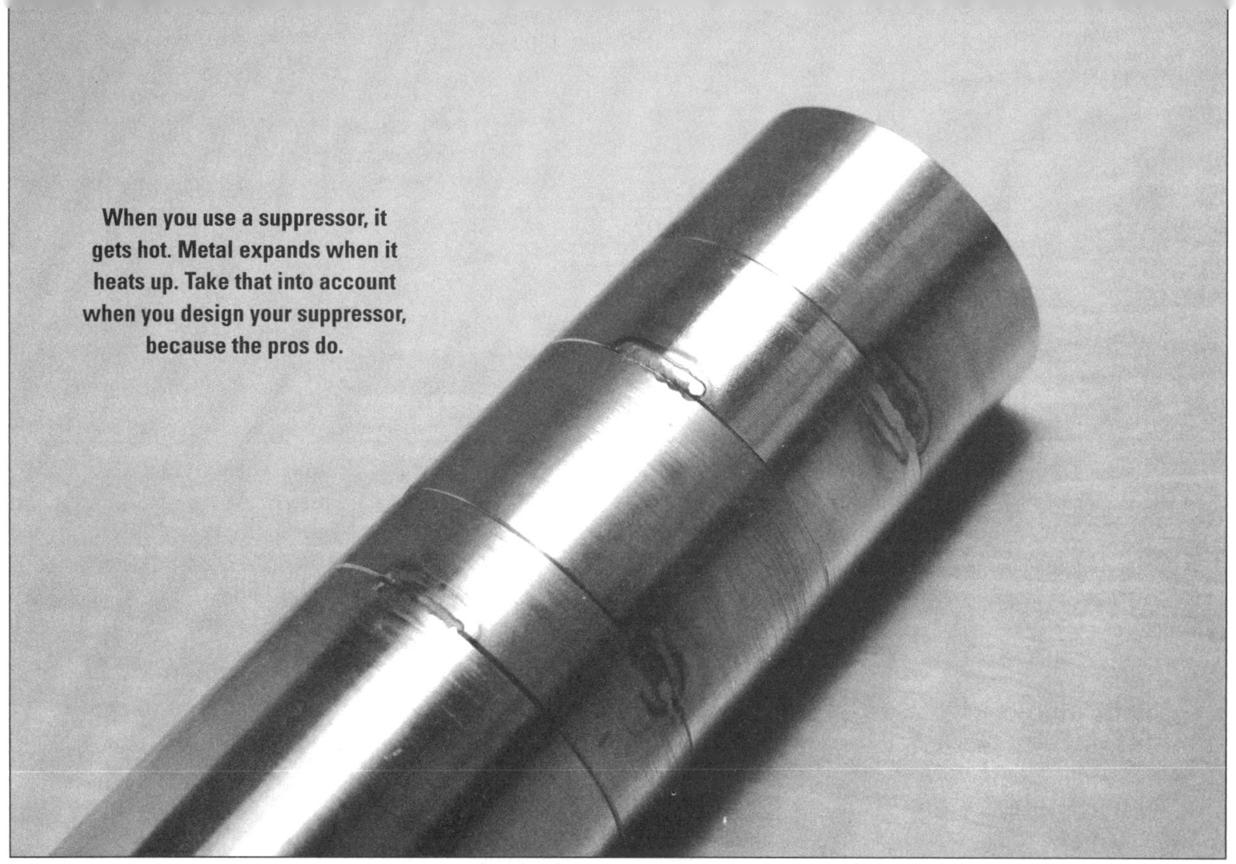

When you use a suppressor, it gets hot. Metal expands when it heats up. Take that into account when you design your suppressor, because the pros do.

It takes a lot of work to come up with effective designs, even more to come up with defective designs that can actually be made.

If you are going to design and build suppressors, you will have failures. How to make sure they can't be used, but you can still prove they were destroyed?

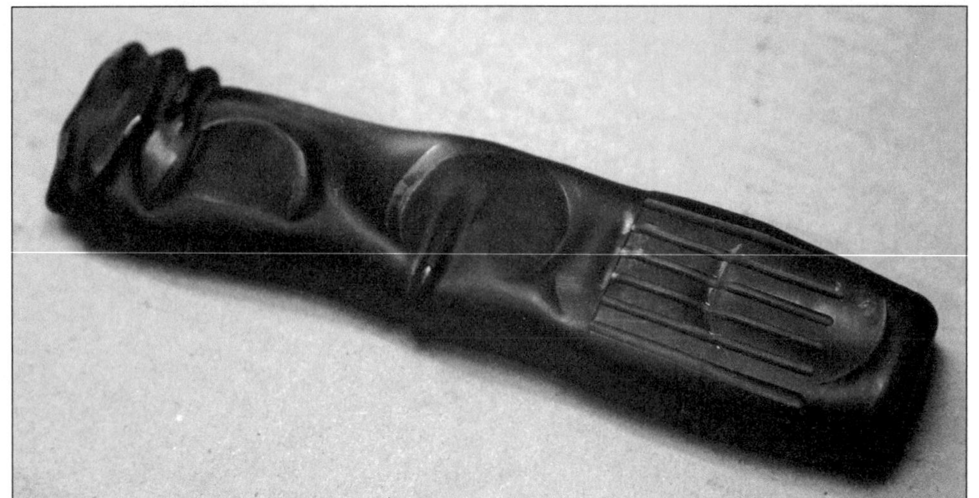

There is a lot of R&D on this table, and if you plan to design suppressors, be sure and take good notes.

Turned so you can see the letters, but not both the direction the bullet travels, you see the K and the M of the classic baffle shape.

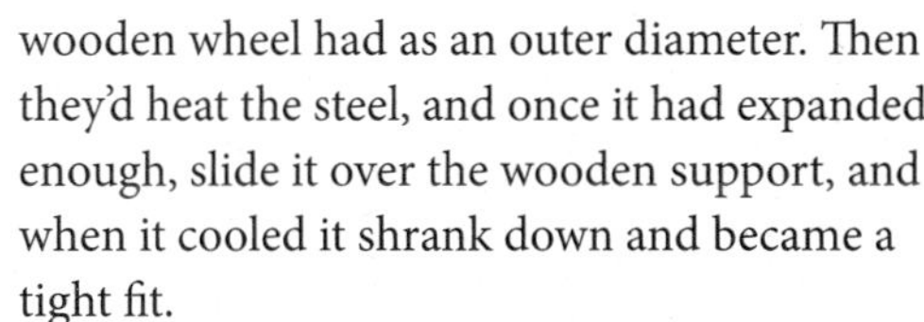

wooden wheel had as an outer diameter. Then they'd heat the steel, and once it had expanded enough, slide it over the wooden support, and when it cooled it shrank down and became a tight fit.

So, you could heat up the external tube (once you had welded the front cap on) and then press the baffle stack into it. When it cooled, it would shrink-clamp the baffle stack tight.

But, but, when it all heated up again when you shot it, wouldn't it come loose? Not really because the baffle stack and the tube would both be heated (the baffle stack would actually bit a bit hotter) and they'd expand at the same rate, if made of the same materials.

Or, you could machine the external diameter of the baffle pieces to the exact same diameter as the inner diameter of the tube, then, use a hydraulic lube to allow them to slide together, and press-fit the baffles in place. The first time the suppressor was fired the lube would be burned out, and the baffle stack would be locked in place.

Now, this would withstand pretty much anyone's use outside of the bearded guys who hunt in dusty places. I can see the excessive use a recon team, SpecOps or some other secret squirrel group subjecting it to could exceed its strength. But then, people who use an M4 as an impromptu SAW are not going to be happy with most suppressors. For the rest of us, a properly-built, non-welded suppressor could be a serviceable unit for as long as we are shooting.

One last welding refinement

Take your cones-with-a-can, and weld them together. Except, you design the cylindrical part to be just a bit thicker than otherwise, so the finished wall is as thick as the baffle-and-tube wall thickness would be. Then, you machine the welds down, and call it done. No internal tube, just tube with baffles.

This is brilliant, but also very exacting manufacturing. If you do anything wrong, there is nothing to salvage, you can only scrap the whole thing.

If the front cap won't tighten flush, that means you have a tabbed baffle out of alignment. Unscrew the cap and start over again.

This is the approach that Sig Sauer takes, and there are definite advantages. I've had a series of long discussions with John Hollister, the engineering guy who works for Kevin Brittingham, the head of the silencer division. For one, the approach they take solves some of the problems we've talked about, or will talk about. By using a single material (some are all-Inconel, other all-titanium) they completely sidestep the thermal expansion and galvanic potential problems. Also, by using a no-tube design (they weld the baffles into a single, tubeless array), they can have a greater internal volume, which makes them quieter.

But, this does not come without cost. It takes a significant capital investment to have the proper welding machines. (Think about it, a continuous, circular weld of Inconel or Grade 5 titanium? Wow. And then repeat, for each baffle joint? Double-wow.) Once welded, the assembly has to be finish-reamed for a straight and axial clearance shaft.

Belt and suspenders

Ever notice that some suppressors have an extra band of metal on the outside, at the rear? They are commonly made of a thin sheet of metal, slotted or drilled full of holes, on the rear portion of the suppressor. Reinforcement. The expansion chamber takes the brunt of the gas pressure. A suppressor can be well served by some extra support there. One way to add support is to simply machine the rear of it with thicker walls. To save weight, the extra thickness can be slotted to partial depth, or drilled with golf ball-like holes.

Another way to add reinforcement is to use the heat-shrink method described above, but to do it adding a sleeve of reinforcing metal.

Heat the reinforcing sleeve (and maybe even cool the suppressor body) and then slide the reinforcing band over the tube. When it cools, it shrinks, and it adds reinforcement in two ways. One, it is an extra layer of metal. The second is the tension created by the shrinkage. When the gas impulse hits the expansion chamber, the first thing it has to do is counteract the compression created by the shrink-on reinforcement band.

This can be especially important for a suppressor that is designed for use on an SBR, where the pressure in the expansion chamber can be intense.

Beyond the stack

Now we come to the monocore. Here, instead of a stack of cylindrical parts, we take a solid bar, and we carve the expansion chamber and baffle stack from that one solid piece. Then, we slide it into a tube, creating the suppressor.

The designers of monocore baffles have in many instances taken advantage of computer modeling of gas flow, and have created "stacks" that appear to have more in common with modern art than with suppressors. The stack will appear to be a sequence of waves, rather than Ks or Ms.

Being one-piece "assemblies," they are not subject to the problems of baffle stacks, of alignment, or deformation. Oh, I'm sure they can be deformed, but the amount of abuse, heat and pressure it would take is beyond what your firearm can generate. That's what computer modeling can do for a manufacturer.

With a monocore design it is a simpler operation, in that the alignment of the bore and the threads or mounts are all done on the CNC lathe. The baffle stack cutting is a lot easier, and then it is a simple task to figure out how to hold it all together.

Looking at a monocore suppressor of modern design and alloys, I'm not sure what Maxim would have been more amazed at – the design, the machine it was made on, or the alloys it was made of. In any case, I have no doubt he'd be impressed.

Having it all

Let's look at a few limitations. One is known as the dielectric constant. Basically, if you place two metals against each other, and their relative permittivity is too great, one will sacrificially corrode as a result. We do cover this in more detail in a later chapter, for those who want the gory details.

You can't have two metals in contact, that have too high a relative permittivity (denoted by K), or one will rust away. The more extreme the environment, the higher the temperature or the higher acidity of the environment, the lower the allowed K can be.

So, if you had two metals, each "perfect" for their application in a suppressor, but with a too-high K, and you assembled them, you'd have a self-rusting suppressor. No good. And it would be worse the more you shot it, heating it up, in effect turbo-charging the dielectric constant.

Then there is expansion with heat. The coefficients of thermal expansion of the metals used in a suppressor have to be close enough to each other to withstand the intended use. The coefficient, αV is something every engineer has to deal with, in every application. And fluctuations at room temperature levels won't do. Ever see buckled pavement on a hot summer day? That's the coefficient of thermal expansion at work. The pavement heated up, expanded, and when it couldn't take the compression (it was all expanding, with no place to go) it popped. So, let's say we make a suppressor with super-duper baffles, but the coefficient of expansion of the baffles is greater than that of the tube they are in.

When you heat the suppressor, the baffles expand outwards, but they do so at a greater rate than the tube. If the tube can take the stress, it holds and contracts when it cools, and all is fine. But many materials weaken when they are heated. So, let's say you heat it up too much and the tube bulges. The bulge will not contract down to its original dimension when it cools, and the baffles will now be loose inside of the bulged tube. Oops. Or, the tube is strong enough, and instead the baffles are in effect crushed inside the tube, trying to expand, and being restrained from doing so. Oops again.

Designers have to keep in mind the dielectric constant, thermal expansion, weldability, machineability, cost of materials, wear-and-tear on production machinery, as just a few of the variables. And that's even

Each alloy has its own requirements for forging temperatures, heat-treatment, annealing and welding.

before they make an R&D sample and go to the range with it.

So you want to be a suppressor maker? Designer?

Well, first of all you'll have to get licenses. As in, a fistful of federal paperwork. Let's start with the easy one, the extra one, the one called the "S.O.T.," short for Special Occupational Taxpayer. This is also what a lot of people call a "Class Three" dealer's license. It is the special piece of paper that lets you deal in NFA-controlled items such as suppressors, machine guns, short-barreled rifles and so on.

With it, you can buy them from the manufacturers (or wholesalers) and then sell.

But, to get this one you already have to have another one. And that is either an "01" or an "07." The 01 is the general gun dealers' license, the FFL, or Federal Firearms License. This is the vanilla-plain retailers license, to buy and sell general firearms. The 07 is a manufacturer's license. With an 07 you can make anything that is within your skills and manufacturing capacity. You can even sell them to 01 and SOT holders. (I'd check on your need for insurance, local business licenses, etc. before starting to ship suppressors.)

You'll notice the singular lack of mention of the license known as the "03," or Curios and Relics. It is a collector's license, and not a dealer's license. If you manage to find a suppressor that can meet the definition of being a Curio & Relic, then you can acquire it. But then, if you live in a state where you can own a suppressor, you

Regardless of who made it, the suppressor has to be marked. If you are making your own, you can hand-stamp it. But manufacturers have higher standards.

could own it regardless.

What being an 01/SOT or 07/SOT (and you do have to have both the license and the SOT) does for you is this; items transferred to you that stay "on the books" do not require you pay the transfer tax. They are inventory. Which leads me to the next fun-crushing detail.

You have to be in the business.

You can't acquire an 01 and an SOT just so you can collect guns and suppressors for your own fun and amusement. You can acquire an 07 and an SOT for R&D, but that leads to the next problem – cost. You see, a regular FFL costs you $90 for a three-year period. The 07 costs you $150 for three years. The SOT costs you $500 per year. And as an extra-fun detail, if you are an 07, you also have to be ITAR complaint. ITAR is the international export regulation/treaty that the government uses to control the flow of defense goods.

It apparently wasn't good enough for the Feds to essentially say, "You want to sell tanks, planes, helicopters and other goodies overseas, you have to get permission," they had to sweep everything firearms-related into the mix. This involved a treaty. Then, in a fit of "hey, let's all compromise," POTUS determined that it would be good if this didn't cost the government anything. So the whole regulatory cost was thrown onto the shoulders of those who had to comply.

This is the long way to say your 07 license also has a price tag of $2,250. A year.

So, each year you are an 01/SOT it costs you $530. To be an 07/SOT costs you $2300 per year. That's a lot of cash to "avoid" the transfer tax. Oh, and if you decide to quit being the R&D guy at your gun club, and let your various licenses lapse? You have to do one of two things: transfer all the NFA goodies off your books to someone else with the correct licenses, or pay the $200 per item transfer tax, transferring them to yourself. One way or another, the government is going to get its $$$.

And what does it entail to be "in the business?" At a minimum I'd say (and I'm not an attorney, so take this with a grain of salt) you'd have to have a place and times of business, advertise, demonstrate that you were at the very least trying to drum up business, and show income. And all of this would be of interest not just to the ATF, but to the IRS as well. As a general rule, the IRS considers it a business if you can show a profit in three out of the previous five years of work. If you can't, they are likely going to define your enterprise as a hobby, and disallow expense deductions.

And if you were doing suppressor R&D? You'd be able to show the test samples you made, and tested, and measured, and destroyed in the process, right? Because if you aren't actually making anything, you don't need a license. The ATF doesn't require a license to do 3D computer modeling of suppressors, only the actual metal objects.

One-offs

But you can still make a suppressor. All you have to do (and those are simple words that end up taking a whole lot of time) is fill out a Form 1, with the required FBI fingerprint cards, etc, etc, as if you were transferring one. But the transfer is a Form 4, this is a Form 1, an "Application to make and register a firearm" and you send it in just like the Form 4. "But, I'm not making a firearm." Yes you are. The ATF considers a suppressor to be a firearm, and this is the form.

You can do all the drawing, measuring and considerations you want while your Form 1 is being considered, but you cannot so much as touch saw to metal until the approved form is in your grubby hands, complete with its Tax Stamp.

That's the good news. The bad news is, once you make it, it is yours forever. You aren't a dealer, so you can't sell it. You aren't a manufacturer, so you can't sell, all you can do is own and enjoy. But we go into this in excruciating, gory detail in the chapter on buying, so on to the next chapter instead.

Chapter Six

HOW THEY ATTACH

Consider the stresses on this muzzle brake, due to gas flow. This is why you need to securely attach your suppressor to your firearm. *U.S. Army photo by Spc. Michael Blalack.*

You are not going to attach your expensive new suppressor to the firearm of your choice with hose clamps and duct tape. You need something more permanent, rigid, aligned and reliable.

The mounting methods to attach a suppressor to a firearm fall into a few categories: direct thread, quick-attach, booster, integral, and exotic and rare.

Direct thread

Luckily, the mechanical engineers of the 19th century solved the mounting problem for us; they called it threading. Threads are old, but before the industrial revolution each one cut was one-of-a-kind, and there was no real interchangeability. Standardized threads of a certain and specifically-defined pitch, size, shape and length are a brilliant 19th-century invention, and have become ubiquitous such that we now take them for granted. The people who have been making silencers in the modern era, being practical types, settled on a few of these thread pitches that would work as the default for standard calibers. So, for instance, in the .22 centerfire, we have $^{1}/_{2}$X28, that is, threads of twenty-eight rotations to the inch of threaded length, with a nominal diameter of half an inch. .30 rifles get a pitch of $^{5}/_{8}$X24, and so on. This way, a silencer of one caliber can't be inadvertently threaded onto the muzzle of a rifle of the wrong caliber.

A quick aside here; threads are also further defined by the shape of the cross-section of the thread itself, as well as the plus-or-minus tolerances allowed and the strength of the materials. So, you have "V" thread and

Direct-thread is simple, cheap, sturdy and durable. You just need a wrench to tighten/remove it, and you need the correct threads for your caliber. This Innovative Arms 556 suppressor will fit on the AR barrel, but not the .45 1911 barrel. (Thank goodness.)

Whitworth thread; you have classes of fit 1, 2, 3; you have bolts graded from Grade 1 to Grade 8; and you have standards as defined by various industry associations. Luckily for us, the suppressor manufacturers knew all this and settled on the common, 60-degree V thread, which is the vanilla-plain American basic thread. They have it squared away (so to speak) so don't worry about other dimensional standards. The grade part? That is a measure of how strong the metal is, and thus how tightly it can be, or must be, torqued. Barrel steel is strong. Suppressors are made knowing that. You do not need to get anywhere close to the torque limits of the metals involved to keep your suppressor tight.

While putting a .30 suppressor onto the muzzle of a .223-chambered rifle would not be a disaster (it might be a tad inefficient), going the other way would be. The thread differential between calibers is not an absolute assurance, however. It is easy enough for someone with access to a lathe to make an adapter, or thread a barrel, so you could mount that .223 silencer on a .30 rifle, but it would be quite unwise.

One area where you might get into trouble is with the various sizes of .22s. You see, ½X28 is also the common thread pitch for .22LR rifles and handgun suppressors. Mounting a silencer built to withstand a .22LR onto a .223 is asking for trouble. Oh, it will probably work, for a short while, anyway. But when it quits, you'll find it an expensive repair, more likely a full-cost replacement because the pressures of the .223/5.56 are likely to break the .22 rimfire suppressor to pieces.

A different problem works the other way; mounting a centerfire .22 suppressor onto a rimfire. Rimfires are amazingly dirty, so they are made to be taken apart and cleaned. Centerfires are high pressure, and it is best if they are permanently welded shut. Fire grubby rimfire ammo through a sealed centerfire unit and it will get dirty. Once it becomes too dirty, it will be less effective, and since it is sealed you can't take it apart to clean it. In this instance, if you do make a habit of using a centerfire suppressor on your rimfire rifle or handgun, swap it back to a centerfire rifle every 100 rounds or so, and use the centerfire heat and pressure of firing a couple of magazines or so through it to blow it clean. Better yet, buy a rimfire can and clean it when it gets dirty, and leave the centerfire can on the centerfire rifle.

But back to mounts.

A threaded muzzle is inexpensive, easy, compact and simple. On a centerfire rifle, it is just fine, because centerfire rifle suppressors are pretty much self-cleaning. You won't have to dismount it to scrub it because

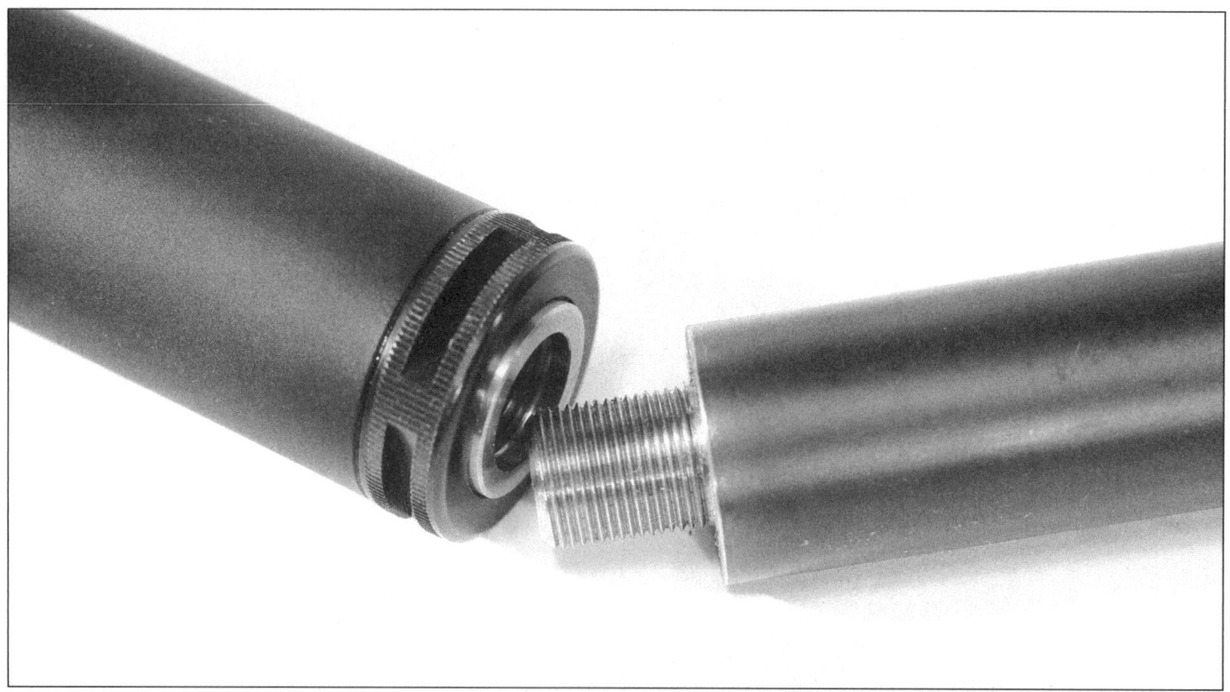

Direct threads are easy, simple, and now common on factory models. If you do not have one already threaded, a competent machinist can thread the muzzle for you.

the suppressor will outlast whatever barrel it is mounted on. Not abused, a well-built centerfire suppressor will outlast five to ten barrels. On a rifle, that is. Rimfire and pistol-caliber suppressors need to be disassembled and scrubbed on a regular basis, and there a quick-detach system can be useful.

The uncommon threads are odd to the American thread proportions, or metric (the "M" designation) for use on imported pistols. You would have to place a pretty big order with one of the European handgun companies to get them to make your barrels in American, not metric, thread pitches. In many instances it is easier to simply have an accessory barrel made for your Euro-shooter, one from an American barrel maker, who can cut American, English/inch pattern threads for your suppressor. Or, prevail upon the suppressor maker to provide a metric-thread rear cap or booster adapter, to fit on your European pistol.

The threads on the muzzle of your barrel are lathe-turned when the barrel is profiled, that is, turned down to its final contour. Depending on the process used by the manufacturer, the threads will be more-or-less centered, straight and uniform. However, unless the barrel maker is very detailed, they will not be precise. If you were to measure centered-ness of the suppressor as it was screwed onto the barrel, you'd see an alarming amount of wobble and wandering. This would go away as you torqued the suppressor against the bearing shoulder. However, minor variances in the thread consistency can matter, as we'll see when we get to mounting.

A direct-thread suppressor is the simplest and least-expensive way to mount a suppressor on your firearm. It has become common enough that even some firearms makers who don't make AR-15s now offer at least one model of their firearms threaded for suppressor mounting.

Quick-attach

Quick-attach is a development that comes to us for a particular reason – cost. Direct thread is a secure, rigid and easy method by which to attach a suppressor. But, once a suppressor is torqued in place, you need a wrench to remove it, and you need that wrench to install it on the next firearm. If you have a suppressor and two or three or more rifles you want to use it on, the wrench-and-direct-thread method gets old fast.

So, the makers came up with a mount called a "muzzle device": one that threads onto the muzzle and

Direct-thread pitches and the rifle calibers they commonly fit	
1/2-28	.22LR and other rimfires, and .223/5.56
5/8-24	6.5 Grendel & 6.8 Rem SPC
5/8-24	.308
3/4-24	.338 Lapua
7/8-14	.50 BMG
1-14	.50 BMG
Pistol-caliber thread pitches	
1/2-28	9mm, booster-mount pitch
1/2-36	9mm, non-booster pitch
.578-28	.45, booster-mount pitch
Uncommon threads	
1/2-32, 1/2-24, M13.5X1-LH 9mm, various	
16x1 RH-M, M16X1 LH-M, 9/16-24 M14.5X1 .45, various	

Quick-attach muzzle devices are brand-specific. Each of these accepts its own brand suppressor (and caliber) and no other.

stays there for the service life of the barrel. The muzzle device has a cylindrical or coned bearing surface, and fast-pitch threads and a ratchet or locking system. You can install the suppressor by hand in a few seconds and, assuming it isn't too hot to handle, swap it from one rifle to another as quickly. No wrench needed.

A few details need explaining. "Fast-pitch" in this context does not describe a softball league, but the number of turns it takes to tighten a suppressor, or any threaded fastener. Let's take the common $^1/_2$-28 thread for a 5.56 mount. If the threaded portion, the shank, is half an inch long, then it will take fourteen complete rotations to get it all the way tight. A fast-pitch thread will be so coarse that it takes maybe two full rotations to tighten the suppressor, maybe one-and-a-half. Also, the threads on the muzzle device will often not be the common "V" threads you are familiar with, but have a profile known as Acme threads, which are flat-topped pyramids, not a pointy V.

The ratchet is there to lock the suppressor in place. A fast-pitch thread lacks the torque to stay tight, especially since it is wrenched on by hand and not with a tool. If you had only the fast-pitch threads, your suppressor would vibrate loose once per magazine. The ratchet locks the suppressor on, once you have bottomed out the fast-pitch threads.

Muzzle devices can be, and usually are, more than just mounts. At the very least, they are also flash hiders. So, if you have the rifle with the mount but for some reason are shooting it without the suppressor, you still have a barrel with a flash hider on it. Some are made as muzzle brakes. When the suppressor is on, the muzzle brake feature doesn't happen. When the suppressor is off, the muzzle device works just like a brake or comp on a competition rifle. The shooter next to you will not be as enthused about that as he or she was when you were using your suppressor.

The drawbacks are not inconsequential, even if they are not deal-killers. First of all, a muzzle device is manufacturer-specific as well as caliber-specific. If you have a suppressor from manufacturer "A" you cannot attach it on a muzzle device from manufacturer "B" or vice-versa. Also, each muzzle device costs as much as $125, and you need one on each rifle that you want to put the suppressor on. That can add up. No, you cannot move the muzzle device from rifle to rifle, as if it were simply a direct-thread rear cap-equipped suppressor. Well, you can, but why would you? You've paid extra for the muzzle device, and for the specific model that

This is a fast-pitch thread. The Acme thread on this AAC mount has a grand total of one and a quarter turns to lock. That's fast. Also note the ratchet teeth on the mount itself.

The ratchet for this Yankee Hill muzzle device is spring-loaded, and inside the cylindrical collar.

requires it. Why treat it as a direct-thread suppressor, one of which you could have purchased for as much as $300 less, the muzzle device being half that? Last, the suppressor itself will cost a bit more than a comparable direct-thread model, because it takes extra metal and machining to create the quick-attach rear cap that is welded or threaded or machined into the suppressor.

Finally, all this adds weight. Yes, it is only a few ounces, but it still adds weight. If you went with, for example, a titanium suppressor because you wanted it to be light, and then you go and add a steel muzzle device for mounting it, you just took away some of the lightweight advantage you paid a lot of money for.

A QC/QA suppressor and three muzzle devices (to mount on three different rifles) can end up costing as much as two direct-thread suppressors from the same manufacturer. Not to pick on them, but since I've got their catalog open on my desk at the moment, let's look

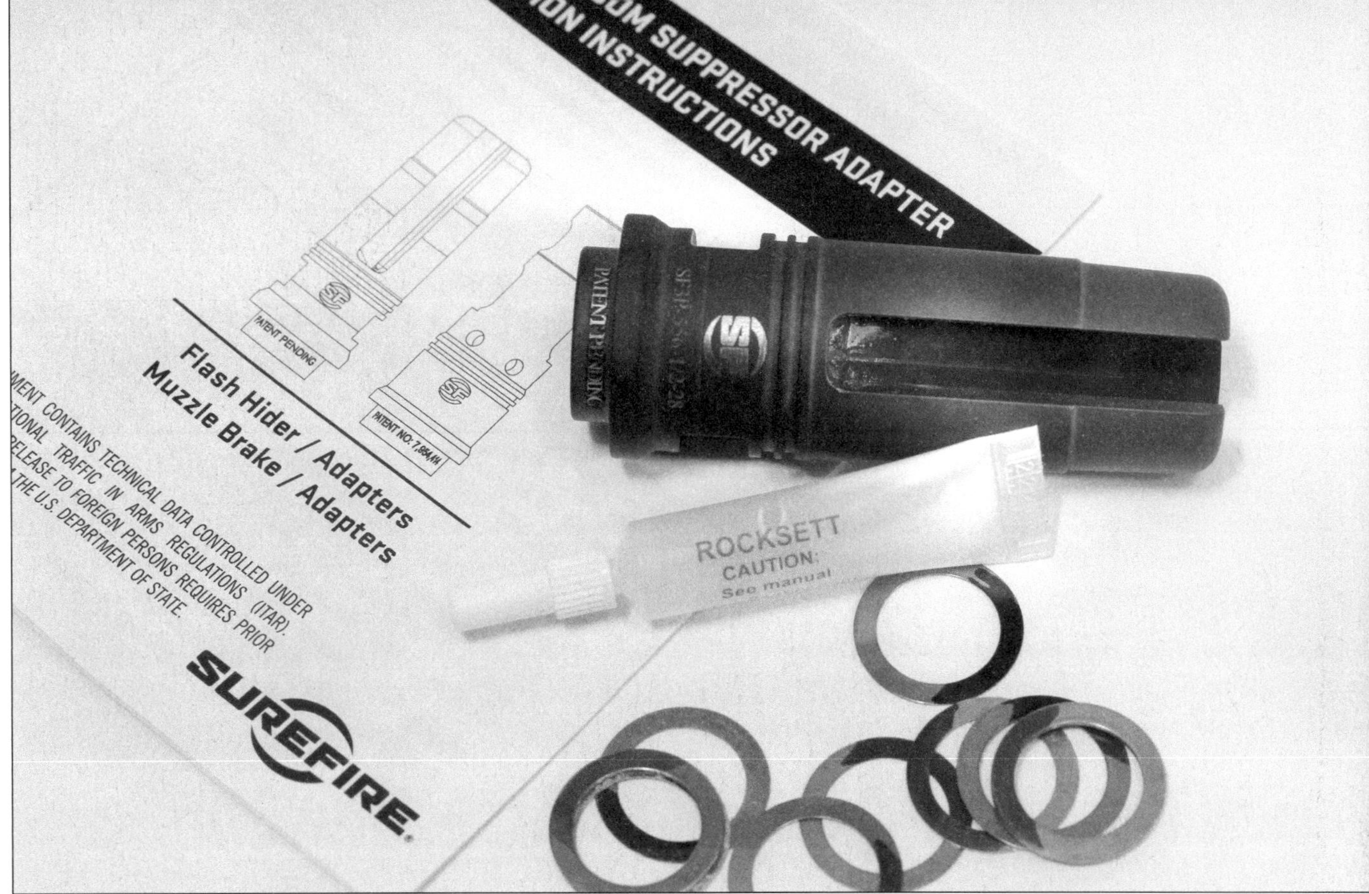

A typical muzzle device package contents: instructions, shims, device, Rocksett. Surefire even color-codes the shims so you can build the correct alignment.

at a pair of Sig silencers (that's the term they prefer), the SRD556 and the SRD556-QD. The QD version costs $100 more and weighs 3.5 ounces more. It does come with the muzzle device, but if you wanted to mount your Sig silencer on another rifle, you'd have to buy another QD mount, at $69. Which, by the way, is half what other muzzle devices cost for comparable suppressors. So Sig is giving you a real break here.

So, if you have two SRD556s that comes to $1090 (MSRP). A single SRD556-QD and two muzzle devices comes to $780. Yes, it will take you a while to get to the point where it is cheaper to buy the direct-thread version in volume, but I hope you get the point. At some point, it is cheaper, and with other manufacturers, it will happen sooner.

QA variants

You can make a fast-pitch thread on a mount and put a ratchet on it to lock it in place, but there are still many ways to do that. One is to make the ratchet spring-loaded and have it engage teeth on the back end of the muzzle device. Once you screw the suppressor down enough to reach the teeth, the ratchet starts engaging. When it bottoms out, you're locked onto the last tooth it could reach.

Another way to do it is to spring-load the latch, but instead of grabbing onto teeth, it overlaps the rear shelf of the muzzle device. Here, when the latch gets past the rear shelf, the spring pops it back down, and it prevents rotation to unlock. Here we have the advantage of directional forces. That is, the suppressor wants to rotate to unlock. But the latch pivots in and out from the bore axis, not in the direction of the bore itself. The rotational forces can't overcome the latch.

Another way to do this is one Surefire uses, a collar with an eccentric opening. The off-center hole of the collar means that when you rotate the collar it pivots to catch the rear shoulder of the muzzle device. Again, the rotational forces act in a different direction than the one the collar moves in.

Neilson devices

Your pistol is designed to work, reliably and effectively, without a suppressor on it. A lightweight suppressor is still at least half a pound of weight, hung on the muzzle. What do you do if your pistol doesn't want to work with that weight out there? You find a way to razzle-dazzle the laws of physics. A booster, or a Neilson device, stores some of the energy of the system, and delivers it back into the system at a time when it keeps

If a manufacturer wants their muzzle device to be "clocked", that is, turned to a particular alignment, they will provide flat shims to let you do so, like this Dead Air Armament mount.

the system working.

The booster is a spring-loaded rear cap assembly, with the baffles and tube ahead of it. When I first considered the function of a booster, I did not consider the timing of it. I thought the gases banged against the baffles, and that thrust pushed the can forward, against the spring. Once the force was absorbed, then the spring snapped the can back.

I was close, just late in the physics of it. What happens (and, thanks to Dr. Phil Dater I've seen high-speed video of this in action), happens due to recoil. As we all know, recoil begins the moment the bullet begins moving. So, the bullet begins moving, and as a result the pistol moves in the opposite direction. Well, when it does, the pistol leaves the suppressor behind. The suppressor tube and the baffle stack as an assembly, hanging in space, does not move back with the initial movement of the pistol. The threaded coupler and the suppressor itself have a sliding, but not locked, fit. When the pistol moves back, but the suppressor does not, the spring inside the booster is compressed as a result. One mass moves – the pistol. One mass doesn't move – the suppressor tube. The spring compresses, loading the kinetic energy created by movement into the potential energy of the spring compression. This is simple physics.

Once the pistol stops moving, the spring can no longer store energy since none is being created. The spring then snaps back to its uncompressed length, releasing the potential energy, delivering the weight of the suppressor back to the barrel, boosting the system and ensuring function.

In fact, the system works so well that a pistol with a Neilson device on it actually kicks ***harder*** than it would without the device and suppressor installed. It is noticeable, and takes some getting used to. "Hey, I just added more than half a pound of weight to my pistol, and it kicks ***harder***? What's up with that?"

You only need this with locked-breech pistols, and not on pistol-caliber carbines. So it is common to make pistol-caliber suppressors with easily-changed rear caps. You can unscrew the booster endcap assembly, and then screw in the proper un-boosted endcap, which has a different muzzle-thread pitch (no getting the two mixed up that way) and then put it on your AR in 9mm, MP5

A Nielsen device, or L.I.D., that allows self-loading pistols to work with suppressors attached.

The linear decoupler uses a spring to store energy and then deliver it back to the system.

(you lucky dog, you) or other carbine.

Your carbine does not need a booster, hence the simple threaded endcap.

Also, since a blowback design does not need to siphon energy from the system to cycle the action, a blowback pistol does not need a booster, L.I.D. or Nielsen device, either. There aren't many you'll be wanting to suppress, but if you do have one, you now have a dilemma. If you go with the standard pistol threads, the only thing you can hang on the muzzle is a suppressor with an L.I.D. If you want to mount it without the booster, you have to go with the pistol-caliber carbine threads.

In 9mm, (or .380) that means you pass right over the $\frac{1}{2}$-28 booster threads and go to the $\frac{1}{2}$-36.

Ease of use & unique

One suppressor I know of doesn't require a specialized muzzle device, and that is the Gemtech Halo. It mounts directly onto the standard A1/A2 flash hider. Unfortunately, simple ideas sometimes require complicated setups and OCD levels of checking for assurance. You see, the mil-spec flash hider is not machined to the tolerances needed for a suppressor mount. The flash hider may be oval, tipped or out-of-round, and any of these can be a problem. And before you object, all of those problems for use mean naught to the military. The specs are meant to define a flash hider (also called a "moderator" in military useage, despite doing just about nothing to reduce recoil) and they didn't know, or care, about suppressors back then. It is what it is, and the military is happy.

When using the Halo on a rifle, you must check clearance with an alignment rod. And, you cannot use a crush washer or split washer to lock the flash hider in place. However, once you have correctly aligned and locked-down the flash hider, you can mount and dis-mount the Halo without any problems ***on that rifle***. But any rifle that hasn't had the flash hider correctly mounted, locked and aligned is a hazard.

Exotic & rare

There's a special mount, developed by Knight's Armament for a government contract. Known as the "Snap-on" mount, it uses a vertically-sliding gate, with two rods in it, to pass along two grooves machined into the sides of the barrel. Made for the U.S. Navy from 1985 to 1989, it is a product of its time. The idea was simple, fast-attach for use on pistols. And it is, it goes on and off quickly, when it goes on and off. I had a chance to try the fit of a sample in the collection of a suppressor maven. One drawback to this system is the precision

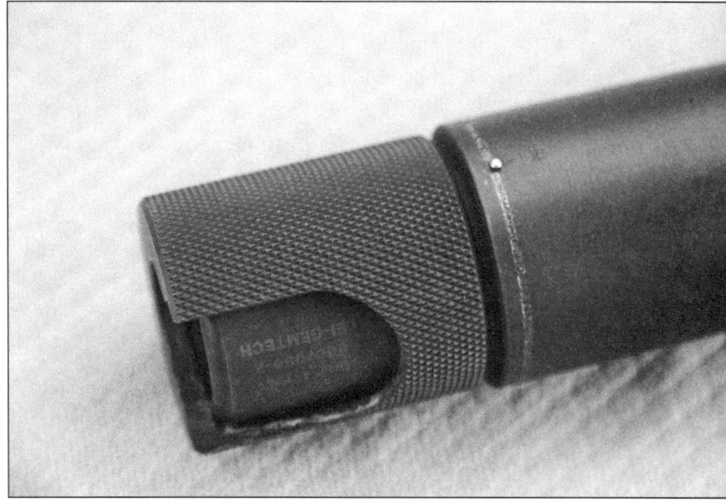

The Gemtech Halo mounts on a standard A1/A2 flash hider. Make sure the flash hider is aligned, or there will be trouble.

The SpecOps folks used a lot of this generation of 5.56 suppressors, complete with the gated, or Snap-on mount.

The Knight's sliding lock, aka Snap-on.

needed to make it work. The surface of the barrel and the interior of the endcap of the suppressor all have to be precision-ground to exacting dimensions. This is expensive work. And the two transverse grooves, and the bars to fit them, also have to be made to a high level of precision. Any looseness will lead to baffle strikes.

When new I'm sure it worked like a charm. But as the parts on the M9s involved wore and were subjected to normal use, the potential for problems were great. I was standing in the vault with a selection of cans and barrels all built for this system, and two pistols with barrels in them, and found there were combinations that simply wouldn't fit together. And this was in a non-stressed, air-conditioned environment, where I could experiment for as long as it took to find a combo that worked.

If you are going to make a suppressor and mount for general, or even limited but not unique, distribution, they all have to fit all the guns in use. As an added complication, the Navy desired that their new pistols (and this was right at the beginning of the adoption of the M9 by the Armed Forces, remember) and their suppressors work like the "hush puppies" of old. That is, the slide could be locked so there was no extra noise from the slide shuttling back and forth, and of empty brass hitting the ground, walls, etc.

Well, the old hush puppy was built on the S&W frame, and those could at least be made of steel. Plus, the slides on S&W pistols are robust, and closed on the top. Beretta M9s, on the other hand, were only ever made for the government with aluminum frames, and the slides are open on the top. Apparently, the locking notch the slide lock fit into took quite a beating when the pistol was fired with the lock engaged. After breaking enough guns to learn their lesson, the Navy said, "good idea, but it won't work," and bailed.

Having to keep fitted sets of barrels/pistols and silencers together is no fun, even less so in a place where people will be shooting at you. And when a simple threaded mount solves the problem, it is easy to see why this system wasn't adopted for wider use.

In asking my circle of acquaintances, spies and informants about this, I had a report of one of these being sighted in an SF armory, stateside, right after we

Here you see the rifle gate open. Unlike the pistol mount, the rifle gate was not spring-loaded.

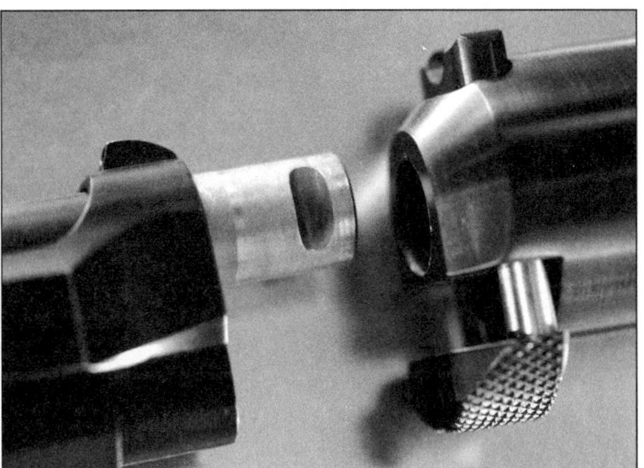

The Snap-On, close up, to show the grooves in the barrel.

The Knight's Snap-on system, as it aligns with the pistol.

let ourselves be chased out of Somalia (1994 or so). So, it may have been made for the Navy, but they apparently got around. I have also heard that these were standard issue for pilots flying over Iraq in Gulf War One. Not to shoot from the cockpit, but as an emergency item, if they got shot down and had to stay hidden until the cavalry arrived.

Knight's was quite fond of this approach, and made the same sort of mount for rifle suppressors as well.

Once clever thing Knight's did was to install a bead front sight on the pistol suppressor tube itself, and machine a rear sight notch into the top of the gate. That way, despite the pistol sights being blocked by the tube, you had something to sight with.

Lugs

Then there is the three-lug system, made famous on the MP5. Here, the idea was to make a fast-attach system that didn't use threads. The three lugs (one of them is a bit larger, ensuring there is only one way to fit the assembly together) are machined on the muzzle of the barrel. The rear cap has three slots, and a spring assembly in it. You line up the suppressor over the mount, and press down. The lugs disappear into the rear of the suppressor, and once it bottoms out you rotate the suppressor. Once it stops, you let go, the springs press the suppressor forward, and the lugs fit into recesses in the rear of the suppressor, locking the can in place.

As old as the HK three-lug system is, you wouldn't think there would be a lot of need for mounts for them. You would be wrong.

Two-lug and three-lug rear caps on suppressors. One size does not fit all.

In use, the blast of gases acts to press the suppressor more-firmly against the lugs.

To remove it, press the suppressor back towards the receiver, turn the opposite direction, and lift forward off the muzzle. Fast and easy.

This is a two-lug system from Gemtech, with the lugs on the muzzle device.

Uzi mount

This one is a specialty mount, and if you don't have an Uzi you won't have a need for this mount. Oh, and it has to be an sbr'd or smg Uzi. The mount is simple; the Uzi lacks a threaded barrel. But it has a threaded shank the barrel nut goes onto. So, you replace the barrel nut with an adapter, and the adapter then accepts your regular 9mm suppressor, once you take off the usual rear cap. That usual rear cap would either be a $^1/_2$-36 for carbines, or a booster, for handguns.

Collet

Machine tools are held into a mill head by means of an adapter called a collet. It is simple: a piece of cylindrical steel, slit at ninety degrees and bored through. The outside has a taper on it. When you slide the cutting tool in, it slides in a (hopefully) slip fit, and then when the outside collar is tightened, it clamps the collet and holds the cutting tool.

As a means of holding a cutting tool, it works great. The thrust on the tool is lateral, that is, side-to-side, so the tool moves in the collet up and down. It is a fast an easy way to swap cutting tools, and have them securely held.

So imagine my surprise when I see a suppressor with a collet mount on it. It was meant to slide over the barrel or flash hider, and when the collar is tightened, clamp onto the barrel and stay in place.

However, here the problem is different. The direction of thrust the suppressor experiences is directly in

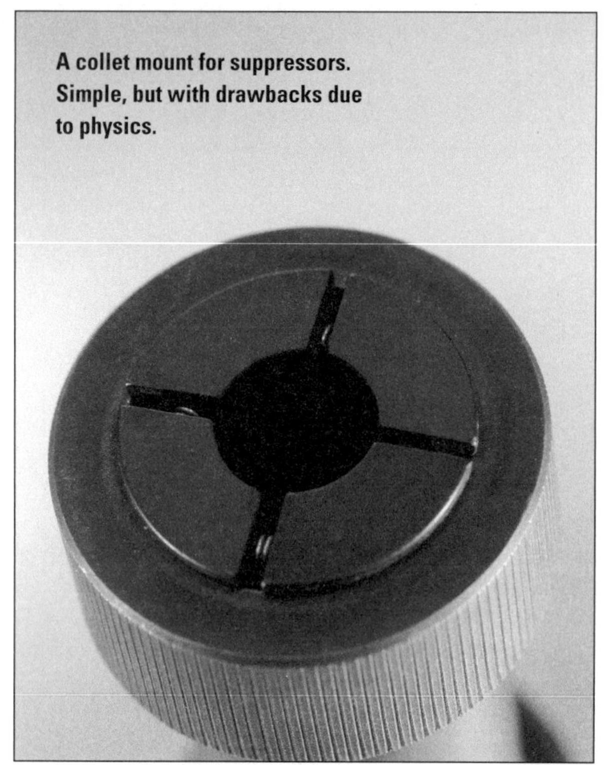

A collet mount for suppressors. Simple, but with drawbacks due to physics.

line with the suppressor. So the collet has to depend on friction to keep it in place, unless the maker machines a lip into it.

In talking with some contacts, I discovered that there were some collet-equipped suppressors to be found in some Special Forces units, back in "the day" but no word on what eventually happened to them. Also, the original Czech Skorpion, the .32 ACP buzzgun the size of a pistol, used a collet design for the suppressors it had, but they featured a lip machined into the barrel, a lip the collet could gain purchase on.

So, rare, and judging by the serial number this particular Uzi/suppressor combo was made in the early 1980s, explaining why it isn't seen any more. Blow a few suppressors off the end of your 5.56 rifle and you give up on a particular mount design.

Thread mounts, extra considerations

If you simply thread a muzzle and screw a device onto it, what keeps it in place, and what keeps it aligned? If

Collets are a long-established attachment system in the machine tool industry. They have severe drawbacks for suppressors.

Flash hiders usually have axial slots, muzzle brakes have transverse slots.

Lugs were not just a rifle thing.

This M9 barrel has a two-lug mount on the barrel.

The taper on this mount (Thunder Beast Arms) aligns the suppressor and provides more bearing area for the fit.

you make the thread a tight enough fit, alignment is controlled mostly by the thread fit. If you do not, and you make it a free-running fit, you can't count on the threads doing the job by themselves. If loose, the device will sag and you may (since we're talking about suppressors here) end up with baffle strikes.

So, you have to use the shoulder of the thread cut as an abutment, to align and keep tight the fit. This means you are depending on the torque you used to tighten it, to keep it tight. Also, you are depending on that shoulder being perpendicular to the axis of the bore and the suppressor. If the shoulder is tilted, then the suppressor will tilt when it is tightened. Even if it doesn't tilt, it will be tight only against the highest part of the shoulder; that isn't a very large bearing surface, and the suppressor is likely to work loose faster than if the shoulder were square to the axis.

One method some suppressor makers use to solve this problem is to machine the bearing shoulder as a cone. A cone has much better axial alignment to the bore than a square shoulder does. It also has a larger surface area for friction to generate resistance to loosening when both are correctly machined. If they are not, both will suck.

Mounting process

Just slapping a suppressor onto a firearm is a good way to end up with a pain in your wallet, and perhaps even a pain in some other part of your body. You see, the bullet has to pass cleanly through the clearance holes of the baffle, without touching anything on the way through. If it touches things, bad results will follow. This can be partly bad, or very bad. My experience with a

Maxim silencers were direct-thread, and since they were offset, they had to be made and fitted "clocked" so they would tighten up correctly.

Gemtech Halo and a police department is illustrative. I was showing the suppressor and how it fits on any A1/A2 flash hider. I turned my back and, next thing I know, an officer was stepping up to the line with my Halo on his M4. The first shot hit the backstop, off the target, high-left. The second was off the target, low-right. By then I'd stepped up to him and said, "Please stop, you're getting baffle strikes." They were actually more like baffle glances, but they were enough to remind me – not all A1/A2 flash hiders are correctly aligned.

Had it been a very bad situation, the bullet would have caught a baffle hard enough to tumble, and the results would have been messy. Or destructive of the suppressor. So, check alignment.

In order to measure alignment, you need a suppressor rod from Geissele. They make two of them, one for .308" rifles, and one for .224". In use they are simple. We will cover the measuring of alignment before we cover mounting, because you have to check alignment before you do any shooting, and knowing what is going on as you assemble your mount is made clearer by knowing the measuring method you'll use at the end.

You take the unloaded firearm, and (in the case of the AR) remove the bolt and carrier assembly from the upper. It is easier to handle if you just have the upper, so separate it from the lower.

If the rifle hadn't been cleaned lately, do yourself a favor and at least run a brush down the bore, followed by a patch to wipe out the crud.

Slide the alignment rod down the bore and use your hand to stop it as it sticks out of the suppressor. Lay the upper down on a level surface and push the rod back until it is flush with the face of the suppressor. Now take a look. What you see will be alignment that fits into one of four categories: centered, off-center but not touching, touching, not coming out.

CENTERED

Here, the rod is dead center in the exit hole of the front cap. Perfect, your alignment-check job is done.

If you have a suppressor and you do not have a Geissele alignment rod, you are risking a baffle strike.

OFF-CENTER BUT NOT TOUCHING

The rod is not on center, but it is not touching the edge of the exit hole in the front cap. This is a judgment call. In most cases the clearance will still be great enough that the bullet will be fine as it passes through, in which case you can leave it alone. However, there is the risk that as the suppressor heats up it will shift on the barrel, and if that shift is in the direction of closest fit, then you could get strikes.

You can re-fit the mounting device and check alignment again. Or you can test-fire and see.

OFF-CENTER, TOUCHING

This is a no-go situation. The rod touches, so it is highly likely that the bullet will touch also. Your choices are simple: re-do the mounting build, get the threads re-cut, or move on to the next rifle.

NOT EXITING

Here, the misalignment is so bad the rod doesn't just touch, but it rubs so hard against one or more of the baffles that it can't pass through the suppressor. If the barrel is long enough, and you can stand the thought of having it shortened by half an inch, you can get a competent machinist to shorten and re-thread. If not, move on and try on another barrel.

Mount up

Now we can talk about the mounting process.

Start by considering the design you have. If it is a direct-thread, then you will need the suppressor, the barrel, a wrench, and maybe some mounting shims. If your suppressor is a QD mount type, then you'll have the suppressor, the mount, and the instructions and shim kit the suppressor maker shipped with the mount.

Let's work with the direct-thread first. Take the unloaded rifle and screw the suppressor onto the muzzle. Use the alignment rod to check alignment. If it is centered, or off-centered but not touching, then you can proceed. Use the torque wrench to tighten the suppressor to the specified torque level.

If it doesn't have correct alignment, you have the choice of moving on or trying to correct the alignment. Using flat shims won't always help, if ever, because they will simply move the suppressor forward by however many thousandths thick they are. But sometimes you can find a combination of shims that corrects alignment (emphasis on sometimes). This happens when there is a

Not quite dead center, but really close, and more than good for our purposes.

Off-center, but not touching the exit plate clearance hole. You're good to go.

Touching the wall of the front cap. This is risky. It might be OK, it might not, but I wouldn't risk it.

The rod will not pass through, indicating a serious misalignment. This won't work. Find another rifle, or re-fit the mount or threads.

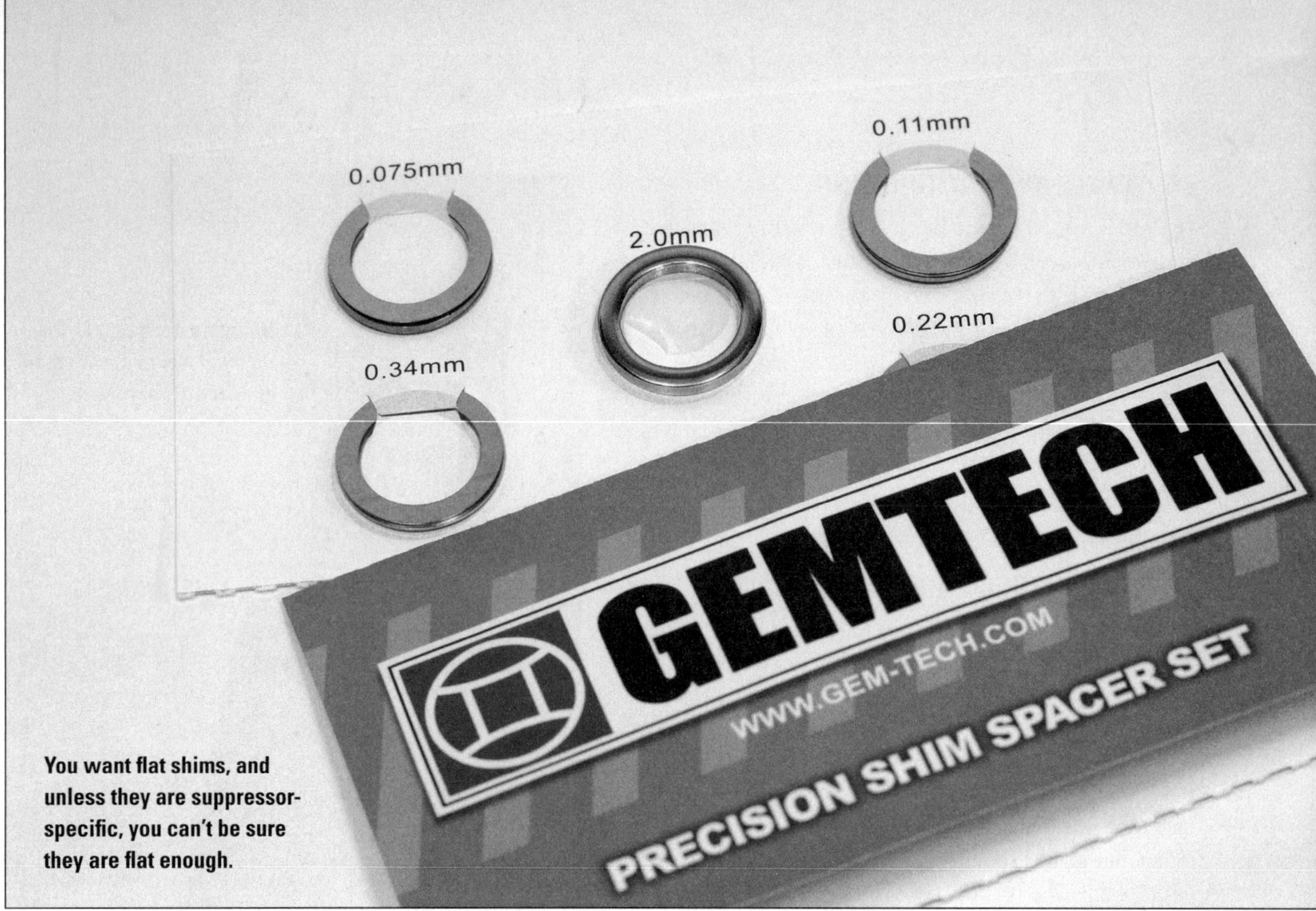

You want flat shims, and unless they are suppressor-specific, you can't be sure they are flat enough.

slight inconsistency in the threads at some point or section of the threaded portion. By moving the suppressor out from the bearing shoulder, and filling the gap with flat shims (not all shims are flat, use the correct ones) you can get the suppressor threads bearing on a section of barrel threads that allows everything to line up.

There is no pattern to this, you will have to install and try, remove, install more, and try again. If you can't get the suppressor to properly align with a few shims (I'd quit if it hadn't aligned by the fourth one) then move on to the next rifle you own. This one doesn't want to play well with others.

If you have paid a gunsmith or machinist to thread your barrel for the suppressor, you have a right to be annoyed at this point.

If you have found that you must use flat shims to get correct alignment, here's a tip: once on, never take it off. If you take it off, you can't be sure of proper alignment without going through the process again. In fact, if I were doing this, I'd use a thread-locking compound to make it difficult to remove the suppressor.

It would be far better to move on, find a barrel it aligns on properly, and use that as the host.

Threads and clearance

Have you ever looked at the threads on the muzzle of your rifle? No? Well, do it now. Do the threads come all the way back to the shoulder? If not, is the section unthreaded the top height, or the bottom of the threads? If top, your suppressor might stop short. Now look at the back end of your suppressor. Are the threads cut cleanly all the way out to the back surface of the suppressor? Without some relief, you can't really tighten the suppressor properly.

If the two threaded sections (barrel and suppressor) are properly relieved, they have overlap clearance, and the rear face of the suppressor will bear tightly against the front shoulder of the barrel. Lacking clearance, you have the situation where the end of the threads on the suppressor jams against the end of the threads on the barrel. That is a tiny contact point, and it won't hold in the heat and vibration of shooting.

Suppressor makers know this, and know that if it doesn't work they'll be blamed, so they are diligent in making their direct-thread suppressors with clearance.

However, if the barrel is not threaded cleanly all the way back to the shoulder, or given clearance, you may need flat shims to fill the gap that the barrel maker left.

A three- (or in this case, six) jaw chuck is a scrolling chuck, and all jaws move at once.

MACHINE TOOLS AND THREADING Most lathes come fitted (If they are fitted) with a three-jaw chuck, known as a "scrolling chuck." This is a clamping device where all three jaws are moved in unison by the same, single, locking screw. (There's a spiral track machined on an inside plate, and the jaws ride in the spiral, opening and closing in unison.) The jaws come to a more-or-less centered position. In fact, for most uses, it is more rather than less centered. As a "more" example, let's say your three-jaw chuck (and this is just for the purpose of illustration) clamps to center and is actually centered plus or minus a thousandth of an inch. If the work you are doing has an allowable variance of five-thousandths, the chuck will never get close to being the problem. On the other hand, if you are machining for an aerospace application, and the tolerance on the blueprint is five ten-thousandths, then your chuck is twice the allowed maximum and you are in trouble before you even start. Most uses aren't aerospace, and most users find a three-jaw chuck works just fine.

But suppressors aren't most uses.

For this, you need a four-jaw chuck, also known as an independent-jaw chuck. Here, each of the four locking jaws is moved by its own screw. The machinist/gunsmith uses a precision-ground index rod, inserted in the bore. He or she then adjusts the jaws one at a time, using a readout gauge, until the index rod is absolute dead-center in the lathe. Threads can then be cut that are centered and parallel to the bore, not the external surface, and will keep your suppressor centered as well.

Thus, if you are having someone thread your barrel, find a way to casually ask, "So, you've got a four-jaw chuck for this, right?" In talking with Ned about this, he told me of a different type of chuck, a six-jaw scrolling/adjustable. It has the adjustments of both. You clamp the piece into the six jaws, which open and close simultaneously. Then, you adjust the chuck as a unit, to get the piece dead-centered for work. You get the best of both worlds. If you don't adjust the offsets, then the chuck is a regular, scrolling chuck, and you use it as you normally would. When you need an independent-jaw chuck, you don't have to take the scrolling chuck off of the lathe, stash it away, install the new chuck, setup, adjust, cut, then take the independent chuck off and re-install the scrolling chuck.

Instead, you have one chuck, to turn them all.

A four-jaw chuck allows the jaws to be adjusted independently, so the operator can make the barrel (as shown here) absolute dead-centered in the lathe.

These threads are not "cleared" on the back, the shoulder is the full height of the threads. This might cause problems with a direct-thread suppressor, unless the manufacturer cut clearance into the suppressor threads.

You want your suppressor to torque up on the front face of the threaded shank of the barrel.

QD mounting

QD mounts are another and more involved proposition. First, unpack the muzzle device, count the parts and make sure they are there. Then read the instructions. Yes, yes, I know, we are men, we don't read instructions. We don't ask for directions, and we don't drink flavored lattes. Get over it. If you don't, and you screw this up, you risk destroying a thousand dollars or more of equipment, plus hurting yourself or others.

Many of the muzzle devices have a specific orientation at which the manufacturer wants it installed, or that works best, and you must know this going in.

Take the muzzle device and hand-screw it onto the barrel. See where it stops. Compare that to the instructions. If they have shims to adjust orientation, check which ones, remove the mount, slide the shims on and re-thread the mount on.

A quick note here, and not to pick on the guys at Surefire. The instructions have a diagram for which shims to use. The instructions also have a chart, for each thread pitch you might use. Be sure you use the right one. If you keep trying to stack shims to get a $^{1}/_{2}$-28 mount to screw up right and you are using the $^{5}/_{8}$-24 chart, you will keep getting it wrong. You know how I know this. (A breeze flipped the page on me, and I hadn't noticed. That's my story, and I'm sticking with it.)

Once you have the mount in place, use your wrench to torque it to the final position. Now, install the suppressor. And finally, do the alignment check with the Geissele rod. If you find you have done all this and the suppressor is not aligned, then I agree – life sucks. You'll either have to start all over again on another barrel or rifle, or you will have to have the threads re-done, or done properly. If alignment is correct, then life is good, move on to the next step.

Once you have everything tight to the correct position and have checked alignment, take it all off. Degrease it with an aerosol degreaser, twice. Then read the instructions for the tube of Rocksett, apply, then slide on the shims, thread the mount on by hand, and use the wrench to torque it the last bit.

Then ***leave it alone***.

Rocksett works like magic, but if you don't give it time to set, it won't set very rock-like. Don't plan on shooting your suppressor-equipped rifle until the next day.

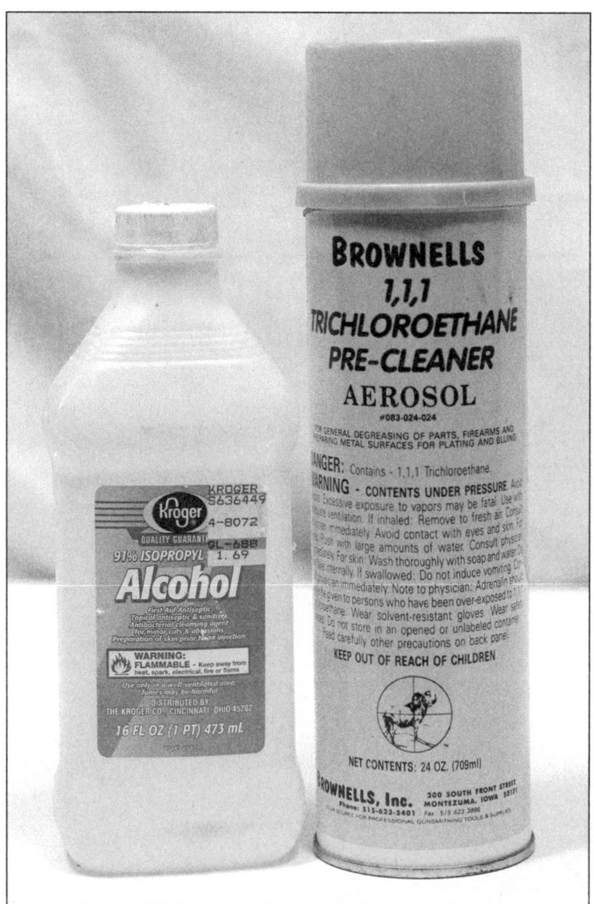

Make sure you degrease the barrel threads and mount threads before you do your final assembly. If you don't, they may not stay tight for long.

Chapter Seven

MEASURING EFFECTIVENESS

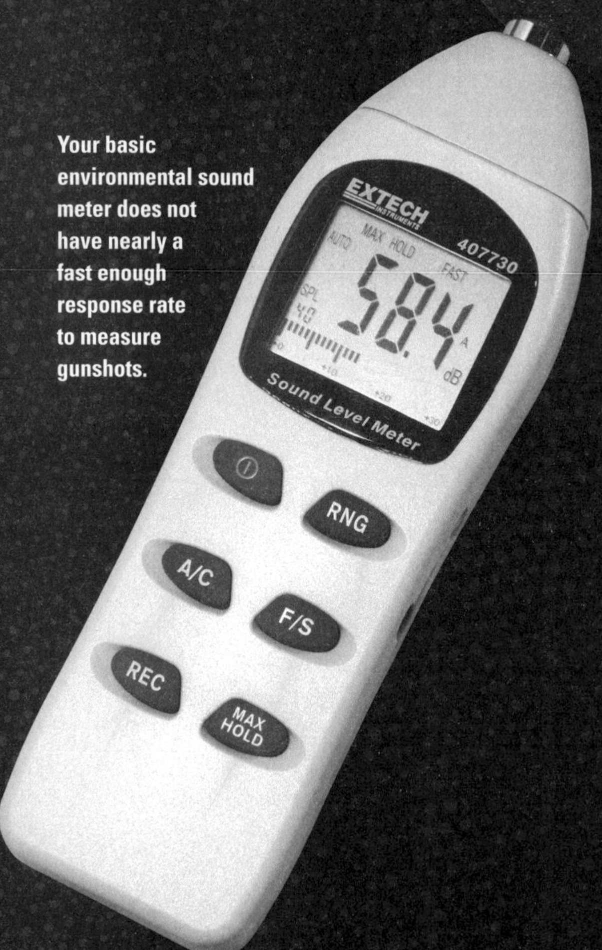

Your basic environmental sound meter does not have nearly a fast enough response rate to measure gunshots.

Cool, you jumped through the hoops, you have a suppressor and all your friends are agog. Range days are fun, as you are the envy of the gun club, and everyone wants to hear, or rather, not hear, your new toy. Invariably, someone will ask to try it. After they have, expecting the Hollywood-level mouse-fart, comes the question, "Is that it?" The nagging question arises, just how quiet is it?

Your friend has an app on his smartphone, one that cost him all of five bucks, and it tells you just how loud things are. Sorry, but it doesn't help here. Sound takes more than an app to measure, at least gunshot sound.

As we covered earlier, sound is a compression wave. To measure it, you need a microphone that can record the compression wave as it goes by. OK, let's make a comparison. You've learned that when it comes to the TV, your wife doesn't want to hear the commercials. So you get in the habit of muting the TV when the commercials come on. When the break is over, if you wait until the show is clearly back on to un-mute, you miss the first few words of dialogue. Your response time is too slow. Between your reaction time, the fire-up time of the

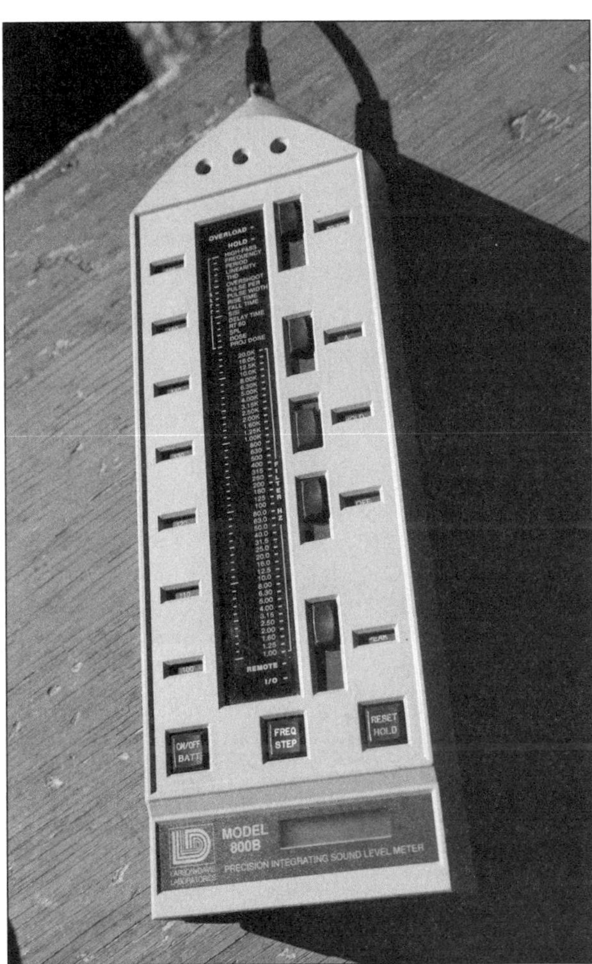

An old Larson-Davis 800B, the pinnacle of old technology. ('Old' here meaning a couple of decades.)

You need to hold the microphone securely, and without adding vibration to the system.

remote, and the response time of the TV, you can miss a few seconds of audio on the show.

A measuring microphone with a too-slow response time will not accurately reflect the true decibel level of the sound you are "measuring." It wakes up and starts responding to the compression wave only after it has already passed by. In technical terms, you need a microphone and meter with a response time of no more than two microseconds, or you will not have an accurate measurement. And no, you cannot back-calculate from a slower response time. That is, you cannot take a ten microsecond response mic, measure it alongside a two microsecond mic, and calculate "Hey, the ten is always X decibels lower than the two, so I can buy the much cheaper ten, and just add on the X on each measurement." It doesn't work that way.

I had a perfect example of this a while back, on a police range, while teaching AR-15s for Patrol Rifle. One of the instructors had a new app on his smartphone, and he was quite happy to show that, standing a couple of feet behind and to the side of a shooter, the phone was registering 105 decibels. Nice, but wrong. At that spot, an AR-15 carbine, with factory ammo, is hammering you at more like 150 dB. The slower response time of the phone was failing to register the other 45 dB, the ones that our ears would still be subjected to.

The newest and current best for the price, the Larson-Davis 831.

If you plan to be accurate, you need a calibration can. This goes over the microphone to test, and set, sound levels.

Mil-spec gone wild

When it comes to measuring sounds and decibel levels, the military has to have published standards. However, the military is concerned with a lot more audio problems than small arms. In fact, that's the least of their problems. There are big internal combustion engines, machine tools, jet engines, helicopter turbines, all manner of cannon and artillery to consider.

So it comes as no surprise that there are mil-spec standards for noise and noise abatement in the services. What might come as a surprise to most is that the number of pages devoted to our subject, small arms, is few, compared to the rest.

The relevant document is Department of Defense Design Criteria Standard, Noise Limits. The 197 pages of that document lay out noise measurement, control and restrictions for not just small arms, but shipboard, aircraft and rotary-wing aircraft. This is MIL-STD-1474D, dated 12 February 1997, and it supersedes all previous documents on the subject.

Combat is a loud business. And rifles are not even close to being the loudest tools. U.S. Marine Corps photo by Cpl. Ricky S. Gomez.

Oh, and speaking of superseding, the original specifications of measuring sound, developed by the Frankford Arsenal back in "the day" called for the measurement to be made five meters from the side of the muzzle, not one meter as we do today. This was due to the relative unresponsiveness of the equipment and the lower maximum threshold. As a result of the change in distance and equipment, it is not possible to compare in a realistic sense the measurements made back then and the measurements today.

As a government document covering technical/engineering situations, it is as involved as you'd imagine, and also chock full of information. I have to warn you, if you want to acquire a copy and read it, you will have pages and pages of technical info on stationary equipment and measuring noise around it. You will learn all kinds of awful things about how noisy helicopters are. But you will be well educated on the subject of noise, its attenuation, and blocking it.

The process

Reading military manuals is a sure cure for insomnia, so how do you actually go about recording gunshot noise levels, and the effects that suppressors provide? If you are going to have a temporary or portable setup, you'll need a pair of tripods. One will be the indicating point, the location of the muzzle (or you can place the rest right behind it, to spare it the scorching experience, as the rest of us do) and the other is the microphone stand.

The regular, normal, and non-combat environment on a ship is noisy beyond belief. The navy has standards, and Petty Officer McDonald has earplugs in. U.S. Navy photo by Petty Officer 3rd Class Brian Sloan.

They should both be 1.6 meters above a level, grassy surface. This is five feet, and the microphone is located one meter (39.34 inches) directly to the side of the muzzle. The angle of line of fire to microphone is 90 degrees.

In an ideal world, the testing would be done in a "quiet room," one with complete sound-absorbing walls, ceiling and floor, and where the temperature, humidity and ambient pressure were controlled and at the ambient standard. Good luck with that, as such a room will cost you a lot of money, even before you rig it so you can discharge a firearm in it.

If you think about it, you'll have to look closely at your potential locations. Obviously, trying to measure gunshot decibel levels right next to a freeway will be dif-

You thought your .300 Win Mag was loud? Really? Even the Uruguayan navy has louder firearms.

One meter to the direct side (left) of the muzzle.

Rather than be "close enough" holding the rifle, you need to have a rest, for consistent distances for measuring.

ficult. (That's even assuming there won't be other problems.) An indoor range, with concrete walls and steel plates for bullet control, would be pretty much hopeless. Ideally, you'd measure out in the middle of nowhere, with the grassy terrain flat to the horizon. Lacking that, any grassy area with screening vegetation around you will do, to block out as much extraneous noise as possible, and yet produce not much, if any, echo.

Use the calibration tool with the meter to check the meter reading, and adjust if needed to bring it to the calibration device's output. One trick you can use, if you are faced with measuring decibel levels at or above the limit of your meter, is to audio-offset. Put the calibration device on the microphone, and have it produce its 120 dB sound level. Then adjust the meter to "read" that as 110 dB. This way, you have a 10 dB offset, so if you are testing, say, a .300 Win Mag, and it is peaking at 172 dB, too high for your meter, the meter will "hear" it as 162 dB. Just be sure and record in your notes that this is what you did, and add those 10 dB back in. And, when you are done, re-calibrate your meter to the correct calibration device level.

Then, the process is simple; record the temperature, humidity and pressure as best you can, then fire a shot, record the dB, and repeat. If you want to see how well a suppressor reduces noise, you have to test it there and then, with the same ammo used in the un-suppressed firing.

Changes in temperature, humidity and air pressure can alter the results, as can wind strength and direction. So, test on the same day. If you do not have professional-level temperature, humidity and atmospheric pressure reading equipment, then record the time of day and exact location where you were working, check with a barometric pressure map, and discover the pressure.

Sound levels vary only slightly with changes in temperature, pressure and relative humidity, but having them recorded lets you adjust, if you wanted to convert them all to the values they'd have at standard conditions. Of course, there are "standard" and then there are "standard" conditions. If you decide you want to do the brain-numbing number-crunching, be sure and note in your work which standard you are using; IUPAC, NIST, SATP, or the U.S. Army Standard Metro.

Short of doing all that, your task is simple: measure the sound levels un-suppressed; then measure the sound levels suppressed, with same firearm, ammo and conditions. Subtract the latter from the former, and you have the "quiet" rating, how many decibels your suppressor knocked off. Don't be surprised if it is a decibel or two less than the promised value. It could simply be the difference between your conditions and those used by the manufacturer or testing lab they contracted with.

Each shot has to be recorded, and then the total averaged, before moving on to the next test.

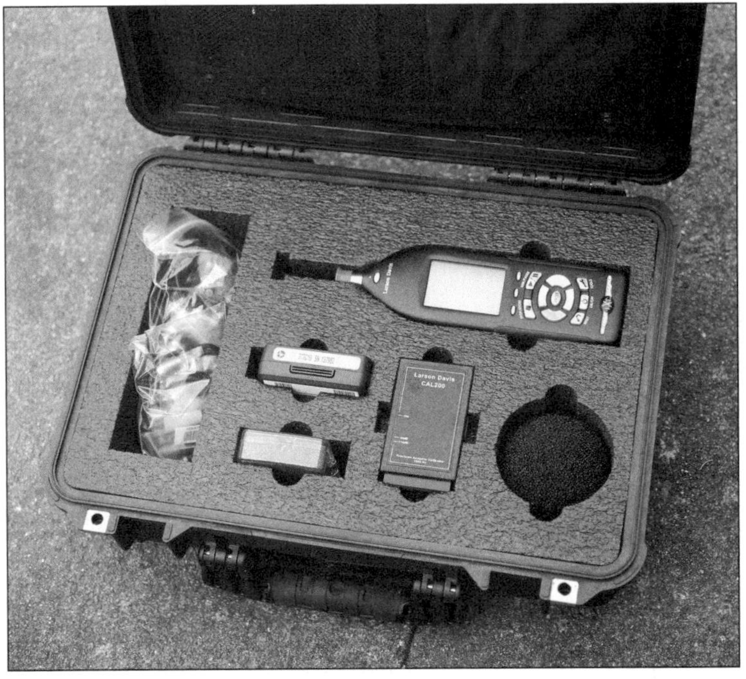

This is the microphone that measures for us. Tiny, delicate, expensive and essential.

The complete kit, meter, microphone, instructions, calibration, hard case for storage and transport.

Chapter Eight

RIMFIRE SUPPRESSORS

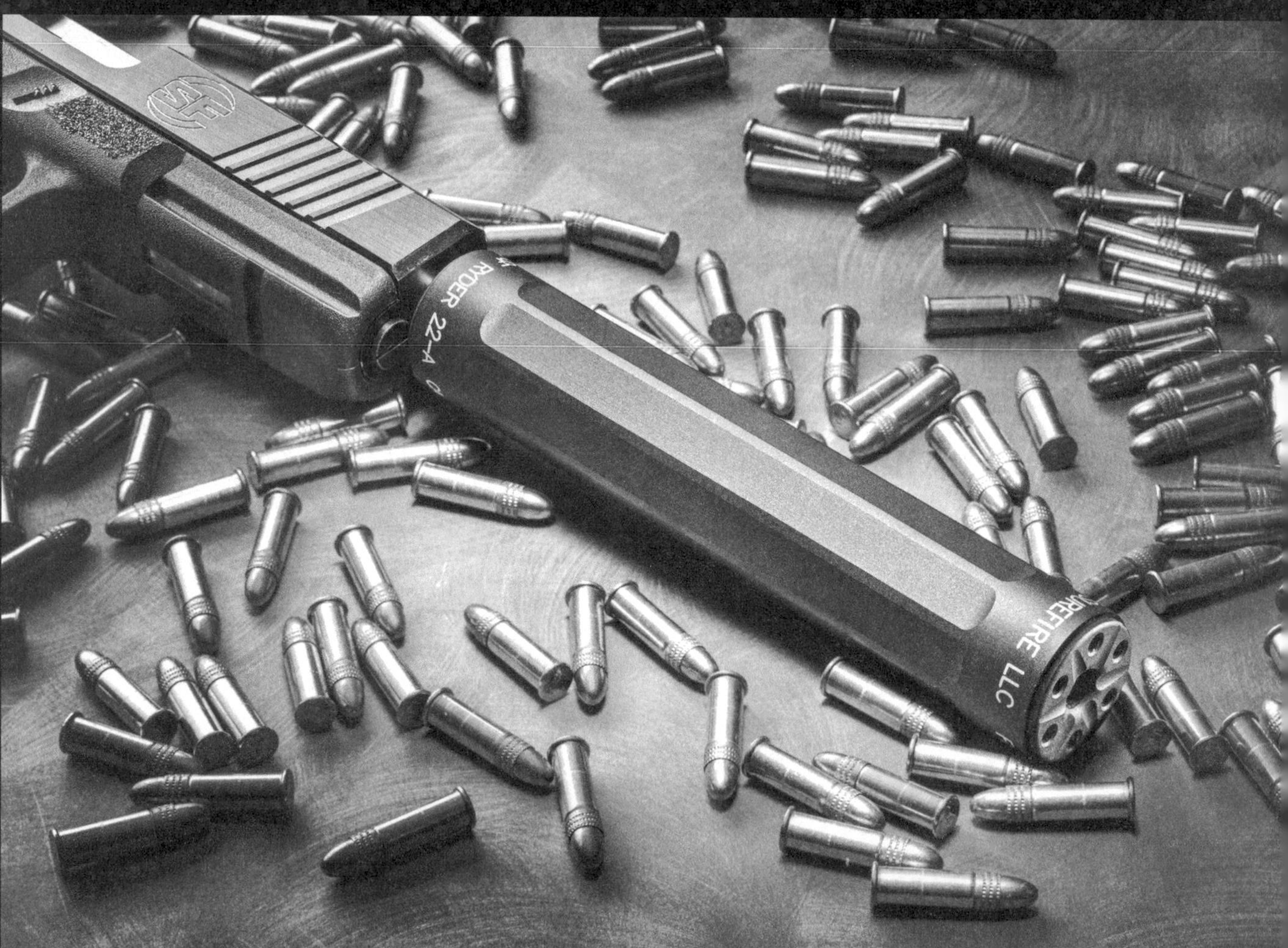

When it comes to cheap quiet, it is hard to beat the lowly rimfire.

When it comes to shooting, cheap is good. Shooting isn't the most expensive sport, but it does cost, and .22LR takes a lot of the sting out of that.

When talk at the gun club turns to suppressors, everyone wants a suppressor for their AR. Something in .223 or 5.56. Or, they want a suppressor for their .308, their long-range precision rifle (aka sniper rifle) or their AR in .308. But, what I find from the manufacturers is that they make a lot of suppressors for rimfire firearms. My personal term for disparities of this magnitude, the numbers made compared to the numbers estimated, is "metric buttload." They make *a lot* of rimfire suppressors, compared to the centerfire ones.

Why? Why do they, in some instances, make four, five, ten times as many rimfires as they do centerfires? (And that's just the companies who make both. There are companies that do not make centerfire suppressors, only rimfire ones.) It comes down to a few things, all revolving around cost. It costs money to buy a suppressor. It costs money to go shooting, and if there's one thing we can all relate to, it is that there's no such thing as too much money.

Now, as "expensive" hobbies go, shooting isn't one of them. Oh, some can be. If you shoot registered trap, you're going to be essentially burning twenty-dollar

With the right array of rear caps, you can put a rimfire suppressor on just about any brand of rimfire firearm.

bills at the gun club. But, it still isn't like auto racing. A previous neighbor of ours raced two different classes of cars, at local tracks, nothing national. He was an engineer and builder, so the cars cost him pretty much his time and the parts, which he could often get wholesale. But he could not make tires, and he calculated that if he was careful in racing, he could make two sets of tires last a season, for each of the cars. $4,500 a set, per car, comes to nine grand in rubber a car a season, so eighteen thousand dollars a season just for tires.

Inflation has a factor in this but I don't think I spent $18,000 on handgun shooting in any year, for everything, when I was a serious competitor. Granted, I was reloading all my ammo and building my own guns, but entry fees, travel, etc. didn't add up to the tire cost for our neighbor. Shooting may cost, but not like *really* expensive hobbies.

But, if you have a family, then the mortgage, clothes, food, orthodontia, car maintenance all gobble large amounts of money. If you are prudent, then you are pumping money into the kid's college fund, and your own IRA or 401K. A suppressor is a splurge. One way to ease the impact of that splurge is to buy a rimfire suppressor for $400 instead of a centerfire one for $900-1200. And then feed it .22LR ammo, which costs less than .223, and certainly costs less than .308.

And they are quiet.

Why does a rimfire suppressor cost so much less? Materials – type and amount. A rimfire suppressor may be only a one-inch tube, instead of the 1.5 inches of a centerfire. Also, it will be made (in most instances) of aluminum, since the .22LR does not generate nearly as much pressure or gas as centerfires do. That all adds up to less material, which happens to be easier to machine, and thus lower cost. There's also the smaller effect of economies of scale. If you are making a thousand of one item, and a hundred of another, you can bargain for lower costs on materials for the former.

If you place an order for a literal truckload of seamless aluminum tubing, one-inch O.D., you're going to get a better price than you would buying it one

The trend to monocore rimfire suppressors is good. It makes them more durable and easier to clean.

tube at a time.

As a further price decrease, rimfire suppressors do not need a booster, like pistol-caliber suppressors do for handguns. And, it is rare that someone wants a quick-attach mount system on a .22LR suppressor. Direct-thread rules here, and that brings down the cost even more.

Ca-ching, ca-ching, ca-ching.

And the quiet?

Well, the .22LR isn't all that noisy to start with. Oh, it will make you go deaf if you don't protect your hearing from it, but the amount of gas to deal with is pretty small. And, the expansion ratio of a .22LR, even a handgun, is pretty large. This soaks up a lot of the gas energy, as the pressure drops and the gases cool. So, it doesn't take much to deal with it. If you then go with target ammo, which is subsonic for accuracy, not noise reasons, or straight-up subsonic ammo, you get the Hollywood "phht, phht, phht" sound from your Ruger 10-22.

Where rimfire suppressors make you pay is in the grubbiness department. Twenty-twos are pretty grubby just as they are. But when you start trapping the muzzle gasses via a suppressor, the carbon deposits become impressive indeed. Remember, there's lead in there too, so wash your hands after you wash your suppressor.

And if you don't? Well, if you don't disassemble and clean your rimfire suppressor after every 500 rounds, you may find it carbon-welded and you can't take it apart. Then, the aluminum construction works against you, as it may not survive heavy-handed attempts to disassemble. If you don't scrub your hands after cleaning, you may (read "will") absorb some lead, which is not good for you. Your body may spend the next year expelling the lead you absorbed from one failure to scrub. That's right, our moms were all correct; wash your hands, and things will be fine.

Dead Air Mask .22LR

The Dead Air Armament mask, a most excellent rimfire suppressor, complete with instructions, takedown tool and carry bag.

The Mask baffle, with a complex shape and side ribs to keep the baffles from binding in the tube when dirty.

OAL	5.14"
Net OAL	4.64"
Diameter	1"
Materials	titanium & 17-4 stainless steel
Weight	6.7 oz
Finish	Matte black CeraKote™
Calibers rated	.22LR
Full auto rated	Yes
Mount system available	direct thread 1/2x28
Construction	User-serviceable
Baffle design	billet, modified K baffle
MSRP	$459

Dead Air continues their no-holds-barred approach, with the Mask. Who makes a rimfire suppressor out of titanium and 17-4 PH stainless? And as if that wasn't enough, it can be disassembled for cleaning. With the same matte Cerakote finish as the bigger suppressors, the Dead Air Armament Mask will fit right in with the rest of your Dead Air lineup.

As is normal and customary with rimfire units, the Mask is direct-thread, not QD.

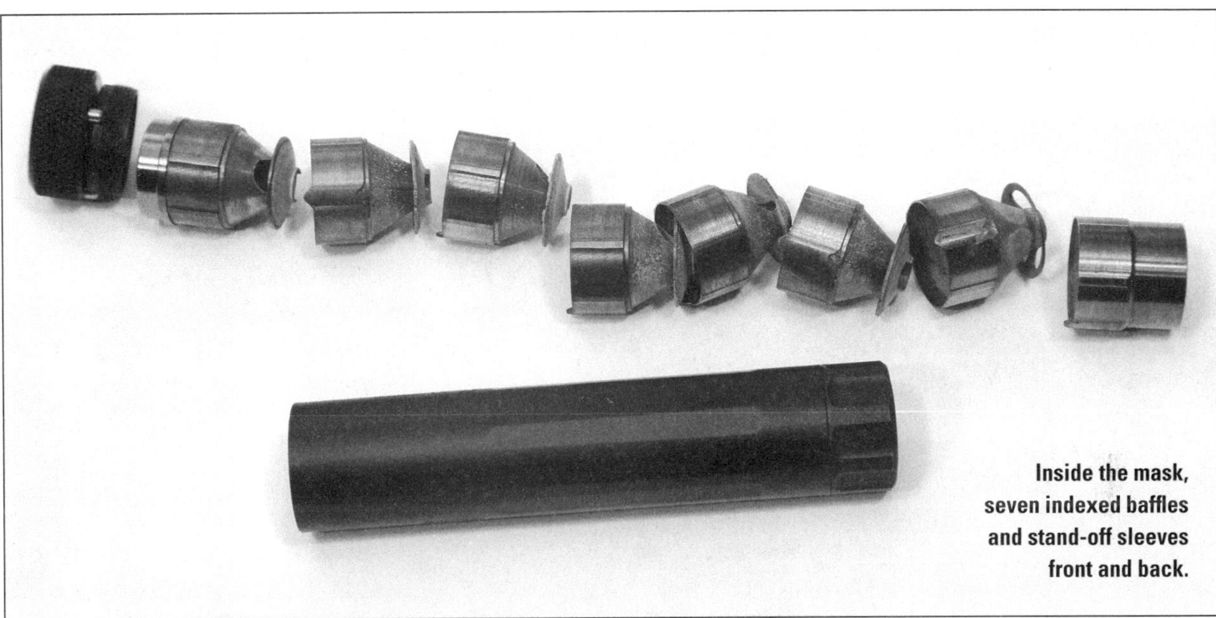

Inside the mask, seven indexed baffles and stand-off sleeves front and back.

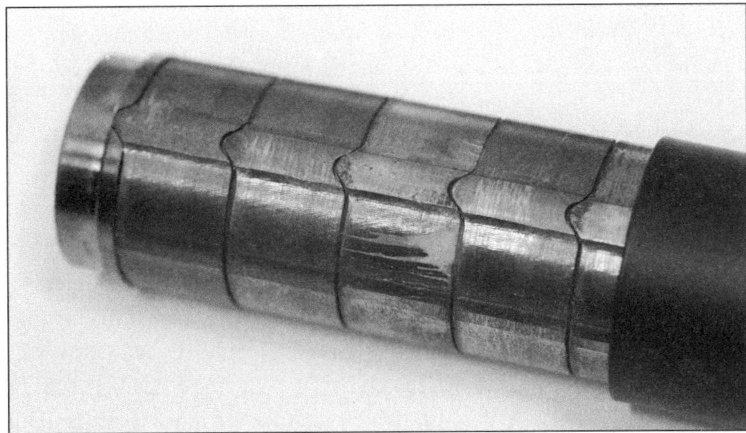

The Mask baffles have indexing tabs to keep them correctly aligned as you reassemble.

The takedown tool fits onto the end of the front cap.

Gemtech Outback IID

Once apart, you can clean, scrub and inspect.

The Gemtech Outback II comes with a disassembly tool, which you use on the front cap.

The Outback is a rimfire suppressor of the modern classic type, but with a few twists. First, the construction is almost all aluminum, but with improvements. The Outback is your basic threaded-on-both-ends tube, but the rear cap has an insert made of titanium, to take the wear-and-tear of mounting and dismounting on the steel threads of the barrel. The baffle stack is made of a series of K baffles, but they are tabbed so you offset the turbulence notches when assembling, and you also get the first and last baffles in the correct places, because they matter.

The first baffle, or blast baffle, is stainless steel, while the rest are aluminum, which accounts for the extreme light weight of the Outback IID, at 2.7 ounces.

Gemtech lists it as having a decibel reduction of 39.4 dB, which is about the most you can wring out of any suppressor of any design, until you start making suppressors the size of gallon milk jugs. With subsonic .22LR, you truly have the "Hollywood" silencer noise on firing. Disassembly is easy, although a pronged wrench or angle pliers (available at many tool stores) makes it a lot easier.

At one inch in diameter, the Outback is going to blend in with the barrel profile of pistols like the Ruger 22/45, and other versions of the various Marks. It also does not look bulky on a rifle barrel. The light weight means you won't have balance changes, at least not much to notice.

The Outback IID is a .22LR-*only* suppressor. If you

The baffles of the Outback II are tabbed, so get them together properly.

Only the front-most baffle lacks tabs, and that is so it clears the front cap.

want something to use with a .17 HMR or .22WMR, you have to move up in weight, to handle the higher pressures. Gemtech makes those, and they are backwards compatible with .22LR, so consider the Outback IID as a trade-off suppressor; you get the ultra light weight (the magnums-rated suppressors are in the 6-7 ounce range) but the cost is .22LR only. Works for me.

OAL	5"
Net OAL	4.5"
Diameter	1"
Materials	Aluminum, Ti threads, one SS baffle
Weight	2.7 oz
Finish	Matte black anodized aluminum
Calibers available	.22LR only
Calibers rated	.22LR only
Full auto rated	No
Mount system available	direct-thread only, $\frac{1}{2}$ x 28
Construction	Serviceable
Baffle design	Oriented, sequential & tabbed
MSRP	$325

Innovative Arms Apex

The Innovative Arms Apex, and its disassembly wrench.

Innovative Arms is a small shop in South Carolina, but with big ideas and a wide array of suppressors. The Apex is a .22LR only suppressor, made mostly of aluminum but with a stainless steel thread insert. This takes the brunt of the wear and tear of mounting and dismounting on your steel-threaded rifle or handgun barrel.

The tricky part of the Apex is the baffle stack, an aluminum monocore. Machined from billet aluminum, the monocore makes it easy to assemble or disassemble, since you can't get the sequence wrong. It does add a

The wrench fits into the slots machined into the rear cap.

The baffle stack is a monocore, and a complex one at that. No way you could make this as individual baffles.

bit more weight (an ounce, if that matters to anyone) simply as part of keeping the monocore strong enough when it is un-shrouded for cleaning.

At an inch and an eighth in diameter, the Apex has plenty of internal volume to keep the noise down, and as a result it is as quiet as it gets with subsonic .22LR ammo. However, it is not rated for the .17s, or for rimfire magnums, so don't abuse them with the brisker ammo.

It comes with a wrench to reach into the slots on the rear for disassembly, but unless you have weak hand strength, or you haven't cleaned it often enough, you should find it no problem to hand-tighten and hand-loosen the assembly for cleaning. If you find you do need the wrench, take that as a sign that you are slacking off the cleaning routine.

OAL	5.25"
Net OAL	4.75"
Diameter	1.125"
Materials	Aluminum, stainless steel
Weight	3.6 oz
Finish	Type 3 hard coat anodized
Calibers available	.22LR
Caliber rated	.22LR
Full auto rated	No
Mount system available	direct thread, $\frac{1}{2}$ x 28
Construction	Serviceable
Baffle design	Monocore
MSRP	$299

Sig Sauer SRD22

Sig makes their own suppressors now, and they made sure they works with their pistols, as well as anything else you care to install it on.

The Sig SRD22 is a modern classic design, although here the baffle stack is oriented but non-sequential. The baffles have a look that would lead me to believe they are cast, not machined, which is fine. Proper castings are just as strong (and can be even stronger) than machined, and while the rougher surface may make them a bit tougher to clean, not enough to worry about.

The baffles are a modified K baffle, oriented so the wide end is towards the muzzle, but they are not notched for turbulence. They are, however, vented on the back surface, to allow gas flow between the baffle arms and the tube.

The front and rear caps are stainless steel, threaded to the tube. The SRD22

The Sig suppressor uses modified K baffles with vent holes.

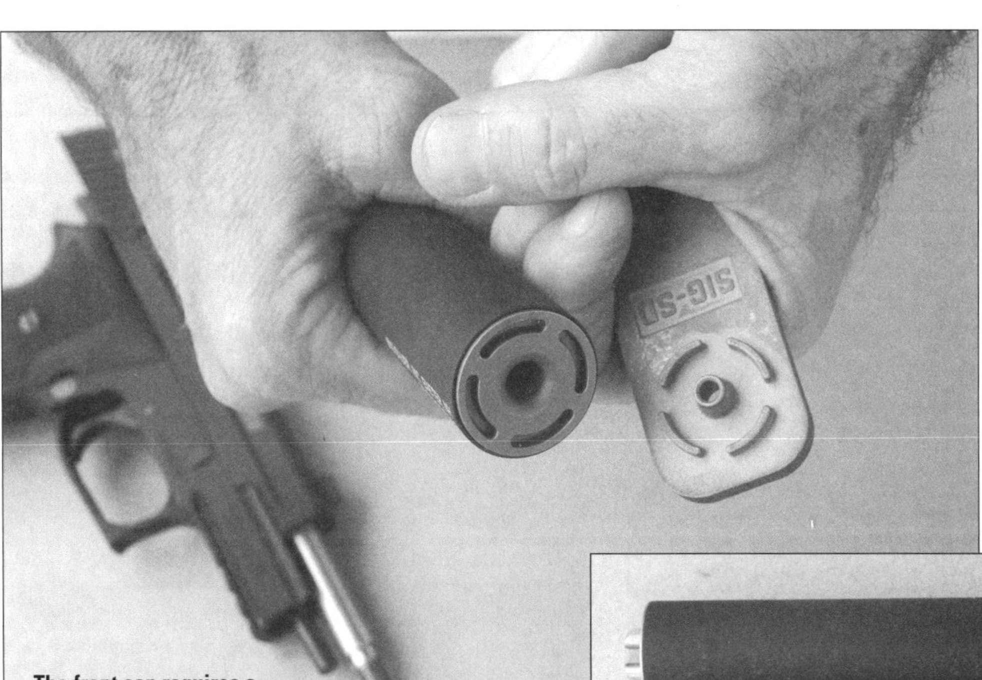

The front cap requires a special wrench to remove, which Sig provides.

The baffles are not sequenced, not tabbed, but you do have to get them in the correct direction.

OAL	6.25"
Net OAL	5.75"
Diameter	1.25"
Material	Aluminum & stainless
Weight	7.7 oz
Finish	Anodized aluminum outer tube
Calibers available	.22LR, .17 HMR, .17 Mach II, .22 Magnum
Calibers rated	Same as above
Full-auto rated	n/a
Mount system available	direct-thread, $\frac{1}{2}$x28 & M9x.75
Construction	Serviceable
Baffle design	K shape, oriented, non-sequential
MSRP	$395

comes with a disassembly wrench, and it has tabs to fit the slots in the front cap and an open-end wrench end to fit the nut of the thread extension on the rear cap.

At an inch and a quarter in diameter, it is a bit larger than other rimfire suppressors, but the advantage gained with the extra volume is the ability to handle all the smaller rimfires. Not just .22LR, but .22WMR, .17 HMR and .17 Mach II. It is not rated for the .17 Winchester magnum, but that is a new cartridge, and plenty robust as rimfires go, so I do not expect to see suppressors made/rated for it until it has proven itself in the marketplace and sells guns and ammo.

The barrel thread extension makes for a different, not-flush appearance when attached to a rifle or handgun, but for the performance you can get used to that.

SLR Rifleworks Aero SS

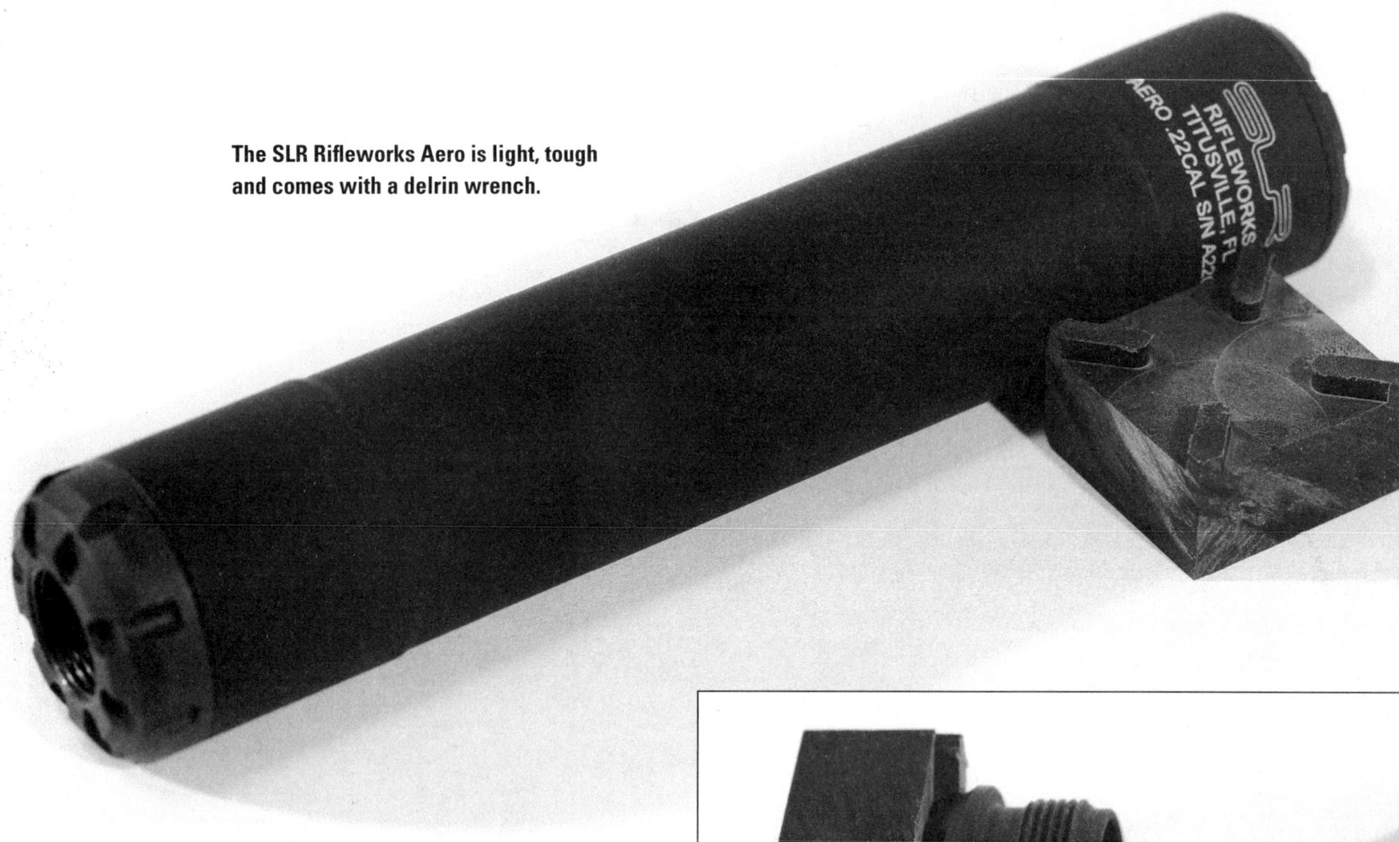

The SLR Rifleworks Aero is light, tough and comes with a delrin wrench.

SLR Rifleworks only makes one suppressor at the moment, the Aero. However, it is a well-designed and well-built one. The tube is an extruded seamless aluminum tube threaded on both ends for front and rear caps. The rear cap is 4140 steel, parkerized to match the black anodizing of the tube, while the front cap is aluminum. What makes the Aero SS stand out are the baffles, which are made of stainless steel. They are a modified K baffle, which I'll call a "cupped" baffle, as SLR takes the basic K shape and then adds a cylindrical extension to create standoff between each baffle. The baffles are oriented, and the first and last must be correctly placed, but those in the middle can be swapped around.

The tube and front cap are 6061 (obvious, since they are extruded, but I still have to mention it) and SLR includes a takedown tool to unscrew the front cap.

The delrin wrench is plenty strong enough to remove the front cap. If you need more force, clamp the wrench in your vise and use both hands on the Aero. And clean more often.

The Aero baffle stack, stainless steel, really tough, and easy to clean.

It is dead simple: a delrin block with ridges in it, to match the slots machined in the front cap. Since rimfire suppressors are only supposed to be assembled hand-tight, that is plenty. And if you lose the tool, it is easy (although you risk marring your suppressor) to use a straightedge as a takedown tool.

The baffles also incorporate a turbulence lip on the entry hole and a vent hole on the in-between tube, to release gas towards the tube and out of the bullet path.

The stainless baffles add a bit of weight, but the stainless also adds durability. You could, if you wanted to and needed to, get really aggressive in cleaning the stainless baffles, where you could not were they aluminum.

OAL	5.2"
Net OAL	4.7"
Diameter	1.0"
Materials	stainless steel, 6061 Aluminum
Weight	6.5 oz
Finish	Matte anodized
Calibers available	.22LR
Caliber rated	.22LR, .17 HMR, .17 Mach II, .22 Magnum, 5.7X28
Full auto rated	Yes
Mount system available	direct thread, 1/2 x 28 (threads are 4140 steel)
Construction	Serviceable
Baffle design	oriented, sequential
MSRP	$250

Surefire Ryder 22

The Surefire Ryder is at first glance a plain old aluminum rimfire suppressor. But then, it isn't. First, the rear cap has a stainless steel insert, threaded, to fit onto the steel threads of your barrel. But the exterior tube is fluted to reduce weight, and the end caps are also machined to take some weight off and to reduce the "edginess" of a machined cylinder.

The included disassembly/assembly tool is what you need to see the next part. Unscrew the front cap, and the baffles slide out. They are anodized red, aluminum, and they are not only tabbed to keep them in correct alignment, they are numbered.

They are numbered because Surefire has spent a lot of time and effort to get them the correct spacing for maximum effectiveness. The baffles are kinda-sorta K baffles, but they have been changed so much, from testing and computer modeling, that they are now cups with turbulence entries, which Surefire called "pig-nose." OK, whatever, I haven't hung out around too many pigs, but I've never seen one with a nose like that. But that's what they call them, and they are patented.

They are also quiet, quieter than you might expect a one-inch tube to be, but the five-inch length helps. That, and the spacing of the baffles.

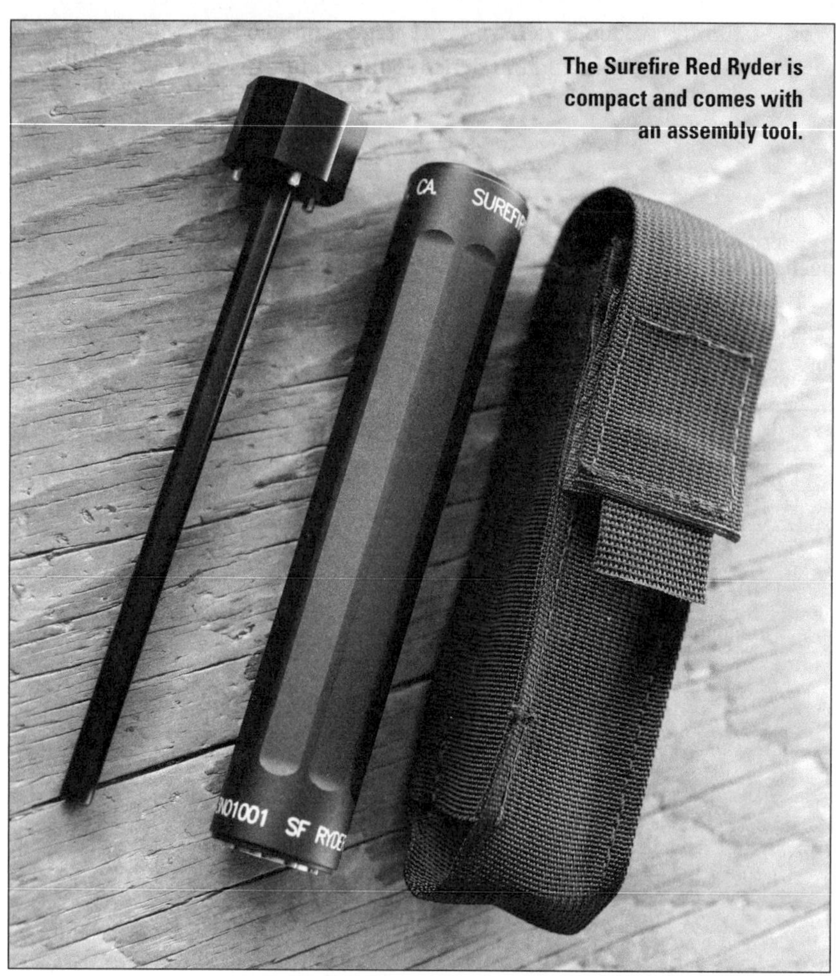

The Surefire Red Ryder is compact and comes with an assembly tool.

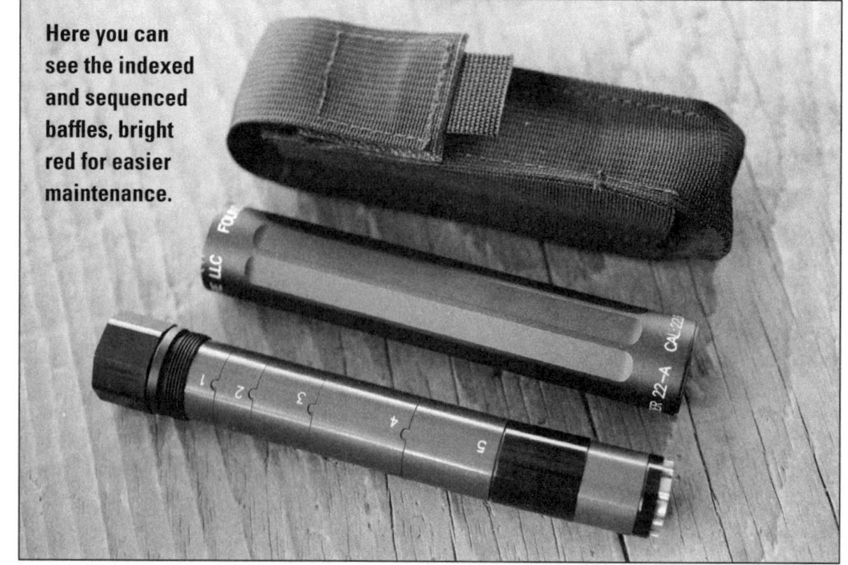

Here you can see the indexed and sequenced baffles, bright red for easier maintenance.

The order matters, for most effective silencing.

Use the assembly stick to keep the baffles in line and in sequence, before stuffing the whole thing back in the tube.

The red anodizing helps to get them clean, as much by not being black as by being a very smooth and hard anodizing.

At a smidge over three ounces, it is hard to fault the Ryder, and it will keep your handgun or rifle very quiet. The included tool serves several purposes. First, you can loosen or tighten the front cap with it. You can use it to push the baffles out, when the Ryder is perhaps a bit too cruddy. And you use it to align and stack the baffles, before stuffing them back into the tube.

A very nice rimfire suppressor, and one that will last for years.

OAL	5.4"
Net OAL	4.9"
Diameter	1.0"
Materials	Aluminum, stainless steel
Weight	3.1 oz
Finish	Mil-spec hard coat anodized
Calibers available	.22LR
Caliber rated	.22LR
Full auto rated	No
Mount system available	direct thread, ½ x 28
Construction	Serviceable
Baffle design	Oriented, sequential
MSRP	$429

Tactical Solutions Axiom

The TacSol Axiom, the neatest rimfire suppressor anyone at your gun club will own.

Tactical solutions pulled out all the stops when they came up with the Axiom. First of all, the tube and the baffles are made of titanium, so no worries about heat, not that a .22LR is likely to get that hot. But the real jump forward is in the assembly. The baffles ride inside a stainless steel tube, a split tube, one that slides into the titanium outer tube.

What this means is simple; if you forget and don't clean your suppressor as often as you should, you can still get the Axiom apart. The carbon-welding of the baffles to the tube now means the baffles are welded to the inner tube. And there is little-to-no carbon between he stainless split tube and the titanium outer tube. You can

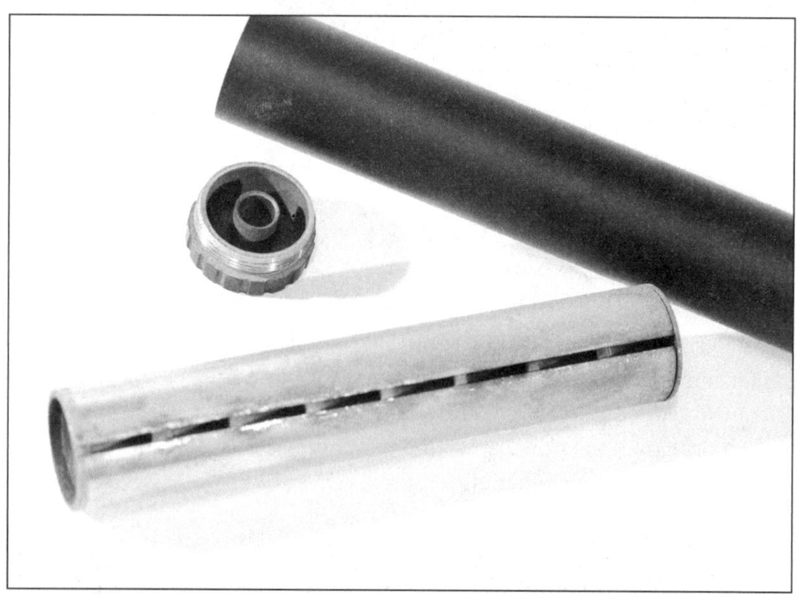

The titanium baffles ride inside of a stainless steel sleeve, to make it easy to assemble and disassemble.

easily slide the stainless and baffles assembly out of the titanium tube. And then, because the split tube flexes, it won't grab the titanium baffles as you press them out.

And, because the load-bearing parts of the suppressor consist of titanium baffles inside to a stainless tube, it is rated for all the rimfires except the biggest. And as a bonus, it will even withstand use on a 5.7X28, should you have one of those.

One of the attributes that makes rimfire suppressors so quiet is an aspect of the firearms they are on: expansion ratio. As explained in Chapter Sixteen, the higher the expansion ratio, the lower the bore pressure at the muzzle. The rimfires have tiny cases and, in rifles, sixteen inch or longer barrels. This means the gas pressure and volume at the muzzle is easy to handle, and also explains why the manufacturers can use one-inch or barely-larger tubes, and make them out of aluminum.

OAL	5.9"
Net OAL	5.4"
Diameter	1.0"
Materials	Titanium baffles & tube
Weight	6 oz
Finish	Matte black
Calibers available	.22LR
Caliber rated	.22LR, .17HM2, .22WMR, .17HMR, 5.7X28
Full auto rated	Yes
Mount system available	direct thread, ½ x 28
Construction	Serviceable
Baffle design	Oriented, non-sequential
MSRP	$440

The TacSol wrench grabs onto the slots they cut into the rim of the front cap.

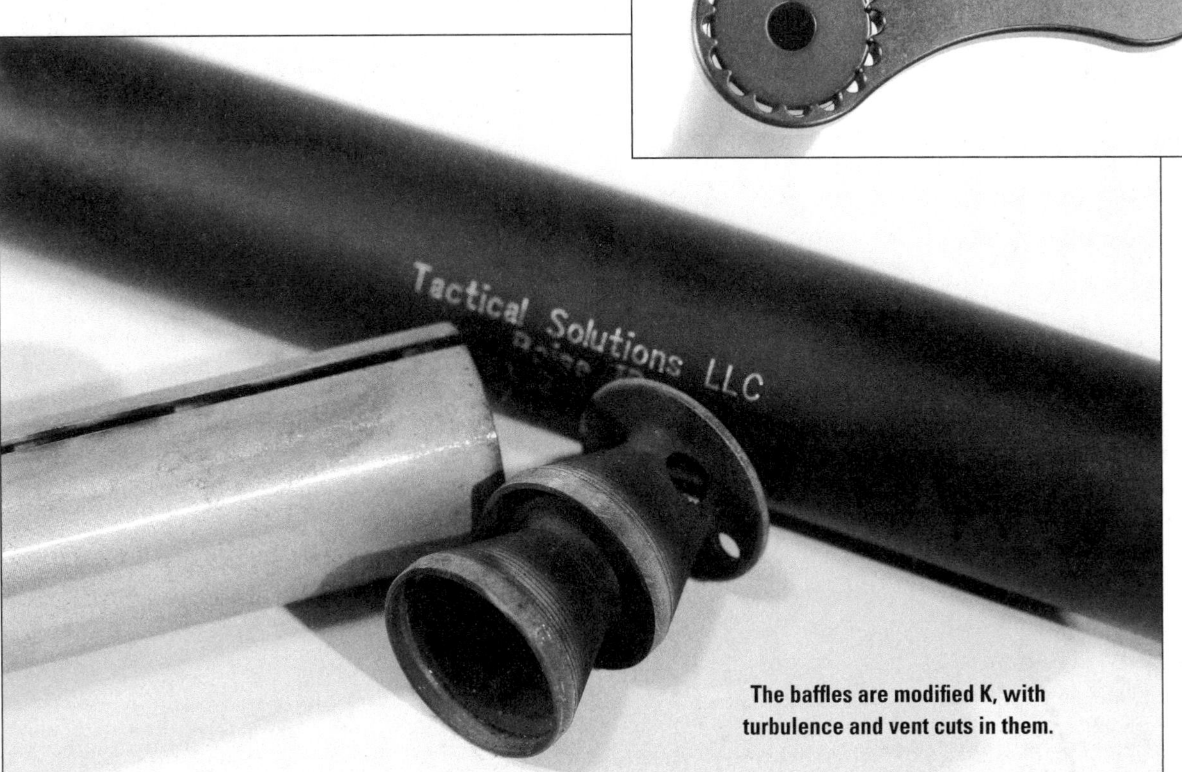

The baffles are modified K, with turbulence and vent cuts in them.

Chapter Nine

HANDGUN CALIBERS

Pistols are cool with suppressors, as you only have to swap barrels to make your pistol suppressor-ready.

Like those for rimfires, handgun-caliber suppressors are made to be taken apart, and they need to be taken apart and cleaned on a regular basis.

When I took Dr. Dater's course on suppressor design and history, he had sample suppressors to show us. Some of them were sectioned, and the pistol-caliber suppressors he had were impressively choked with carbon residue. So much so that they were markedly heavier in the hand than a similar, clean, suppressor. It had taken tens of thousands of rounds to pack them like that, but it hadn't taken that many to seize them and make them incapable of disassembly. That had happened before the first thousand rounds were through them.

With a little care and maintenance, they would not have been so packed. The packing cut their efficiency, but not by much, they were only a few decibels louder than their original, un-packed siblings, but we don't pay good money for "close enough" performance. So why allow neglect to create it?

There are .22LR handguns, but those cans are covered in the rimfire section. Here, we're concerned with suppressors for 9mm, .40 and .45 ACP. You'll notice the list of calibers is short. Well, putting a suppressor on a revolver is something we've already covered. And this section, like the rimfire section, covers suppressors that can go on both handguns and rifles. You see, there are rifles chambered in pistol calibers. Your basic 9mm AR readily comes to mind. But we'll cover their uses in the next section, where we look at rifles.

One advantageous aspect of pistols is that it is possible to simply swap the existing barrel for one that is longer than normal, and threaded for a suppressor, in order to have a suppressor-ready handgun. This leaves the sights as a problem, but you can solve that problem.

Where the suppressors here differ is that a .22 rifle or handgun does not need a booster, an L.I.D.

The booster, the Nielsen device, is needed to cycle a locked-breech handgun. The carbines, being blowback, do not need a booster. And, the Sig MPX, despite being a locked-breech, does not need a booster either. It operates from gas pressure, not momentum, and the suppressor has no effect on barrel movement for the simple reason that the barrel doesn't move. Finally, blowback pistols don't need boosters.

You can use a suppressor "down" in caliber, but not up. That is, you can use your .45 suppressor on a .40 or a 9mm, if you can find a thread adapter, but not up from 9mm suppressor to a .45 pistol.

Also note that many pistol-rated suppressors are also rated by the manufacturers for the .300 Blackout cartridge, as long as you use *only* subsonic ammunition. Supersonic ammo has too high an uncorking pressure, and will eventually or quickly damage a 9mm can.

So, owners of pistol-caliber suppressors often have a set of rear caps and boosters, so they can use their suppressor on anything they own in the appropriate calibers.

Gemtech Multi-Mount

The Gemtech Multi-Mount is a modern classic wet or dry pistol-caliber suppressor, using K baffles. The baffles have indexing tabs and relief cuts, not because they have to be assembled in a particular order, but to have correct alignment of the turbulence features. The first and last baffles, obviously, have to be first and last, but in-between the order doesn't matter, as long as the tabs line up.

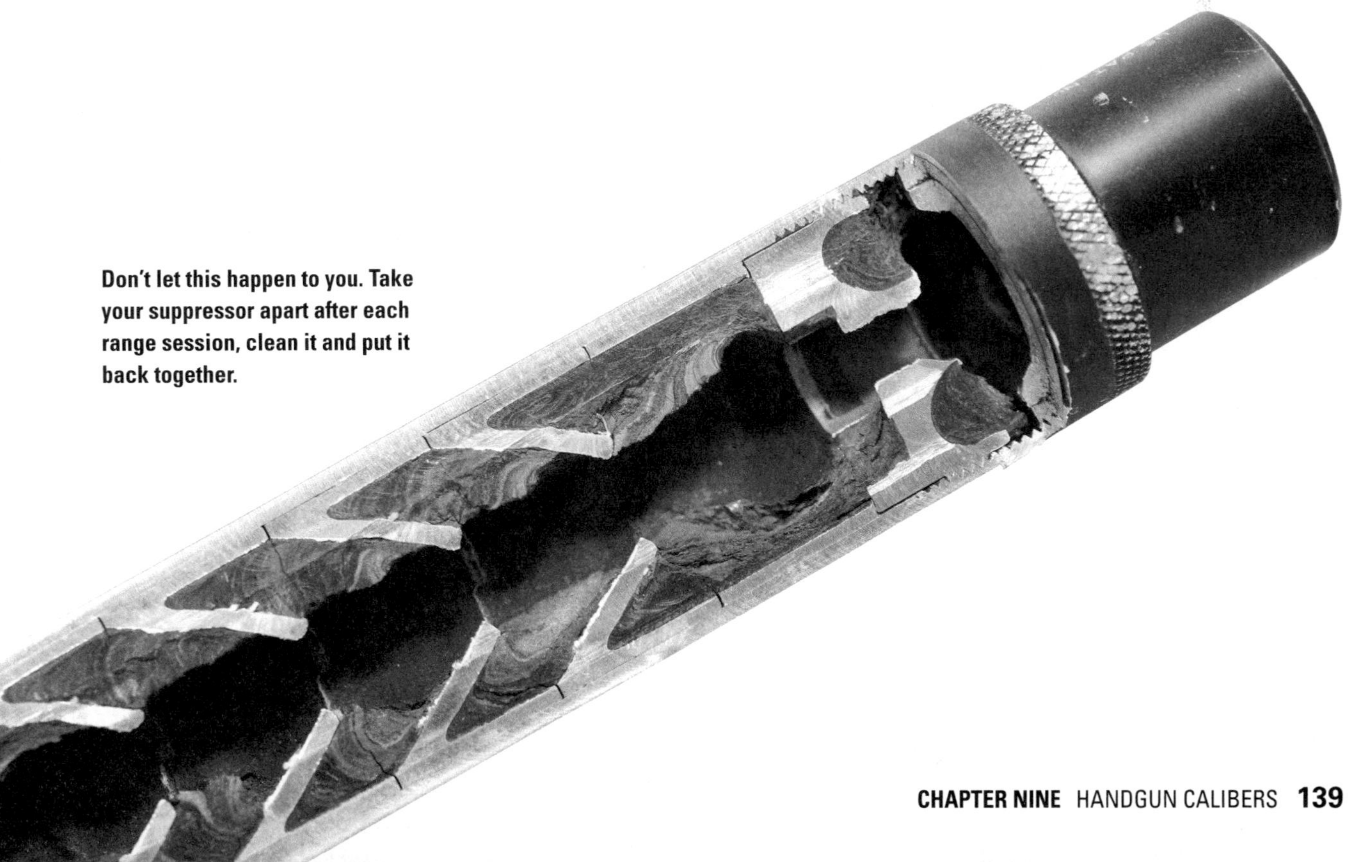

Don't let this happen to you. Take your suppressor apart after each range session, clean it and put it back together.

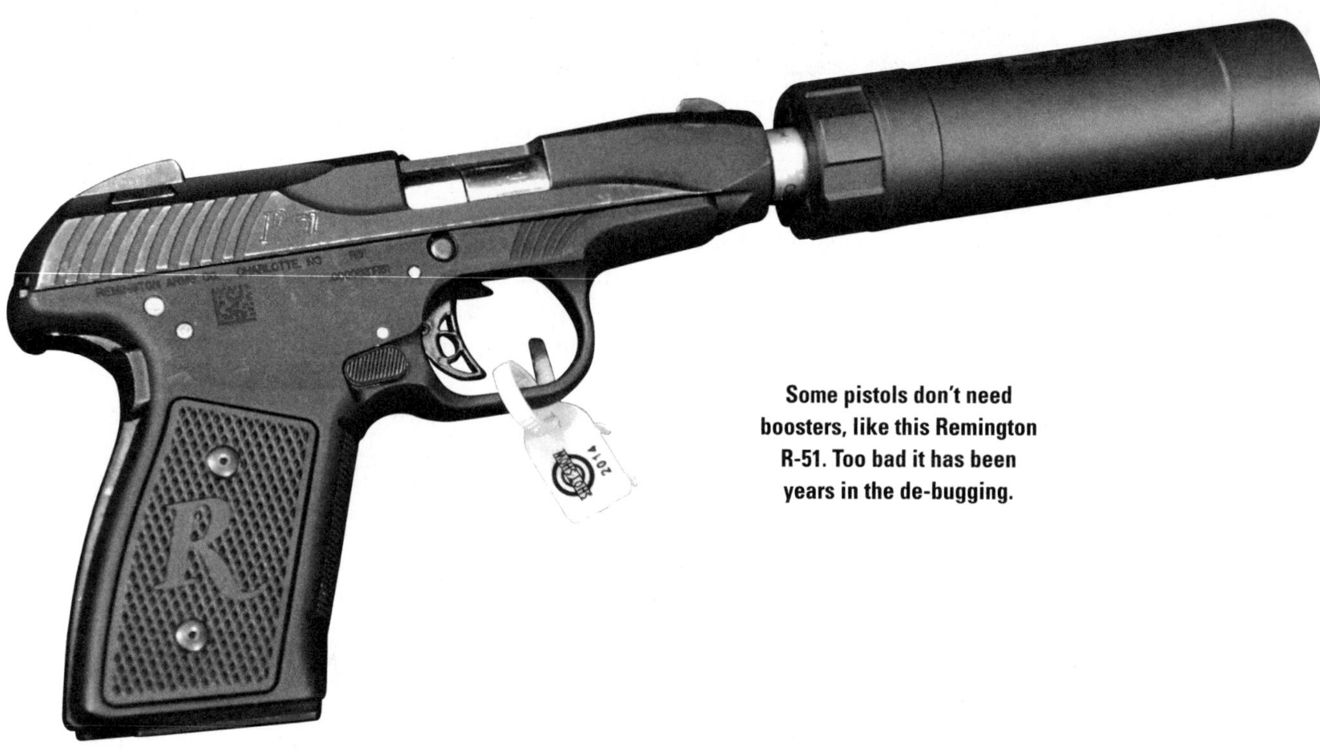

Some pistols don't need boosters, like this Remington R-51. Too bad it has been years in the de-bugging.

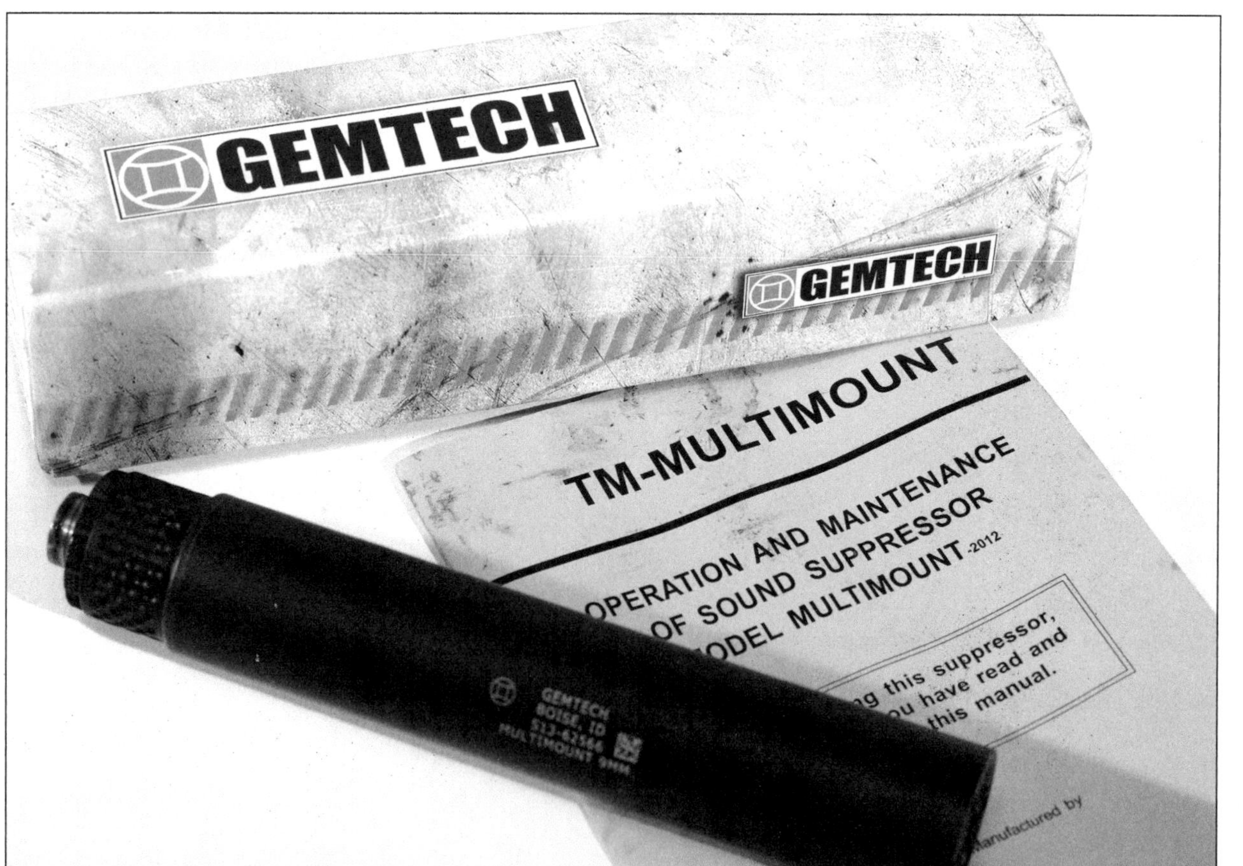

The Gemtech Multi-mount is a suppressor for all seasons. Well, almost, but it will fit on a whole rack of firearms.

The rear cap assembly for the Multi-mount, in this instance the L.I.D. for a 9mm.

The turbulence cuts and the relief cuts are meant to be arranged in a particular orientation to each other, to maximize effectiveness, but that is the only reason for the tabs.

The tube is 7075 aluminum, with the tube threaded for the front cap, and the mount on the rear. Since it is meant for use on pistols, it has to have the capacity to accept a Nielsen device, a booster, which Gemtech makes. And since there is not just one thread pitch, the booster cap itself can be had in several different thread pitches.

But there is more. This is why it is the Multi-Mount. You can also replace the booster with a "dead" rear cap, threaded for the muzzle of a carbine. Or the three lugs of an HK, or to fit on an Uzi.

One suppressor, with the ability to fit it onto a whole rack of firearms, using the correct rear cap or booster.

What it doesn't do is work on anything but a 9mm or the .300 Blackout, subsonic only. *Only*! If you use supersonic Blackout ammo, and bust your Multi-Mount, don't go crying to Gemtech. They told you not to, the rest of us told you not to.

Since you can disassemble it, you can scrub the internals and keep it clean and quiet for a long time.

OAL	7"
Net OAL	6.5"
Diameter	1.375"
Material	Aluminum, 7075
Weight	6.5 oz
Finish	Matte black CeraKote™
Calibers available	9mm
Caliber rated	9mm, .300 Blackout subsonic ONLY
Full-auto rated	Yes
Mount system available	direct-thread, Nielsen device, 3-lug, Uzi
Construction	Serviceable
Baffle design	Oriented, non-sequential
MSRP	$600

Gemtech GM9

If the Multi-Mount is so good, why the GM-9? Simple: monocore. Gemtech used their experience of the Multi-Mount and their Tundra, and the GM-9 is rated for full-auto 9mm, and subsonic .300 Blackout. The GM-9 accepts all the mounts that are made for the Multi-Mount, so if you have a drawer full of those, you are good to go with a new GM-9.

If you can't decide between the old Multi-Mount and the new GM-9, here's the answer: the GM-9 will be quieter, more durable, lighter, easier to clean, and easier to re-assemble after cleaning.

OAL	6.5"
Net OAL	6.5"
Diameter	1.25"
Material	Aluminum, 7075
Weight	5 oz
Finish	Matte black CeraKote™
Calibers available	9mm
Caliber rated	9mm, .300 Blackout subsonic ONLY
Full-auto rated	Yes
Mount system available	direct-thread, Nielsen device, 3-lug, Uzi
Construction	Serviceable
Baffle design	Monocore
MSRP	$595

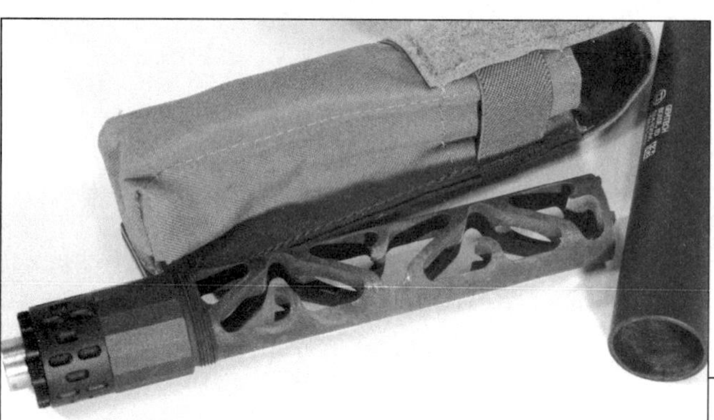

Here you see the monocore of the GM-9, which is a lot easier to clean, and a whole lot easier to assemble.

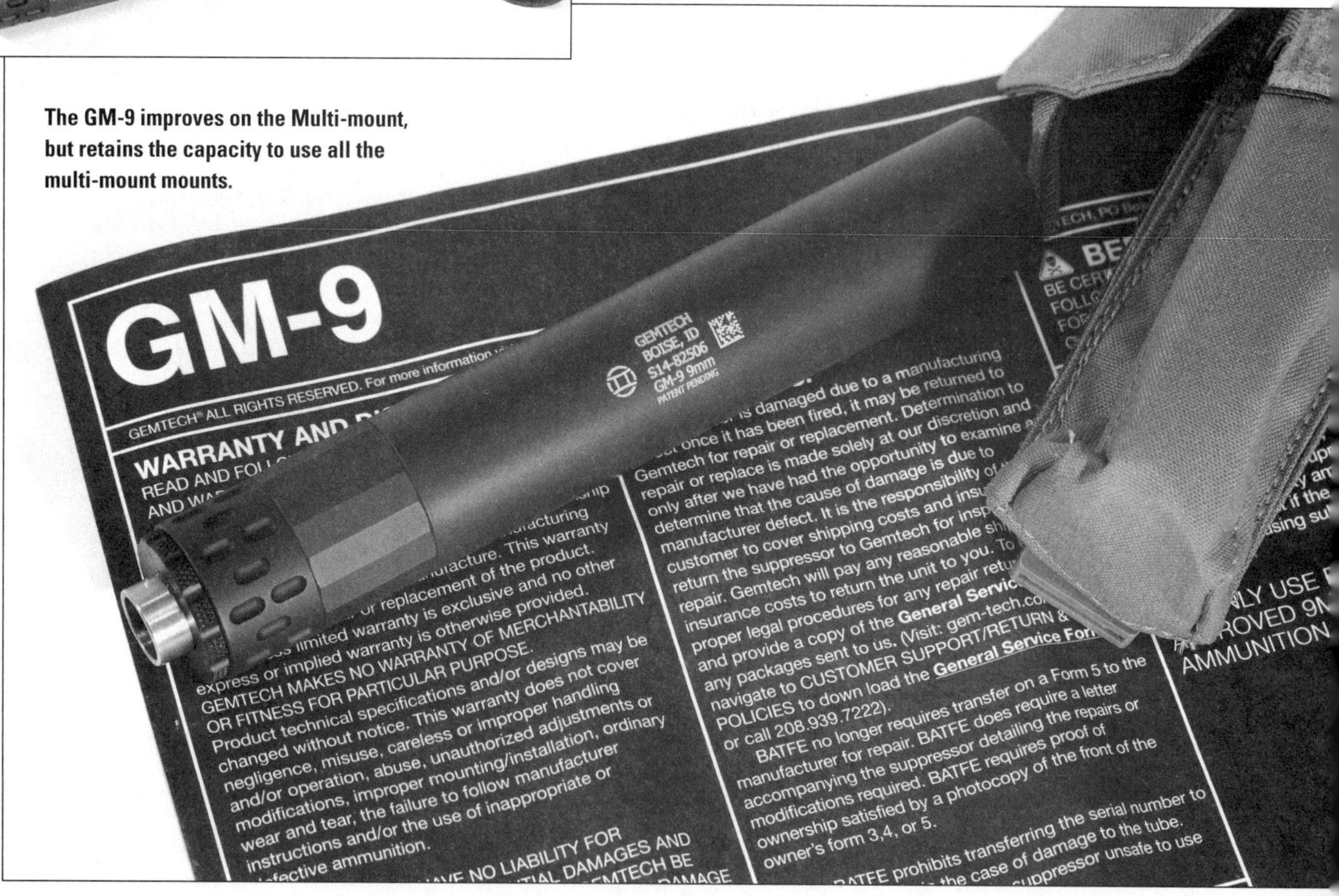

The GM-9 improves on the Multi-mount, but retains the capacity to use all the multi-mount mounts.

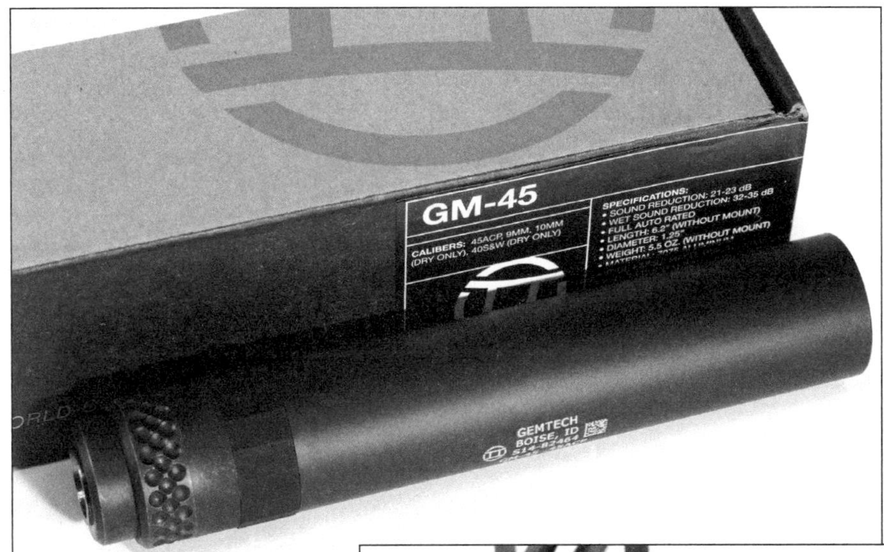

The GM-45 is the big brother, and can handle all normal pistol cartridges, plus .300 Blk.

The GM-45 monocore looks a lot like the GM-9, but bigger, and that is good.

Gemtech GM-45

Whats to say? The GM-45 is a monocore, user-serviceable suppressor, with the same multi-mount system as the 9mms. As if that wasn't enough, since it is the big boy of the handgun cans, it can be used on lesser calibers. So, if you have a .45, 9mm, 10mm or 40, you have a suppressor that will work on them all. While the GM-45 can be used wet, it is a dry-only can for 10mm and 40.

OAL	6.2"
Net OAL	6.2"
Diameter	1.375"
Material	Aluminum, 7075
Weight	5.5 oz
Finish	CeraKote, black standard, OD Green & FDE optional
Calibers available	.45
Caliber rated	.45, 9mm, 10mm, .40SW
Full-auto rated	Yes
Mount system available	Nielsen device, selection of threads
Construction	Serviceable
Baffle design	Monocore
MSRP	$595, mount included

Thompson Machine Poseidon, 9mm

The Poseidon is a rarity in the modern suppressor world: it uses wipes. Well, it uses a wipe, as there is but the one, the last item the bullet encounters before it leaves the muzzle. The big deal here is weight. The Poseidon is so small, compact and light, that it does not need a booster. Inside the wipe there is a monocore baffle stack, so you have the best of both old and new – the quiet and durability of a monocore, with the compactness and wet-ability of a wiped suppressor. Yes, it can be used wet, that's the whole point of the wipe.

OAL	4.125""
Net OAL	3.875""
Diameter	1.25"
Material	Aluminum, 6061 T6
Weight	3.8 oz
Finish	Black, hard-coat anodized
Calibers available	9mm, 40, 45
Caliber rated	9mm
Full-auto rated	Yes
Mount system available	Direct-thread, 1/2 x 28, 1/2 x 36, 13.5x1LH (metric)
Construction	Serviceable
Baffle design	Monocore & wipe
MSRP	$379

Here is the Poseidon disassembled, with the wrench, monocore, tube, cap with wipe, and a punch to make new wipes once the old one is used up and destroyed.

Poseidon, god of the sea. And a really great suppressor, with a monocore and a wipe.

The Thompson Machine wrench, for loosening grubby caps.

The Thompson Machine ISIS-2: monocore, no threads on the tube, efficient and multi-caliber adaptable.

OAL	8″
Net OAL	7.5″
Diameter	1.375″
Material	Aluminum, 6061 T6
Weight	7 oz
Finish	Black, hard-coat anodized
Calibers available	9mm, 40, 45, .300 Blk subsonic
Caliber rated	9mm
Full-auto rated	Yes
Mount system available	Direct-thread, 1/2 x 28, 1/2 x 36, 13.5x1LH (metric)
Construction	Serviceable
Baffle design	Monocore
MSRP	$399 (9mm & 40) $569 (.45 ACP)

Thompson Machine ISIS 2, 9mm

The ISIS 2 is Thompson Machine's standard handgun adaptable suppressor. You can use it on handguns (if you get the .45, you can use it on smaller calibers, such as 9mm and 40), you can use it on rimfires, and you can use it on .300 Blackout, subsonic ammo only.

Thompson makes rear caps for all those applications, including the various lugged versions. As an additional bonus, the baffle stack is not only monocore, but the tube, the actual suppressor with the serial number, is not threaded. So, if you do lock it up from lack of cleaning, any threads you knarf won't be on the serial-numbered part.

Still, clean it.

The insides of the ISIS-2: simple, monocore, easy to clean, durable.

Innovative Arms Shepherd

There's improving, and there's making life easy. The Innovative Arms Shepherd is a versatile, durable, suppressor meant to fulfill many desires. First, we have a booster-equipped pistol-caliber suppressor, made of aluminum with stainless steel mount. In .45, the version here at Gun Abuse Central, it can also handle 9mm and 40, as well as .300 Blk subsonic.

The Shepherd can be used on pistols from rimfire to .45 ACP, and on pistol-caliber carbines as well.

Innovative doesn't list rimfires for the Shepherd, but I would have no reservations about using any of them in this suppressor. Well, a

OAL	7.75"
Net OAL	7"
Diameter	1.5"
Material	Aluminum, 7075 T6
Weight	10.5 oz
Finish	Black, hard-coat anodized
Calibers available	9mm, 40, 45, .300 Blk subsonic
Caliber rated	,45 ACP
Full-auto rated	Yes
Mount system available	Direct-thread, L.I.D., .578x28, M16x1LH, 5/8-24, 1/2 x 26
Construction	Serviceable
Baffle design	Indexed, no-sequential K baffles
MSRP	$625

Innovative Arms makes the Shepherd. Here in .45, big, durable, quiet and reliable.

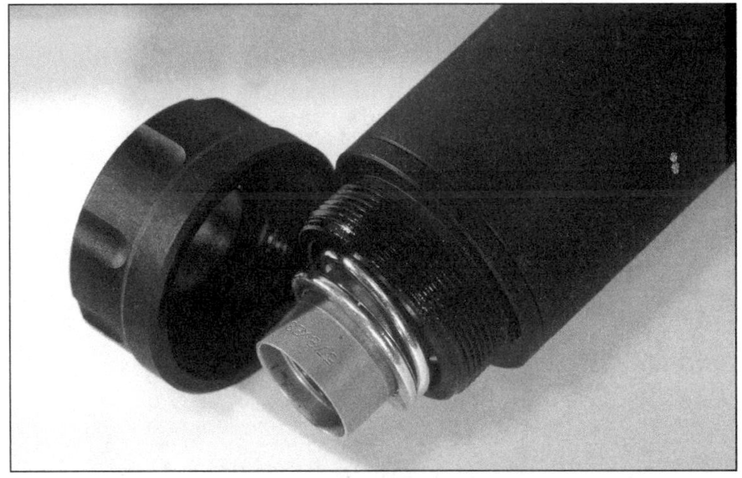

Here you see part of the insides of the Shepherd's Nielsen device.

.221-inch bullet, trundling through a bore reamed for a .452-inch bullet, leaves a lot of room for gas blow-by, but how much can a .22LR have?

The baffles are modified K, anodized, and big enough to handle while you clean them. The Shepherd comes apart into the rear cap assembly, the front cap, tube and six baffles. Full-auto rated (which means it is tough) and finished in your basic black.

Handgun-caliber suppressors are always fun, and they are made in large numbers, relatively speaking. They are not made in the numbers that rimfire suppressors are, and they do not have the panache of the 5.56 suppressors, but if you were to get just one, and wanted to use it on as many firearms as possible, then a .45 ACP, with lightweight design, and a drawer full of rear caps will fit it onto anything from a .22LR, up past .300 Blackout, to .45 ACP.

There's a lot to be said for that level of versatility.

Shooting suppressed handguns is fun, make no mistake about it.

Chapter Ten

RIFLE SUPPRESSORS

The Ruger 10/22 is the best rimfire to suppress, because you can simply bolt in a new, threaded barrel.

Pistol calibers are really quiet in smgs and carbines. When it is a historical item, like this British 34, it is almost embarrassingly fun.

When most people think of buying a suppressor, this is what they are thinking about. The smallest, and those that have the least demanded of them, are the rimfire cans put on rifles and handgun suppressors on carbines.

The rimfire rifles are easy; you simply unscrew your rimfire suppressor off of your .22 handgun, and screw it onto the threaded muzzle of your rifle. What, the muzzle isn't threaded? Well, if you have a .22 rifle where the barrel is easily changed, like a Ruger 10/22, then you can simply buy a new barrel and swap the threaded one in place of the un-threaded.

If not, you have two other choices: you can have the existing barrel threaded, or you can buy a new rifle. Considering that a new Ruger 10/22 Takedown, factory-threaded for a suppressor, lists for $429, and can be found at retail for a lot less, buying new seems attractive. Of course, if you know, or can find, a gunsmith or even machinist (the barrel isn't a firearm, anyone can do it, if they know how) who can thread properly, then a plain, blue-and-wood 10/22 lists for a mere $289.

The trick is getting it properly threaded, something we've already covered.

The pistol-caliber carbine is a lot easier in this regard. If someone is making a carbine in 9mm, 40 or .45, then they are quite likely to have threaded the muzzle, if only for a flash hider. If there are threads there, you can get a suppressor on it.

But the main course here is .223/5.56, and pretty much in the guise of an accessory to an AR-15 or clone. It is the biggest inexpensive centerfire rifle to shoot, in both ammo and rifle cost, and generally speaking, a .223 suppressor costs less than the same brand and model

.308 rifles make greater demands on suppressors than 5.56 ones do, and that means bigger, stronger cans.

in .30 or bigger. Most guys who own a suppressor, once they have a rimfire, jump up to something sturdy enough to be put onto their .223. It will be a rare centerfire rifle suppressor that is capable of disassembly, but they are not unknown, and if you opt for that feature by all means take advantage of it.

The next step up is to cover a .308. This is a special case for rifle suppressors. Unless you are putting a suppressor onto an AR, Stoner-type, rifle, it is not likely to be a self-loader. Oh, there will be the guy at the gun club who has a SCAR, the AK guy, and maybe a few others, but most of the .30 suppressors you'll see are meant for the .308. This matters because of the gas pressure and volume medium-bore rifles generate. It takes a lot more design and engineering to make a suppressor stand up to a .300 Winchester Magnum than .308, and the .308 takes a lot more than the .223/5.56. And even then, the maker may only warranty it on a 24-inch barrel, not the special, compact, 16-inch-barrel rifle you had built. (And while we're here, why trim it? Chop a .300 WM down to 16 inches and you might as well have a .308 as far as performance is concerned, but your gas pressure is way up.)

The bulk of the .308 suppressors you see will likely be on bolt guns, sniper rifles. There, the heat-resistance and ability to stand up to full-auto fire are not needed.

Black Rain ordnance and their Aris, the .223/5.56 suppressor.

The Aris, disassembled.

.223/5.56 suppressors

BLACK RAIN ORDNANCE .223/5.56

The Black Rain Aris is designed for ruggedness, and as a result is a few ounces heavier than others. If you want to spend all day hosing down a prairie dog town or a day in a training class and not worry about your suppressor, here you go.

It is user-serviceable, the baffles are big, sturdy and made of stainless steel, and it is done in a glossy matte finish that is subdued but not ultra-tactical.

OAL	6.1"
Net OAL	5.5"
Diameter	1.5"
Materials	stainless steel
Weight	21 oz
Calibers available	.223/5.56 plus smaller calibers
Caliber rated	As above
Mount system available	direct thread, 1⁄2 x 28
Construction	user serviceable
Baffle design	epsilon baffle design
Finish	black nitride
MSRP	$799

ELITE IRON

Located in Montana, Elite Iron makes a full line of suppressors, from .22LR all the way up to .50 BMG. The smallest ones are thread-on rimfire suppressors, but unlike other manufacturers, Elite Iron isn't impressed by the long-term durability of aluminum in rimfire suppressors. The lowly .22LR gets a lot of use in a suppressor (unlike more-expensive-to-feed centerfire guns), so don't be put off by the slightly higher weights listed in their catalog. One advantage you get with a stainless .22LR suppressor is the ease with which it handles the rimfire magnums and 5.7X28.

Their centerfire rifle suppressors are made of differing stainless alloys, with 304 used in the tube, and 17-4 PH, a precipitation-hardening stainless. 17-4 has very good strength and corrosion resistance, and with its short heat-treatment cycle, minimizes warpage.

Not that a small amount of warpage in a suppressor is a problem, since Elite Iron finish-reams all suppressors after they have finished their 100% weld assembly.

OAL	6"
Net OAL	5.5"
Diameter	1.5"
Materials	304 & 17-4 stainless steel
Weight	21.8 oz
Finish	Matte black CeraKote™
Calibers available	.223/5.56
Calibers rated	5.56 & Smaller
Full auto rated	Yes
Mount system available	Elite Iron mount
Construction	Sealed
Baffle design	billet, modified K baffle
MSRP	$760 (includes mount)

The sample I had to spend time with was a CQC-1, and it worked very well.

Elite Iron has instructions on how to correctly time a suppressor installation so as to minimize zero-shift changes, with and without a suppressor. You would do well to read them, but a quick summary: treat your suppressor like a wood baseball bat – keep the logo up, at top dead center.

GEMTECH HALO

The Gemtech Halo is unique in that it will mount onto an A1 or A2 flash hider. This is its strength, and also its weakness. If your flash hider is not axial and aligned, you will be sorry in short order. So, check alignment before you go out for a day of plinking, practiced, training or varminting.

Tough? The titanium version has been tested to SoCom standards and passed. The steel one is heavier, but as tough as an anvil. And the ability to mount it on any AR you own, without a special muzzle device? Priceless.

OAL	7.25"
Net OAL	6"
Diameter	1.5"
Materials	Inconel, stainless steel
Weight	21.8 oz
Finish	Matte black CeraKote™
Calibers available	.223/5.56
Calibers rated	5.56 & SMALLER
Full auto rated	Yes
Mount system available	A1/A2 flash hider
Construction	Sealed
Baffle design	n/a
MSRP	$750

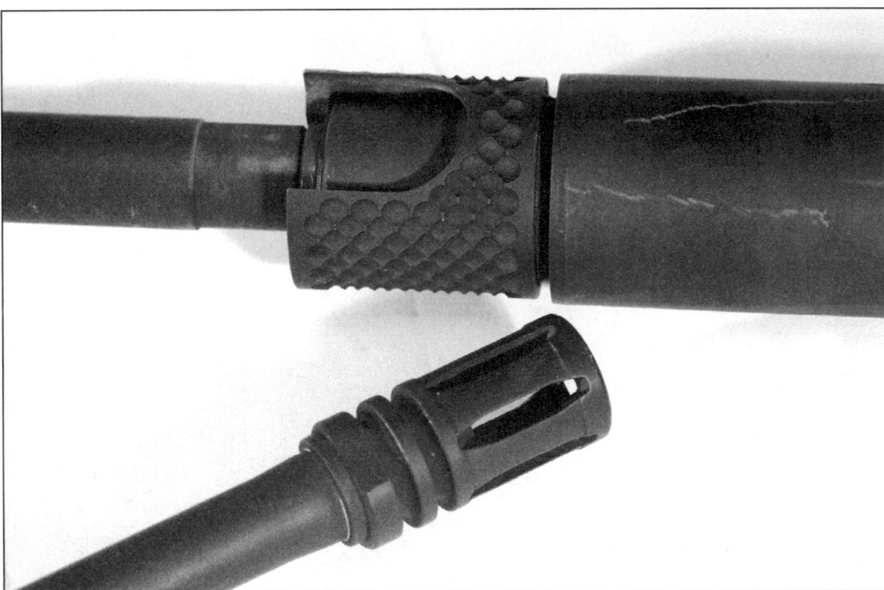

From the first A1 flash hider to today, the Halo will fit them all. Just be sure and check alignment.

The Gemtech Halo, the only suppressor to use a standard A1/A2 flash hider as the mount.

SIG LE 5.56

This is the initial Sig suppressor design, intended for law enforcement, and in direct-thread only. It is made of stainless steel, it is tough (I heated one to well over a thousand degrees in one test) and it holds zero. This particular design has been upgraded, but since it is what I have, it is what I tested, and it is what you get to drool over.

OAL	6.25"
Net OAL	5.75"
Diameter	1.5 & 2.0"
Material	17-4 & 316 stainless
Finish	none
Calibers available	5.56 plus anything smaller
Caliber rated	As above
Full-auto rated	Yes
Mount system available	direct-thread, 1/2x28 for 5.56
Construction	Sealed
Baffle design	n/a
MSRP	$ n/a

The Sig LE 556 suppressor, on a Sig M400, and fun.

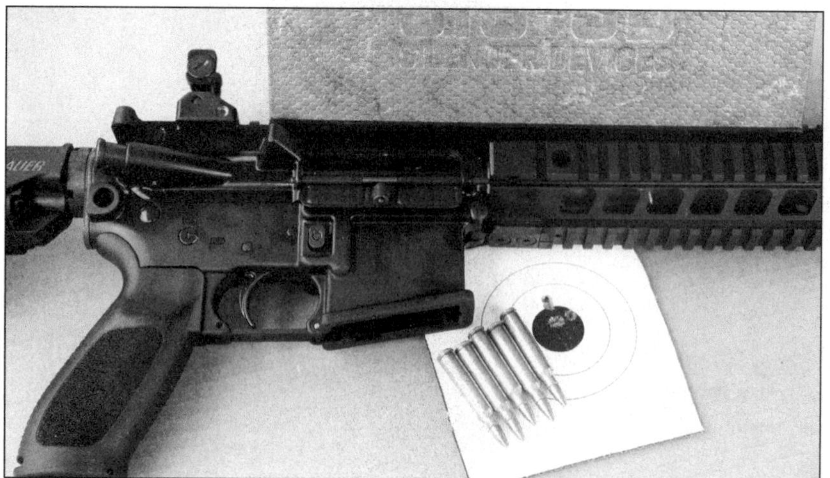

No problems here with accuracy.

SUREFIRE SOCOM M556-RC

This is the gold standard of compact, quiet, repeatable-zero suppressors. It uses a unique locking system, it is compact and shaves a few ounces off of many other 5.56 designs, and it is good for a long time. In talking with veterans of SOF-D, when the Surefire was tested, the only problem they had was when they carbon-welded the suppressors onto the mounts.

Having gone a bit far with shooting before cleaning myself, and having to wrestle a Surefire off the mount, I can understand. Despite that abuse, it still holds zero. The mount is also a very good flash hider, unless you opt for the muzzle brake, and then it is a very good muzzle brake for its size.

OAL	6.2″
Net length added to firearm	4″
Diameter	1.5″
Weight	17 oz
Finish	Cerakote™
Calibers available	.223/5.56 (other models for other calibers)
Calibers rated	5.56 and smaller
Full auto rated	Yes
Mount system available	Surefire quick-mount
Construction	Sealed
Baffle design	n/a
MSRP	$1,375

Surefire makes most excellent suppressors. The 5.56 SoCom is great.

The Surefire suppressors use an eccentric end collar that rotates around the rear of the mount. Secure hardly begins to describe it.

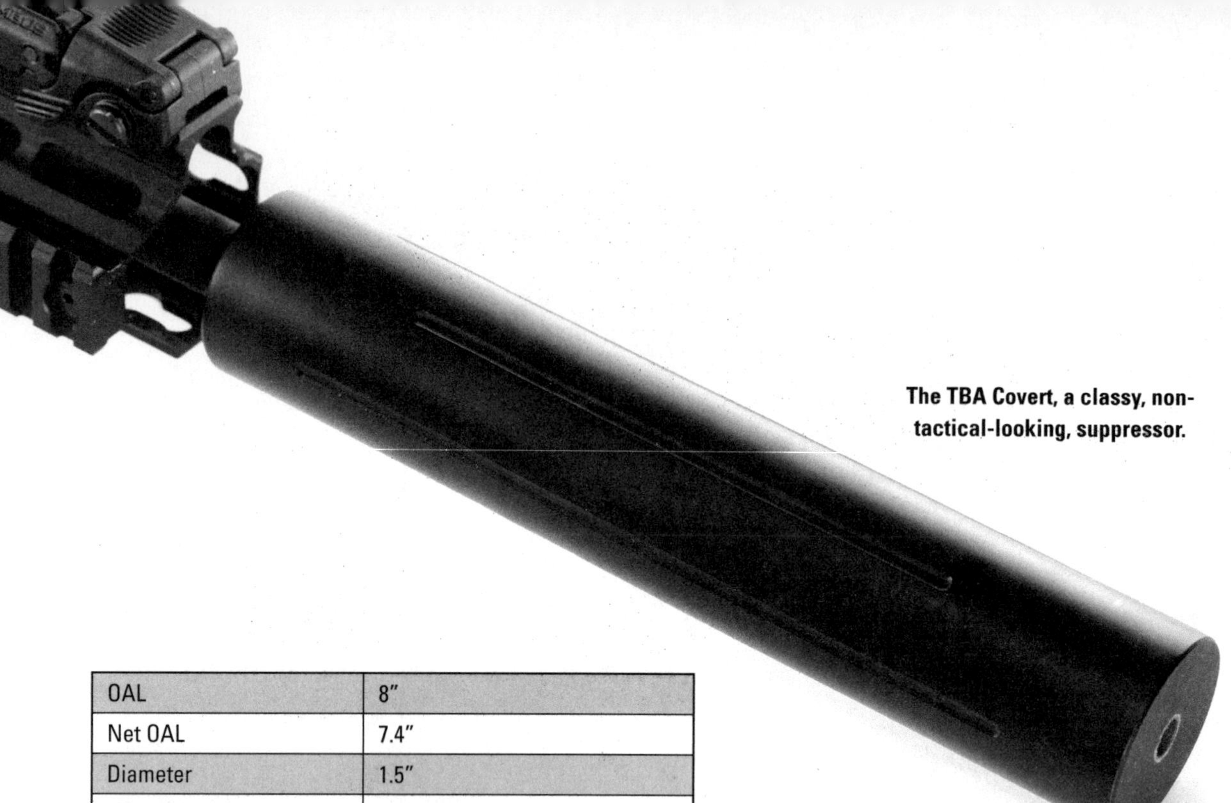

The TBA Covert, a classy, non-tactical-looking, suppressor.

OAL	8"
Net OAL	7.4"
Diameter	1.5"
Materials	316, 300 series, inconel
Weight	24 oz
Finish	Norrel moly resin, flat black, polished stainless, matte stainless
Calibers available	.223/5.56
Calibers rated	As above and all smaller
Full-auto rated	Yes
Mount system	direct thread, $\frac{1}{2}$x28 & QD
Construction	Sealed
Baffle design	n/a
MSRP	$725

TBA SUPPRESSORS COVERT .223

A fully-welded Inconel and 300 series stainless core, sealed inside a 316 stainless tube, and made in a direct-thread design, the Covert is not made to look "tacti-cool" and that can be a good thing. You don't need to camouflage yourself from the prairie dogs you are blasting, and a big, durable can is a good thing on a pleasant day expending ammo.

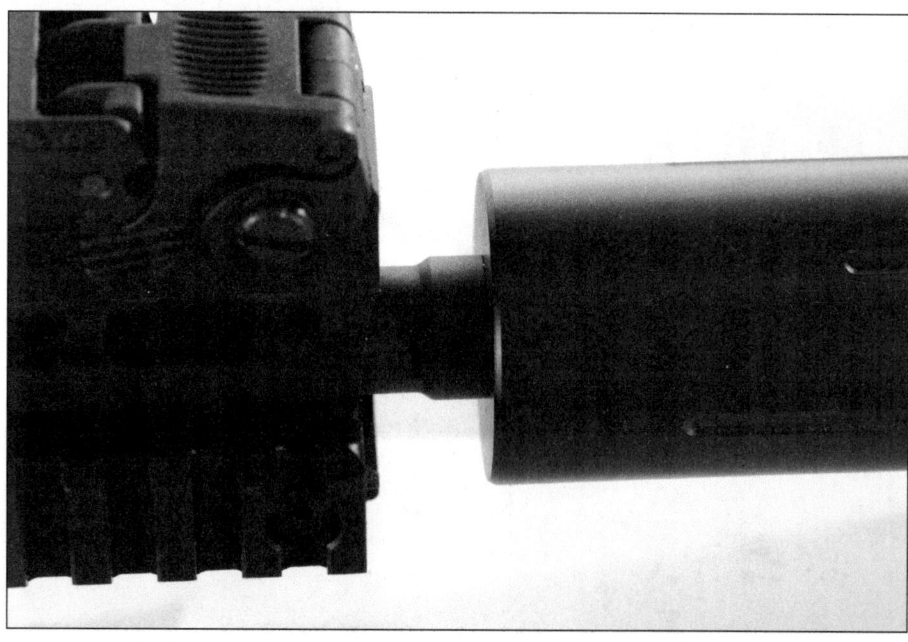

No complicated QA mounts for TBA, they use direct-thread to mount the Covert.

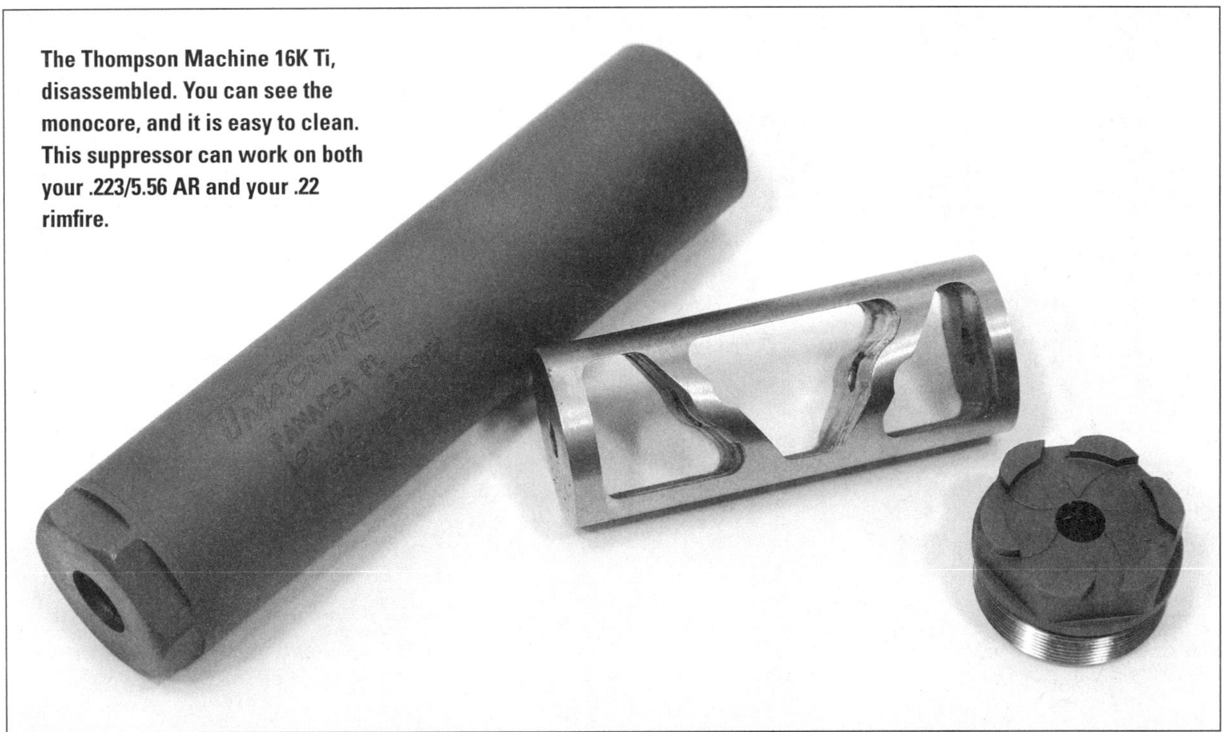
The Thompson Machine 16K Ti, disassembled. You can see the monocore, and it is easy to clean. This suppressor can work on both your .223/5.56 AR and your .22 rimfire.

THOMPSON MACHINE 16K TI

Thompson Machine started this line with their Sixteen, a take-apart monocore rifle suppressor. Both were good things; monocore was stronger and quieter, and self-serviceable meant you could take it apart and clean it. While it was a cracking good suppressor, it did have the small problem of being a bit on the large and heavy side for a 5.56 suppressor. Not that the users minded, even at seven inches and 27 ounces, it wasn't heavy, and it is quiet.

So, Thompson Machine came up with the 16 K. Made of the same high-strength alloy steels, it chopped an inch and a half off the length of the Sixteen, and seven ounces of weight. What was left? Titanium.

The 16 K Ti is an all-titanium suppressor, user-serviceable, with a monocore baffle stack, and to keep it as compact and as light as possible, it is a direct-thread design. To keep the price down, and to make it as user-adaptable as possible, they left it in the bare titanium. So if you want it black, paint it black. If you want it camo, paint it camo.

And, since it is a suppressor you can take apart, you can use it on any smaller caliber than .223/5.56, such as all the rimfires, and all the centerfires smaller than .223. Just make sure, if you feed it .22LR, that you take it apart and clean it on a regular basis, otherwise you'll end up with a non-take-apart suppressor. That would be bad.

OAL	6.75"
Net OAL	6"
Diameter	1.5"
Materials	Titanium
Weight	17.6 oz
Finish	bare Ti
Calibers rated	5.56 and smaller
Full auto rated	Yes
Mount system available	direct thread, 1/2x28
Construction	user-serviceable
Baffle design	monocore
MSRP	$1095

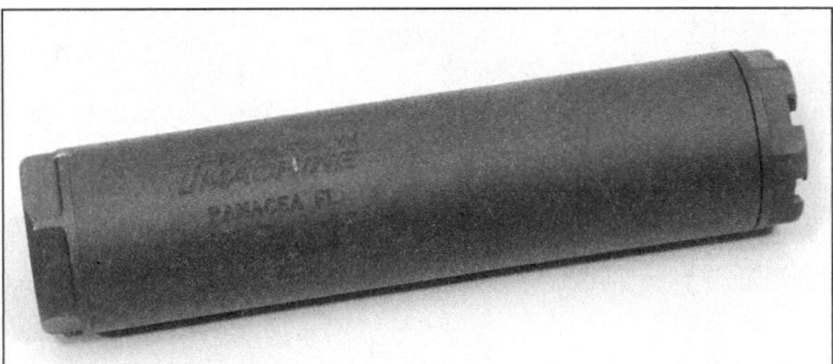
The Thompson Machine 16K Ti, a first-rate thread-on suppressor for everything .223 and below.

The Yankee Hill Phantom, being abused, heated, doused, run over, and still working.

YANKEE HILL PHANTOM PHANTOM 3100 QD

The YHM 3100 series are suppressors with Inconel baffles inside of chrome-moly tubes. This is the definition of tough, as I have seriously abused one for a year, up to and including driving over it with multiple vehicles, heating and dousing it, all to no avail. It just kept on working, right up to the point where I had to send it back because Yankee Hill wanted to see just what I had done to the poor thing.

OAL	6.875"
Net OAL	5.5"
Diameter	1.5"
Weight	20 oz
Materials	Chrome-moly steel & Inconel 718
Finish	matte black
Calibers available	5.56
Calibers rated	5.56 and smaller
Full auto rated	Yes
Attachment	YHM QD muzzle device, many thread pitches available
Construction	Sealed
Baffle design	n/a
MSRP	$626

The Yankee Hill 5.56 Phantom on a Mossberg. A bolt gun? Yes, when you are shooting a qualification course meant for ARs, it is real work keeping up.

The YHM quick-attach mount is also a very good flash hider, and when you do not have the suppressor installed you won't have to worry about protecting your muzzle crown.

The Innovative Arms Grunt, getting a thorough thrashing. It didn't care.

Innovative Arms makes the Grunt, and it is anvil-tough, but not anvil-heavy.

INNOVATIVE ARMS GRUNT

First, Innovative Arms does something I had not heard of before – they make a monocore baffle stack. They machine it out of billet stainless steel, then slide it into a stainless tube and weld the whole thing together for $600! This is one tough suppressor.

Tough? I've had the Grunt on half a dozen different ARs and M4s, semi and select-fire, as well as a selection of bolt-action rifles and even an AK-74. (That took some doing, to make sure it was aligned and fit. Damn left-handed, metric threads.)

It has never failed, never had a baffle strike, and never failed to provide exemplary service. And all that for six bills. What a deal.

OAL	6.25"
Net OAL	5.5"
Diameter	1.5"
Materials	Stainless steel
Weight	17.5 oz
Finish	InnoArmor, black OD Green, FDE
Calibers available	.223/5.56
Caliber rated	.223/5.56
Full auto rated	Yes, down to 10" barrels
Mount system available	direct thread
Construction	Sealed
Baffle design	n/a
MSRP	$599

INNOVATIVE INDUSTRIES

Innovative Industries is one of your AR-15 retro sources. They specialize in the AR before it was the ubiquitous black rifle, and the near-pariah "mattel toy." Among the products they make and carry is a truly retro suppressor, a faithful copy of the XM177 moderator.

As a faithful copy, it will not be as quiet as a modern suppressor. That isn't the point. The idea is to have as much as possible, an exact copy of the Vietnam-era LRRP carbine. It would be difficult to make a modern suppressor that is as short and thin as the XM177, and were you to try, you'd be putting a .22 rimfire-made suppressor on, and that would be bad.

OAL	4.25"
Net OAL	3.875"
Diameter	1.0"
Materials	4140 steel
Weight	8.6 oz
Finish	black oxide
Calibers available	.223/5.56
Caliber rated	.223/5.56
Full auto rated	Yes
Mount system available	direct-thread
Construction	Sealed
Baffle design	n/a
MSRP	$325

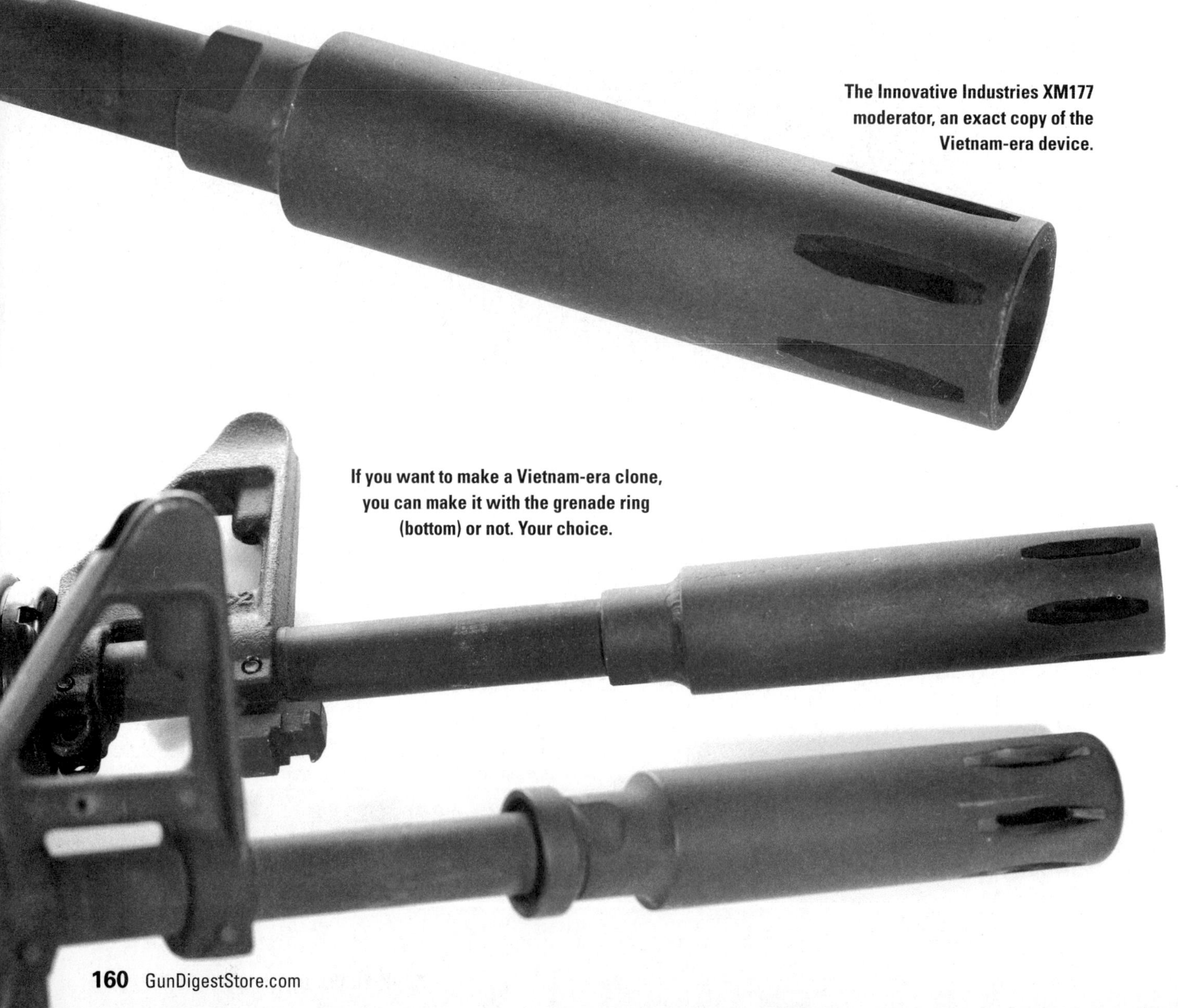

The Innovative Industries XM177 moderator, an exact copy of the Vietnam-era device.

If you want to make a Vietnam-era clone, you can make it with the grenade ring (bottom) or not. Your choice.

.30 suppressors

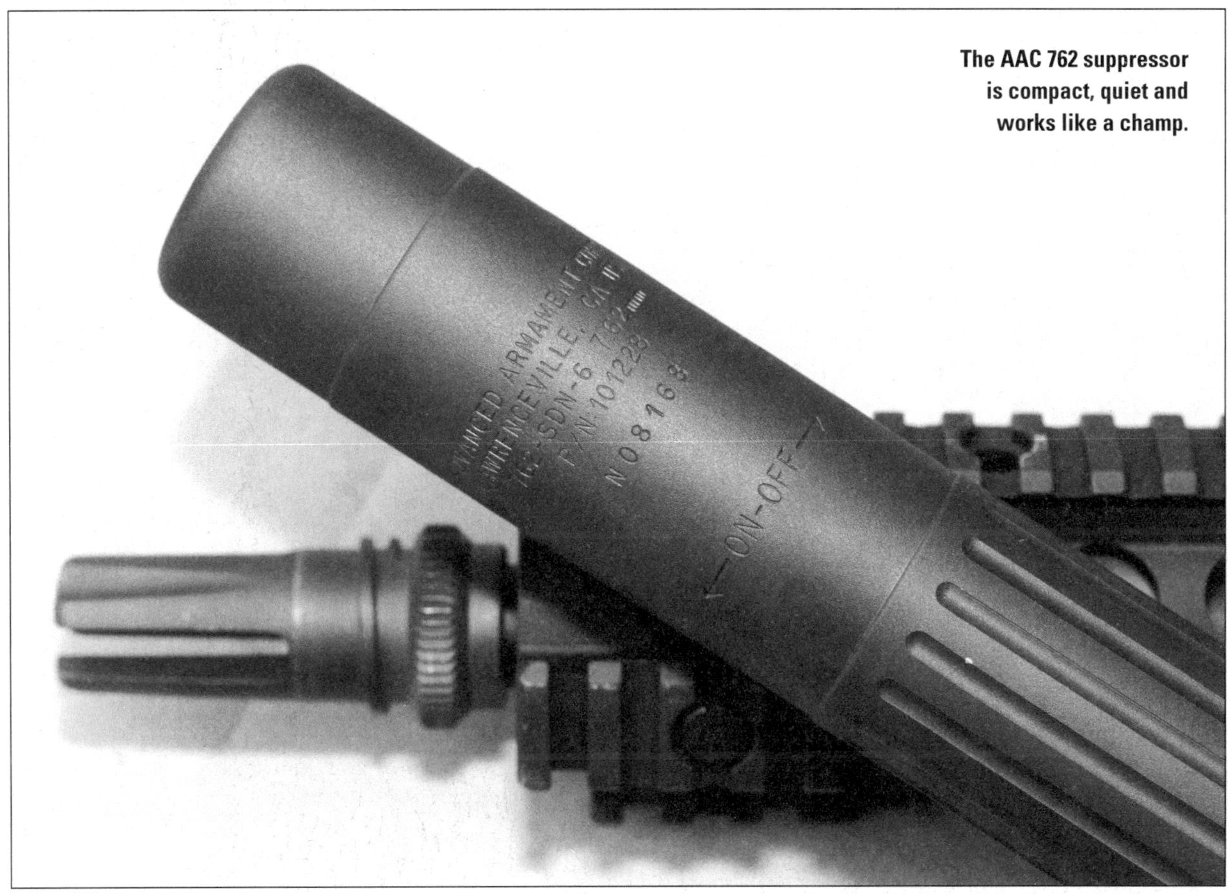

The AAC 762 suppressor is compact, quiet and works like a champ.

AAC 762-SDN-6

Advanced Armament makes a full line of suppressors, this one being their .308-and-less suppressor. Designed to be the most compact .308 suppressor possible, it works with all lesser cartridges, to include the very popular .300 Blackout.

One detail that AAC is very proud of is that the 762-SDN-6, when fed .300 Blackout subsonic ammo, is quieter than the old-school, earlier generation benchmark, the HK MP5-SD. Having fired the 762-SDN-6 with subsonic ammo, from a 16-inch-barreled carbine, I can attest to just how quiet it is. It is truly a giggle-worthy experience.

To have a six-inch suppressor in .30, be full auto rated, and to tip the scales at a pound and a quarter is pretty amazing.

OAL	7.66"
Net OAL	6.10"
Diameter	1.5"
Material	Inconel
Finish	CeraKote, black standard, OD Green & FDE optional
Calibers available	.30
Caliber rated	.308 Winchester, .300 Blackout
Full-auto rated	Yes
Mount system available	AAC QA mount
Construction	Sealed
Baffle design	n/a
MSRP	$896, mount included

On a carbine or an SBR, especially in .300 Blackout, the AAC suppressor is a blast. Or rather, not a blast.

Two AAC uppers and a suppressor, and you have lots of fun options.

BLACK RAIN ORDNANCE M30-A

Big brother to the Aris, the Black Rain Ordnance .30 suppressor, the M30-A, is big, smooth, quiet and durable. With all-stainless construction and baffles sturdy enough to be used as impact weapons when disassembled, you are going to have to win the lottery to put enough ammo through this suppressor to wear it out.

That durability costs you a few more ounces, but on a ten-pound rifle (and what .308 these days isn't that heavy?) you aren't going to notice it.

OAL	8.5"
Net OAL	7.9"
Diameter	1.5"
Materials	stainless steel
Weight	28 oz
Calibers available	.308 plus smaller calibers
Caliber rated	As above
Mount system available	direct thread, 1⁄2 x 28
Construction	sealed
Baffle design	n/a
Finish	black nitride
MSRP	$999

The Black Rain Ordnance wrench is used to disassemble the .30 suppressor.

The .30 BRO, apart and ready to be cleaned.

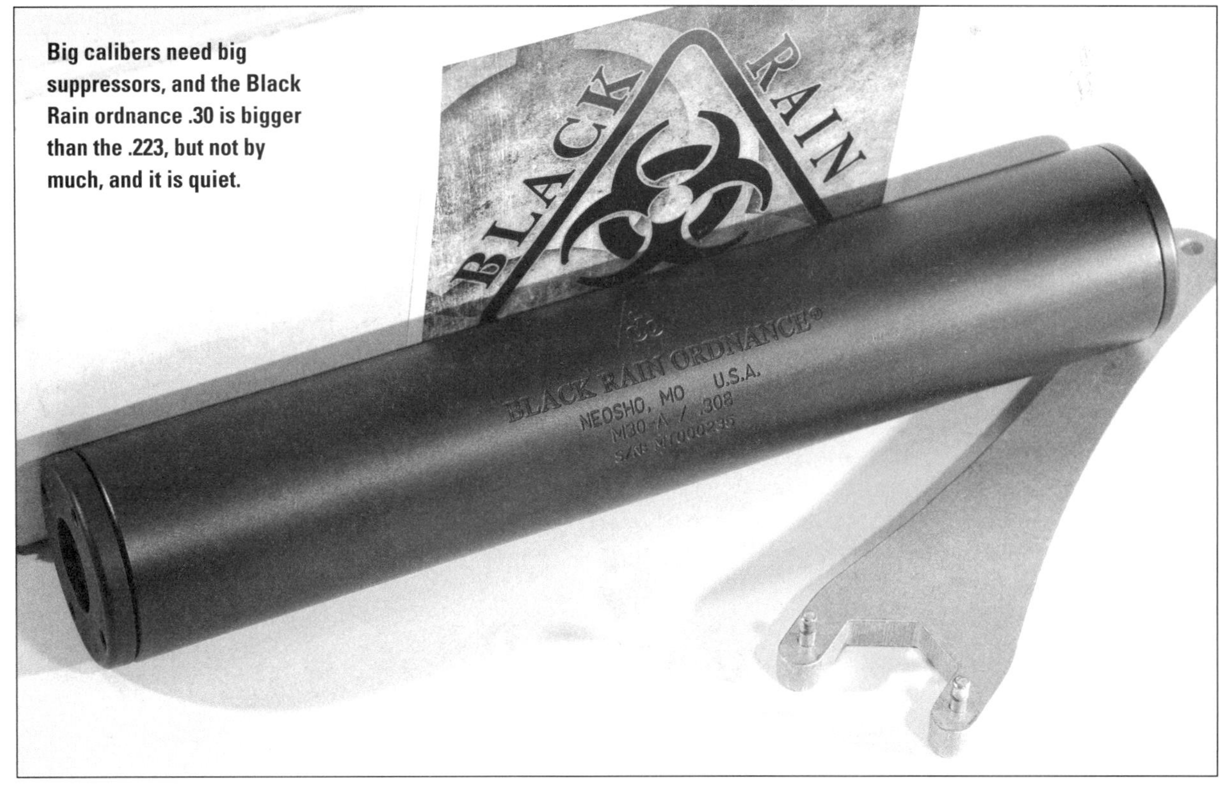

Big calibers need big suppressors, and the Black Rain ordnance .30 is bigger than the .223, but not by much, and it is quiet.

DEAD AIR ARMAMENT

The owner of Dead Air Armament, Mike Pappas, has been involved in the modern silencer manufacturer field for a number of years now. As the head of his own company, his goal now is silencers that have the best performance.

To that end, he manufactures his rifle suppressors with seamless steel stainless, precipitation hardened (that most-likely means 17-4 PH) and with stellite baffles.

But, that is just the start. The stellite baffles are welded into a unitized stack, for rigidity, strength and durability. The suppressors are sealed, but the front cap can be unscrewed. Why? Well, there is the chance of a range "oops" and a suppressor dropped off the table will fall onto the concrete range floor, and land on the part most likely to cause problems. If your front cap is dented or damaged, you can unscrew it and replace it. Plus, the front cap has a built-in flash hider, so any residual flash left by the end of the can is summarily dealt with.

There's also the "oops" of a baffle strike. The first one to get hit is the one farthest from the muzzle, and that's the front cap. If you get a damaged front cap, you can unscrew it and replace it.

The mount system is a QD design, and the muzzle device is a muzzle brake, and is also nitrided for added durability.

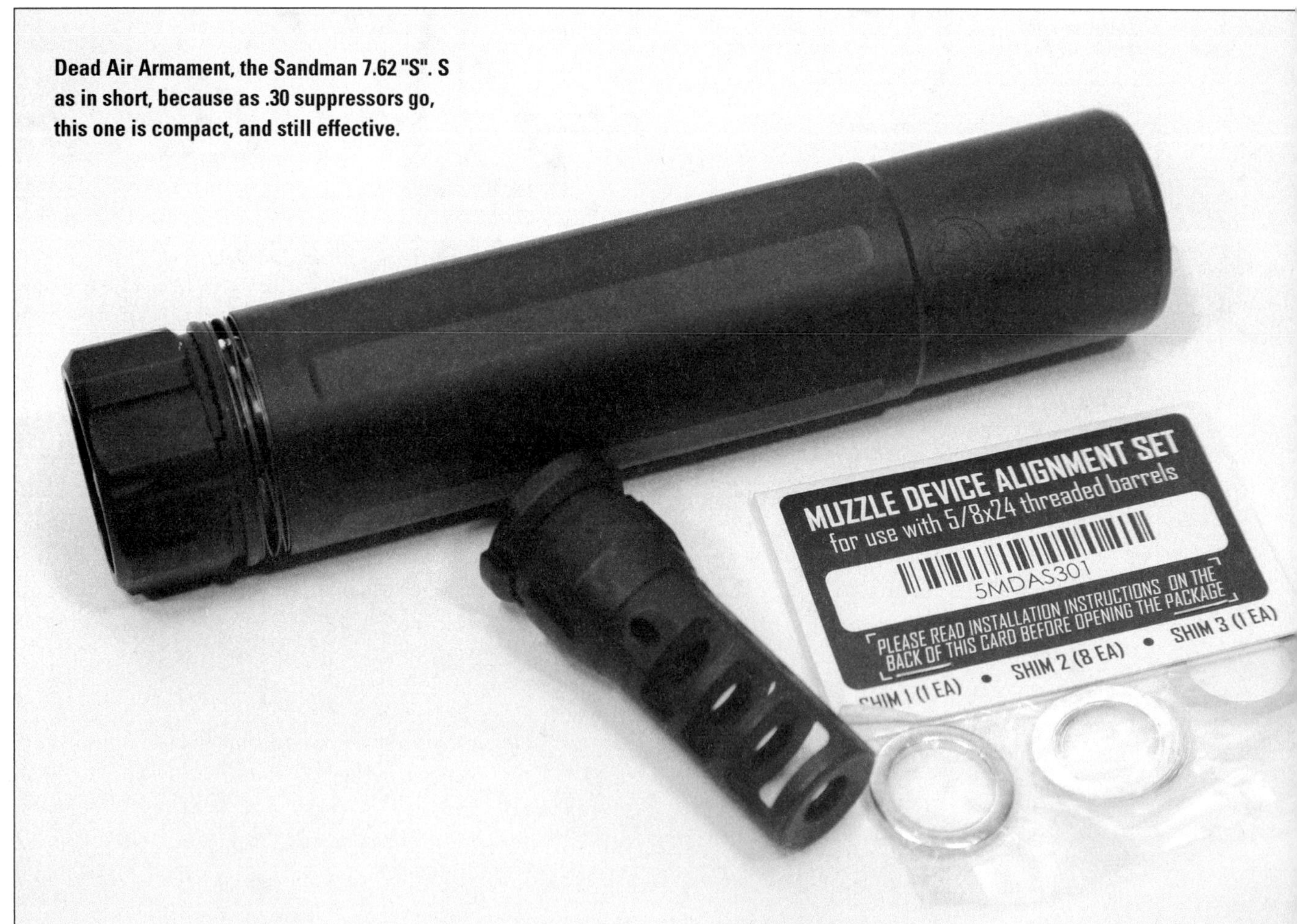

Dead Air Armament, the Sandman 7.62 "S". S as in short, because as .30 suppressors go, this one is compact, and still effective.

SANDMAN S, 7.62

The "S" stands for short, and the compact Sandman is that. Dead Air Armament intends this to be the compromise suppressor, an interesting idea for a company built on no compromises. The compromise is that it is a small and light-enough can to be used on a 5.56, it handles .300 Blackout like a dream, and still does a really good job on 7.62, and can stand up to a .300 Win Mag.

OAL	6.8"
Net OAL	5.8"
Diameter	1.5"
Materials	17-4 stainless steel & stellite
Weight	18.5 oz
Finish	Matte black CeraKote™
Calibers rated	Up to .300 win Mag
Full auto rated	Yes
Mount system available	Dead air QD mount
Construction	Sealed
Baffle design	n/a
MSRP	$1,049 (includes mount)

The Dead Air Armament S compared to the L, with a muzzle brake/mount in-between them.

SANDMAN L, 7.62

The big brother to the "S", the L is the full-sized and meant to be even quieter. The L is for those who want to wring every decibel they can out of the muzzle signature, even with the biggest-bore .30 rifles. Longer and heavier, but built to the same specs and materials as the S, the L adds length and weight, but the benefit is a quieter can.

OAL	8.9"
Net OAL	7.9"
Diameter	1.5"
Materials	17-4 stainless steel & stellite
Weight	23.4 oz
Finish	Matte black CeraKote™
Calibers rated	.300 Win Mag & smaller
Full auto rated	Yes
Mount system available	Dead Air QD mount
Construction	Sealed
Baffle design	n/a
MSRP	$1,199 (includes mount)

The Dead Air suppressors are marked as to which is which, but do you really need that, to tell that one is a lot shorter?

The Gemtech Quicksand is their quick-attach titanium suppressor for the .308 crowd.

GEMTECH QUICKSAND

Gemtech took their Sandstorm and made the rear cap a quick-attach two-lug system, producing a tough, light, quiet .30 suppressor. And as a bonus, it works well on .223/5.56 as well. I'll be the first to admit that a nine-inch suppressor on a 5.56 carbine is a bit long, but it is light and quiet, so quit complaining. Made with an all-titanium tube and baffles, and 100% welded for durability, this is a difficult suppressor to beat. Or beat up.

OAL	9.2"
Net OAL	8.5"
Diameter	1.5"
Materials	Titanium
Weight	17.5 oz
Finish	matte titanium, CeraKote optional
Calibers available	.308/7.62
Caliber rated	.308/7.62 (smaller w/correct QD mount)
Full auto rated	Yes
Mount system available	Gemtech two-lug QA mount
Construction	Sealed
Baffle design	n/a
MSRP	$1300

The Gemtech Quicksand uses their two-lug mount.

The Saker comes in a case with extra caps and the muzzle device, which is a muzzle brake.

SILENCERCO SAKER

First among the many, the Silencerco Saker baffles are made of stellite, stronger and tougher than Inconel. Another unique feature is the front cap, which can be changed for caliber and use. If you go to put the Saker onto a 5.56 rifle, you can change the front cap to a 5.56 cap, for less clearance and more quiet. (But be sure you swap it back when you go back to .308.) It also comes with two other caps, a flash hider and a barbed wire/rebar cutter.

SilencerCo Saker, in 7.62, is the only suppressor to use satellite for baffles.

A .223 cap, flash hider, barbed wire breaker, someone will figure out how to open beer bottles with this.

Using a rifle to cut barbed wire is an old trick, the problem is keeping the wire aligned with the bullet's path. Well, the Saker MAAD cap does that for you.

If you don't want the adaptability, or want something a bit smaller and lighter for your 5.56 rifle, then the Saker comes in two 5.56 models: the regular, at 18 ounces and 6.67 inches; and the "K," which is 14.7 ounces and 5.8 inches. Needless to say, they won't work on a .308 rifle.

OAL	7.5"
Net OAL	7"
Diameter	1.5"
Materials	Stainless steel, stellite
Weight	20.7 oz
Finish	Black oxide
Calibers available	.308/7.62
Caliber rated	.308/7.62 (smaller w/correct QD mount)
Full auto rated	Yes
Mount system available	SilencerCo QA mount
Construction	Sealed
Baffle design	n/a
MSRP	$1365

THUNDER BEAST ARMS CORP. 30BA

Where a lot of suppressor makers are oriented towards satisfying the "CQB" customer, the guy who figures an AR is good to 100 yards and isn't looking for more reach, Thunder Beast Arms are sniper guys. They look at anything less than 600 yards as "nearby" and will not give up sub-MOA accuracy for anything. The 30BA is a legacy model; they have improved and upgraded their designs since then, but this one works like a champ, and delivers the goods.

The "BA" means brake-attach, and they made a muzzle brake that was also the mount. One cool thing about the design is that the bearing surface of the mount is a cone, so the suppressor automatically aligns as you tighten it the last thread.

Thunder Beast is precision, and the 30BA is accurate.

The Thunder Beast mount is also a muzzle brake, in case you are shooting your .308 rifle unsuppressed.

Mine is mounted on a bolt-action sniper rifle, built on a Kinetics Research Group chassis, and the only reason it sometimes doesn't shoot sub-MOA is that I've either had too much coffee, or I'm feeding it surplus ammo, good only for sub-2-MOA accuracy.

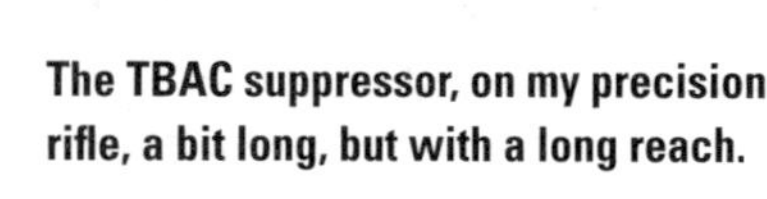

The TBAC suppressor, on my precision rifle, a bit long, but with a long reach.

OAL	9"
Net OAL	8.25"
Diameter	1.5"
Material	Titanium
Weight	16.7 oz
Finish	CeraKote, black standard, OD Green & FDE optional
Calibers available	.30
Caliber rated	rated for .300 WM plus anything smaller
Full-auto rated	No
Mount system available	BA brake/mount, stainless, eight thread pitches for installing the mount
Construction	Sealed
Baffle design	n/a
MSRP	$1245, mount included

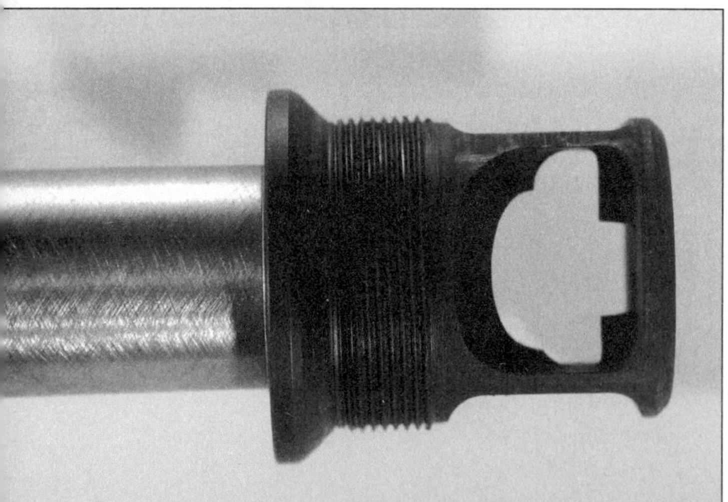

The Thunder Beast mount uses a taper to ensure alignment of the suppressor.

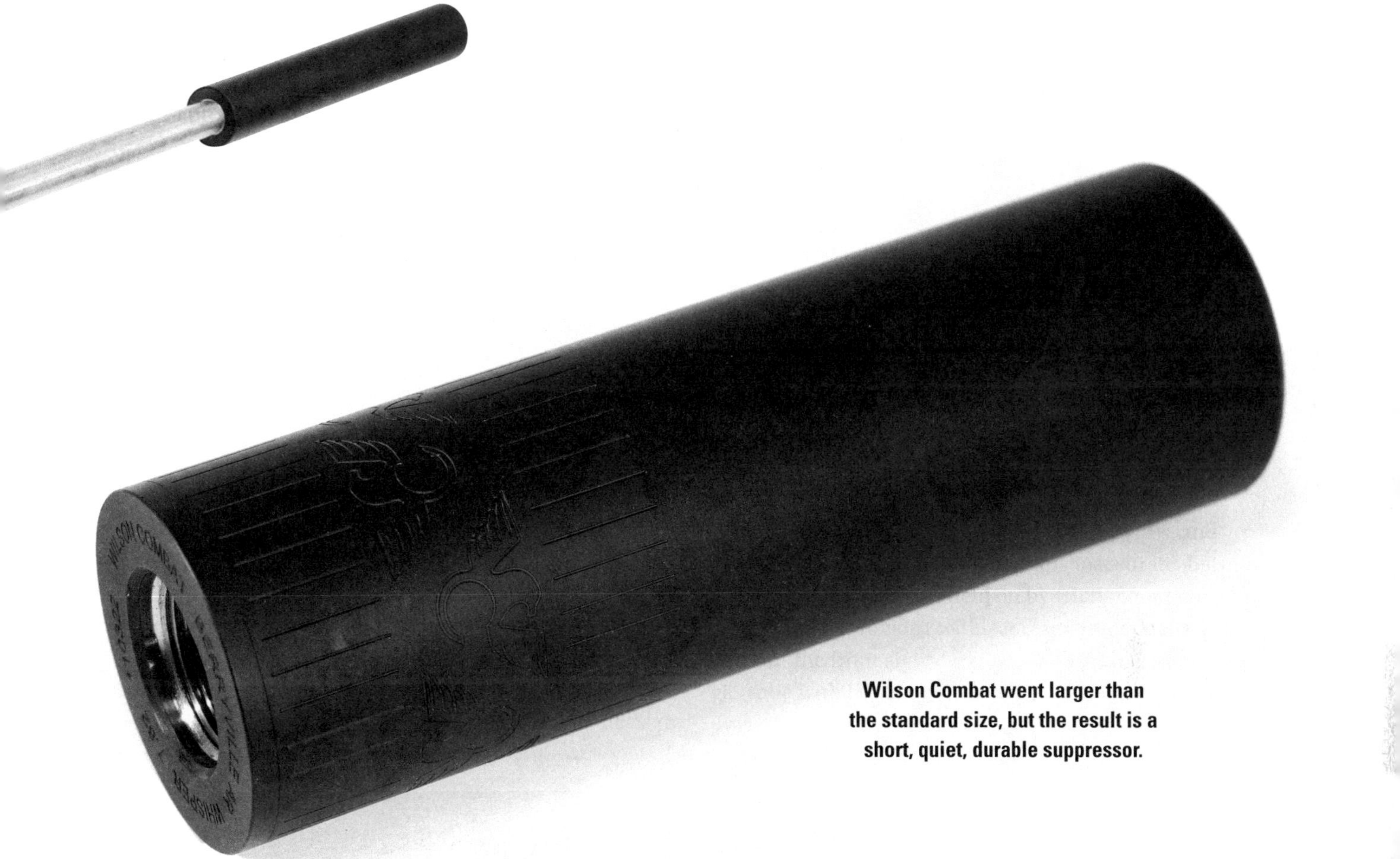

Wilson Combat went larger than the standard size, but the result is a short, quiet, durable suppressor.

WILSON 7.62 WHISPER®

Bill Wilson makes a suppressor? You bet. And this is a compact, quiet one. Wilson Combat starts with an oversized titanium tube, 1-7/8 inches in diameter. They then fill it with titanium baffles and seal the whole thing up. It mounts on a proprietary Wilson Combat mount, which is a muzzle brake, made of stainless steel, and melonite treated for durability.

The baffles are 100% welded, so you won't have to worry about breaking one

Wilson Combat also went with their logo as the gripping, no-slip area to tighten the Whisper.

The Wilson Combat muzzle brake is the mount, and it is tight, repeatable and sturdy.

loose if you abuse it. It is made for .308 and lesser calibers, so you can, if you want, mount it on a 6.5, 6.8 or .223/5.56. There are other models for 9mm and .458 Socom. If you want a 5.56- or 6.5/6.8-specific suppressor, Wilson Combat can make one for you.

It comes in standard bead-blasted titanium, or with one of the five colors of Wilson Armor-Tuff.

OAL	6.25″
Net OAL	4.5″
Diameter	1.86″
Materials	Titanium
Weight	18.2 oz
Finish	Wilson Armor-Tuff® in Black, Gray, O.D. FDE, Desert tan
Calibers available	.308/7.62
Caliber rated	.308/7.62 (smaller w/correct QD mount), 9mm, 5.56, 6.8, .458 Socom
Full auto rated	Yes
Mount system available	Wilson Combat rapid-thread muzzle brake
Construction	Sealed
Baffle design	n/a
MSRP	$1195

The Yankee Hill .30 suppressor also works on .223/5.56 rifles, as this crusty muzzle device shows.

OAL	8.5"
Net OAL	7.5"
Diameter	1.5"
Materials	Titanium & Inconel
Weight	15.4 oz
Finish	matte titanium
Calibers available	.308/7.62
Caliber rated	.308/7.62 (smaller w/correct QD mount)
Full auto rated	Yes, but limited
Mount system available	YHM QA
Construction	Sealed
Baffle design	n/a
MSRP	$1130

YANKEE HILL TITANIUM PHANTOM

The 30S is a big but light suppressor, meant for use on .308 and smaller rifles. It is capable of handling anything smaller than .308, provided you have the correct Yankee Hill QA mount. (The mount is the same for all, but the threads to attach to the barrel vary, according to the rifle's caliber.)

Titanium is light and stands up well to much use, but there are limits. So Yankee Hill warranties the titanium suppressors to only limited use on the short barrels.

The best part is to get two mounts, one in .308, and one in 5.56. That way you can swap your Yankee Hill Ti suppressor from a .308 to a 5.56 rifle (once it cools) and have even more fun.

Yankee Hill titanium Phantom in .30. You could make this one do everything from .308 down.

Suppressed armament Systems and the Resistor.

SUPPRESSED ARMAMENT SYSTEMS RESISTOR

An all-titanium .30 suppressor, the Resistor is designed with the idea of reducing the back pressure on the system, and thus less gas in the shooters face. At eight inches it is not the longest .30 suppressor out there, and not the shortest. It is, however, one of the lightest, tipping the scales at a mere 12 ounces in the direct-thread version, and 14 in the QA.

Even if you plan on putting it on a bolt gun, that is compact and light, in the .30-'verse.

The Resistor uses a muzzle device, with a threaded shank, to keep the suppressor axial and aligned.

OAL	8"
Net OAL	7.5"
Diameter	1.5"
Materials	titanium
Weight	14 oz
Finish	Matte black
Calibers available	.308
Calibers rated	.308 & .300 Mag
Full auto rated	Yes
Mount system available	SAS QA mount
Construction	Sealed
Baffle design	n/a
MSRP	$960 to $995

You can see the band of reinforcement around the expansion chamber of the Resistor.

A note to the product lists: In the process of this book, Sig Sauer changed their approach. They went from over-sized, sealed, tubed suppressor designs to QA, titanium, and welded baffles with no external tubes. It takes time to change production, fill inventory, and fulfill the paperwork obligations required to send one or more to a gun writer. So, I have the old design to test, even while the new ones are on their way to me. Deadlines being what they are, dead lines, I deliver this to you knowing there will be more to come. (And Sig is not alone in this.)

We can look forward to more goodies in Volume 2.

Rifles with suppressors are way fun, whether they are pistol-caliber and thus very quiet, or centerfire rifle, and comparatively less quiet but still quiet and fun. If you are using a suppressed rifle, you are protecting your hearing, being less annoying to your neighbors, and engaging in that most American of all pastimes – enjoying the freedom we possess.

Have fun, be safe, and keep your finger off the trigger while you are giggling.

Sig has changed the design of their suppressors, and here Kevin Brittingham shows the new .30 suppressor on a Sig 716.

And then there are the ones that are neither rifles nor pistols. The HK MP7 is a kinda-rifle cartridge, but in an smg sized package. As compromises go, it isn't so good.

What can I say, this is a great job.

Chapter Eleven

BIG BORES – YOU WANT TO SUPPRESS WHAT?

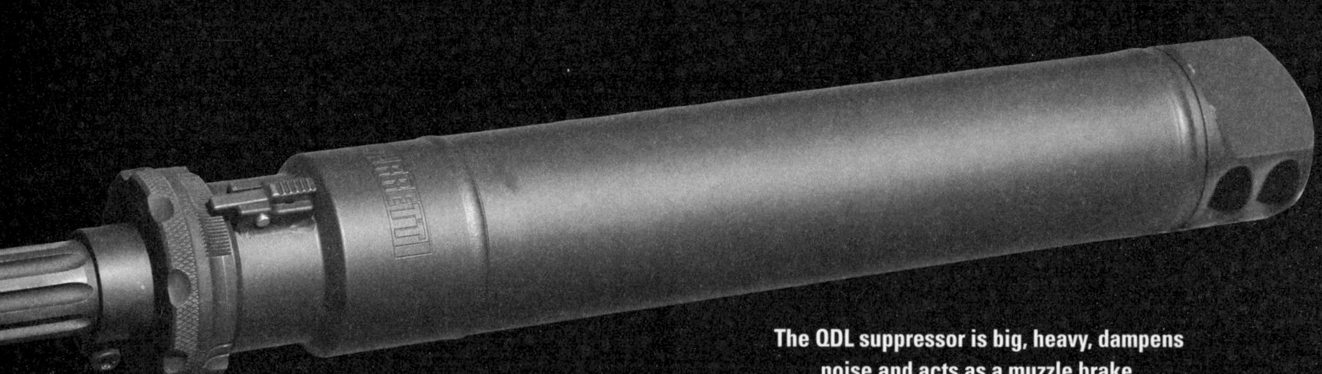

The QDL suppressor is big, heavy, dampens noise and acts as a muzzle brake.

Big caliber, big suppressor. This Barrett M107A1 is complete with a Barrett QDL suppressor. The rifle weighs 28 pounds, the QDL adds another 5.

Once we get up past the more-or-less normal hunting calibers, we get into territory that is truly an engineering exercise. The military services used to use match grade .308 rifles for long-range sniping, basically because it was what they had or could get. The problem is simple; you don't get enough range, or oomph, to make it worthwhile. Your normal .308/7.62x51 cartridge fires a bullet that goes subsonic before it gets to 1,000 yards. This is bad for a couple of reasons. One, it means you'd now got a projectile that is acting more like an M1 Carbine does at the muzzle, than a .308.

The second, and more difficult, problem is that as the bullet slows down and passes to subsonic, going through the transonic region, the turbulence it experiences has an adverse effect on accuracy.

There are ways to solve that problem, but they only eke out a few hundred extra yards or so. Best-case, you can keep a bullet supersonic to 1,500 yards, but you really have to work at it.

So, the services looked at .50 BMG. This was good, in that the weight and velocity kept the bullet supersonic to a much greater distance. It wasn't so good, in that regular .50 BMG ammo was not made to (and we're being generous here) match-grade accuracy levels. When you're using a belt-fed machine gun, a little bit of built-in dispersion is a good thing. It widens the beaten zone, increasing the likelihood of hitting your target. For snipers, not so much.

So, they and the ammo companies spent a bunch of time and effort improving the accuracy level of the ammo. This was also a project of the various .50 shooting organizations, for shooters who had enough elbowroom to plink at 1,000 yards and beyond. The military and manufacturers also spent time developing cartridges that wouldn't knock your fillings loose from recoil. Enter the .338 Lapua Magnum.

Basically a .416 Rigby case, necked down to .338 inch, it offers bullets with ballistic coefficients that are practically off the scale. The BC is a measure of how much drag a bullet experiences, traveling through air. The higher the number, the more "slippery" it is. The higher the BC, the better a bullet retains velocity downrange. Your typical 7.62 bullet, a 147-grain flat-base or with a miniscule boat-tail, has a BC of about .320. If you go to a heavier, boat-tailed bullet, like a match 175-grain

Take a four-foot long precision rifle, and to quiet it you have to add nearly a foot of extra length, in the form of a suppressor.

bullet, your .308 now has a BC of around .490. If we jump up to the big .50, a plain old FMJ found in M33 ball ammo, can have a BC of .620. If we really pull out all the stops, and use ammo loaded with a Hornady A-max, the BC is 1.050. Wow.

But that is a 750-grain bullet, one that we are doing our best to launch at 2800 fps. That's a lot of recoil. To tame it means either a really hefty rifle, or a humongous muzzle brake, or both.

If we take a step back, and go with the .338 Lapua, we can be firing a 285-grain bullet, one with a .780 BC, at 2800 fps. That means we're dealing with one-third the recoil of the .50 BMG, while still firing a bullet that stays supersonic out to 2,000 yards and change.

All this is to give you a bit of background as to why the military, in Iraq and Afghanistan, were plinking at bad guys with big-bore rifles, out to more than a mile distant. If you are firing from one ridgeline to another, and your first shot misses, the bad guy might not even know someone has fired at him. Especially if you were using a suppressed .338 or .50 BMG.

But it takes a lot of engineering to do that. I don't have either a .338 Lapua or .50 BMG rifle in the racks in the shop. Since I don't have such a rifle, I haven't asked a suppressor manufacturer for a sample, since there wouldn't be much point. So this is a chapter on range

As big as the .338 Lapua seems, it is compact, efficient and mild in recoil compared to the .50 BMG.

Of course I'm smiling. I don't have to pay for the ammo, clean the rifle, or pick up the brass when I'm done. You'd smile too.

tests at industry gatherings.

To give you an idea of the level of engineering and effort it takes, let's take a quick look at a couple of manufacturers I know of, who make suppressors for both .30 and bigger bores.

Gemtech makes their Dagger suppressor for .308/7.62 (and anything smaller). It is titanium, and it weighs 15.3 ounces. It is your basic inch-and-a-half tube, and it is a smidge under nine inches long. MSRP is $1050.

The Gemtech Arrow is meant for the .338 Lapua and smaller. It is twelve inches long, it weighs 27 ounces despite being made of titanium and aluminum, it is two inches in diameter, and the MSRP is $1895. That's what it takes to get a handle on the gas volume of the .338 Lapua.

Thunderbeast Arms offers .30 and .338 suppressors. Their Ultra 5 is a .308 can (good up to .300 WinMag/RUM) and it is five inches long, 1.5 inches in diameter, weighs 9.4 ounces of titanium, and costs $945. Their .338BA is ten and a half inches long, 1.8 inches in diameter, weighs 25 ounces of titanium, and costs $1795.

And we haven't even gotten up to .50 BMG yet.

Advanced Armament makes their excellent 762-SDN-6, and it is a really good .308 and smaller silencer. It is 7.66 inches long, 1.5 inches in diameter, weighs 20 ounces, and costs $896. If you want to install an AAC on your .50 BMG, then the Cyclops is the anvil. First of all, it is 79 ounces. That's four pounds, fifteen ounces worth of high-strength alloys.

It is almost sixteen inches long, although in its defense the net added length is less than thirteen. It is 2.5 inches in diameter, and it costs $2501.The big bore suppressor field is one in which you really have to be well-heeled to have fun. Where we are gritting our teeth as .308 ammo comes down past the dollar-a-shot range, and will never get much below fifty cents each, .338 Lapua costs $1.50 to $2 a shot. And .50 BMG? Feeding a big fifty rifle is like owning a yacht; if you have to ask, you can't afford it. But, just to keep you up to speed, the ammo cost search at this moment turns up the lowest cost as $2.85 per. And that's XM33, not particularly accurate ammo. If you want the primo accuracy stuff, the MSRP is $8.30 per shot. No, that's not a typo, eight dollars and change per shot.

Now, the cost of the ammo and the suppressor isn't the end of things. Apparently, for those at the top of the long-range competition circuit, the thousand-yard .50 shooters, a rifle barrel for a .50 BMG is considered to have a service life of 2,000 rounds. Considering what a match barrel in 5.56 or 7.62 costs, I don't want to know what a 30-inch match tube in .50 BMG costs, fitted to a receiver. And while 2,000 rounds probably represents three years of competition shooting, it is still $16,000 in match ammo. You can see why I don't own one of the beasts, at least not until after I win the lottery.

Chapter Twelve

SHOTGUNS – AND THEY SAID IT COULDN'T BE DONE

Despite the low pressures of shotguns, there is a very large volume of gas to deal with. This requires a big suppressor. The SilencerCo Salvo 12 has as much internal volume as three or four of the rifle suppressors behind it.

Time for a little movie trivia. Who has seen the movie, "No Country for Old Men"? Who thought it deserved the Oscars it received? Who found Chigurh totally creepy and would have wasted no time in whacking him, given the opportunity? (Not like he'd have given you any.)

And who watched the movie, thinking "Nobody makes a suppressor for shotguns, that's just silly."

Well, no more.

SilencerCo has developed a shotgun suppressor. The big problem with making a suppressor for a shotgun is a technical detail that is the very essence of the shotgun: the payload is not a single unit. In birdshot, you have a fistful of small pellets held in a plastic cup, and the cup is designed to peel away and drop behind when the whole thing leaves the muzzle.

Buckshot is worse, there may not even be a plastic cup.

Slugs can be better, but you really don't want a fiber wad, even one screwed to the bottom of the slug like a Brenneke, just trying to hang up on a baffle.

Keeping the payload under control has been the hang-up. Although, now that I think about it, there's no reason you couldn't drill a bazillion holes in the shotgun barrel, and then put a tube around that, to contain the gases. An integrally-suppressed shotgun. But, SilencerCo saved us all the work, with the Salvo 12.

The essence of the Salvo 12 is the rails. What they did, in essence, is construct a new screw-in choke design, which has as part of it a collection of rods. The rods act like a barrel, constraining the payload, while the gaps between the rods allow gas to bleed off behind the shotcup. The pellets are contained, the gases bleed off, and life is quieter.

This does not come without cost. The expansion ratio of a 12-gauge shotshell is pretty big. But there is still a lot of gas volume to contend with. And, by the time you make the rod assembly, and then wrap it in a container, you have a bulky package. The Salvo 12 is a foot long, two and a quarter by three inches in size, and weighs two pounds.

Here's an interesting quirk in the law; you have to receive it as the full-sized package, and then you can, with the necessary parts from Silencerco, re-build it to a shorter size.

Why? Apparently, if SilencerCo were to ship the compact ones and allow you to re-build it bigger, you'd in essence be making a quieter suppressor. And that is bad. No, I don't get the logic, either. I mean, you've paid for, and been approved for transfer of, a suppressor. As long as it reduces sound by 1 dB, what does it matter to the ATF if it is any good or not? Or better or worse?

But bureaucratic requirements do not need to be rational, logical or consistent. They simply are. So, your Salvo 12 will arrive in its entire one-foot glory. After that, you can do what you and your checkbook want.

The big question is, does it work? Yes. I spent an afternoon on a TV set, while we had fun with the Salvo 12. While it does make the shotgun a bit muzzle-heavy, that can be a good thing, making you follow-through. I'm sure you'd get some odd looks on the skeet or trap range, if you were the first to ever show up with one, but once they got used to it (and everyone got tired of "Hey, can I try?"), no-one would give you a second look.

Chapter Thirteen

ACCURACY

You can't judge a suppressor and accuracy if you can't shoot. This was thrown, and called, so this group is a waste of ammo when it comes to determining if this is an accurate combo.

When it comes to accuracy, we have competing dynamics at play. On the one hand, the suppressor should cause a shift in point of impact, and perhaps even accuracy itself, because we've just parked anywhere from half a pound to a pound and a half of metal on the end of the barrel. When you fire a rifle, the barrel hums like a tuning fork. The muzzle whips around like crazy. The point of impact depends, in great part, on just where in the cycle of whipping around the muzzle is when the bullet pops out of the crown.

An inaccurate barrel has inconsistent harmonics, and the bullet leaves when the muzzle is basically in a random location in space at each shot. An accurate barrel is one that either has little or no movement, or the bullet leaves at the same location in space of the muzzle's movement.

The Browning BOSS system was an attempt to tune the barrel harmonics so that you have a consistent release. The BOSS has an adjustable weight, one that moves back or forth, so it changes the harmonics, and you do a trial-and-error test to see which position is best. (I can't help but wonder just how much of the improvement in accuracy is created simply by the shooter getting more practice. That's just cynical old me.)

So, hanging a chunk of metal on the muzzle should change accuracy. And just as an aside, I asked some of the gun writers I know, hunters who would have been more involved with Browning, how well the system worked. The consistent answer was, "Don't know, haven't shot one since they were new and I had to write about it." So I guess the shooting public decided it just wasn't worth it.

On the other hand, the suppressor can improve accuracy by stripping away the turbulent gases from the muzzle, the location where the bullet is at its most unstable and most suggestible to change. Which one wins?

It turns out that the gas-stripping variable is larger than the random harmonic change variable. (Maybe that's why Browning let it fade, the improvement wasn't worth the effort?) Most suppressors actually increase accuracy. Few change the point of impact, and when they do, it is by a minimal amount. While the direction and distance of the change is random on each pairing, it is consistent with the pair. That is, if you slap a suppressor on your rifle, and find it shifts the group half an inch low-left, the shift will go away when you take the suppressor off. And, it will return, in the same direction and amount, when you put it back on.

But, it will not necessarily have the same change on the next rifle in your rack. You have to try it and see.

Now, there is accuracy, and then there is accuracy. For most shooters (and I don't mean to be insulting here), the accuracy shift is one they will not notice. For example, I tested a 9mm suppressor on a high-end 1911, a pistol built with a bank-vault-like fit. Over sandbags, the pistol was capable of less than two-inch groups at twenty-five yards. If I knocked off my usual and excessive coffee consumption, I could get groups down to close to an inch, center to center. That's basically five shots touching, at twenty-five yards.

The suppressor I tested shifted the group center maybe an inch. So, a shift at twenty-five yards that isn't even half the apparent width of the front sight blade, this when shot over sandbags? Admit it, how many of you can shoot a sub-two-inch group, even off of a rest, with your current pistol, ammo and practice level? On demand? If I had handed the pistol to someone who could shoot a three-inch group at best (which is still pretty darned good, by the way) the change in point of impact would not be as great as the group itself. The overlap of the groups would mean no change was apparent, and it would take some very careful measuring to even indicate there had been a shift.

I did the same thing with a top-flight AR, using match ammo. And the numbers were pretty much the same. If I changed my regular scope to a high-X one (Leupold 6.5-20) I could shoot sub-MOA groups, and the suppressor caused a change of almost an inch. At 100 yards. If you could not shoot sub-MOA groups, you would not be able to determine if any change at all had occurred.

Now, this is not a guarantee. It is entirely possible that a suppressor on your rifle, or handgun, will cause a significant and unwanted change in accuracy. If it does, then there are a few things you can do.

First, take a quick look, or use the Geissele gauge,

to determine that the problem with accuracy is not that you are experiencing baffle strikes. If you are experiencing baffles strikes, stop shooting!

Rifle procedure

The first thing to do is to remove the suppressor and then re-mount it. If you have a direct-thread suppressor, you may find it has come loose. If you torqued it on bare-handed and it is loose, use a wrench. If you did use a wrench and it was properly tight, take it off anyway and use a stiff brush to brush the threads and bearing shoulder clean. Re-install, re-torque and try again. What may have happened is that some grit or other tiny object got into the threads or on the bearing shoulder, and the suppressor torqued-up not quite cleanly. That could introduce unwanted harmonics into the system.

If doing this does not change the situation, and your accuracy is not good, then you have to move on to another rifle. Not every rifle is going to work well with every suppressor. The best of both will be amazingly adaptable, but every now and then there will be a combination of rifle and suppressor that simply do not want to play well with each other. Shrug, move on, and try another rifle.

Oh, you can complain, to the rifle maker or the suppressor maker, but you will not get much satisfaction. They've been down this road before. The rifle maker makes his rifles to a certain accuracy spec or price point. Despite the insistence in today's marketplace that every rifle deliver sub-MOA accuracy, they do not. Many can, with one ammo or load, or now and then, but it is a rare rifle that shoots sub-MOA with all ammo. If you send it back and it shoots within the factory spec, they may do a clean-up and inspection, just to ease the sting, but they'll send it back with a note saying, "everything checks out."

If you send back your suppressor for service, with a complaint of poor accuracy, the manufacturer will do much the same. They'll poke a bore scope inside to make sure there hasn't been a baffle strike. They'll mount it on a rifle of known accuracy and test-fire it. When it produces the expected good group, they box it up and send it back.

And then, there is the human equation. Nothing personal, but can you shoot as well as your expectations think?

Now, if you find that there is no rifle you own that will shoot accurately with that suppressor installed, you need to do some more research. Find someone at your gun club who has a suppressor, whose rifle shoots well, and is willing to experiment. Swap your suppressor onto his rifle. If his rifle now suddenly does not shoot well, then you have your answer.

One last possibility to consider is that your rifle is exquisitely sensitive to suppressor torque. That is, it needs, nay, demands that the suppressor be screwed on with a certain amount of torque, and no other. You're going to have to invest in a torque wrench then. The bad news is, torque wrenches are heavy, and you need to learn how to use them. The good news is, they can be had cheap. The last time I was in the local store, I found them on sale for $17. No, that's not a typo, seventeen whole dollars, and it works, too. I'm not saying it is a plus-or-minus a few ounces tool, but if your $17 torque wrench tightens to a repeatable level, and as a result your suppressor-equipped rifle shoots accurately, do you really care if it is off by a few pounds-feet from the indicated value?

If you have a quick-attach system, remove the suppressor, clean the threads, re-install it and try again. If it won't shoot well, then you will have to remove the muzzle device, re-attach it, and try again. (This is a good reason to test a suppressor and muzzle device before you go and more-or-less permanently attach the muzzle device with Rocksett.)

Handguns

On handguns, we have a lot more to play with and perhaps get things in alignment. You see, a pistol needs a booster, a Nielsen device. They come with a guide tube that has on it a series of notches, just like the notches on the barrel nut of your AR-15. Some have a lot, some have a few, but they all have some. If you look at the booster, you'll see that there is a pin on the body, one that rests in one of the notches. You can pull the suppressor body forward (make sure the pistol is unloaded) and then give the suppressor a small turn, and let it spring back in place, putting the pin into a different notch. Try again. You'll most-likely find that the group moves around, as you change from notch to notch. When you find the notch where your pistol shoots to the sights, or the tightest groups, mark the location.

That's the setting you want to use for that suppressor, on that pistol. If you install a different suppressor on that pistol, the new one will have its own setting that

If you use a direct-thread suppressor, it has to be on tight and consistently, or groups will shift. This is a before and after pair of groups with a Black Rain ordnance rifle and suppressor. No change here.

holds zero. And the first suppressor, onto a different pistol? You guessed it, you start over.

And the booster sleeve has to be machined to tight-enough tolerances that the suppressor can't "droop" on the booster and permit mis-alignment. That leads to baffle strikes.

To test accuracy, I used a Nighthawk 9mm pistol, set up by Nighthawk as a suppressor-ready model. I checked it for accuracy and zero with two loads, Hornady 147 XTP and Asym 147 FMJ match. I chose those two loads for a couple of reasons. One, they are both insanely accurate in pretty much any pistol I haul out of the safe. Well, any 9mm pistol. And two, since the whole point of a suppressor is to be quiet, using subsonic ammo makes sense.

End result: booooo-ring. The Nighthawk showed, at most, a one-inch group shift of point of impact, and no change in overall accuracy, which is impressively tight. And I say "at most" because a one-inch shift, in a pistol that shoots one-inch groups as the maximum, means we're right on the edge of being able to say anything at all happened.

Were I to hand it to someone who could wring 1.5-inch groups out of the pistol, bare, it would be difficult to observe a one-inch shift suppressed. A shooter who could "only" manage two-inch groups would not see any

Once you have a suppressor-equipped rifle zeroed, you should not have to re-zero it with or without the suppressor. If you do, there's something wrong, and it probably isn't the suppressor.

observable zero shift. So, the statisticians among us will declare "No observable zero shift" with this combo.

Rifles, semi-auto

The big deal with accuracy here is heat. With a semi-auto it is easy to get a suppressor smoking hot. Literally smoking hot. When hot, the question becomes, does it change the gas flow properties of the suppressor, and thus accuracy? My testing, so far, is that good ones do not change. However, a good suppressor is, to more than a small extent, dependant on correct installation. If you don't install the muzzle device correctly, or you don't torque a direct-thread suppressor properly, you will not be happy with what happens when you heat things up.

I've done this test with a variety of rifle-caliber suppressors, but for this test I figured I'd pull out all the stops. For a rifle, I used a LaRue Stealth upper, mounted on a Stag lower with match trigger installed. The LaRue Stealth is built on a LaRue billet upper and LaRue railed, free-float handguard, and uses their own barrels, stainless steel, 1/8 twist, with a .223 Wylde chamber. If you put this on a lower with a good trigger, and use a good scope, any "inaccuracy" you see is your bad shooting skills, not the rifle. Well, maybe the ammo can take some of the blame.

The Stag lower is one of my test drones, with a match trigger installed, and it has seen a horde of uppers lashed on top. It has not failed me, even once.

For a scope, I clamped on a LaRue QD scope mount (what else?) and in it I plunked a Leupold target scope. The scope in question is their 6.5-20x40 AO EFR. Translated, it is a 6.5 to 20X scope, with a 40mm objective lens, adjustable objective and target knobs. This allows me to use the objective adjustment to focus at 25 yards, and establish a solid zero, before fine-tuning it at 100 yards. (And changing the focus to there.) The target knobs make it a painless task to move the group around until I have the zero I want.

So, off to the range with the rifle and two primo ammo loads and a couple of suppressors. The ammo I used was Black Hills, loaded with 73 grain Berger bullets, and Asym, their scary-accurate 77 grain OTM.

The suppressors were an Innovative Arms Grunt, a direct-thread that is about as delicate as an anvil, and a Black Rain Ordnance .223, also direct thread.

The process was simple – get the rifle zeroed with the ammo, using the regular A2 flash hider. Then remove the flash hider, torque on a suppressor, shoot for

Even smoking hot, this Sig 556 suppressor holds zero. (50 yards, benched, red-dot sight, boring 55 fmj ammo.)

accuracy and zero, and compare.

Now, this kind of shooting is very environment-dependant, and obviously so. When shooting the smallest groups possible with a handgun, you simply zen out, and press the trigger while keeping the sights aligned.

With a rifle, regardless of the setup (and I used my Sinclair front rest and rear bag arrangement), you can see your heartbeat in the reticle. Thump-thump. Thump-thump. Shooting tiny groups with rifles is hard work. But, the results were clear. If there was any shift in zero, it was smaller than the average diameter of the groups I was shooting. No change in size, no change in zero.

Bolt actions

Unlike semis, a bolt gun won't heat up a suppressor as much. So that makes it easier. But, bolt-action shooters have higher standards than the semi-auto guys. Semi shooters brag about sub-MOA. A bolt-action shooter expects a precision rifle to shoot five rounds at 100 yards where all five holes are touching.

For this test, I used the Thunder Beast Arms 30BA, a model they no longer make (because they improved it so much they changed the name) and the "laser rifle." It started as a blueprinted Remington 700 with a Shilen XX barrel, in .308. I built it without having the barrel profiled, and the result was a rifle that put all its shots into one hole, but was so heavy that hauling it from the

Bolt guns do not have to worry so much about heat on the suppressor, as heat causing mirage.

truck to the firing line was work.

So, I had Ned profile it down to an approximation of the USMC M40 barrel, but while that was going on I ran across Kinetic Research Group at the SHOT show. So instead of a regular stock, I dropped the barreled action into a KRG X-Ray chassis. Now, it would shoot one-hole groups and I could actually haul it around without feeling like a pack mule.

To test, I zeroed it with some Federal XM-118, the current mil-spec sniper ammo. Once it was zeroed unsuppressed, I screwed on the 30BA and proceeded to shoot more groups. Well, I tried. I had the luck on my first range session to have some club members show up, and while I was plenty happy to let them have a go at it, I wasn't going to burn up my limited supply of XM-118, so they got to shoot ball, M80. The biggest problem with an accurate bolt gun, a suppressor, and trying to have fun? Mirage, from the heat of the suppressor.

The next session, I had scrubbed the bore and installed an Armageddon Gear suppressor cover to tame mirage, so I sat down, checked zero (it hadn't shifted) and then installed the 30BA and shot more groups. Spot-on.

I was not able to do this test with more than the one suppressor, because the TBA 30BA uses a muzzle brake with threads for the suppressor. Once it is properly aligned, and the Rocksett has set, I was loathe to remove it just to try another suppressor.

Rimfire

For the rimfire testing, I had an embarrassment of riches. First, I had rimfire cans from a host of makers. Second, I have three different rimfires I could test, four if you include the Alexander Arms .17 HMR in the rack (which I did).

For the handgun testing, I used a Ruger 22/45, their now-old-enough-for-social-security-and-not-showing-it pistol, but with a difference from the original. The grip is shaped to have the same angle and roughly the same feel as a 1911. Also, the barrel is a bull-barrel profile, no taper to it, and is threaded for suppressors. Testing was simple. I used Gemtech subsonic ammo and checked the zero unsuppressed. I then swapped onto it three different rimfire suppressors, checking the zero and group size with each one.

Next is my other Ruger, my 10/22 that I built a long time ago for the Chevy Truck Challenge and the rimfire event at Second Chance. It has a Butler Creek barrel on it, but this one has proven brilliantly accurate. For this book I sent the barrel off to Ned and had him thread it for suppressors. Since it has had the same 4X scope on it for some twenty years now, I figured I'd dip into my supply of Eley match ammo and see if I could really wring out some tight groups.

That done, I swapped on rimfire suppressors and shot the same groups again.

Then, for the AR testing, I had two. One is my Alexander Arms .17 HMR, a real laser-like cartridge. A 20-grain bullet is steaming out the muzzle at something like 2200 fps, even from the carbine-length barrel if the Alexander Arms. Now, this means there is a supersonic crack, but the various suppressors took the muzzle thump out, and didn't change accuracy.

Last up is the CMMG .22 conversion, re-built as a dedicated upper. This is for cheap training, and to introduce new shooters to the AR, without the noise and cost of centerfire .223 ammo. I included it primarily because, as a flat-top AR, it is dead simple to mount a scope; just clamp a scope that is already in a QD mount, and re-zero.

Long range

At my home stomping grounds, I don't have much chance to get out to long distances. The nearest 600-yard range is just down the road, but it is very structured. They are interested in NRA High Power, getting tuned up for it, and the format is set up for that. There really isn't much of a chance to experiment, and they are not at all interested in setting up a 600-yard gong for steel plate shooting.

To shoot that far, or farther, I have to drive four or five hours, depending on which direction I head.

So, I had a good opportunity to do some long-range shooting on a couple of visits to Gunsite on industry junkets. They involved steel plates from 300 to 800 yards, at sometimes odd distances, and all at different angles and directions. The rifle was a Remington Defense bolt gun, chambered in .300 Winchester Magnum, and the suppressor was an AAC MK13-SD, designed for use with both/either 7.62 and .300 WM.

Once I figured out which particular hash mark on the reticle was the desired one, I was able to plink the plates with merry abandon. And, the 800-yard plate was a particular joy. By leaning forward and pre-loading the bipod legs against the recoil, I was able to recover quickly enough that I could follow the bullet's wake

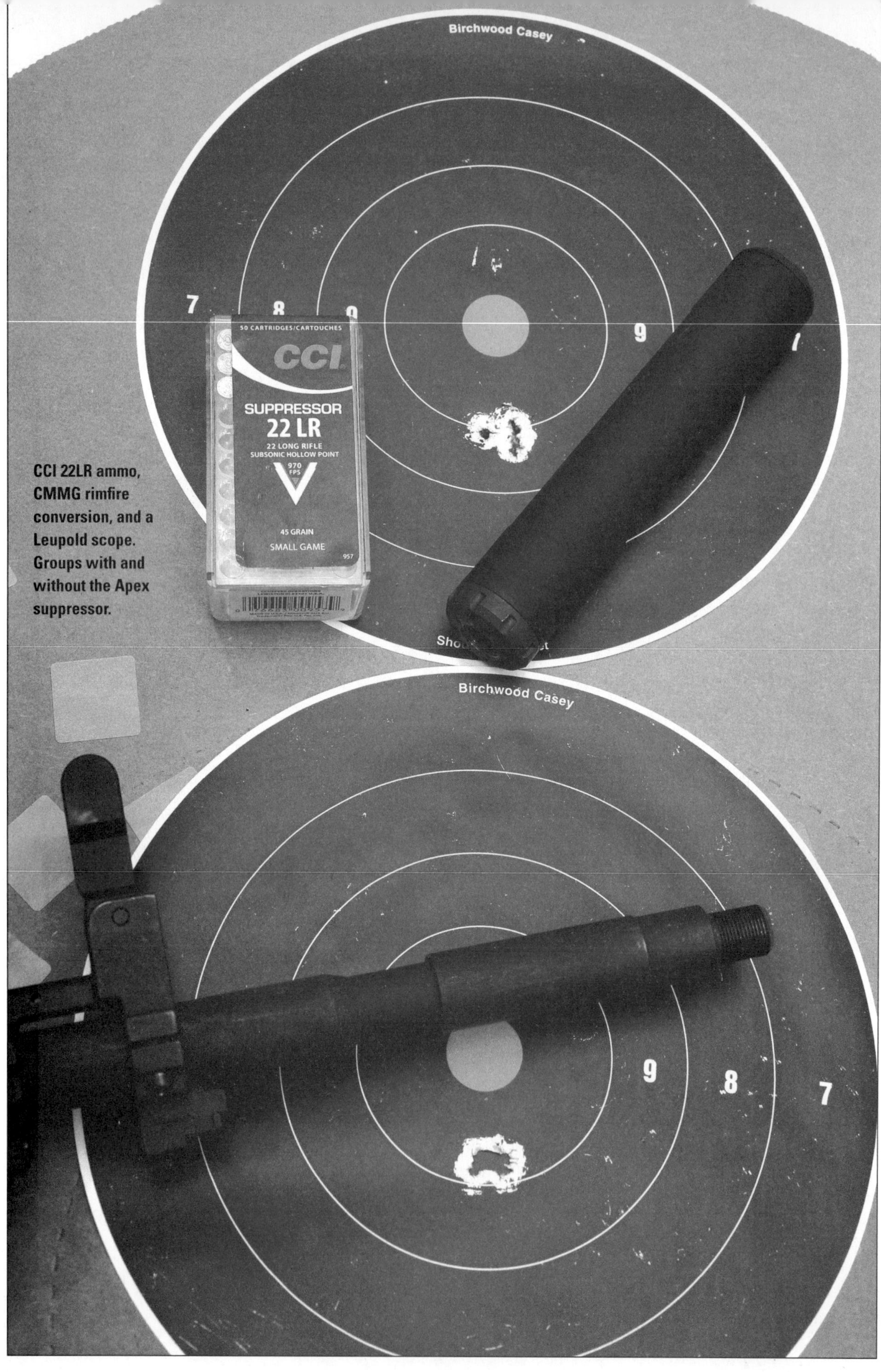

CCI 22LR ammo, CMMG rimfire conversion, and a Leupold scope. Groups with and without the Apex suppressor.

800 yard plinking, with a suppressor-equipped magnum rifle. Fun hardly begins to describe it.

through the air. This was something I've seen before, usually while coaching officers on the 300-meter targets in our LE patrol rifle classes.

Each 180-grain Accutip would rise above the line of sight, drift a bit left, into the wind, then as it began its fall, drift back to the right, until it hit the plate with a visible splash of lead, paint and dust. And, the pattern of dust on the ground, from the fragments splattering off the steel, differed from that of a miss, letting me know I had a hit before the "thwak" of the bullet strike arrived, two and-a-quarter seconds after it hit steel.

I took full advantage of the heap of factory-supplied ammo, and shot the rifle until the mirage made it too difficult to see the target. Until mirage built up enough to make it impossible to see, I was hitting with monotonous regularity. The suppressor-equipped rifle did not shift zero as it heated, so there's another test, and data point.

Summary

Well, in the bad old days it may well have been that suppressors caused a change of impact, or a change in accuracy, or both. These days, the manufacturers who will remain in business have designs that don't cause changes. And we're all the better for that.

Chapter Fourteen

GAS CONTROL AND OFF-LABEL USES

Adams Arms was early into piston conversions. This one has been almost criminally abused, is adjustable, and still works just fine.

PWS makes a long-stroke piston system. Top is an early conversion, bottom is their dedicated piston system on one of their uppers.

When it comes to gas control, you don't need pills or to change your diet. Where suppressors are concerned, you do have to make some effort, or suffer the expected results. As we've discussed, the extended dwell time created by the suppressor does cause problems.

The original DI system is not meant to be adjustable. Unlike the FAL, with an adjustable gas system, the Stoner system depends on the ammunition manufacturer using the correct powder (or a powder within a correct range) when they load the ammo, and if they do, the gas system is more-or-less self-regulating. Throw in a suppressor and it can't regulate that, and there is more gas blown back into the receiver.

This is one place where piston systems have an advantage. As long as the designer or manufacturer builds in a decreased gas flow setting, you can "dial back" the gas flow and keep the suppressor-equipped rifle working just fine. Of course, if you forget, and take the suppressor off but don't return the system to the un-suppressed gas flow, it may short-stroke. That's life.

Colt Competition uses a small adjustment valve on their rifles. It is competition, so it doesn't have to be something you can adjust in the field.

When Ruger does ARs, they do them right. Not only did they start with a piston-driven A, they made it suppressor-ready with an adjustable gas system.

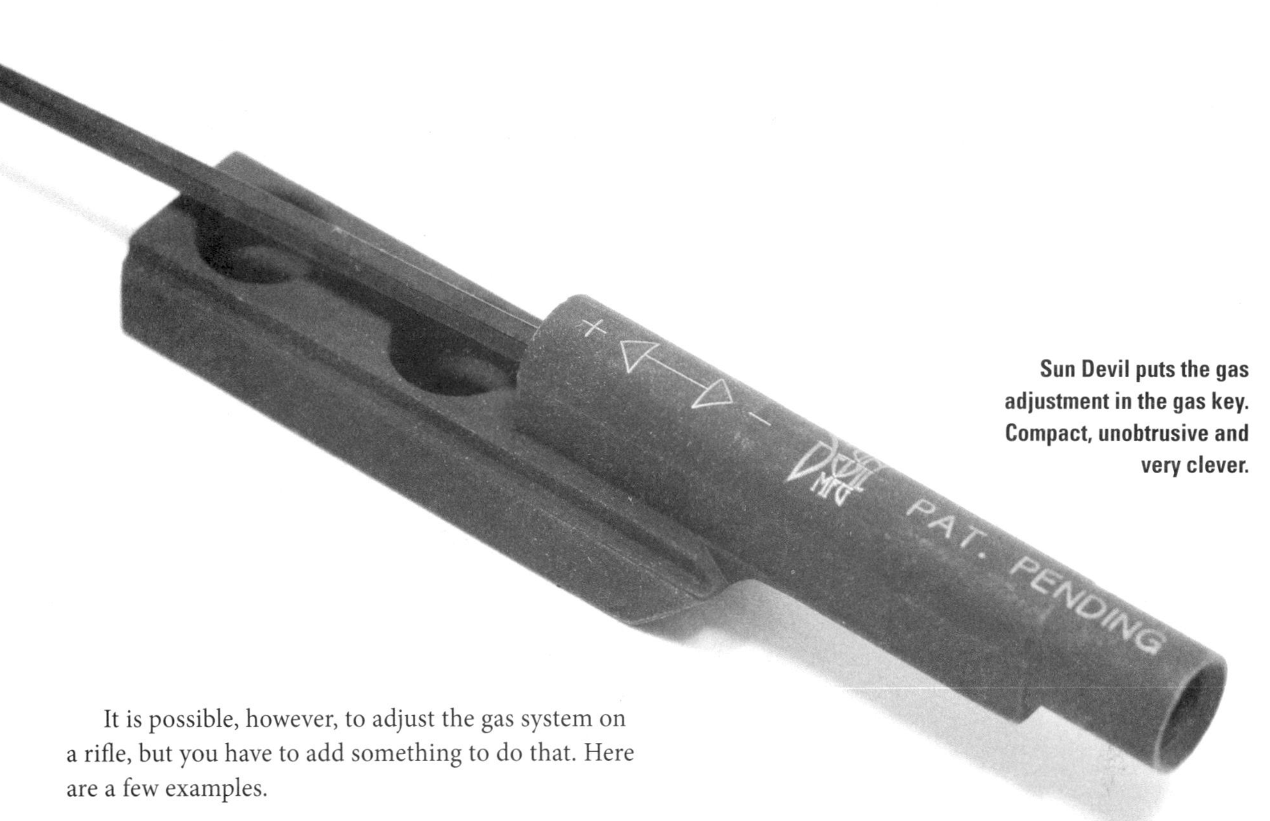

Sun Devil puts the gas adjustment in the gas key. Compact, unobtrusive and very clever.

It is possible, however, to adjust the gas system on a rifle, but you have to add something to do that. Here are a few examples.

Adams Arms

One of the earliest piston conversions, and now makers of all-piston systems, their gas systems are adjustable and removable for cleaning. Mine has been viciously abused and neglected, and has shown no signs of ever wanting to quit.

Gemtech makes a carrier with a built-in suppressor selector. You can read what the setting is, through the ejection port, but you have to remove it from the rifle to change it.

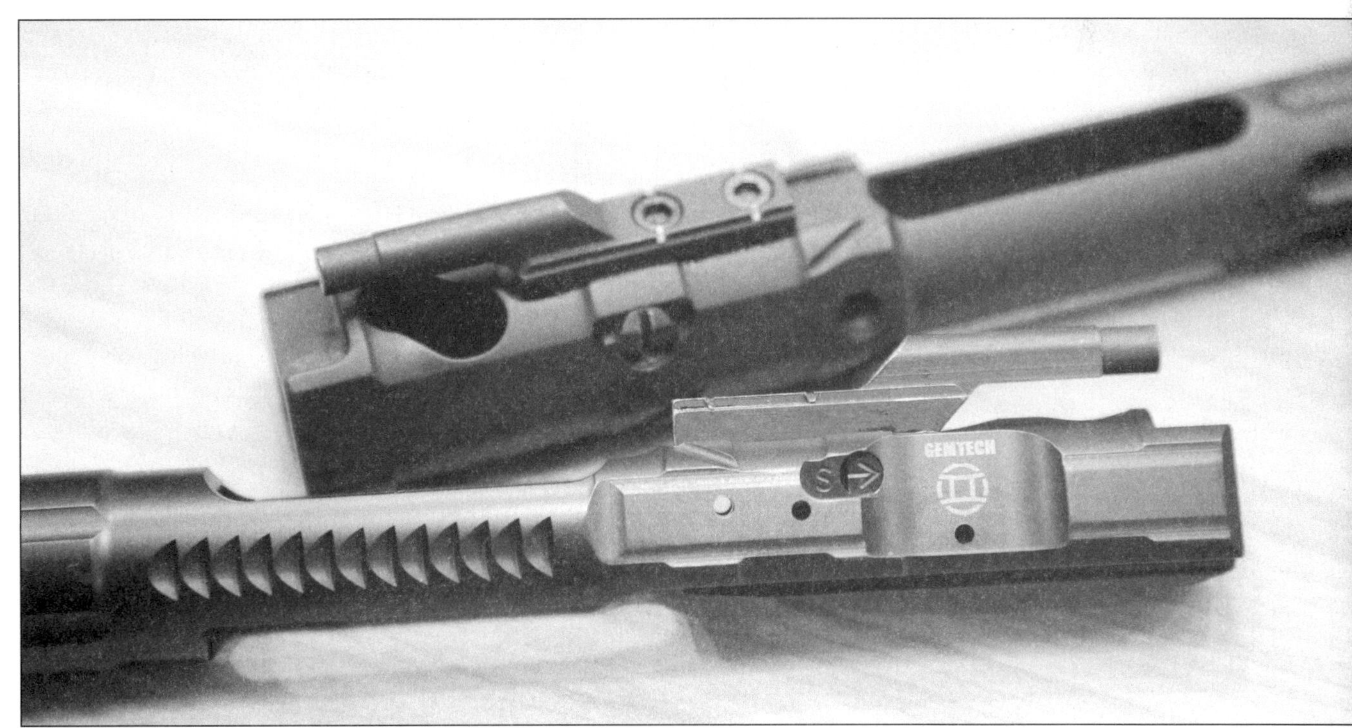

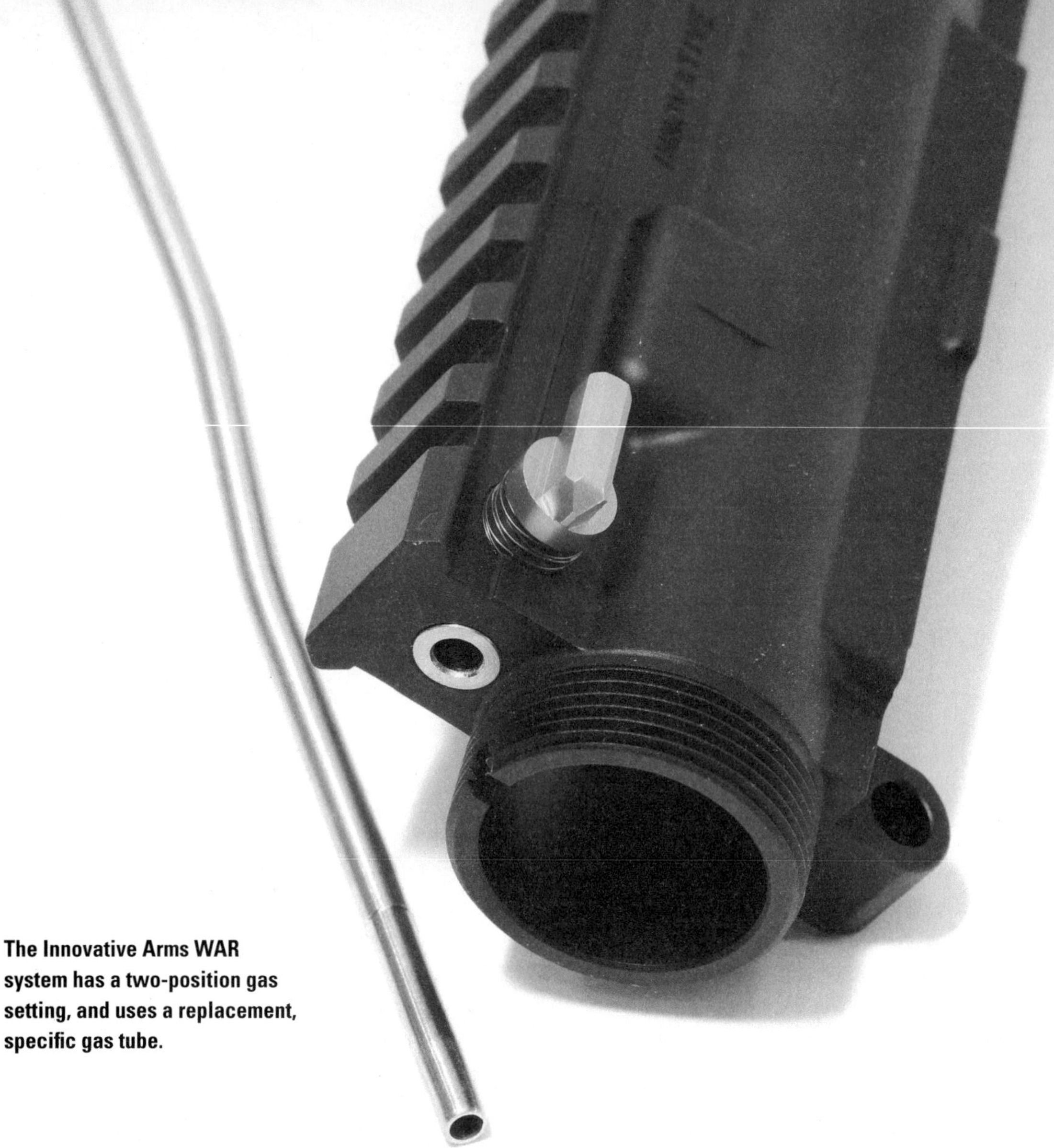

The Innovative Arms WAR system has a two-position gas setting, and uses a replacement, specific gas tube.

Primary Weapons Systems

The PWS rifles and carbines use a long-stroke piston, one where the piston is attached to the carrier. With three or four (depending on the era it was made) settings, and removable for cleaning, it makes shooting suppressors fun.

Colt Competition

Not Colt themselves, but a private company that has licensed the Colt name, offers improved rifles. They offer rifles with an adjustable gas system, using a knurled knob out on the gas block. You can adjust the gas system to ease gas flow with a suppressor, or to tune it for use in competition, to make recoil less "thumpy."

Ruger

If you had walked into a gun shop a few years ago and said, "I want to buy an AR-15 rifle made by Ruger," they would have laughed themselves silly. But now, Ruger is a big player in ARs, and makes both piston and DI rifles. The piston guns have adjustable gas systems, so you are covered there, and they even made them with flash hider that could accept a suppressor (think Gemtech Halo) or with threaded muzzles.

Some piston systems are not user-adjustable, but are self-regulating. This makes it a bit difficult to predict which will be happy with suppressors and which will not. Add to that the constant change we are currently in (some AR makers have changed/upgraded their lines two or three times just in the short time I've been working seriously with suppressors), and what is true when I write this, might not be when you read it. So, I'm letting you know what I have that I have experience with.

Not all adjustments are made on the rifle, in the gas system. Some approaches come at it, literally, from other directions.

Sun Devil

The ADIGS is a replacement gas tube. You have to either replace the existing gas tube key on your carrier, or build a new one with the Adigs, and install your bolt into the new carrier. At the back of the key is an adjustment nut, and you dial this until you have the correct gas flow with a suppressor. This is not an "on the fly" adjustment. You're either set for suppressors, or you are set for un-suppressed.

Gemtech

Gemtech offers a replacement carrier, but the adjustment here is an either/or setting. You simply use a screwdriver to rotate the adjustment (on the side of the carrier) to suppressed or un-suppressed. You have to remove the carrier from the upper to do this, but that isn't much of a problem. And, since you have to remove it from the upper, that reduces the chances that someone can reach in with a screwdriver or knifepoint, and turn your setting, just because they are bored.

A 9mm suppressor, in many instances, can be used with a .300 Blackout rifle, provided you use subsonic ammo.

Innovative Arms

The WAR upper from Innovative uses a different approach. The upper is made with a special gas tube, and a lever on the side of the upper indicates which gas flow setting you have, suppressed or un-suppressed. You can turn it one way or the other, your choice, without having to take anything apart, unload and disassemble, or use a special tool.

Adjustments to avoid

There are adjustable gas flow gas blocks you can install on your AR. They are made for competition use, avoid them. The idea is simple, a competition shooter is using a muzzle brake and wants to minimize recoil. So they will develop a competition load, and use it and only it. They will then install an adjustable gas block and keep throttling back the gas flow until the rifle just barely locks open when the mag is empty. Then give it a bit more gas. This way, they reduce or eliminate the "thump" of the carrier and buffer bottoming out in the buffer tube.

This makes the rifle more sensitive to being dirty, but they will start each match with a clean rifle anyway, so no problem.

If you do this, and you adjust your gas flow to be comfortable in recoil with a suppressor, guess what? When you take the suppressor off, the rifle will short-stroke.

Remember, suppressors turn noise into heat, and with great efficiency. After only one magazine, the oil is already smoking off this suppressor, which wasn't very oily to start with.

One suppressor to quiet them all

You've heard of "off-label use" right? There's a great joke about it on Big Bang Theory. Bernadette is recounting how their new drug, which was supposed to be their great new medicine for heart problems, caused "anal leakage." Oops. So they marketed it as a constipation cure instead. (Apologies if anyone found that just a bit too icky.)

Well, doctors know that what may be a side-effect, or a happy byproduct of a drug intended for use in one area, becomes of help in another. This is known as off-label use. Well, we can do that with a suppressor.

Your 9mm/40/45 pistol suppressor, if you are careful and don't forget, can be used as a suppressor on your .300 Blackout, but with subsonic ammo only. Or, your .30 rifle suppressor, once fitted to your AR, works with your .223/5.56 ammo.

But what is really going on? What the manufacturers have found, or tested, or computer modeled, is that the gas flow, speeds, pressures and heats of the other cartridge fall within or close enough to the limits of the original use.

So, your .300 Blk, as far as the suppressor is concerned, is no different than your 9mm. The 9mm peak pressure, per SAAMI, is 34,000PSI. The SAAMI spec for the .300 Blk is 55,000PSI. The .300 Blackout, despite using three times as much powder, has an operating pressure in its subsonic loadings of 27,000 to 35,000PSI. It uses the max to get the lighter bullets up to max speed, but those pressures are not needed for subsonic. Indeed, they are counter-productive.

So, the pressure difference is why subsonic .300 Blackout is OK in your 9mm suppressor, but supersonic isn't.

And, here's a tip: the suppressor manufacturers tested their products with subsonic ammo to make sure it was OK. Then they also tested it with supersonic, to see how and where it breaks. If you shoot supersonic, and break your suppressor, they'll know. So if you are looking to get it repaired, don't fib.

Now, on the matter of a .223/5.56 begin used in a .30 suppressor. Here, it isn't a gas flow or stress situation. The pressures of the .223/5.56 and the .308/7.62 are pretty much the same. They have so much overlap, there isn't a real difference. So, the pressures are close enough to the same. Here, we have a volume disparity, and it is in the favor of the suppressor. The .308 may be using from 35-40 grains of powder. The .223/5.56 could be down in the 24-26 grains range.

Your .30 suppressor will shrug that off like it didn't happen. What you will notice, if you're careful, is that it isn't as quiet as a similar, .223-specific suppressor would be. And why would you expect it to be? The clearance holes in the baffle stack for the .30 suppressor are reamed for clearance for a .308-inch bullet, and you're pushing a .224-inch bullet through? What do you expect?

Of course, you can use something like the Gemtech One, which has changeable front and rear caps. If you want to use it on your .223, you install the .224-inch-specific front cap, and the .223-threaded rear cap. (Make sure you do both.) It will be a quiet can for .223 use. Then, swap the .308-inch-specific front cap and rear cap, and go back to using it on a .308 rifle.

Chapter Fifteen

SIZE, SHAPE, TOLERANCE FOR ABUSE

Not to pick on, or single out Yankee Hill (but I did), I'd expect much the same results from the rest of the suppressor makers in the market today.

So, if what we learned back in Chapter Four is true, that bigger is better, why do manufacturers stick with the same sizes? Why are they all pretty much an inch-and-a-half for rifle calibers, and more-or-less one inch for rimfires?

One thought comes to mind pretty quickly for me, and that is machinery and materials. Yes, you can source the raw tubing for suppressors in 2-inch diameter, but one and a half is going to be more common, and cheaper. And keeping the tolerances tight on a 1.5-inch tube is going to be easier than with a 2-inch tube, which means they can keep down costs. When it comes to the marketplace, cost may not be king, but it does matter.

There's also the law of diminishing returns. We all "know" what it means, but do we really? In essence, it means that up to a certain point, adding more of something increases what you want to get from that system. You want to go faster? Increase the size of the engine in your car/truck/motorcycle. Each added unit of horsepower will increase your top speed by X mph. However, the law of diminishing returns means you will reach a point where each added unit of horsepower nets you less than one X. Why?

It could be one of a host of reasons. The bigger engine could be so much heavier that its weight becomes a problem, and it can't add a full "X" per horsepower. Or, the speeds you've reached increase drag so much you can't get the full benefit of each unit of horsepower. You've gotten so much horsepower wrestled into the system that the tires, or transmission can't handle them, and your frictional or mechanical losses increase. Something is robbing you of the expected boost.

So you increase a suppressor from 1.5 inches in diameter, to 2.0 inches in diameter, and you get how much extra decibel decrease? One? Two? Three? And for that "better" result you have a suppressor that weighs twice as much, and costs half again as much as the 1.5-inch tube.

There is also the matter of balance. If you add too much weight or bulk to the end of the muzzle, your rifle becomes less handy. We've already seen this over time, where the original XM177 carbine tipped the scales at 5.6 pounds. (I have a clone, that's what it weighs.) But now, manufacturers are proud that their M4gery weighs a mere 7.5 pounds. Add optics, a light, and then put a suppressor on the end, and we're past the starting weight of an M1 Garand, M1A/M14 or FAL.

So, for rifles, a 1.5-inch tube, seven or eight inches long (shorter is good, but now that costs you on dB not decreased) and a pound and a half in weight.

Ditto the variables for handgun and rimfire suppressors. There are good mechanical, sound-reduction, materials and costs reasons for there to be a standard size for the differing applications.

Abuse

How sturdy is a suppressor? And how much babying should you give it? The quick answers: very, and not much. And, what is a Sweeney book without some sort of awful or even heinous abuse of firearms? Not much of a book. Can we continue the tradition? Oh, and to give you an idea of just how seriously I approach this, as a risky endeavor, I make sure I have a tactical med kit on hand, in case I have to stop the personal leaking while I call for an ambulance. No kidding, a complete, tourniquet-and-bandages blowout kit, just in case.

To find out if the tradition can be continued and I can stay in one piece, I abused a couple of suppressors. Now, as I've done in the past, I'll tell you right up front, don't do this. These tests were expensive, somewhat hazardous, and potentially very expensive if I were to break a suppressor. But, as Einstein once said, "If we knew what we were doing, it wouldn't be research." I have to also point out that Einstein didn't do anything that was particularly dangerous. He was, after all, a mathematician and physicist, and didn't wire up gizmos or churn chemicals together. He could be a lot more cavalier about R&D results that ended with, "Well, that didn't work out so well."

Sig SDR-5

The first test was done with a Sig SDR-5, their direct-thread LE suppressor, made of various grades of

Without a select-fire lower to use for heat, I had to heat up the Yankee Hill the old-fashioned way, one trigger pull at a time.

stainless steel. I mounted it on a Sig M400 SBR, to maximize the blast and heat. I then zeroed it with a Sig compact red-dot sight, and made sure it was hitting dead-on at fifty yards. (No point in walking farther, 50 is far enough to see if there's a zero shift or accuracy change, with a red-dot sight.) I then did the "mad minute" drill – sixty shots in sixty seconds – except I did it for two minutes. Four magazines, 120 rounds, with shots fired at one-second intervals over two minutes.

At the end, the SDR-5 was smoking hot, and I sat down at the bench and shot another group for zero. Well, as much as I could, through the mirage caused by the hot suppressor. No change in zero, no change in group size. Shooting at this rate pumps the heat into a suppressor, and the IR thermometer showed a temp up near 500 degrees, which will instantly raise a blister.

But, I wasn't done. At a TV filming session I had an opportunity to abuse this same setup on-camera. I also had access to a select-fire lower. So, we scrounged up all the magazines on hand (we hadn't planned on this) and found we had eight of them. We loaded all eight, and the plan was simple; I'd check the zero on a steel silhouette at 200 yards (with the same red-dot as before) before we started. Then, I'd do full-auto mag dumps of all eight mags, in a row, as fast as I could stand to shoot the rifle, and then we'd check zero again.

I had an off-camera assistant take the first empty mag and stuff five rounds into it, for the "after" zero check.

This was work. First of all, I had the foresight to wear a glove on my left hand. The heat, smoke, and back-blast were quite impressive, and when I was done, the IR thermometer, when I trained it on the suppressor, zoomed past 1,000 degrees F (its max reading) so fast I couldn't even see numbers. I then went prone, and tagged the steel without a problem.

Then, to cool it off, I poured water on it. At that temp, the water doesn't even flow off of an object normally, as it would off of a cool one. The heat is so great it instantly causes steam where the water touches it, and the water then flows off the suppressor, supported by a film of steam. It is an interesting optical effect.

I was not surprised by the result. I later spent time on the range, not heating up the suppressor, with a scope on top instead of the red-dot, just to see how much accuracy was left. Any accuracy loss would be more due to the wear on the barrel (that kind of heat really works a barrel hard) and not the suppressor.

Everything was just fine, but I'd bet I took more than the 240 rounds worth of life off the barrel. Probably more like the equivalent of a couple of thousand, semi-auto firing, rounds worth of barrel life.

Yankee Hill Phantom

For this test, I didn't have access to a select-fire lower, and I also didn't want to put all the wear on one barrel. So, I mounted four Yankee Hill QA muzzle devices to four different upper receiver assemblies. My plan was simple; shoot the suppressor hot, then swap to a cool barrel, and continue. The suppressor in question is the Yankee Hill Phantom, made of chromoly steel and Inconel. Yes, not the most expensive, and certainly promising to be the most durable, but can you blame Yankee Hill? I was going to do my level best to essentially trash a suppressor, and make it useable for not much more than a display wreck in the locked case at trade shows. What would you do, send the most expensive one you made? I thought not.

So, off to the range, install four muzzle devices on four uppers, and get to work. Check zeros, before and after, no changes, check. Lots of ammo on hand, check. Oven mitt, check. The first one gets a mad minute, sixty rounds in sixty seconds, and the IR thermometer reads 395 degrees. Yowza! Slide on the mitt and unscrew the suppressor. Ow, ow, OW!

"Dammit, Jim, I'm a doctor, not an assistant machine gunner." (Bonus points if you know that reference, and laughed.) Your basic oven mitt isn't made for that kind of heat, at least not for the hand pressure needed to unscrew a suppressor. I'm not going to go through this for every swap of the suppressor, especially when it gets even hotter. Time to re-think this.

If I'm going to toast a barrel, I'd better toast a crappy one. And I have just the candidate. A take-off, it came off of a police officer's carbine in a class, and it is wondrously bad. Not in that it is inaccurate, but in that the front sight is held on by friction and four tiny setscrews. It won't withstand any rough handling without the front sight slipping, and this mis-aligns the gas tube with the gas port, and then it stops cycling. To get it working again, you have to bang the front

This is a more leisurely testing of the Sig 556 suppressor. I did this at the Sig Academy, and the clever fellows there only handed me two magazines for each firearm.

Here is the mount for the Yankee Hill suppressor, after some of the abuse.

Running over the Yankee Hill in sand made no impression. Except in the sand.

What looks like marks are simply bits of sand clinging to the Yankee Hill.

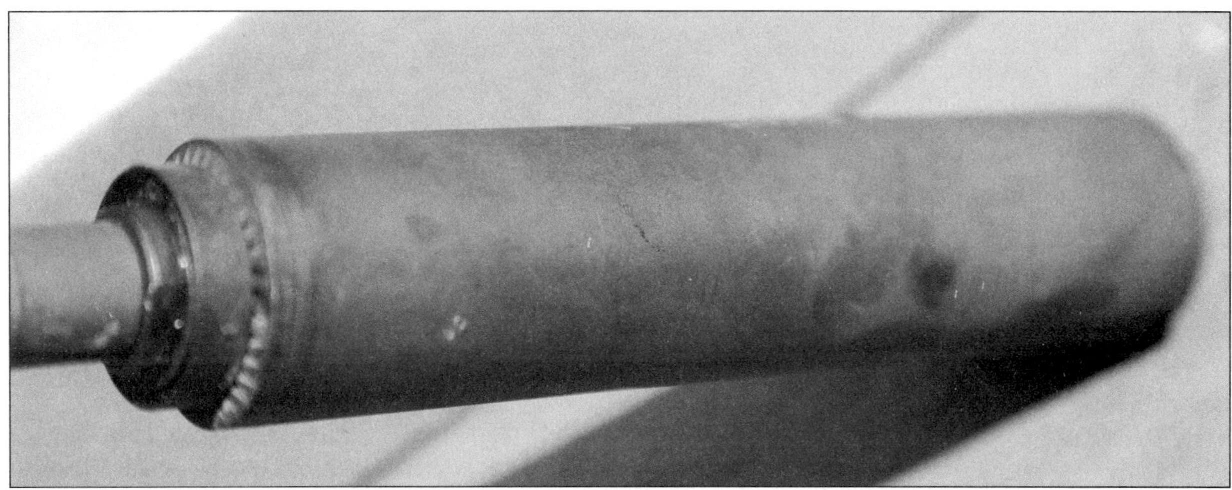

The first heating episode left the exterior mottled in color, from the metal reacting. No change in accuracy or function.

sight assembly back into position. This also changes the zero, so even when the rifle is working you can't hit anything.

So, I move on to other things for that range trip, and take all the uppers with Yankee Hill QA mounts home to rebuild for the test.

I build an upper using that bad barrel, and put it on one of my SBRs. I mount the Yankee Hill muzzle device on, and proceed to thrash the barrel and suppressor. I heat it up, I douse it with cold water. I heat it up again, I leave it in the sun to bake. I periodically swap it (cool) back to the first upper, which happened to be my Colt, and check accuracy. No problems.

As a preliminary to the full-on abuse, I took a couple of test runs, driving my car over the suppressor. No problem, it shrugged that off like it didn't happen. Then again, my gun club parking lot is either sand, or grass-covered gravel. Not the worst environment.

I took the rifle to an LE class, and during one of the demos, worked it hard. One of the class demos is to have an array of rifles on the line, each with its own target. All the students cycle through all the rifles, firing on the target, to get a feel for the differences between various barrel lengths, sights, and in this case, suppressor. Also, the composite target of all students using one rifle on one target demonstrates that a "pool" gun is a possible, but not desirable, approach.

Once they were done, and the rifle and suppressor were good and hot, I then fired the class qualification course, and posted a clean score.

Next, and once it had cooled enough to handle, I used some duct tape to cover the front and rear opening, and put a small piece over the serial number. I then tossed it out into the gravel driveway leading to the range, and let (actually, encouraged, and guided) the officers to drive over it with their vehicles. One kept a close eye out of his window, stopped on the suppressor, and then gunned it. He tossed the suppressor out into the roadway.

I had to dash out, pick it up, and toss it back into the driveway, where several other officers tried the same thing, but didn't succeed. They did drive over it, however. There were a couple of officers who were too squeamish to drive over it, and they actually veered around it. Imagine that, not abusing equipment.

Once they were all in the parking lot, I picked up the suppressor, peeled the tape off the rear, mounted it, and shot the qual course again. Clean.

Of course, I had to heat it up once again, if for no other reason than to melt the duct tape and make it even uglier than it had become.

Through all this, the Yankee Hill Phantom did not change zero, change accuracy level, or do anything but stubbornly resist my efforts. The exterior is scarred, gravel-marred, and has the residues of melted duct tape on it. The flash hider/muzzle mount is green with oxidized copper, from being doused to cool it. The barrel is probably done for, but I'm going to see if I can scrub it clean inside, install a low-profile gas block, and use it with optics.

After even more use and abuse, I set the rifle aside for a while. When I got back to it, the suppressor was

Second go-around at heat, and we can quickly run the suppressor temp up to 358 degrees Fahrenheit.

Duct tape, while protecting the serial number from marring and keeping gravel out of the tube, doesn't react well to heat.

Now, run it over in a gravel parking lot, and you start getting some results.

Some police officers gleefully ran over the Yankee Hill, others avoided it.

With a short respite from abuse, the mount had time to rust, locking the Yankee Hill suppressor in place. Everything still worked.

rusted to the mount. I checked accuracy, it hadn't changed. So, I simply clamped the suppressor in my bench vise (stop cringing, you know how this goes) and forced it off the mount.

The lesson of all this: suppressors can be very tough. You might want to keep it in good repair, but you do not need to store it in a velvet-lined lockbox, and carefully dust it off after every round is fired. It isn't made of candy, it won't melt in the rain.

A "wet" suppressor is something else entirely, as we've discussed.

Chapter Sixteen

EQUATIONS AND STRESSES

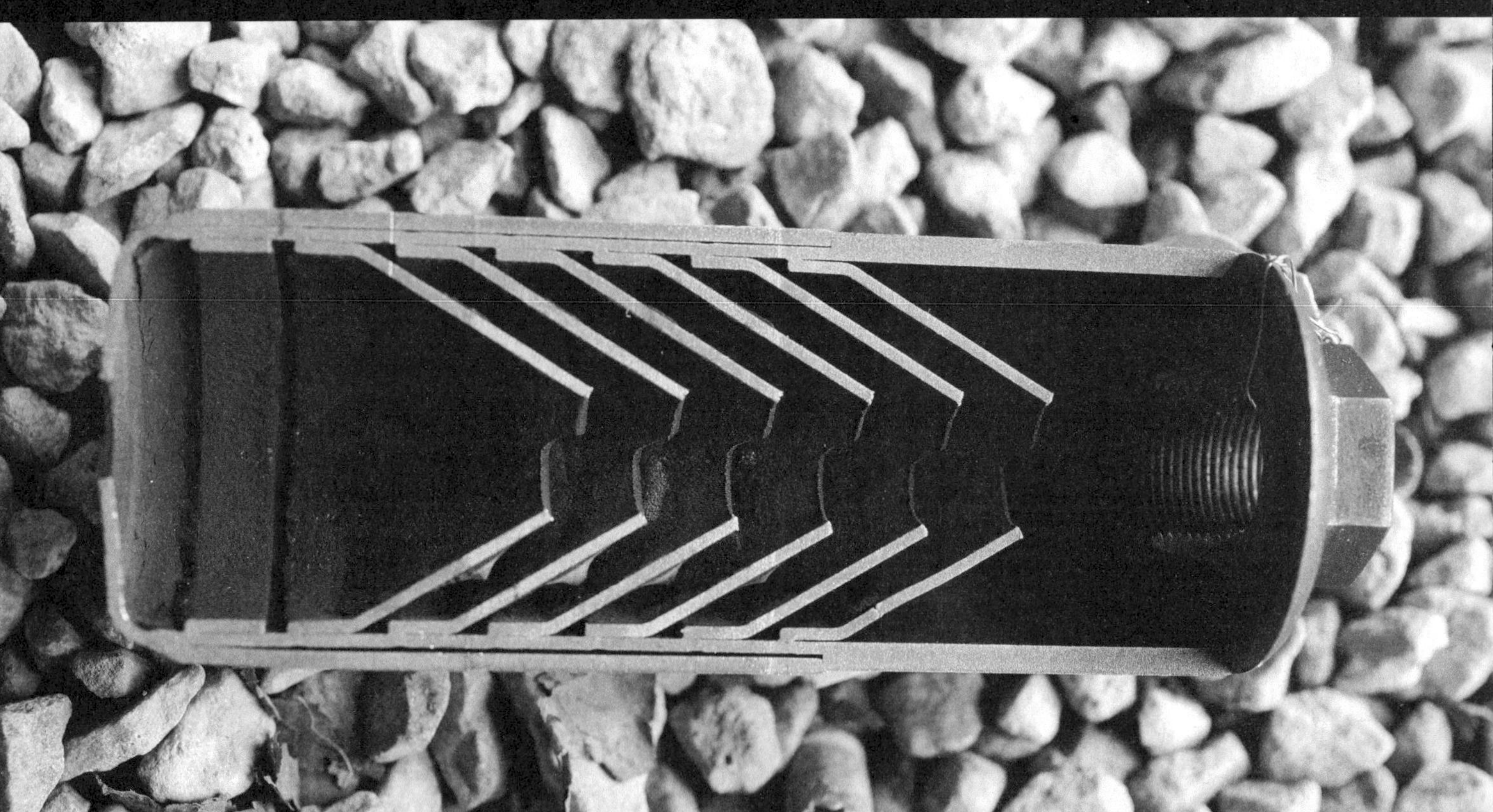

Hoop stress is greatest in the expansion chamber, where the bullet exits the bore, and the gases first expand. (On the right, in this suppressor.)

The gas laws

Since we'll be discussing them, we should know what they are and what they tell us. Let's start with the first, from a guy by the name of Robert Boyle, an Irishman in the 17th century who determined the relationship between volume and pressure.

Essentially, if you keep the mass constant, then when you increase volume, pressure goes down, and vice-versa. The equation:

$PV = k$

P is pressure, V is volume, and k is the constant. The constant k is not an absolute number, like the speed of light. It is whatever it is. So, if you take a scuba bottle, and you have filled it to a certain pressure, say, 200 PSI, and you hook it up to another, empty bottle, and valve them together, you end up with two bottles with 100 PSI each. You say, "duh, of course," but this was not obvious before Boyle proved it experimentally.

This works for us along with an aspect of firearms and internal ballistics called the "expansion ratio," which is, in essence, the ratio of the case capacity to the bore capacity. Let's get our heads out of the tactical realm for a bit and take as an example a couple of hunting cartridges: the .308 Winchester and the .300 Winchester Magnum. The case capacity of the .308 is around 54 grains of water, while that of the .300 is around 91. The powder that burns in a case has the length of the barrel to expand and accelerate the bullet. If we take the comparative volumes, we can see that a .300 WM rifle would have to have a barrel that was two-thirds longer to have the same expansion ratio. If they start with the same chamber pressure, Boyle's Law tells us that in order to have the same muzzle pressure as a .308 rifle with a 20-inch barrel, the .300 Win Mag would have to have a barrel that was 33 inches long. Since the .300 does not, it will have a higher muzzle pressure than the .308 does, and that is why your .30 suppressor may be rated for a 16-inch .308, but with the .300 WinMag it will not be warrantied by the manufacturer on any barrel shorter than 24 inches.

It also explains why your 9mm carbine or .22LR rifle is so quiet. Look at that stubby case. Look at that 16-inch barrel. The expansion ratio is off the charts.

Next up is Jacques Charles, whose assertion was actually proven by another Frenchman by the name of Gay-Lussac. Here, we take the same vessel that Boyle described, but instead of varying the volume, we change the temperature. Charles' law:

$$\frac{V}{T} = k$$

Where volume divided by temperature equals a constant. So, we take our scuba bottle at 200 PSI and we leave it lying on the fantail of the dive boat in the hot tropical sun. When we check it before going into the water, it reads 300 PSI, but when we hit the "relatively" cool water, the pressure reading drops back to 200 PSI. The air inside did not change except in its temperature. The internal air mass did not change, pressure changed when we pumped heat into it. And then it dropped when we sucked the heat out.

Gay-Lussac further refined this, when he came up with the smashing idea that the pressure is linked to the absolute temperature. Well, for us working with suppressors it isn't a really obvious thing, but it does tie things up. Basically, with any given mass and volume, pressure is directly related to temperature.

This leads us to the Ideal Gas Law, which takes all the previous work, plus the efforts of an Italian Chemist and Count, Avogadro, forces them into one law, and makes them play well with each other. The Ideal Gas law:

$pV = kNT$

Where pressure times volume equal the number of gas molecules k, times the absolute temperature T, and N, the Boltzmann constant. What? Who is Boltzmann, and how did he get in here? He was a physicist, and his contribution is the physics-chemistry equivalent of an accounting shortcut, statistical mechanics, to clean up the various things that can cause our calculations to go kerflooey.

But, we're getting deep into the weeds here. So I'll leave you with this thought; you go through school, and in a lot of instances, some wise-cracking slacker will comment "We'll never use this, why learn it?" Well, if you had paid attention to the Ideal Gas Law when you were going through physics class, you'd have been able to comment intelligently on the New England Patriots and Deflategate.

Knowledge is kind of like a firearm; you never know when or where you're going to need to use it. If you have it, and you need it, cool. If you need it and you don't have it, you're in trouble.

In the interests of going completely over the top, and seeing who can keep up (not that it's a contest or anything) I have to say; we're not done. If you really want to get a handle on how this works, you have to take into account that simple fact of heat, something the various gas laws don't address as closely as we'd like. In this step, we consider not what heat you pump in, or the changes in temperature you get with a corresponding correction in the system. No, we'll consider what you do when the system itself creates heat. That's right combustion.

For that, we have to go to a refinement of the Ideal Gas Law, known as the Noble-Abel equation of state. And just so we don't have a whole branch of firearms physics described by a bunch of French experimenters and mathematicians, Sir Andrew Noble, a Scottish artillerist, and Sir Frederick Abel, an English chemist (real chemist, not a pharmacist), worked to first improve the performance of black powder and then solve some of the thorny problems with the first smokeless powder the British adopted, cordite.

Our problem here is we have to account for the fraction of the mass that is converted to gases, i.e., burned, and the mass of the combustion gases created. I'm going to risk exploding your brain by introducing a simple concept, but one that defies many who try to grapple with it: the molar equivalent, or the Avogadro constant. Instead of dealing with mass we are dealing with the constant number of molecules. If you have one mole (the scale used for Avogadro's number, as it used to be called when I went to school) of hydrogen, and one mole of water, you have two different masses. But you have the same number of constituent particles, atoms or molecules, in each.

If you go through chemistry or physics, you will wake up in the middle of the night, sooner or later, shouting "six point zero, two, two, times ten to the twenty-third power," that's how many atoms/molecules are in one mole.

The Noble-Able equation of state is:

$$pV = \frac{C_0 ZRT}{V}$$

Where we have our good old stand-bys, pressure and volume, but we have a few new things to explain. C-zero is the co-volume, the combined volumes of the burnt and unburnt powder, and R-prime acts to control for the heat generated.

The ideal gas law does a good job accounting for the changes in a system, as long as the intermolecular forces are weak in the gas under consideration, and the densities are low. However, it does not do so good a job when you have hot, dense, gases, such as those in the chamber of a firearm, right after you've dropped the hammer.

What? Where'd this come from? As much as I'd like to thank the automotive industry for this, as with so many things, I can't. While you are designing (or refining) an internal combustion engine, the basic Ideal Gas Law doesn't do you much good when you are also burning a given amount of gasoline at the peak of compression. But, the Noble and Abel efforts on interior ballistics were being discussed in the end of the 19th century, before automobiles came about. Then, it was being used mostly to calculate artillery ballistics, with the still relatively new smokeless powders.

They are still being referenced today, with all sorts of high-energy combustion, explosive and ballistics applications.

You can relax now, the hard part is over.

Durability

Suppressors are a lot tougher than a lot of people seem to think, but they still have limitations, and they still need to be taken care of. What are the stresses that a suppressor is subjected to? In short, the impact/thrust of the blast of gasses, the heat, and the oxidation that happens at extreme heat and in acidic environments.

When you fire your firearm, your suppressor, if only for a moment, emulates those propane cans you see in the rack at the local gas station. They become thin-walled pressure vessels. As such, they can be described by the equations covering stress. Our main concern is hoop stress. Think of the stresses as three arrows. Hoop is the arrow going straight out from the axis of the bore, at a right angle in all directions to the line of travel of the bullet. The cylinder of your suppressor is being stretched, and the stress can be significant. The other stresses are the circumferential stress, basically the expansion of the cylinder's circumference, and lateral, the attempted stretching of the cylinder in the direction of bullet travel.

Now, the stack of propane bottles you see at the gas station are sturdy for the job they do. They aren't that thick-walled, but then they aren't subjected to that much pressure. Depending on the size and application, they are pumped to 100 or 200 psi of propane. Compared to the (just a rough starting point for our discussion for now) 12,000 psi of a muzzle blast, that's puny. Also, the propane cylinder receives that pressure as a constant, where the interior of your suppressor is basically subjected to a low-grade explosion on each shot. It has to be tough.

How can we calculate hoop stress? The following equation:

$$\sigma_\theta = \frac{F}{tl}$$

(OK, I lied, the hard part isn't over just yet.)

Where the Hoop stress (delta, subscript theta) is equal to the force exerted on the walls of the cylinder, divided by radial thickness of the cylinder and is the length of the cylinder. Before your head explodes, let me clarify; this is the total stress, and we're interested in the momentary stress, at the highest point of stress. So, we simplify. We take some mathematics developed by a couple of French math wizards in the early 19th century, Young and Laplace, modify them with the work of Gauss, and throw in a dash of Bernoulli. Warning; if you want to know all the gory details, you'll have to spend about two years on college-level math to get through the differential equations needed.

Or, you can simply use the equation below:

$$\sigma_\theta = \frac{Pr}{t}$$

Where the hoop stress, delta subscript theta, is described as the pressure P, multiplied by the inside radius of the cylinder, r. Divide that by the wall thickness, t, and *viola* you're there. Let's take the hoop stress formula for a ride, shall we? We'll assume you have the standard inch-and-a-half diameter rifle suppressor, and for this exploration we'll call it the Super-Duper-Tactical, and our first run is the V1. Also, let's take our starting assumption for pressure, 12,000 psi, at the muzzle. If your suppressor has a wall thickness of a quarter-inch, then we have:

$$\sigma_\theta = \frac{12{,}000X0.625}{0.250}$$

Which gives us a hoop stress of 24,000 psi. Given that the tensile strength of a good grade of steel can be as low as 65,000 psi (a low-alloy annealed steel) and as much as 200,000 (full heat-treated 17 stainless alloy)

The CRC handbook has been a staple for nearly a century, but it will tell you about elemental metals, and not many alloys.

this isn't really all that much. A basic engineering principle is that you always allow for an absolute bare minimum of double the tensile strength to the maximum load that will ever be applied. So, our 24K load demands at the very minimum a 48K alloy. No problem, right?

What about heat? As a metal heats up, any metal, its yield strength goes down. That is an unavoidable aspect of physics. Let's assume, just for the sake of argument, that when an alloy in question reaches 1,000 degree Fahrenheit, its tensile strength has been reduced to 40 percent of its original. All of a sudden, our low-alloy steel isn't good enough. The yield strength drops to 26K, marginally better than our hoop stress, and we're risking a burst can.

The 200K alloy, at 40 percent strength, is still triple the amount of the stress. Whew, we're safe there. Other than choosing a more-expensive (hey, you want stronger, you have to pay more money) alloy, can we address this with design? Sure, but it won't be easy. First, we double the wall thickness, and call this one the V2 suppressor. The extra steel gains us both a smaller radius (and thus less "leverage" for the forces to work on) and a thicker wall. But, remember, the wall thickness is the divisor, and we decrease expansion if we make it thicker working on the inside. There, the result is a hoop stress of only 6,000 psi. However, we've doubled the weight of the suppressor.

A sharp reader might call a halt to the proceedings. "Waitaminit, less stress with a smaller expansion chamber?" The formula calculates not the pressure inside the vessel, but the stress experienced by the steel containing it. Thicker walls experience less stress, in part because there is more steel to offset the increased pressure. As for the pressure inside the expansion chamber, we can go back to the equations in the first part of the chapter and calculate them, if we want to.

At this point it may be instructive to point out a favorite acronym of the late Robert Heinlein: TANSTAAFL. That is, there ain't no such thing as a free lunch. So, you can use a low-alloy steel for your suppressor, you just have to make it heavy. Of course, heavy also means it will absorb more heat without zooming up in temperature. That same amount of shooting that ran your V1 up to 1,000 degrees might only run the V2 up to 600-700 or so. (No, in this instance the heating is not linear.)

Let's take a different approach; we'll make the walls thicker, but we'll do it on the outside. Again, we add a quarter-inch, making the walls the same thickness as before, but heavier even more. (Think about it; thicker on the outside is more steel than thicker on the inside. I'll leave it as an independent exercise to figure out how much.)

V3 is 1.75 inches on the outside, with 0.5-inch-thick walls. The hoop stress here is 18,000 psi. What happened? Simple, we have increased the surface area that the expanding gases have to work on, and that area made the difference. We've both added weight and made the stress greater. This is not the direction we wanted to be going.

On the other hand, the increased expansion volume will most-likely make the suppressor quieter.

Welcome to the sometimes bizarro world of the suppressor designer.

So, what the suppressor designer is trying to do is balance performance and cost. A suppressor that is big enough to offer expansion, and thus be quieter, but

A rapidly expanding bubble of hot gases, this is kind of what your suppressor "sees" on each shot. Well, if your suppressor was on the end of a 120mm tank gun, that is. U.S. Army photo by Sgt. Alan Brutus.

Scan from left to right, and you can see how the baffles eroded, at the entry port and the turbulence cut, as the rounds piled up.

not so big it gets in the way. After all, if we took that propane bottle you see at the gas station and made that into our suppressor, it would be really quiet. Clumsy, but quiet.

A designer also has to consider materials. Cheap metal works, but you need more of it. And you pay for the more at a ferocious rate. Another example, and for this one let's step outside of suppressors and steel, and consider the ceiling on your house. Your average 2x4 can hold a certain amount of weight. What if you wanted it to hold more? You could double them up, but you do not double the floor capacity. Each acts pretty much independently, until the stress is distributed across the ceiling (from the floor above) and spread to the adjacent beam. Once a beam reaches its breaking point, it breaks, regardless of how many of them there are in the floor/ceiling.

OK, so you secure them together. You use really good glue and nails, and you make 4x4s. You still don't double their strength. First of all, you've added the weight of the nails and glue to the beam you've made. That comes out of the total weight the beam could support, the net weight. Second, you have a little matter of a rule used in engineering call the "square-cube law." The strength of a beam goes up by the square, the cross-section of the beam. But the weight of it goes up by the cubic volume.

The example I was told, a long time ago in engineering class, is the mouse versus the elephant. You can apparently toss a mouse out of a window of any height, and unless it hits concrete, it will survive the fall. An elephant can't fall more than six feet without being killed. Their weights go up by the cube, the volume, but the structures they are made of, the bones, sinews and muscles, get stronger only by the square, the cross-section.

So, you quickly run out of strength with wood, regardless of how thick you make the beams, and you have to move up in material strength. That's why we make big buildings of steel and concrete today, and use wood for decoration in them. And you never thought to ask why there were no wooden skyscrapers? Shame on you.

Your cheap-steel suppressor can work, but you have

Testing the tensile strength of metals involves a precisely-crafted bar, one that is pulled apart by means of powerful hydraulic presses. Photo courtesy Professor James Higley, Purdue University.

The bad news; Once erosion gets started, it just keeps on "eating" your baffles. The good news: even seriously eroded, it only "loses" a decibel or two.

to make it thick-walled for strength, and thus pay the weight penalty.

Expansion, not to be confused with inflation

When the barrel uncorks, the bullet begins its free-flight travel and the gases expand into the suppressor. As we've discussed before, that expansion is pretty much on the order of a low-grade explosion. One moment, atmospheric pressure, a millisecond later, 12,000 PSI of hot, debris-laden gases. What else gets stressed? The first baffle, for one. The baffle stack does not begin directly off of the muzzle. Experimenters and engineers with elaborate gas flow calculations have determined that a certain amount of space, the first chamber, is needed for best effect.

Just how far forward of the muzzle that first baffle is depends on what you want out of your system. Moving it forwards or back can and will change the characteristics of the suppressor. One direction makes it quieter on average, but increases the magnitude of the first-round pop. A different direction raises very slightly the average, but makes the first-round pop not so noticeable, and much more like the rest of the rounds. It is all in what you want, and what you are measuring for.

But the gas slams into that first baffle with some force. How much? Let's do a first-order estimate of the impact.

The relevant equation here is Boyle's law. Basically, it states that the product of the pressure and volume of any container is constant, given an ideal gas (which propellant gases are not, but we'll save that for later) and a constant temperature. So, you have ten pounds per square inch in a bottle, and you valve the gas into another, equally-sized bottle, and the result is two bottles with five psi in them.

To determine how much impact the first baffle receives, we have to determine a number of variables: first, the volume of the bore and chamber, at the moment of uncorking; next, the pressure at uncorking; finally, the volume of the first chamber.

Let's use a carbine-length barrel, in 5.56. Bore is .224 inch in diameter (we'll ignore the rifling for the moment) and 16.5 inches long. That gives us a volume of 0.650 cubic inches. (I know, it doesn't sound right, but there it is. I checked the math three times.)

The pressure is our old favorite, 12,000 psi.

The volume of the first chamber? Let's assume it is a robustly built 1.5-inch OD suppressor. So, the internal diameter is one inch. The length of the first chamber is two inches. That gives us 1.57 cubic inches.

So, the pressure (at least momentarily) of the first chamber is the uncorking pressure, divided by the volumes of the bore and the first chamber combined. The maximum, first estimate pressure of the chamber is 5,405 psi.

The impact on the first baffle is the pressure multiplied by the surface area of the baffle. So, we take a circle one inch in diameter, and we poke a hole through it for bullet clearance. Let's call that a quarter-inch. That gives us a surface area of the baffle of 0.736 inch, and a maximum impact of 3978 pounds. Impressive, the first baffle takes almost two tons of hit on each shot.

In doing my research, and asking the long-time experts in the field, I received this reply to a different question, which was quite gratifying: "At the moment of firing, there is between 2,000 and 4,000 psi pressure in the entrance chamber pushing on the blast baffle."

Refining our estimate lowers that quite a lot. We'll leave the muzzle pressure figure alone for the moment. In traveling two inches, the gas loses speed and cannot arrive at the baffle with the full 5400 psi. Second, another gas law comes into play, and that is Guy-Lussac's law, where volume and temperature are inverse. That is, when you expand a gas, doing so lowers its temperature. That is why your aerosol can gets cold when you spray with it. So, our gas drops in temperature when it expands into the chamber, and that lowers pressure. It also transfers heat to the walls of the suppressor, lowering pressure even more.

So, the impact is probably half the initial estimate, more like a ton. Which, returning to a different use for gas flow, explains why muzzle brakes work so well.

That stress is not borne solely by the first baffle. Since the baffle is welded (one hopes securely) to the suppressor tube wall, the thrust forward of the impact has to be taken up by stretching of the suppressor wall, and the thread of the muzzle attachment. And now you know specifically why it is so important to have a proper machinist cut the threads to attach your suppressor.

Thermal expansion

Things expand when they are heated. Thermal expansion can be calculated easily (compared to the Federal budget, by comparison). The equation is:

$L = \alpha \times L_1 (T_2 - T_1)$

Where L is the linear expansion, alpha is the coefficient of linear expansion, L_1 is the initial length, and T_1 is the start temperature while T_2 is the heated temperature.

You find the expanded length by using the temperature change, and multiply it against the coefficient of expansion and the initial length. So, you take a ten-mile long length of railway line, welded to be a continuous length. You subject it to a change of temperature of one hundred degrees, and what do you get? Buckeled rail. Why? The expansion compressed the rail at the end where it butted up against something it wasn't welded to, and when the compression load exceeded the buckle-load limit of the steel used, it popped to the side.

Coefficient of expansion is measured either metric or English, so let's do English. We're talking about α (alpha) being 10^{-6} in/in°F, that is, how many inches of expansion, per inch of length, per degree Fahrenheit of temperature increase. And ten to the minus sixth means we're measuring 0.000001 or greater increases. Not a lot, but it adds up.

What happens when we heat up a suppressor? Why, it gets bigger. Let's do some calculations. Let's take a stainless steel rifle suppressor, 1.5 inches in diameter. If we select the stainless alloy 304 (you'll see why in a bit) we can calculate expansion. Just as a mental experiment, let's section it so we make a ring, and then cut the ring and straighten it. We end up with a length of steel that is 4.7124 inches in length (1.5 inches times pi). The linear expansion is 0.04524 inches, so we add that in, wrap the length back into a circle, and calculate backwards to get the new diameter. (We could have built it into the equation, but this way it is a bit more intuitive. I hope.)

We end up with a hoop with a new internal diameter of 1.509 inches, more or less. Nine thousandths doesn't seem like much, but let's see what else happens. Lets insert a baffle stack made of Inconel, and somehow (I haven't any idea how) we weld the stack to the cylinder walls.

The expansion coefficient for 304 is 9.6×10^{-6}, while

Suppressors get hot, and jet hot gases out of the end. And this is nothing, compared to what goes on inside.

that of Inconel is 7.0×10^{-6}. If we assume (and we're making things easy here) a flat disk of Inconel, then the expansion of the disk will be .0105 inch, for a total of 1.5105 inches for the disk. The difference is not much at all, a thousandth of an inch.

But you can make problems for yourself. If you use a complicated baffle design, one that has more mass and length with which to expand, and you select differing materials that have greater differences of thermal expansion than our example, you can set yourself up for trouble. How different can you get? Well, the 304 stainless was 9.6 (we'll drop the scientific notation for the moment) and the Inconel was 7.0.

How about aluminum baffles inside of a titanium tube? Aluminum has a thermal coefficient of 12.3, while titanium, has one of 4.8. If we were to construct such a suppressor, and heat it up to one thousand degrees above ambient, what would we have?

The tube would expand by .0004 inch for a tube of 1.5004 inches diameter. The aluminum baffles would expand to 1.5185 inches, or eighteen thousandths; fourteen thousandths more than the tube would. Is this enough to buckle the baffles? I don't know, and anyone who shoots an aluminum-baffled suppressor up to a thousand degrees can report back.

This is just background info, and I'm laying it out so you can understand when a particular manufacturer is not so hot on your idea of a suppressor design with a

This is what goes on inside of your suppressor, on each and every shot. Photo from New York Air National Guard by Staff Sgt. Christopher S. Muncy.

tube of X material and baffles of Y material "because it would be so light, or so cool, or so tactical."

And, there is a much bigger problem to consider, if you want to make a multi-alloy, really durable suppressor: welds. You've got this great idea – use Inconel baffles inside of a stainless or titanium tube and weld the baffles in place. Well, the coefficient of thermal expansion is so much greater between Inconel and stainless steel that you may find your welds cracking, or the tube buckling, when it cools.

And welding Inconel to titanium? You'd have to be a Jedi Knight of welding to accomplish that. Some metals just can't be welded to each other, and others aren't worth the effort.

Oh, and the buckled railway line? If we take a ballpark steel alloy coefficient of 6.7, and we apply it to a hundred-degree increase and ten miles, we get 35.376 inches of expansion. Just shy of three feet of more rail than the bed was laid for. Back in the days of sections of railway track, they'd leave gaps, and the gaps are what caused the "clickety-clack" of railroads. Today the rails are welded into one continuous length, and the rails are pre-stressed and/or fastened in such a way as to constrain expansion.

Galvanic corrosion

Galvanic corrosion is a whole other bag of worms. Each

The U.S. navy uses cathodic protection to combat corrosion. The USS Fort Worth uses water jets, not props, increasing water exposure, and making it even more important to inspect and protect. U.S. Navy photo by Senior Chief Mass Communication Specialist Donnie W. Ryan.

metal has what is called its anodic index, that being its measure of the electrochemical voltage that will be developed between it and another metal. The index metal is gold. So, if you take a chunk of cast iron, and place it against a gold nugget, the anodic index will be -0.85 volts.

If you place two metals with sufficiently different anodic indexes against each other, the one with the most negative index value will experience accelerated corrosion. You could say, with some truth, that the sacrificial one experiences all the corrosion that both metals would have.

The difference depends on the metals involved, and the effect depends in part on the environment. In a cool, dry environment, you can get away with a greater anodic index differential than you could in a hot, wet, acidic one. (Hmmm, does that second environment sound familiar?)

Let's take an example. Say you have, oh I don't know, a boat. And you have brass uprights bolted to a stainless steel deck, and the brass has an aluminum railing bolted on top. (You did this because you wanted weight down, and lighter stuff up, to keep the center of gravity lower. Weren't you clever.)

Hmm, anodic index of stainless steel: -0.50. Anodic index of brass: -0.40. Anodic index of aluminum: -0.75 to -0.90. If you leave your boat in the air-conditioned warehouse, things will be fine. But once you hit the seas, you'll have trouble. The relative index differential between the aluminum and the brass is at least -0.35, and can be as much as -0.50. That means the brass is going to corrode, and fast. If you left your boat in the cool, dry warehouse, you could get away with that much of an index differential, but where's the fun in that? Out on the open seas, where it will always be wet and salty, you don't want a differential greater than 0.15 between metals. So, swap the aluminum rails for brass, and you'll be better off. Hey, polishing all that brass will give your crew something to keep busy, right?

What does that mean for suppressors? First of all, they are a hot and acidic environment. Second, you'll have them out in the rain, snow, humidity, and maybe even salt air. So, we can't be having an anodic index differential of 0.50, that's for sure. More like the salt-air max of 0.15. Can you believe it? There is even a mil spec for anodic index, and it provides a galvanic table. (Anyone who bets against the Navy or USMC needing this, sit down and do your homework again.) The relevant mil-spec is MIL-STD-889B, and it dates back to 1976.

The U.S. Navy takes this seriously, as drydock costs can be ferocious when you're maintaining a fleet. And it's not just the navy. It is so common to use sacrificial anodes to protect a hull and running gear that you can buy them as a normal item of boat maintenance. Well, not so much bass boats, but anything that goes into salt water, for sure.

What we find is that the really reactive metals don't have much utility in suppressors.

Titanium is so passive (cathodic) that it will never be the sacrificial anode to anything else. At the other extreme, magnesium, zinc, beryllium and cadmium are so anodic they will sacrifice to anything else. All the materials we use, or are on common use, in suppressors are smack-dab in the middle of the galvanic response charts, and there is not much concern. But, in extremely harsh environments, you can see why an end-user might be interested in a suppressor that does not have different metals in it. If it is all titanium, or stainless steel, for example, you cannot have galvanic response problems.

The usual approaches in industry to solve this problem are one or both of two: to select exotic alloys, or to plate. Since we are not going into the aerospace realm when it comes to cost or environmental harshness, there isn't a need to go beyond the usual suspects when it comes to alloys. (And after all, Inconel is a pretty exotic mix already.) The second approach, plating, adds a lot of work and cost to a simple (relatively speaking) engineering problem. Yes, you could plate baffles with something like hard chrome or NP3, but the protection is limited. The first time you scratch the plating through, or drop one and dent it, the break in the coating will be the point of attack. The abrasion of the gases and particles inside the suppressor will erode the plating pretty quickly.

And are we all going to be using suppressors in the surf zone, in burst mode, and cooling them off by letting the salt spray suck the heat away? (Maybe in a video game.)

So, as fascinating as galvanic response is, it is not something we have to worry about, much.

Full-auto rating

What does this mean, and why does it matter? A rifle firing in full auto presents a suppressor with all the problems at once. It is going to be hammered repeatedly by the gas expansion (as a matter of fact, at the cyclic rate of the firearm). It is going to be heated, because there isn't time to cool between shots, and probably not much, if any, time to cool between bursts. And then once it is hot, the loss of strength that happens with heat gets hammered some more, by the next burst and the next.

So those who make their suppressors stout enough to stand up to it will say so. This means exotic materials, sometimes. And thicker walls and cross-sections. Sometimes. It may take the form of an external reinforcement, a ribbed or pierced sleeve that was heat-shrunk on the rear of the suppressor.

The rule of thumb here is simple: unless the manufacturer specifically says it is rated for full-auto fire, it isn't. Now, for most of us this is a moot point. We don't own a full-auto gun, and if we did, and could afford to feed it, the rating of a suppressor wouldn't be a big deal. Except it would. If you over-heat a suppressor that isn't rated for full-auto fire, and it sags, buckles or warps and you get a baffle strike, it could be bad, with fragments of literally red-hot metal flying. At the least, you lost the suppressor. Worse, you could damage the heinously expensive and nearly-impossible-to-replace machine gun. And you could get injured.

Two things come to mind. One is the range day where the gun club guy who owns a machine gun shows up and someone gets the bright idea, "Hey, what does a suppressed machine gun sound like?" Is your suppressor full-auto rated? If not, politely decline the chance. The other is the Slide-Fire stock. Since it pretty easily mimics a machine gun, you can create machine gun-like conditions for your suppressor. Again, if your suppressor is not full-auto rated, turn down this opportunity to show off.

Much beloved of poets and noir cinema directors, fog is humidity you can see. This is one of the times when it varies from being an ideal gas, not that it matters much to us.

Ideal gas

All fraternity jokes aside, what is an "ideal gas?" In physics-speak, it is a gas that has only elastic collisions, random motion, and no chemical interactions or phase transitions. Most gases act pretty much as ideal gases within some range of their existence. Some are quite obnoxious in that they have no regard for our interest.

An example of a gas that screws with the gas laws would be water vapor. In a certain range of pressures and temperatures, it is close enough to being an ideal gas. But, move too far from that range and you get problems such as condensation. Oops, there went your gas, it is now fog or dew.

For our purposes, all the gases we'll be dealing with are ideal gases, as defined by the various physical, chemical or thermodynamics laws.

Thermal transfer

This one is instinctively obvious, but still bears a bit of discussion. Heat moves. Some things, it moves through faster than others. Your hot barrel radiates heat to the aluminum forearm, and you have to wear gloves. The plastic M4 handguards don't conduct heat as readily as aluminum, so your hand stays cooler, longer. The thermal conduction rate of materials is something we take advantage of in suppressor design. By sucking heat out of the gases, we cool them and make the noise less. But, there's a cost. (Isn't there always?)

We risk getting burned. Suppressors get hot, and you forget that at your peril. So, we want to keep them from burning us. Also, the heat radiating off of the suppressor transfers heat to the air. Hot air rises, which can be put to a useful purpose, as the Montgolfier brothers proved

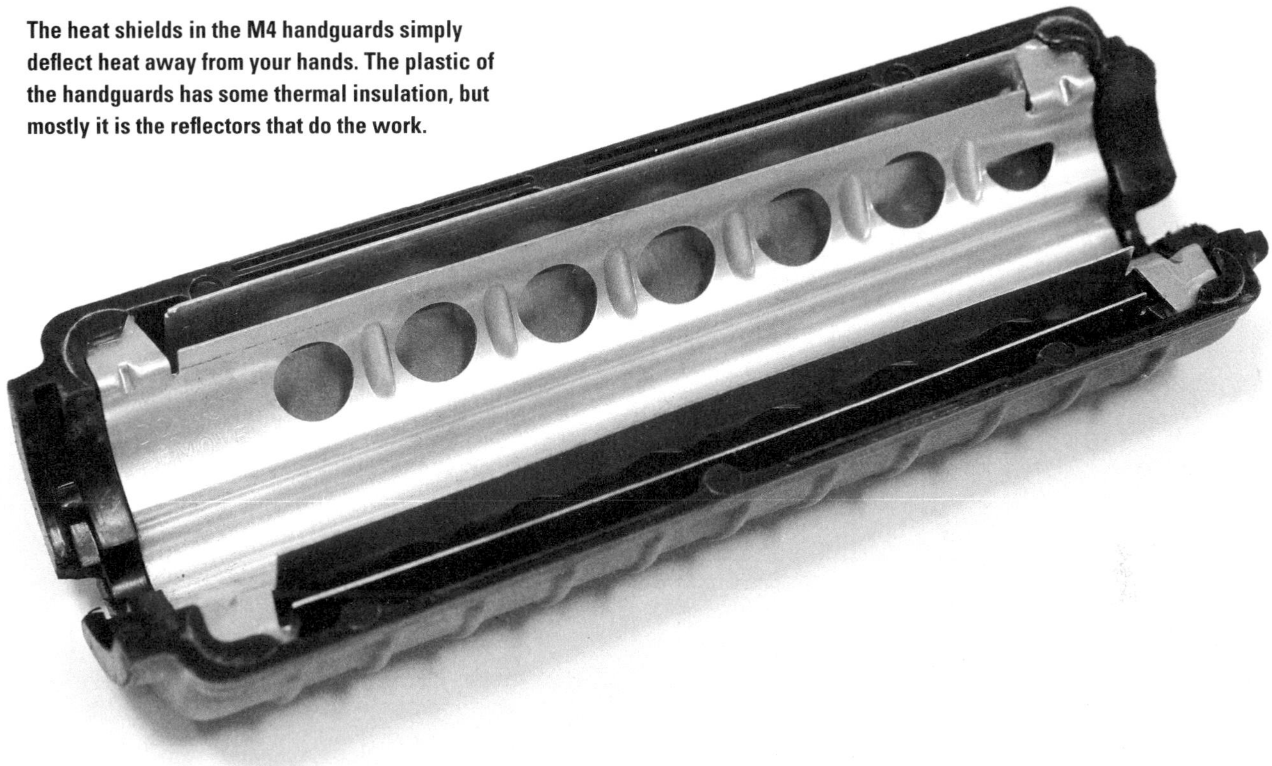

The heat shields in the M4 handguards simply deflect heat away from your hands. The plastic of the handguards has some thermal insulation, but mostly it is the reflectors that do the work.

in France in 1783. For our uses, the hot air causes mirage, which can be a distinct hindrance to aiming. For that reason, we wrap that rascal and put a suppressor cover on it. Made of a material that does not conduct heat at all well, the suppressor cover slows the rate of air-cooling, and decreases mirage. It can't eliminate it entirely, as the front cap of the suppressor is still open, as is the barrel.

And, for those of you who think everything can be solved with some duct tape, fuggedaboudit. Any cloth you use, unless it is specially designed for heat, will char or melt. Oh, you can probably strip the layers out of an old Kevlar vest (but why would you want to?) and have it survive a bit longer than anything else. But in the end, and quickly, it will give up the ghost. No, you have to have specialized gear for this sort of task.

You need a purpose-built suppressor cover.

Manta

Starting as a rail cover company, with the intention of also managing light switches and other gear, the Manta guys took advantage of the thermal properties of modern polymers to produce rail covers and suppressor covers that are very heat resistant. How tough are they? They make a barrel cover that fits on the outside of an M2HB barrel, just forward of the carry handle. Yep, a cover to keep a hot .50 machine gun barrel from burning the AG who is changing barrels.

Here, there is no outer sleeve covering a thermal barrier. They just mold the whole thing in one piece. And you have a choice of three colors or camo.

Armageddon Gear

Armageddon Gear makes a suppressor cover that has a nylon outer cover and an inner insulation liner. Why the two? Simple, nylon is easy to cut, sew, wrap and dye into interesting camouflage patterns. The inner liner is the heat-resisting part of it, and that you can't dye. Now, the folks at Armageddon Gear make great stuff, but they are also straight up about what their gear will and won't do. They intend it to control mirage. As such, while it will protect you and your gear, they can't guarantee that,

The interior is ribbed, both to make it easier to install and to provide air flow for cooling.

Manta makes suppressor covers, rail covers and other goodies. They are made of a synthetic that is so heat-resistant that you probably could make a lava surfboard out of it.

so they don't. You can still burn yourself with a hot suppressor.

Also, since the ends are open and there's only so much they can do to wrap that rascal, they will tell you that it controls mirage, it doesn't eliminate it.

And finally, they do not rate their suppressor cover for full-auto use. Having heated up more than one suppressor with full-auto shooting, I'd be leery of anyone who says their cover is fine with it.

Sounds good to me, and you have your choice of seven colors or camo patterns.

Griffon Industries

Six color or camo patterns, four lengths, wrapped in shock cord to keep them tight on your suppressor, Grif-

Armageddon Gear makes suppressor covers, and they are nearly indestructible.

You can see why you can't escape mirage, just slow it down. The suppressor has to poke out the end of the cover, or bullets can't leave, and that means heat can escape.

fon Industries makes suppressor covers that will make your gun club buddies envious. They also make an enticing line of gear for your AR – mag pouches, holsters, sights and bags – that will risk melting your credit card.

A suppressor cover slows down the inevitable, but inevitable it is. Physics wins, heat wins, and you'll have to either stop shooting and let the suppressor cool down, or keep fighting the mirage. If you do stop, also understand that the very cover that slowed down the onset of mirage will slow down the cooling you desire.

Life is like that.

Rainman

How to keep water, snow and mud out of the muzzle? The front-end opening of your suppressor.

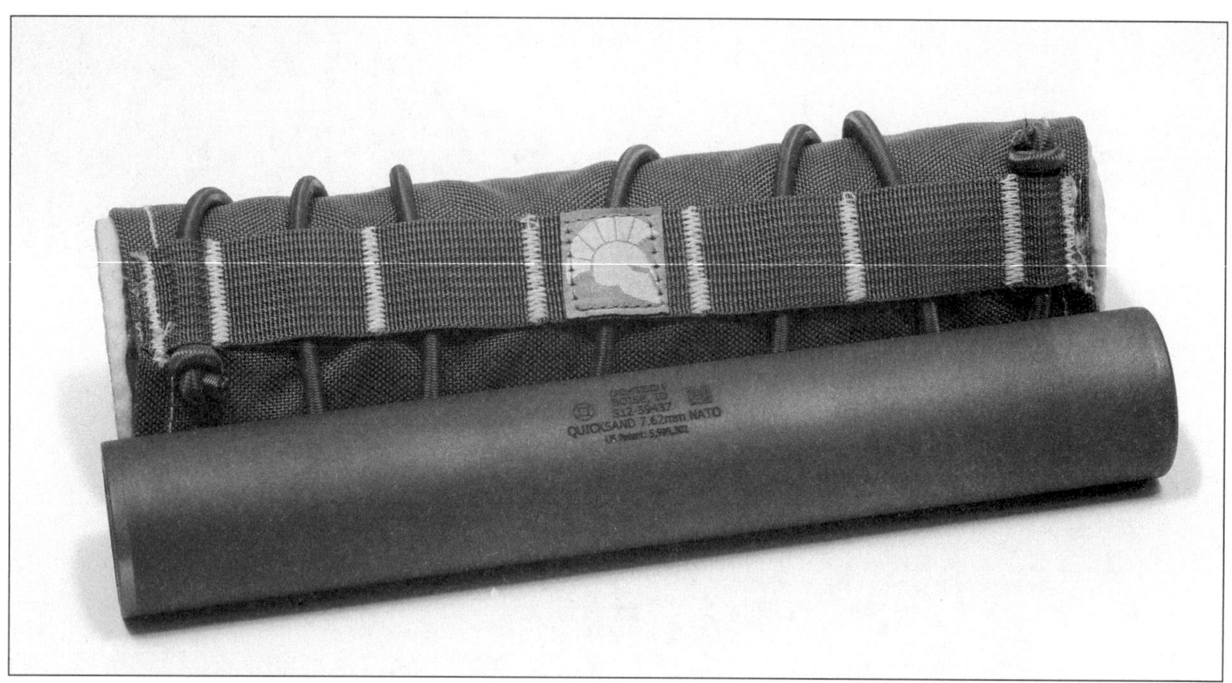

Griffon Industries suppressor cover, next to a big titanium .30 suppressor. Wrestle the cover over the can and have fun.

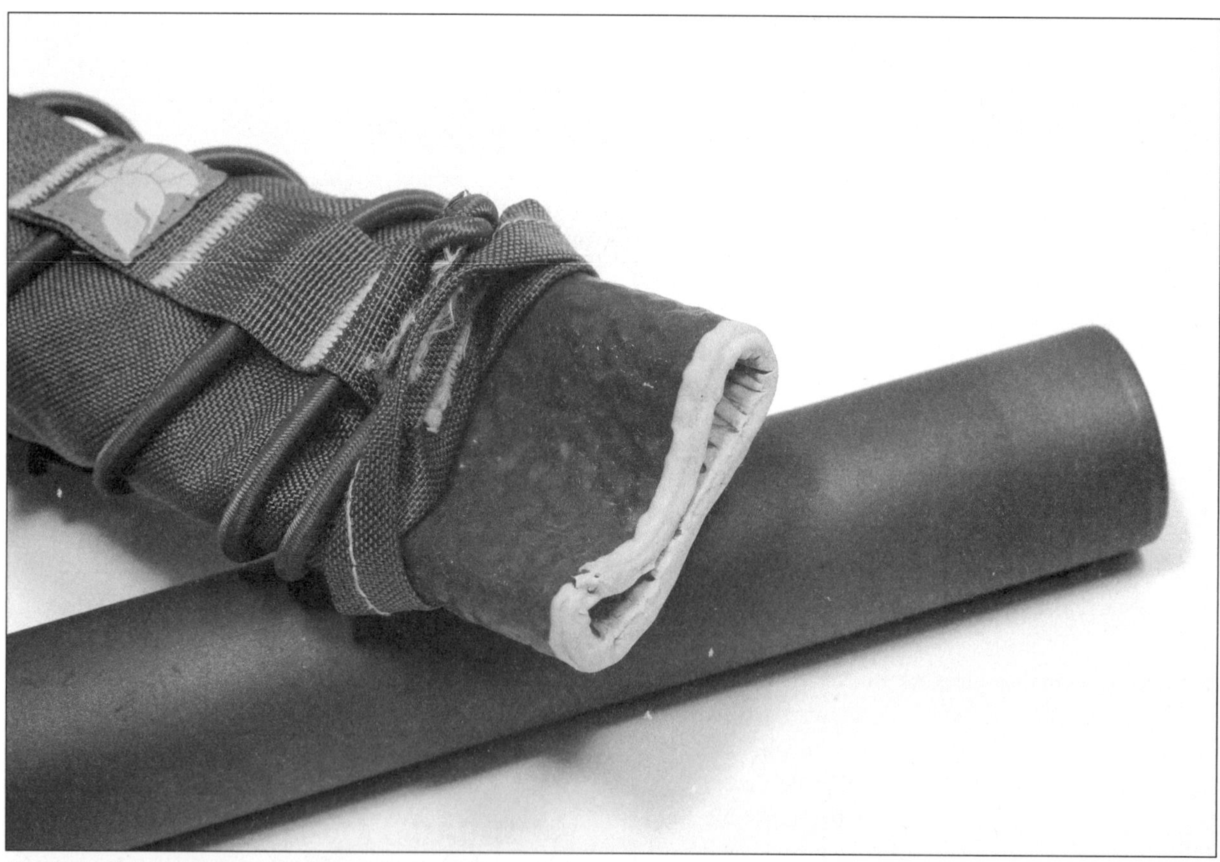

The Griffon Industries cover, with the nylon peeled back to show the insulating liner. Tough stuff.

The McMaster-Carr endcap, one that costs a pittance, keeps rain, mud, snow and other stuff out of your suppressor.

Back when my father was getting the walking tour of northern France and Germany, he and his cohorts used government-supplied condoms. (They didn't have many occasions to use them in the expected role.) They slipped them over the muzzles of their rifles, machine guns, smgs, etc., and kept the rain out.

The common external diameter of rifle and many pistol-caliber suppressors is one and one-half inches. The McMaster-Carr round cap, flexible vinyl, with an I.D. to accommodate a 1.5-inch suppressor, with an internal height (length over the end of the suppressor) of 1.5 inches is part # 9753K72. The cost is $9.00 for a box of twenty-five caps. Thirty-six cents seems like a paltry price to pay to keep the muzzle of the suppressor clear, and to prevent the inevitable mess of various tapes.

If the cap is left on, it will simply be blown off of the suppressor on the first shot. The low mass and large area will limit travel distance and velocity.

You can go crazy with the McMaster-Carr catalog or web page, and order up a box of "suppressor condoms" for everything you own, in specific diameters. They will all be black, however.

Chapter Seventeen

HOW TO BUY ONE

The popularity of suppressors has caused a growth in the number of outlets where you can buy them. Gun shops that were "01 dealers" only had to add an SOT to their license wall, and then they could begin selling suppressors. As a measure of their popularity, you can now find suppressors in the Brownells catalog.

Buying is easy. Frustrating because of the wait and the paperwork, but easy.

First, do you have the money? Suppressors aren't cheap, even an "inexpensive" .22LR suppressor can cost more than the rifle or handgun you are putting it on. And, you have to have a suppressor-ready firearm. Do you have one of those? No? Then can you afford to also buy a gun onto which you can put the suppressor?

Second, do you live in a state that allows them? In a lot of areas of the legal landscape, the federal government has been more than happy to trump state law. There was that whole 55 mph on the freeways thing, a while ago. Oh, a state could tell the federal government, "We don't think 55 is right, we're going to post a higher limit." The federal response was simple, "OK, but you aren't getting a dime of federal money for road building, maintenance, and anything else we can think of, relating to roads, while you are over 55."

Federal law has a path to buying a suppressor, but they won't insist on it over the objections of a given state or local jurisdiction. So, if your state doesn't permit it, the Feds won't help you. "Application denied, money refunded."

So, the first two hurdles? Money and state.

Next is your own background. Have you bought a gun recently from an FFL holder? Or do you hold a CPL? If so, cool, you have already gone through the kind of background check the ATF will do on you for your suppressor application. If you passed those, you'll pass the next. If you haven't, then you have to do some deep thinking about your past behavior. Be honest with yourself. Ever been arrested? Ever skipped on child support payments? DUI? Have you ever had *any*

U.S. Department of Justice
Bureau of Alcohol, Tobacco, Firearms and Explosives

**Application for Tax Paid
Registration of Firearm**

ATF Control Number

2a. Transferee's Name and Address (Including tradename, if any) (See instruction 2)

Billy bob's suppressor Shop
123 country lane
Dirt, North Dakota,

2b. County
Agricultural

3a. Transferor's Name and Address (Including trade name, if any) (Executors: see instruction 2k)

Upstanding Citizen
1 Main Street
Old Town, NY.

3b. Transferor's Telephone Number
Area Code
212-555-1234

3c. If Applicable: Decedent's Name, Address, and Date of Death

The above-named and undersigned transferor hereby makes application as required by Section 5812 of the National
below to the transferee.

4. Description of Firearm (Complete items a through h)

a. Name and Address of Manufacturer and/or Importer of Firearm	b. Type of Firearm (See instruction 1c)	c. Caliber, Gauge Size (Spec
Secret Gear manufacturer Nowhere Place	silencer	.30

additional sheet if necessary)

Yes, it is a four-page government document. Yes, if you get any part wrong they will bounce your application back. But the dealer has done this before, many times, so work with the dealer when you fill out your Form 4.

kind of a run-in with the law? Do you have an ex who bears you no good will? Because the ATF will check, and if they find you have some sort of disqualifying problem, and you haven't gotten the situation cleared up, then your application will be cheerfully denied.

So, have a clean record and you're good. If you don't have a clean record, your problems need to be resolved before you apply.

Next, find a dealer. This isn't as hard as it used to be, as the manufacturer of the suppressor you are interested in will be more than happy to tell you the dealers in your area, and which of them might even carry their product in inventory.

With a dealer or dealers in mind, go there and see what they have, or what they can order. You have this book, you have magazine articles, hopefully you've done your research.

Shop, discuss, work out a price, and pay for it. Once paid for, it is yours, but you don't get to take it home. It may not even be there in the store. This is where the patience comes in. You and your dealer will fill out the form, in this instance a Form 4, a transfer approval application.

This is different from the Brady check you went through when you bought a gun last year. There, they were simply verifying that you weren't a prohibited person. Once that was established, the dealer could sell you whatever gun he had on hand, or order one.

The Form 4 is an application to transfer *a particular item* to you, at this time. That's why the form has your name, the dealer's name, the model and serial number, and manufacturer's name of the suppressor on the form. The form approves the transfer of *this* suppressor, from *this* dealer, to *this* person, on the date approved, and not a minute before. And it is what you will have to go through each time you buy another suppressor.

Once the Form 4 is filled out, in duplicate, take it to your CLEO along with the FBI fingerprint cards. And again, they want specific cards. The ATF does not want to see your local police department's fingerprint cards, or the state police, or anyone else's. They want the FBI cards they specify. Get fingerprinted, get the CLEO sign-off, wash your hands, write a check for $200 and, wait, there's one more step – get photographed. You'll need a pair of passport-quality photos, so comb your hair, put on a smile and get your pics. Then you can send it all, in one envelope, to the address on the form.

Oh, and be a smart guy and make sure the check will clear the bank. If the check does not clear, your transfer is denied, and you won't find out until the paperwork is returned. Don't send cash, don't send anything but approved funds. Now, if you want to make sure that there is no question, sending the ATF a U.S. Postal Service money order will likely work. I mean, a USPS MO is as good as cash. But they do accept personal checks, and that is easy.

Then you wait. And wait. It takes as long as it takes, and phoning to "see how things are going" simply delays the process.

Now, there was an electronic form that was used for a while, and may well be back by the time this hits print. This sped things up quite a bit, as the examiner didn't have to wade through piles of forms, all arriving in the mail in one big bag, to do the work. However, as with so many things, some smart-alec (stronger words were used at the time) screwed it up for everyone else. What I have heard from those on the inside was this: some too-clever outside programmer figured out how to "jump the line" and get their own electronic transfer applications moved up to the head of the line.

Once this was discovered, the ATF figured, and rightly, that if the system could be "gamed" that way then they had to close it down until it could be made secure. So, we went back to the paper system. I had a bunch of electronic transfers in-process at the time, and when the ATF decided they couldn't continue, they voided all of them (mine and everyone else's) and told us to go back to paper.

Thanks to whoever was responsible for that.

OK, you've been patient, you've been approved, and your form has come back stamped and ready to be used. There's still one more form you have to fill out, the 4473.

You see, as defined by law, a suppressor is a firearm, which means it requires the 4473. Your dealer is familiar with this, and will mark it as "other" when you get to the box on the form. (Hey, it isn't a rifle or shotgun, it isn't a pistol or revolver, what else can you call it?) You finally get to take your new toy home. Make sure you take care of it, keep it locked up and know where it is. It would be bad enough to explain to the local police and insurance company that you "don't know where" your deer rifle is, but a suppressor? That one brings in the Feds.

Trust

No, not the feeling you get when you see your grandmother (I hope you can trust granny), but a legal trust. A legal trust can take a number of different forms, and these forms have variations from state to state. But the essence of a trust is that it is a legal entity that can possess property or items of value, and those items are not considered to be possessed by the individuals who hold the trust.

The whole idea of a trust, and why it even exists, is a matter of historical and philosophical legal arcana. But they exist, and for our situation they can be very useful tools.

You see, your Form 4 must have a signature from the "Chief Law Enforcement Officer" of your area. We've covered this in chapter three, Myths, but it bears repeating: you form a trust because the CLEO won't sign. If you do form a trust, it would be prudent for you (and a good idea for the rest of us) to make sure no one who has access to your suppressors might be in a prohibited category. Prudent for you because handing a suppressor to a prohibited person is a crime, and good for us because if the trusts are abused, they will go away.

It is one thing to be at the range on a beautiful day and, after handing your daughter's boyfriend your suppressor-equipped firearm to plink with, find out later he is considered under the law a "prohibited person." It is something else to have had him named on the trust papers as having access to the suppressor, and all the other toys, for who knows how long. The first can be laid at the feet of inadvertence, and "I didn't' know at the time." But to put someone on the trust, you'd be smart to make sure you know what you need to know.

There's also the matter of taxes. A trust pays a tax on the transfer, just like a person does. If the trust has to be dissolved, then the transfers out of the trust will also be taxed to the new owner or owners of the suppressors. If, on the other hand you own them personally, your inheritor may not have to pay the transfer tax. As with so many things, it depends.

And, in a curious twist, it wasn't that long ago that the ATF themselves suggested that the CLEO requirement be done away with. After all, with instant, digital background checks now the norm, and readily available to any law enforcement agency, and since the ATF was doing it themselves, what did they need the local LE to be doing it for?

That was entirely too rational a suggestion for the administration in place at the time, and it wasn't but a couple of years after that the "suggestion" came floating down from the administration that the CLEO sign-off be added to trusts.

When someone tells you that voting for the "lesser of two evils" is still voting for evil, remind them that we probably wouldn't be dealing with nonsense like this, were it a Republican administration. Sure, we'd be dealing with different bone-headed ideas, but they'd be less hazardous, and easier to quash.

Trust extras

Let's assume you own a suppressor or a bunch of them and you finally run out of luck. What happens to your suppressors? Well, if you have them covered in your will, your executor can handle things, but they won't like you for it. You see, while the inheritor of your suppressors waits on their paperwork, the items in question are in legal limbo. You own them, but you are dead. The new owner doesn't have approval to own them. Where do they stay? In the bank safe deposit box? In the desk drawer of your attorney who is handling the will? It is entirely possible that your state law will require them to be handed over to the custody of the local police until the new paperwork is approved.

And there is also the matter of publicity. You see, a will is good, but it will not prevent you from going through probate. And when the court gets involved, and your will goes through probate, it all becomes a matter of public record. As a friend of mine pointed out, when Bob Hope died, and his property was disposed of according to his will, it all became a matter of public record. But, when Bing Crosby died, he had formed a trust (no idea if there were suppressors involved) and no one outside of the inheritors know what was involved.

A trust solves all that uncertainty. You die, and the other named trust officers still have access, and the trust still owns the items.

And if you have set up a trust to cover the disposition of your property, there is no probate, there is no public record, and no one with the search software can simply troll court records and find out what you owned and to whom you left it.

Even if don't form a trust to transfer suppressors, get yourself a trust to cover your property disposition instead of just a will.

Chapter Eighteen

DO IT YOURSELF

Yes, you can use someone else's lathe, and even have them do the work while you supervise. But if you get the bug, sooner or later you're going to want to do it yourself, and that means your own lathe. It need not be expensive.

Yes, Virginia, you can make your own suppressor. First, the pesky technical and legal details. You have to file a Form 1, an application to manufacture a controlled firearm. Except for the number of the form, this is the regular process as it would be were you buying one: the forms, the fingerprints, the check, the waiting. And while you wait, that's all you do. You do not "get ready" by acquiring materials. You do not "make a test cut" to see how things work.

And when the approved form returns, you do the work yourself. This is the part that is the real stumbling block for a lot of would-be suppressor makers. You see, you have to be the one actually driving the machine that does the cutting, threading, boring, etc.

And the ATF has gotten lot more picky about this of late.

In part, that's because of the excesses of the AK guys a while ago. You see, back in the first decade of the 21st century the really hard-core and involved shooters were buying AK parts kits (back when parts kits could be had for less than $100) and building up AKs on new receivers, or even bending their own receivers from "flats." This typically took mostly some simple hand tools, but a few fixtures and a hydraulic press made things a lot easier. Starting as a solitary endeavor, it evolved until a bunch of guys from a gun club, or a local area, would show up at someone's machine shop on a weekend. On that Saturday or Sunday they'd help, coach, share info and tips, while they each built their own AK from the parts kit and the bare receiver or flat they had brought with them.

As long as the guy who owned the shop did nothing, no problem. When he accepted money for the time, and the wear-and-tear on his machines, that was a grey area. And if he assisted, by working a particularly difficult or expensive machine, well, he was a manufacturer. Enough people pushed the boundaries far enough, long enough, and hard enough that the ATF had to step in and say, "this isn't kosher."

(We'll leave aside for the moment the question of whether the ATF should be doing this at all, and just focus on what is.)

So, to stay kosher building an AK, you've got to do it yourself, you have to work the machines, and you can't participate in a "build party" with a bunch of people doing the same thing. Now, if you were to rent a shop, be there by yourself, and the owner wasn't present, would that be kosher enough? Maybe, but what machinist would rent his shop out to the un-trained, and not be there? But that's making AKs, or rifles such as "80%" AR lowers, into rifles. What about suppressors?

Well, when in doubt, consult the relevant sections of the federal regulations. For us, it is Section 6.4, Approval of Form 1. In the third paragraph, we get down to the nitty-gritty, which, in the interest of clarity, I'll start out by quoting:

"If the applicant on the Form 1 lacks the skill, ability, and/or equipment to manufacture the NFA firearm, the applicant, after receipt of the approved Form 1, can have the firearm created or modified at a premises other than shown on the approved Form 1 as long as the creation or modification was done under the direct oversight of the applicant, thus having the applicant retain custody and control of the firearm. If the location is outside the applicant's state and the firearm being made is a short barreled rifle, short barreled shotgun, destructive device, or an unserviceable machinegun which is being reactivated, the applicant will also need to request permission to transport the firearm interstate as required by 27 CFR 478.28."

This is pretty clear; you can have someone else do the machine work on your suppressor, but with some clear guidelines: you have to be there the whole time, supervising the process. No drop it off, "I'll be back after lunch, the drawings are all clear," sort of thing. They can't "keep it overnight" because they are backed-up with work, or say, "You'll have to come back tomorrow, something came up." If you leave, the parts leave with you. It may be possible, if you have a friend who is a machinist, who will let you baby-sit your suppressor being made. If not, then you are on your own.

What if you want to, or must, do it yourself? You need a lathe to make a suppressor. A mill is useful, if you plan on making it with a monocore, and a drill press can be useful if/when you want to vent the sidewalls of your baffles. Now, this is not impossible. What you are looking for is called an "engine lathe" and it cuts metal. A wood-turning lathe won't do you any good, regardless of how good a deal it may be. For a suppressor, you'd need something that can handle stock up to 1.5 inches in diameter, and a foot long or so.

A lathe sufficient for the purpose of making a suppressor can be had for about $1,500 to $2,000, depending on the features you need or desire, and how hard you shop. Be aware that this is not like buying a vacuum cleaner, something you plug in, run when you need, and then put away and forget until the next time. This will draw enough electricity that you can't run it on the same circuit as other power equipment, even if you buy one that requires only 120 power. The lightest will still tip the scales at over 200 pounds, and will require its own solid bench, no sharing with other gear. They can be had with their own stand, but that adds cost and weight.

All this means you need a dedicated space. A garage won't do, unless it is heated and kept dry. And you have to learn how to use it. That will end up costing you time (but if you view it as entertainment, then it is time well-spent) and tools. You'll have to buy materials, and materials aren't cheap.

Now, you can practice your lathe technique before your approved form is returned, but don't go trying to push the boundaries and work on suppressor parts. Do us all a favor and keep your nose clean. Instead, invest in a subscription to one of the newsstand machinist's magazines out there, and learn on their projects.

Once your approved Form 1 arrives, you're good to get started.

You need four things: front and rear caps, tube and baffles. I ran into one of the members of my gun club, coincidentally while both of us were testing suppressors, and he had to show me his that he had made. He had found a cool source of materials for the tube and front cap – an expired Mag-light flashlight. He centered the tube, sans the emitter head, and bored the clearance hole for the suppressor front out of what had been the end cap of the light. He then turned it around, parted-off (that's something you have to learn before your Form 1 is returned, so get to work, on a non-suppressor project) and threaded the rear. Then he turned, threaded and fit a rear cap, and then with the main tube back in the lathe, bored and threaded it for the muzzle threads.

Now all he had to do was make baffles. Of course, if he didn't he'd still have a suppressor, just one that didn't shave off all the decibels that he otherwise could have.

Making baffles is the hard part. This will require a bar of aluminum (you aren't going to be lathe-turning titanium, Inconel or stainless steel as an amateur) that is an inch and a half in diameter, or one that matches or is slightly larger on its O.D. than your suppressor tube has as its I.D. I just checked with McMaster-Carr, the big industrial supply house. A bar, a rod actually, of 6061 aluminum 1-5/8 inches in diameter, runs you twenty bucks for a foot-long piece.

You'll probably cut up and ruin one of them just learning how to turn, bore, part and not scrap baffles.

At the end of all this, you'll have a bare aluminum suppressor, the tube of which you have to stamp with your name and the city in which you live (the Form 1 and the regs require it) and you can paint it if you want. What you can't do is get it anodized at home.

You see, anodizing is not a home-workshop process. It requires more than a stovetop. This is where things get a bit dicey. You are the owner of the suppressor, and the maker, but you are not a manufacturer. The anodizer has an SOT (they must, or this is a complete non-starter) but they are not the manufacturer of the suppressor you own.

So, you'd think you couldn't ship it to them for service or repair, as you would the manufacturer of a store-bought suppressor, because they aren't the manufacturer of it. And you would be wrong. The "suits" are amazingly rational about this. You want your home-built suppressor anodized, you can ship it to an anodizer who has an SOT, and may I suggest U.S. Anodizing?

To make the job as un-hassled as possible, tell them exactly what everything is made of. If you, as my fellow club member did, made your suppressor body out of a Mag lite body, then include that info. If you made your baffles out of 6061 you bought from McMaster-Carr, say so. This makes life easier for the anodizer, and anything you can do to make life easier is appreciated.

Oh, and as with pretty much all things related to suppressors, make a copy of your approved Form 1, mark it as a copy (you'd better just buy a rubber stamp from the office supply store, that says "copy") and include the copy with your suppressor.

Experimenting

Now you have a tube with front and rear caps and no baffles. It is an approved suppressor, but you want it to be more efficient. Gotta make some baffles, then. OK,

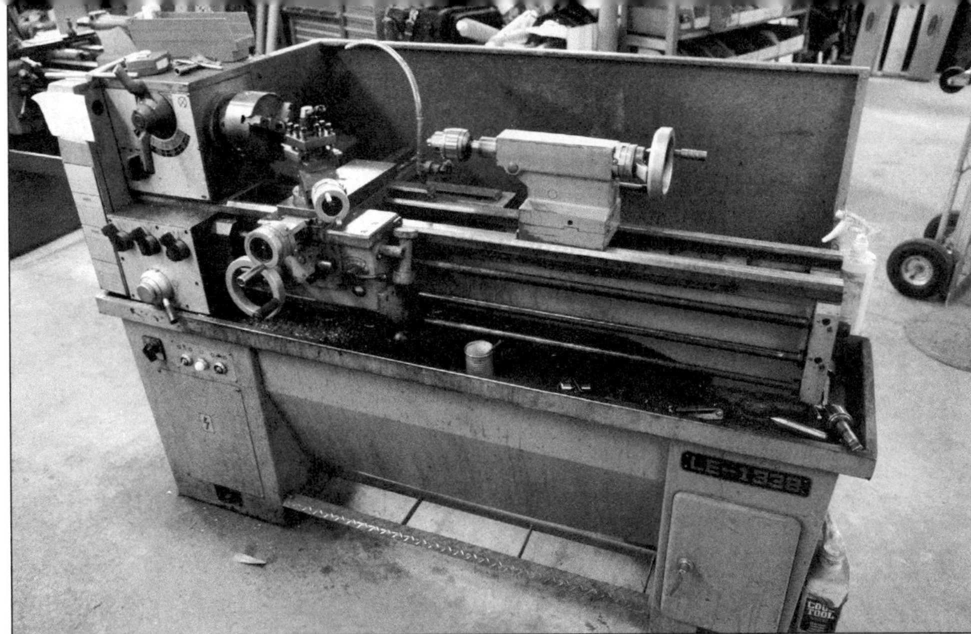

One nice thing about having a lathe of your own is that you can be absolutely sure your muzzle threads are axial, concentric and correct.

no problem.

This is where your time spent practicing beforehand, but not on suppressor parts, will come in handy. What you have to do is bore a K or an M baffle out of your bar of aluminum, bore a hole down the center, and part it off. You have to do this one at a time, and you have to make them precisely enough that when you assemble them into the tube, they are not loose and they fit with the caps on tight.

Success! You have baffles, and they work. But, being the kind of guy who makes his own suppressor (try not to brag) you wonder, "Can I make better baffles?"

Of course you can. But here's where the previously accommodating regulators are not so accommodating – you can't make spare baffles. You can't have any spares, and you can't make a second set to compare to the first, because they have declared that spare parts constitute suppressors, and that's a no-no.

What? How? That's crazy!

Yes, and no. This takes us far back into the history of shooters who were too clever by half. (Not that we have a monopoly on that particular attribute.) Back in the 1980s or so, suppressors were just the serial-numbered part. You owned a tube back then, and everything else was "just parts" and the tube itself could be just a part, because, well, it was just a tube.

So, you had the situation where you could go to a large gun show in a suppressor state and find a guy who was selling "just parts." He'd have all the baffles you wanted, in various shapes and dimensions. Two aisles over, there'd be another guy, who had spare front and rear caps, "just in case" you damaged the ones on the suppressor you owned. And in the corner was a guy, with an immense pile of gear, who happened to have a cardboard box of blank tubes.

One day at the show, and you could have all the parts you needed to assemble a suppressor and they are all "just parts."

We all like to complain about how bone-headed various regulatory decisions have been, and how they could have "done it better, if…" Well, sometimes they can't. You see, the tools available to many regulators are limited, sometimes by tradition, sometimes by regulatory purview, and sometimes by statute.

And, they want to make it easy on themselves, too. So, the ATF decided, "all parts of a suppressor are parts of a suppressor." That means no spare parts, with a few exceptions. Those exceptions basically are in the mounting device and the front plate. You can have a rear cap that lets you mount a suppressor onto different calibers, or thread pitches of barrels.

But you can't have spare baffles.

That means, if you want to try a different design of baffle, you have to destroy the existing baffle stack, and then (and not before) make a new and improved one. If you want to compare two baffle designs, side-by-side, you have to apply for two Form 1s (or a second one), and once approved, make two suppressors with two different baffle designs and test them.

If you want to try a third iteration, you can file for a third Form 1, or destroy the less-effective baffle array, make the new one, and test again.

This applies to wipes, also. If your suppressor uses one, you get to have one. If you want to replace it, chop up the old, used one and then punch out a replacement. Having a box of "spare wipes" on the shelf is just asking for trouble, if you ever have a visitor.

It does make things a bit cumbersome, but hey, you were they guy who wanted to make his own suppressor.

Chapter Nineteen

TRAVELING WITH SUPPRESSORS

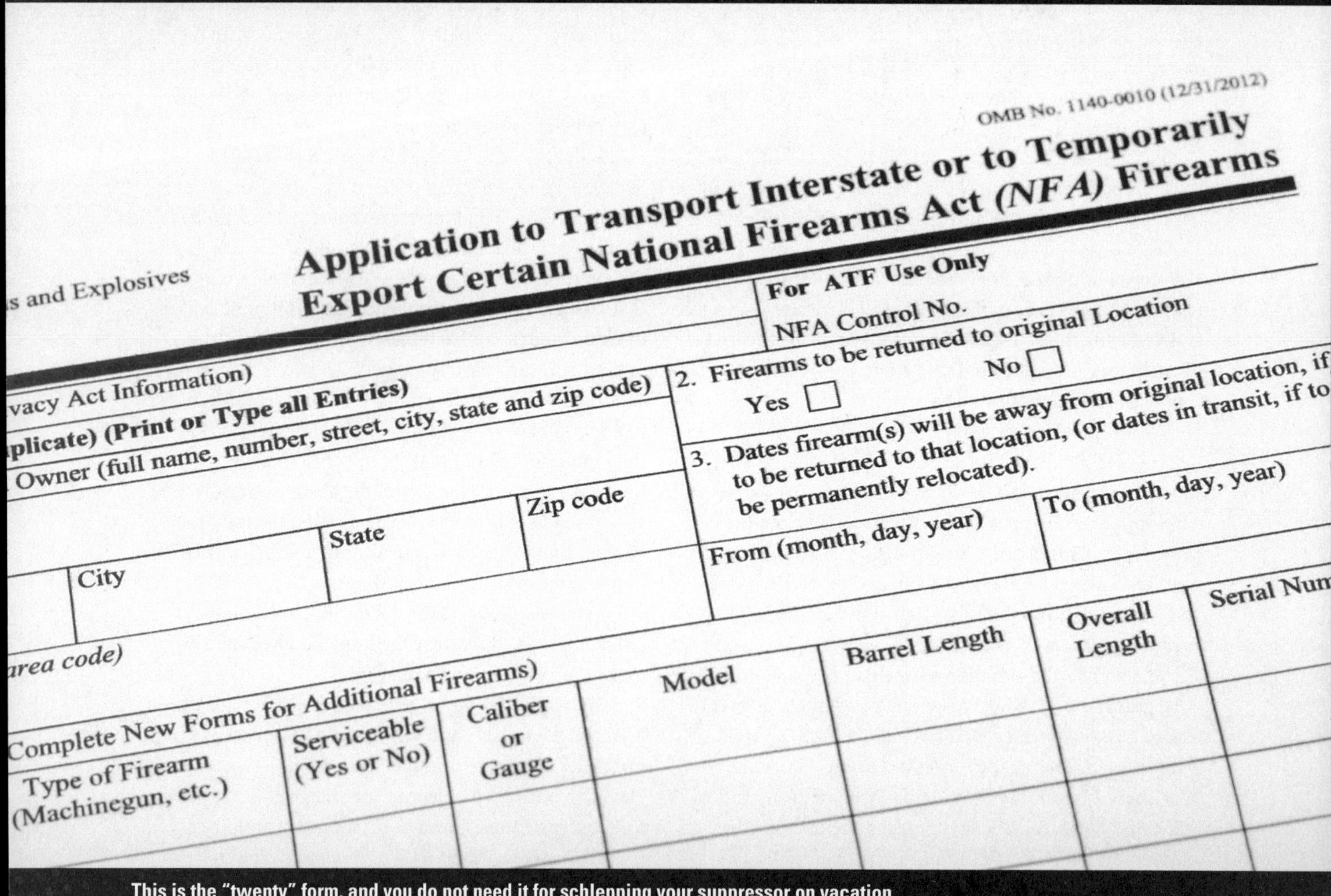

This is the "twenty" form, and you do not need it for schlepping your suppressor on vacation. Just be sure you stay overnight in states where they are allowed.

Welcome to the bizarro world of, "No one has a clue, not even the people in charge." First of all, as far as the ATF is concerned, your suppressor is a firearm. It says so right in the definition, and that's what you would think you'd mark on the 4473 when you picked it up. You would be wrong. It gets marked as "other" on the form, because, well, I don't know why, and I'd bet most of the ATF agents you asked wouldn't know, either. Except, for the paperwork and subsequent tax status, it isn't "other," it is treated as a machine gun. When it comes time to travel out of your home state, they consider it a plain old firearm.

You'll see people recommend that you go and file a particular form with the ATF – the 5320.20, also known as the "Twenty form" or the "Machine Gun Travel" form. To grasp the full irony of this, you have to know what you'd have to do, were you traveling with your machine gun.

If you want to travel to the state next door to shoot in a match with your machine gun or your SBR, you have to fill out the Twenty form. What 5320.20 asks you, among other things, is your name, the firearm, the current location, where it is going, and the dates and reason. You get a lot of leeway in this.

You can for instance, list a whole raft of states, list the dates as January 1 to December 31, and put down competition or training or both. You don't have to file a form for each and every trip, individually, one at a time for each item. They want to know if the move is temporary or permanent. So, if you're traveling to compete in a match, you mark it as temporary. If you are traveling to move, because you're tired of the heat/cold/wet/dry and want to live someplace else, then you have more forms than just the 5320.20 to fill out, but you've got to fill that one out, anyway. Oh, and one more thing, they want to know that you know that your machine gun/SBR, etc. is legal where you're going. If it isn't, they deny the application. You don't get to use the ATF as a shield and the form as approval to go live someplace that would otherwise throw you in jail for owning your goodies, because they will. Throw you in jail, that is.

Now, let's suppose you're a "snowbird." You live "back home" in the summer months, and you travel south in the winter and live there for 3-4-5 months, whatever. That's right, you fill out a new 5320.20 for each year, listing travel to and from the locations.

A final bit of "let's make this not-so-clear": if you are moving, that is, changing residences, but remaining in the same state, you are strongly encouraged to fill out the 5320.20 form, for your machine guns, SBRs and suppressors. It isn't required, but it is "strongly recommended." If you are changing permanent residences to another state, you are required to fill out a 5320.20, for all the gear, even suppressors.

Here's the good part – you do not have to file the form for traveling with a suppressor. (Unless, of course, it is attached to a machine gun, SBR, etc. C'mon, get a grip.)

But, you do have to be taking your suppressor to a place where it is legal to own.

And in that regard, it is just like travel with a regular firearm. In other words, plan your travel. For instance, the Firearm Owners Protection Act of 1986 protects you while driving through jurisdictions that might otherwise prohibit your firearm. So, theoretically, you could drive through New York State (even NYC) with an AR, and be legally protected. Theoretically.

I've got to tell you, I did just that many years ago, to compete in the USPSA 3-gun Nationals, held on Long Island. Talk about nervous. I could just imagine getting in an accident and having to explain to the officer why the back of my pickup truck was full of gun gear. And no, I did not stop for anything but traffic lights.

However, the big Blue cities have taken upon themselves to parse the law, and declare that travel by plane is not covered. If you fly through NYC, Newark, or one of the many other socialist hellholes that hate guns, you risk incarceration. So don't. Plan your flights accordingly and do not change flights there, or other locations with similar attitudes.

Next, don't stop. Let's say you're driving from Indiana to Iowa to compete in a match. Driving through Illinois is covered under FOPA/86. Staying in a motel in Iowa is covered. Stopping for gas, to take five minutes in a rest stop, get some food, that sort of thing, is covered. But staying in a hotel in Illinois isn't. You can't stop, so don't. Plan ahead.

Let's say you are flying. You dutifully check your baggage with firearms, declare them, and open the case for inspection. When the clerk asks, "Unloaded?" you either say yes, or show them. The clerk has probably been instructed to say, "Show me," even if they don't know a Mauser from a mouser. Be polite, and just show him or her. Keep your mouth shut about the suppressor, because saying anything will only confuse them, and confusion means delay and most likely a missed flight. It can't be loaded, anyway, so questions about its loaded status are meaningless. Best to keep it wrapped up, out of sight, and let them simply see it as more incomprehensible shooting gear, like the other mysterious objects in the case.

If anyone asks, your choices are few and fraught with peril. "Oh, that's unloaded, too." Might be met with, "Show me." "It isn't a firearm" isn't the truth, and that might be bad. Getting caught in a lie, I mean, as a prelude to other inquiries. Me, I just figure that they are interested in what is visible, and what clearly looks like a gun. Let them see that it or those are unloaded, and the rest is just so much shrapnel to them. Lock up and move on.

As an extra bit of insurance, you can make use of those cable locks that every gunshop in America has a bushel basket full of. Thread the cable through the suppressor, lock it, and then stuff it in the hard case you are flying with. If anyone says, "Show me," all you have to do is point to the mysterious object, with the obvious cable lock through it, and they will most likely be satisfied.

If you think you are planning ahead and covering all contingencies, you have not met the federal agent I was in a class with. His lockable hard case had a sign taped to it. The sign read, "The owner of this case is a federal agent, traveling under official orders. Inspection must be conducted in his presence. If you need to look inside, call this cell phone number [number printed] and he will unlock it."

His agency had seen too many cases show up with cut locks, and was tired of the paperwork. I wish I could have been listening in to those phone conversations, between his bosses and the TSA, over those locks and any missing items.

Now, those of you with trusts are probably asking, "What about me?" I've got some bad news for you. Unlike being a dealer, an FFL holder who has an SOT (also known as a Class 3 Dealer), you don't get any extra consideration. Dealers can travel into the various people's republics (although there are limits even there) to demo product. It is, after all, what they are supposed to do.

But as a member of a trust, you are an individual. Even if you are a trust board member, or officer, or however your state arranges it, you are an individual. You have to fill out the forms for the relevant items. And you best not tarry in the banned states.

You filled out the form anyway

On the advice of your buddy, the gun club guy who "knows everything," you filled out a 5320.20 to travel with your suppressor to another state. What next? The ATF examiner who gets it in his/her in-box will chuckle, shake his or her head, stamp it approved, and mail it back. The ATF doesn't require it, but you are making the rest of us wait. You see, even if the form isn't required, he/she (the examiner) has to do their due diligence: open it, read it, consider it, approve or deny it, and then put it in the "return" stack. All of this delays the applications of the rest of us, who are waiting for our suppressors.

The examiners would rather you did your due diligence, and made sure where you are taking it is a place you can possess it.

Unless, of course, you're trying to tell him or her you want to travel into [fill in the blank] it being one of one of the few remaining oppressive states that do not allow suppressors, and then he will mark it "not approved" which should be a clue.

And, there are probably places (poring through state statutes to parse out the details is beyond this book) where it is legal for the residents there to own suppressors, but not for you to arrive with one as a vacationer.

Pay more attention to what you have to ask for, and where you can go. Don't get in trouble, it makes things more difficult for the rest of us.

Licensed owners

If you've paid any attention at all to the differences in state law concerning firearms, you have to wonder what is in the water. Well, brace yourself, travel with suppressors can be even more strange.

There is another group of owners who can travel with suppressors, and those are the federally-licensed ones. These worthies fall into two groups, both with an SOT: Special Occupational Taxpayer. These being the regular FFL, also known as an 01, and the 07, aka manufacturer. And consider all this as interesting (or not) information, that probably won't impact your life, but can make for "Didja know?" talk at the gun club.

An SOT has two kinds of suppressors: those they personally own, and those still held on the Acquisitions & Dispositions book, also known as the bound book.

The personally-owned suppressors can only be taken to states where a suppressor may be individually owned by a non-sworn person or agency. That is, if a resident of the state in question can own one, if you the traveler can bring one, you can bring one with you. If suppressors can't be individually owned, then you can't bring one that is individually owned. Even as an SOT, if it is personally-owned, you can't take it there.

However, as a dealer, that is, a Class 3 seller, a holder of both an FFL (01 or 07) and an SOT, you can take them there, with a few provisos. First, that it is still in the bound book and has not been transferred. That is, "company" property. It would be prudent for there to be an official reason for you to be there. In other words, you are there to show them to a police department, not for a weekend of prairie dog shooting. Now, this holds for the "usual suspects" the states where they are approved for police use, but not individual ownership.

But, there are exceptions. (There are always exceptions.) Two states, Illinois and Massachusetts, do not think it wise to allow even dealers, 01 SOT holders, to be bringing suppressors into their state. For those, you have to take another step up and be a manufacturer holding an 07 license. With an 07 and an SOT, you could travel to those states, but you'd best be there in a bunch of them for the purposes of demo'ing them to the police, otherwise you will be in trouble.

And as a final, "you've got to be kidding me," there are two states where you can't even do that: Hawaii and New Jersey. (Admit it, you knew that New Jersey was going to be in here someplace, didn't you?) Even as an 07 manufacturer and an SOT, you can't transport suppressors to those two states. So, how do the police departments there acquire suppressors? Besides, "I really don't give a flying bleep, they can go bleep themselves," I can only imagine that, being police departments, they can acquire them directly from manufacturers. No need to involve grubby dealers in this, is there? (OK, a bit unfair, only some dealers are grubby.)

On second thought, I'm not in a particularly charitable mood, after all this. I don't care if a department or agency in New Jersey acquires suppressors or not. But that's just me.

It is at times like these that I shake my head when anti-gun people ask the stupid question, "Well, we license cars and drivers, don't we?" If guns were treated like cars, once you owned and had your suppressor papered, you could take it anywhere. After all, if your Nebraska plates are up to date, you can drive in Manhattan without a hassle, right? Morons.

Chapter Twenty

CARE AND MAINTENANCE

This is what happens when you shoot a pistol-caliber suppressor, and never clean it. The baffles get choked with residue.

As far as care and maintenance are concerned, your suppressor is probably the least-maintenance-requiring expensive thing you own. Still, you shouldn't neglect it. As we've discussed repeatedly, suppressors come in two flavors: sealed and user-serviceable.

The sealed ones are dead-simple. Keep them clean, scrub off whatever collects on the outside, and keep them from rusting. If they are made of steel, that is. The other materials won't rust - titanium, aluminum and Inconel. If you find yourself in the rain or snow, and your sealed suppressor gets wet, shoot it enough to heat it up and drive out whatever moisture might be in it. That's pretty much it.

If you and/or your suppressor take a dive and it ends up submerged, then you have a different problem. Water is an incompressible substance. That is, you can press on it all you want, but it won't take up any less room as a result. Which is good, or else boats wouldn't float. The problem is, if you fire a suppressor that is filled with water the gases still try to expand. Only now there is less room, and as a result, the internal pressure in your suppressor will skyrocket. Yes, some can be fired "wet," but if they aren't that kind, then doing so is not a good idea.

Modern baffle designs defy using drainage as a means of getting all the water out. It won't drain. That leaves heat.

A sloshed suppressor, if it is a quick-detach type, is easy: turn the oven on to "warm" and leave the suppressor in there until you can't hear water sloshing when you shake it (the suppressor, not the stove). A direct-thread will require you get out the wrench and barrel blocks, remove the suppressor, bake it, and then re-install it.

There is no need to try to get any kind of solvent into it, or to brush, scrub or swab the interior. A sealed, rifle-caliber suppressor gets hot enough that it burns out whatever might precipitate on the interior. There is no need to try and reach inside there, all you can do is make trouble for yourself.

Normal maintenance

For a sealed suppressor, all you really have to do, and then only if it is a QC/QA design, is brush the mounting system clean between uses. That way it will always tighten onto the muzzle aligned with the bore, and to the same spot.

User-serviceable suppressors, on the other hand, are another situation. And the user-serviceable ones are made that way for a reason.

The typical user-serviceable suppressor is a rimfire or pistol-caliber can. Some rifle-caliber suppressors are made to be disassemble-able, but most of them are rimfire or pistol cans. And there's a good reason for that.

Rimfire suppressors in particular can have a great deal of build-up. You really can't shoot a rimfire handgun or rifle enough in one session to heat up the suppressor sufficiently to burn out the residue. If you could, the (typically) aluminum construction would complain. And .22LR ammo is really, really grubby. As a result, a rimfire suppressor builds up an incredible amount of gunk inside. The usual manufacturer's recommendation is to disassemble and clean a rimfire suppressor after each 500 rounds fired. If you don't, you can easily build up enough residue inside that you essentially carbon-weld the suppressor together. If you get too much build-up, the force needed to unscrew the end caps can exceed the strength of the aluminum, or the threads. Or your wrench makes a mess of the wrench flats so carefully machined into the end caps.

Pistol-caliber suppressors can have the same problem, which is why you really don't want to be using lead bullets, cast or swaged, through a suppressor. You can build up enough powder and lead residue that you seize the assembly. Oh, it will still work, but once you can't take it apart, you can't clean out the build-up and it will gradually get heavier and less effective as a suppressor.

The end result isn't great, but it can be enough to notice. If you have, for example, a full-packed 9mm suppressor and a brand-new one of the same model, you can tell the packed one is heavier just by hefting the two, side by side. And it will be noticeably, albeit marginally, less quiet.

So you want to clean the ones you can clean.

Scrubbing a fired suppressor is straightforward, but messy. After all, you have both end caps, the tube, and if it is a baffle stack, 5, 6 or 7 baffles. If a monocore, you have a framework tube that has a dozen grubby surfaces. The big problem here is the mess. If you are used to cleaning a much-fired pistol, you can scrub the bore, and scrape and wipe out the packed powder residue in the slide and on the frame. A pistol-caliber suppressor is like that, except there is something like ten times as much surface that has collected residue.

Back when I was a gunsmith, I had a love-hate relationship with the parts cleaning tank. I suspect all gunsmiths do, or have had. The cleaning tank is simple – a basin or sink, with a tank under it holding cleaning solvent, usually mineral spirits, and a pump. The drains drain down to the bottom of the tank, and the tank has water in the bottom, and the pump pumps cleaning solvent off the layer of mineral spirits that float on top. (Mineral spirits, being a hydrocarbon, are less dense than water, and float on top as a layer.) The water acts as a filter, and the grubby stuff gets separated.

It works, and you can scrub guns more-or-less-clean pretty quickly. But it is messy, and the compressed air you use to blow the parts dry sprays solvent (and the grub still in the solvent) all over the place. And, you end the workday smelling of mineral spirits. After a few months, you really don't want to look inside the barrel, because the slime down there, cleaned off of guns, is enough to make you go pale.

As bad as it got, and as much as I came to loathe the parts cleaning tank, it sure would come in handy

After a class' worth of police cars, this Yankee Hill suppressor is ugly.

Pretty much any lube will do, but the better it penetrates, the better luck you have, and less time spent waiting. A day or two soaking in any lube, while you score a bottle of Kroil, is better than not doing anything.

now that I've got a steady supply of suppressors I'm testing.

Cleaning a suppressor

To clean a suppressor, you do the same things you'd do with a firearm, just over a much larger surface. Powder and lead solvents, brushes, wiping cloths, but keep in mind what you are scrubbing on. Often it is aluminum, sometimes titanium, occasionally something far tougher, like steel or Inconel. Aluminum parts means no steel wool, no stainless steel brushes, nothing aggressive.

One approach that gets suggested from time to time is to use a solution of vinegar and hydrogen peroxide. It rapidly dissolves powder residue, and even loosens lead deposits, but there is a down side, and it is not a small one. The chemical reaction of this solution, with the lead in the residue, creates lead acetate as one of the byproducts (this particular form is Lead (II) Acetate $Pb(CH_3COO)_2$). Now, people tend to think of lead as a dangerous metal. In some situations it can be fairly hazardous. Lead bullets lying on the ground is not one of those situations. If you simply consider that the National Park Service is still picking up lead bullets from the battlefield of Gettysburg, 150 years later, and can easily identify them as to which type (and in some instances even which individual) firearm they came from, it is clear metallic lead does not pose a problem.

However, lead acetate is really bad, and is also easily taken up by the body. It is toxic, water-soluble, and as such, once on your hands, easily ingested. You don't want to be exposed to it, and you don't want to be flushing it down into the water system. As if all this wasn't bad enough, it actually tastes sweet. (Or so the historical record tells us, I've never tasted it.) The Romans used a form of it as a sweetener, as have other civilizations before and since. If you are also sucking on a soda or chewing a sweetened gum, you may not notice the extra sweetness the lead acetate you just got a dose of. This is also a good reason to not smoke, drink or chew gun while cleaning firearms.

Another byproduct of this chemical mixture when used to remove lead-containing deposits is peracetic acid (CH_3CO_3H), which is not toxic, but will corrode or discolor metals it comes in contact with. Combined with the vinegar and the hydrogen peroxide, all metals in contact with the solution or exposed to the vapors will be discolored or corroded. The "traditional" solution is a recipe for damage to the suppressor, firearm, ammunition and pretty much anything else in the room where it is employed.

As a final note, discharging compounds of this level of toxicity into municipal water systems is no doubt in violation of EPA regulations. Admittedly the amounts will be small, but it is a bad habit to encourage or indulge in this kind of pollution.

So, don't mix the "really good cleaning solution," and don't use it.

Once the parts are clean, use a small amount of lubricating oil on the threads and re-assemble.

Rusted, crusted and neglected

What if you overlook regular maintenance and end up with a seized suppressor? The best thing to do is to remain patient. If you rush things and try to use force, a busted suppressor means a long wait. First, you have to contact the manufacturer and see if they can, and will, fix it. The digital age is great here, as you can email them, send digital photos, and get an idea of what it will take.

If they can repair, you actually get a break here. You can ship your suppressor directly to the manufacturer (and no one else) without filing for a transfer. Make a photocopy of your approved form (and be sure and mark it as a copy) and ship the suppressor, the copy, and instructions to the manufacturer.

The slow part is if it can't be fixed.

If the manufacturer can't repair the suppressor (the tube itself, for example) then they have to either send it back un-repaired, or having logged it in their books as a suppressor, now note its exit in their book as being destroyed. They then have to replace it, and you have to pay not only the repair costs, but the new transfer tax. That's right, it is a new suppressor, so you have to pay the tax on it. Back to square one, back to the $200 tax, and back to the end of the line while you wait. Oh, and back to the local dealer you bought it from, too. No, they can't ship a new suppressor (for that is what it is) back to you as an "identical replacement" because it isn't. You have to transfer it through the dealer. And no, they can't just mark the next one coming down the line with your old serial number instead of its intended number, and ship that as the "repaired" suppressor.

Life sucks when you get heavy-handed with a mon-

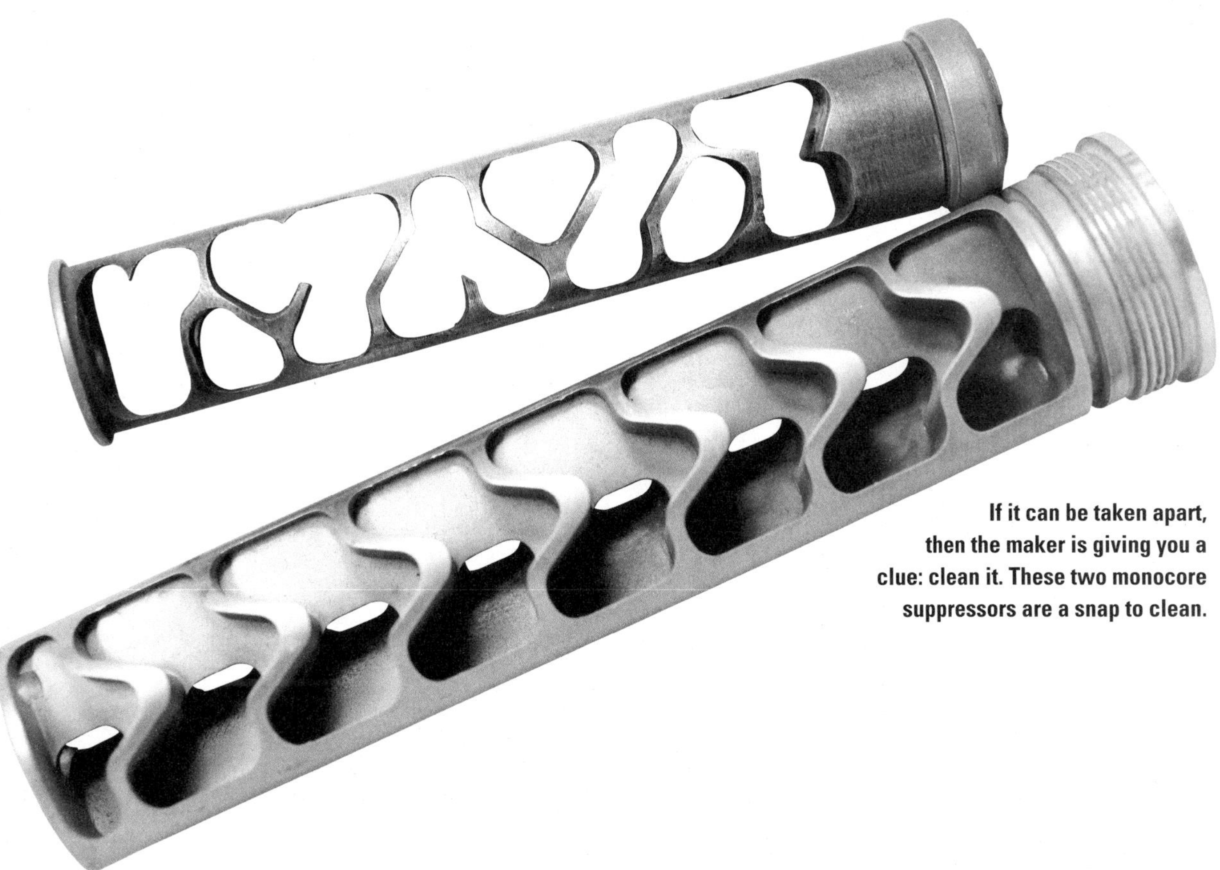

If it can be taken apart, then the maker is giving you a clue: clean it. These two monocore suppressors are a snap to clean.

key wrench.

So, seized suppressor? Go to the local hardware store or big-box home supply store and buy enough Kroil to submerge it. Kroil is a penetrating oil, and it works its way through just about any gap and into every joint. Submerge your seized suppressor and leave it there. How long? As long as it takes.

It took time to get yourself into this predicament, so be willing to spend some time getting out. Days, weeks, a month. I'd suggest leaving it submerged for a couple of weeks at least to start with, sealed in whatever jar or bucket you've chosen. Then take it out and try unscrewing the end cap. If it won't go, put it back and leave it there for another week.

Here's a tip, for those designs where this will work: when you go to try and unscrew things, clamp the rear cap, on the wrench flats, in your vise. Use pads, but get it tight. Then use a strap wrench to unscrew the tube from the cap. Don't try to clamp the tube and wrench on the rear cap, that will leave you with a well-lubed round tube simply rotating inside the vise jaws, as the jaws chew and gnaw score marks into the tube. Check the "lefty-loosey, right-tighty" direction you will apply force, two or three times, and then have a go at it. If it won't move, back into the Kroil.

This was the Kroil-soak process I used back at the gun shop, when it was necessary to take apart something that had been rusted, crusted or neglected.

One cleaning solution recommended to me by a suppressor manufacturer is a $^{50}/_{50}$ mix of automatic transmission fluid and mineral spirits. If you have a favorite penetrating oil or solvent, then use that, but everyone knows Kroil.

Here's the best part – if you use penetrating oil, a strap wrench and are careful, and still it won't come apart, you have not made things worse for the manufacturer. Let them know what you did, and how it fared, in the letter you send. Their hydraulics may succeed where your strap wrench failed.

Once clean, be sure and use a degreaser on the baffles and tube (it is counter-intuitive, to clean off clean parts, I know), because if you don't, the oil left behind will smoke when you next shoot your suppressor.

Chapter Twenty-One

MISTAKES, AMMUNITION AND CORRECTIONS

This was an experimental design with a sheet metal tube. After an obscene number of full-mag, full-auto mag dumps in .308, on an SBR, it finally let go. Think about this before you let your buddies get wild 'n crazy.

This is an ugly, if not catastrophic, baffle strike. Still, this suppressor needs an overhaul and reaming to be sure it is still functional.

OK, what can go wrong? We've spent the whole book discussing the fun, the benefits and the status that a suppressor can confer. What can go wrong and what can you do to prevent or correct problems? First, let's talk about the things that can go wrong.

Misalignment

One problem that you should be alert for is misalignment. Yes, we've covered this before, but it bears repeating, if for no other reason than the fact that it is easily avoided. Well, that and this mistake can end up being very expensive. The suppressor needs to be centered on, and in line with, the bore of your firearm. Off-center or tilted, it risks a baffle strike. Baffle strikes are not good, but they need not be catastrophic. I've had a chance now to see a bunch of suppressors, including some that are nearly a century old. Some have suffered baffle strikes, more like baffle skids, but they still work. If the baffles are still securely fixed in the tube, then a strike means there is some upsetting of the clearance hole, and a little more passage of gases.

It might not be quite as accurate having suffered a baffle skid or minor strike, and it might be a few decibels noisier, but it works. This is a perfect time to inquire with the manufacturer about service. I've talked to most of them about this sort of situation, and the response is pretty much the same: if the unit is still solid, and nothing has broken loose, then they would simply ream it "just enough." That being as little as possible to clean up the mangled metal, and that's it.

Yes, it will be a decibel or two louder, but it could have been a lot worse.

A catastrophic strike means the baffles are bent severely or broken loose, or the tube is bulged. This will likely mean replacement – an application for transfer, a new tax stamp and another 4473 form. How to avoid that? Buy a Giessele alignment rod.

The alignment rod is a ground steel rod of just the right diameter to slide smoothly down a .224- or .308-inch bore (on top of the rifling lands, of course) and poke out through the suppressor. If the alignment rod pokes out through the front cap, centered in the clearance hole, then the suppressor is aligned with the bore. You're good to go. If it doesn't, then there could be problems.

If it is off-center but doesn't touch, you're probably OK. If it touches the edge of the clearance hole, you are taking a risk; and if the rod won't pass through, if it hangs up on the end cap or an interior baffle, then you will bust your suppressor firing it.

Even if you have a QC/QA muzzle device, you are dependent on the alignment of the threads in the barrel to attach the muzzle device. If the threads are out of alignment, no muzzle device in the world can correct that. So I check the alignment of a suppressor on each and every rifle it is attached to, before I shoot it. I learned this the hard way, at an LE class.

I had just received a Gemtech Halo unit and was showing how it could be attached to a regular A2 flash hider. I got distracted with other details and, the next thing I knew, I saw a police officer stepping up to the line with my Halo suppressor on the end of the muzzle of his M4. I stepped forward, but before I got to him he fired two shots. (Thank goodness he hadn't flipped the selector to auto.) The first missed the target low-left, the second missed the target high-right. The Halo had just had a couple of baffle "skips," not really strikes. You can see the baffles that were brushed, but it hadn't changed the accuracy or point of impact, when it was back on my rifle. A lesson learned, at low cost.

As soon as I knew about the Geissele alignment rod, I got one in each caliber.

The thought will occur to some of you, "I know a machinist, I can have one made for less than $75 each." Maybe, maybe not. If you are paying cash for time spent working, no. If you are getting it as a return on a favor, yes. I looked into this before I knew about the Geissele, and steel rods do not come in the diameters we need. You need to have one ground down, and lathe-turning probably won't be straight enough. A bent rod is of no use.

So get the rods, and use them every time your suppressor goes onto a new rifle, be it yours or one of your gun club buddies.

We've already discussed the seized user-serviceable suppressor in the maintenance chapter, so we don't have to go into that, but what do you do if you have it seized onto a rifle? Hmm, I'm not sure exactly how this would happen, but if you have really tightened it down and now it won't come apart, what to do? Back to Kroil, except now you'll be standing the rifle, muzzle down, in a bucket of Kroil. It would be wise to tie, wire or otherwise clamp it in place, because who wants a bucket of Kroil spilled across the shop floor? No one, that's who. Give it a couple of weeks, and then try un-wrenching it.

Wrong caliber

Here we have a two-fold problem. First, how did you get a suppressor of the wrong caliber to even fit onto the other firearm? Suppressor makers go to a lot of trouble to make sure the wrong combos can't happen. And here we're talking, for example, about a 5.56 suppressor on a larger (usually a .308) rifle. This is bad news, and it is bad right from the start. This usually means a one-shot suppressor experience, and then a busted suppressor. It can also happen with smaller over-sized calibers, especially in the AR-verse. A 5.56 suppressor on a 6.5 Grendel, a 6.8, or a .300 Whisper/Blackout is bad news.

The usual result is a busted baffle assembly flying downrange, lead by a front cap in pieces. In some few instances I have heard about, the suppressor held together for a few shots, but the end result was still the same.

The only thing that can be done is replacement. Even if it had been a disassemble-able suppressor, the mounting threads for the front cap are gone, and that's that.

How did this happen? Usually, it comes from someone making a dual-thread mounting adapter – one with the muzzle threads of the barrel and the mounting threads of the suppressor – to put the two together. I don't care how clever you are with a lathe, this is not wise. A thread adapter to fit a larger-caliber suppressor to a smaller? OK, as long as you're good enough to make it all properly aligned. But don't make one to fit a smaller-caliber suppressor on a larger-caliber rifle. (I

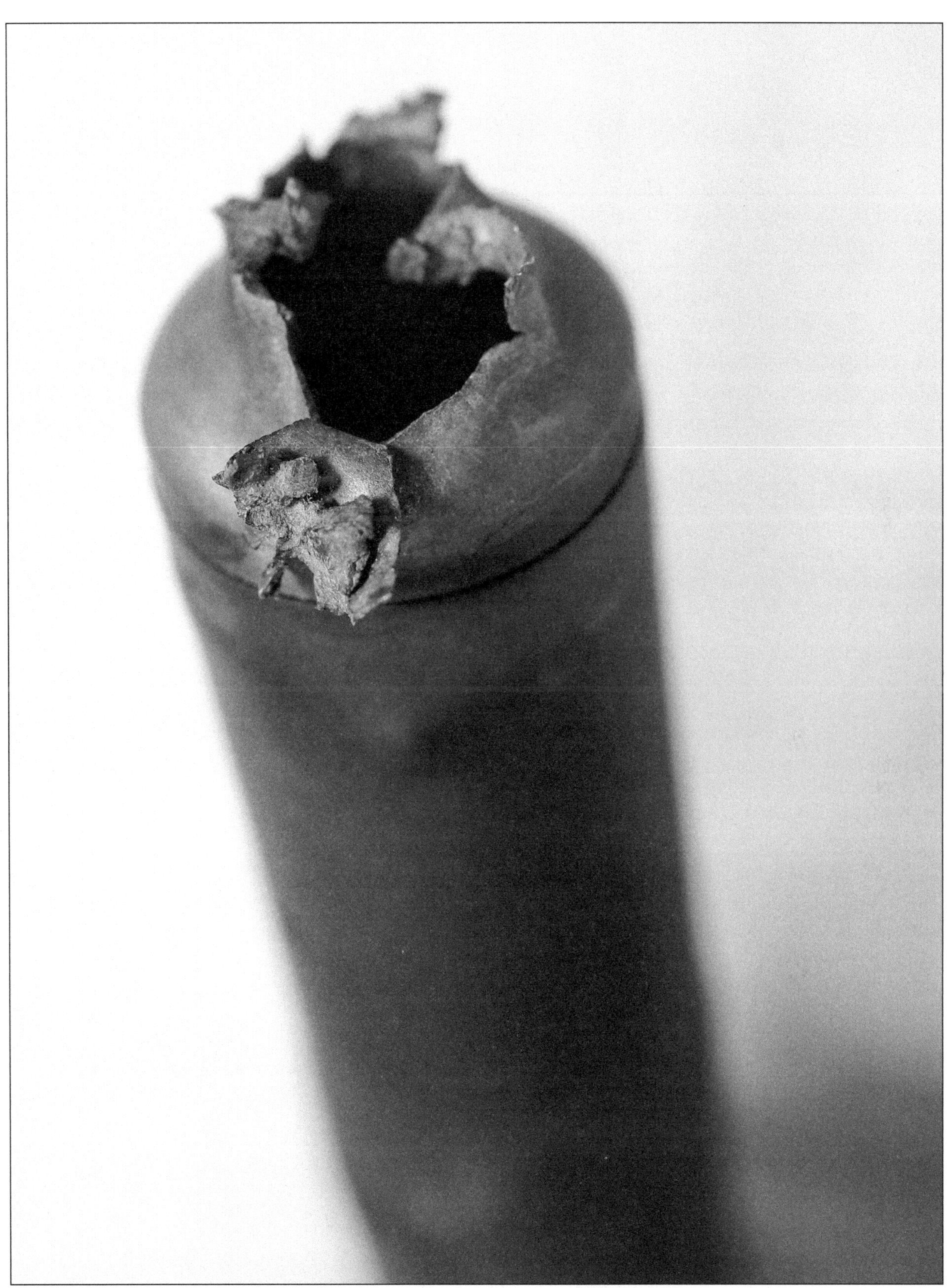

OK, this one is clearly a goner. There are parts rattling around inside, and you put others at risk from flying shrapnel when you shoot.

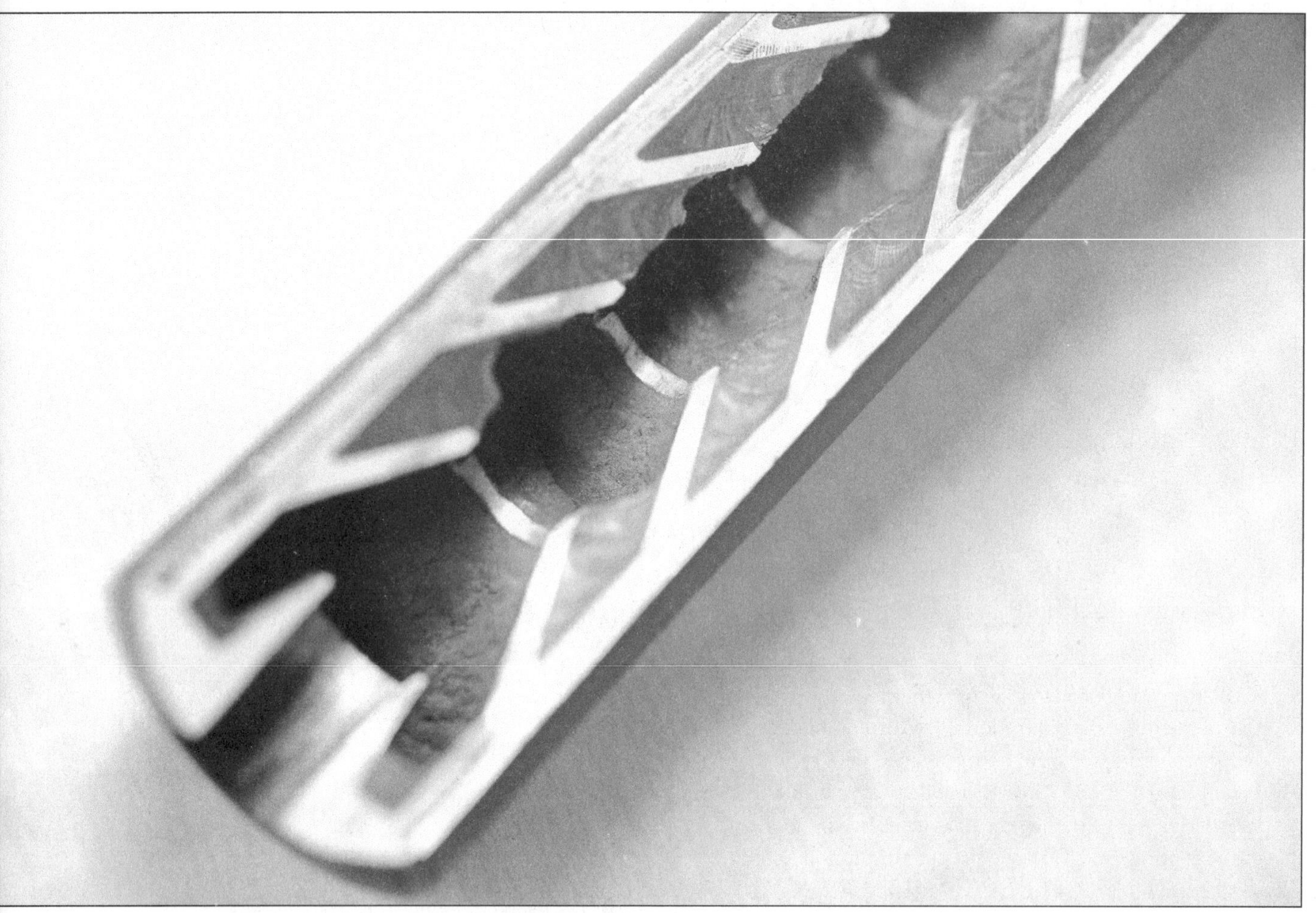

Here we have a pistol-caliber suppressor that was never disassembled and cleaned. It is fully packed with residue, with just enough of a clearance hole for bullets to get out.

mean, what were you thinking??)

The more common (even though it is rare) too-big caliber is when a .22LR suppressor is mounted onto a .223/5.56 rifle. You see, the threads are the same. Both .22LR and .223/5.56 use the common 1/2-28 thread, and there is the hazard. The uncorking pressure of a .223 can be an appreciable fraction of the chamber pressure of a .22LR cartridge. The .22LR runs in the low 20,000s as far as PSI is concerned. The .22LR suppressor is meant to deal with uncorking pressure that isn't that great in the scheme of things. Yes, the .22LR runs at (let's just pick a number) 21,000 psi, but by the time the bullet has reached the muzzle it is far, far less. In fact, we can even calculate it, and for a handgun it is on the order of 1,800 PSI and for a rifle with a 16-inch barrel, the pressure is 492 PSI.

Compare that to the 7,000 psi a .223 can generate at the muzzle, and that's for a regular carbine. An SBR will generate more.

So, your buddy who was so clever, using a lighter, smaller and slimmer rimfire suppressor on his AR because it is "so handy," until the tube bulges? He wasn't so smart, was he? Your only recourse, once you pry it off the rifle, is to send it back to the manufacturer, after considerable email consultation and photography.

Rust & dents

So, you left it out in the rain, and it got rusty? Don't be bashful, scour or buff the rust off. Yes, there will be rust inside, but the only way you can deal with that, if at all, is to shoot it. Shoot it enough to heat it up, and then don't get it wet again.

I should point out that most of the alloys used

inside of a suppressor don't or won't rust, so it is the lowest-cost ones, made of chromalloy steel, that will suffer this.

OK, you unscrewed your suppressor, and put it on the shooting bench while you went to take care of something else. As your back is turned, you heard a dull "thunk" with a definite concrete sound to it. Your suppressor has rolled off the bench, and you have just proven once again the Sir Isaac was right.

What to do? Re-install it and check alignment. If everything is aligned, then you have nothing to worry about. Yes, it is dented and scarred, and those will act as reminders every time you see them. But if it is still aligned, then nothing is wrong and it will work. Suppressors are not delicate little flowers, they can take a certain amount of bouncing around and not care (see Chapter Fifteen).

If there's anything else you can do to bust a suppressor, I haven't thought of it, and I'm pretty devious.

Ammunition sensitivity

Use of the proper ammunition is important, both to keep the suppressor from being clogged with residue and to keep it intact. An errant bullet striking a baffle at 2700 fps can be damaging, or it can be catastrophic to the suppressor. Use of incorrect ammunition will quickly lead to an ineffective or damaged suppressor.

The common-in-use bullets you buy at the big-box store or your local gun shop will pose no problem to suppressors that are properly mounted. These would be full metal jacket, softpoint, hollowpoint, polymer-tipped and monolithic copper projectiles. All of these bullets have sufficient structural integrity such that they would not pose a hazard to the baffle stack. The clearance hole on a suppressor is kept as small as possible by the manufacturer for the simple reason that the smaller the hole, the quieter the suppressor. But there is room enough for the bullet to pass through without a problem, as long as you do your part.

However, all-lead bullets of any type – hard-cast, swaged or otherwise made – are a problem. The soft lead (softer than copper, even with the hardest-cast alloy lead bullet) will when it leaves the muzzle generate a plume of vaporized lead. A full metal jacket bullet with an exposed lead base does the same, but not nearly to the degree of an all-lead bullet. An exposed-base jacketed bullet is not a problem in a suppressor, but all lead is. (It is also a big part of the lead exposure you get at indoor ranges.)

Using lead bullets in a suppressor will cause an accelerated lead build-up in the baffle stack. If the suppressor is a user-serviceable one, it can be disassembled, cleaned and re-assembled. However, if it is a sealed unit, or a serviceable one that is not taken apart and cleaned, the lead will build up until the suppressor loses efficiency, and becomes heavier due to the build-up.

There is no effective way to clean a sealed suppressor that has a build-up in it. The only possible way for a manufacturer to do so would be to cut it open and replace the baffle stack. As this would probably be more expensive than making a new one, the service cost would exceed the replacement cost. That ends up being an expensive lesson.

As there are no full-metal-jacket .22LR loadings, rimfire suppressors have to be different, and are. The

Frangible does not look like "normal" bullets. Learn the look, if you own a suppressor, and especially if you are at a range where you might acquire some frangible ammo.

Bullet length matters. Left to right, these .224-inch bullets are 55 grains, 69, 77, 70, 85 and 90 grains. That is not a typo, the 70-grain bullet is all-copper, and longer than a lead-core bullet.

soft lead of their bullets is the reason they are user-serviceable, and various manufacturers suggest disassembly and cleaning at different intervals, 500 rounds being the average. Unlike a centerfire rifle suppressor, it is nearly impossible to heat up a rimfire suppressor enough by shooting to burn out the deposits. No, do not "solve" that problem by putting your rimfire suppressor in the oven. Don't even think about it.

Hazardous

Bullets that are heavy or long for their caliber can be a hazard to suppressors. Another way to look at it is, barrels with slow twist rates can be hazardous to your suppressor. In the AR-15/M16/M4 use, barrel twist is of continued interest even when suppressors aren't involved. In using suppressors, it is of great concern. A rifle whose barrel has a too-slow twist will not properly stabilize a bullet. The prime example here would be an early AR or M16, with a 1/12-twist barrel. That is, the rifling of the bore makes one turn in twelve inches. This is the correct twist rate to stabilize the normal weight bullet for the early rifle cartridge, the M193, and its 55-grain bullet. Firing the M855 bullet, with its 62-grain weight and greater length, leads to insufficient twist to keep the bullet stable.

M855s fired from a 1/12-twist barrel will produce "keyholes" – bullets literally striking the target sideways.

A non-AR example would be putting a suppressor on your varmint rifle. If you have a bolt-action rifle, in say .223, and you get it threaded for a suppressor, be sure you know the twist rate. It may have a rate of 1/14, even slower than an early AR. If so, using anything heavier than a 52-grain hollowpoint or varmint bullet may risk yaw.

If the bullet begins to yaw quickly enough once it leaves the muzzle, it can tip far enough to strike a baffle as it is passing through the suppressor. It may stay point-on long enough to clear the suppressor, and it

Bullet makers know their wares, Do not assume that you can "get by" with a slower twist. At least not until you've tested it on a rifle without a suppressor.

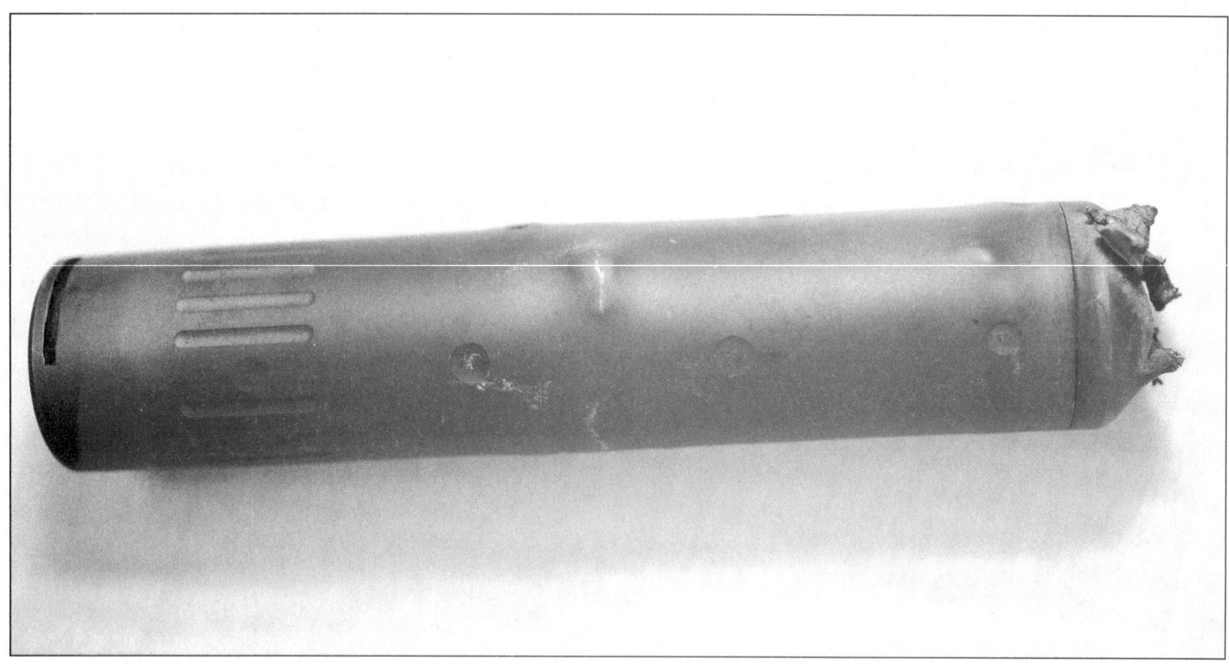

Frangible ammo is cool and useful. But if it costs you a suppressor, then it is too expensive and you should avoid using it.

may not. A baffle strike can be anything from injurious to accuracy to catastrophic, in some cases leading to a burst suppressor and an injured human.

The twist/ammunition combination is usually not injurious in the other direction. That is, use of M193/55-grain bulleted ammunition, in rifles with a twist faster than 1/12 (commonly, 1/9, 1/8, and 1/7), does not create a problem. It can, however, if taken too far in the other extreme. If you have access to, or reload a source of "inexpensive" ammunition stuffed with bullets intended for varmint use, this can be a different problem.

In varmint use, a bullet lighter (in some instances much lighter) than 55 grains, is fired at a significantly higher velocity. It is not unusual for a 20-inch rifle, firing a 40-grain "Blitz" bullet, to achieve velocities of 3600 fps or more. If the 20-inch barrel on the rifle also happens to have a twist of $^1/_7$, that is, one turn in seven inches, the bullet can be rotated faster than its thin, varmint-designed jacket wall can withstand. The bullet in many instances disintegrates before it reaches its intended target. It can disintegrate inside of the suppressor, especially if the barrel and suppressor are hot from an extended firing string, such as in training, practice, or hosing over a prairie dog town.

When you are practicing, or learning what ammo your rifle shoots well or doesn't, a certain amount of experimentation can teach you a lot, and is relatively harmless. Finding out that a particular bullet in a particular barrel won't be stable means you have a target with key-holed hits on it. Experimenting with a suppressor is not wise. So, stay in the safe zone of bullet weights when it comes to rifling twist rate.

If you own a range of rifles and ammunitions, for hunting, competition, defense or other use, careful consideration must be given to which rifles can have suppressors mounted, and which cannot.

Prohibited

Any frangible ammunition, with one design exception, is absolutely incompatible with suppressors. Frangible bullets are most commonly manufactured by the sintering process, where a pellet of powdered metal is compressed (after being mixed with a binding agent) to create a bullet which will more-or-less hold together "long enough" and then break into dust on impact with a hard object.

Frangible ammo is used in training, usually law enforcement, where the idea is to use bullets that won't be so abusive of indoor ranges and shoot-houses.

The problem is that the limits between "not long enough" and "too long" to hold together are not wide. "Not wide" means most suppressor makers will not warranty their products if they have been used with, and damaged by, sintered-bullet ammunition. The sintered ammunition makers will not warranty the ammunition for use in suppressors. These two facts should be a clue.

It is not unusual for frangible bullets to break on feeding, or shortly after leaving the muzzle. In training, a bullet that breaks into pieces as it is feeding causes a malfunction, and as a result becomes the cause for some impromptu transition training. Without a suppressor, a sintered bullet breaking as it leaves the muzzle is not a problem, as it then will penetrate even less on range equipment. But if it breaks apart leaving the muzzle, while still inside a suppressor, it is just another baffle strike in the making.

Federal offers frangible ammunition in 5.56, the Mk311. This was originally loaded for the Navy, for exactly this situation. It uses a sintered core, but one inserted inside of a regular jacket. It cannot break as it leaves the muzzle, but will shatter upon striking a hard object. This ammunition is available for civilian purchase (i.e., non-DoD) and by police departments. It won't be easy to find, as Federal doesn't make a lot (the Navy doesn't need a lot) and it will be pricey. The same kind of suppressor-safe bullet design is available from Extreme Shock, there with a 110-grain bullet that is loaded to subsonic velocities. It is also suppressor-safe due to its construction. The sintered bullet materiel here is also compressed inside of a copper jacket. The jacket keeps the bullet in one piece until it strikes the steel target, and then it breaks apart.

If you are a reloader, you can make your own frangible training ammo that will be suppressor safe by loading Barnes Varmint Grenade bullets. They are jackets with frangible cores pressed in place. You'll have to load your own, and you should not press your luck by trying to reach the maximum velocity the reloading manual offers. Pick a speed in the middle-normal range for your caliber, load to it, and be happy.

IMPROVE YOUR SHOOTING SKILLS

Handgun Training for Personal Protection **is a must-read for anyone who is serious about maximizing their self-defense skills. This latest title from handgun authority Richard A. Mann teaches you how to get the most from your training.**

“This book belongs in every shooter's library. Mann provides a practical, hands-on guide to working with your handgun and the equipment that goes with it. Along the way, common misconceptions are corrected, and often neglected topics are explained. This book will become your go-to reference.”

—***Il Ling New,*** *Gunsite Instructor*

3 EASY WAYS TO ORDER

www.gundigeststore.com (product U2147)

Download to your Kindle, Nook or iPad tablet

Call (855) 840-5120 (M-F, 8-5 CST)